China Turned Rightside Up

China Turned Rightside Up

Revolutionary Legitimacy in the Peasant World

RALPH THAXTON

Yale University Press
New Haven and London

Published with assistance from the foundation established in memory of William McKean Brown.

Designed by Nancy Ovedovitz
and set in VIP Times Roman type.
Printed in the United States of America by the Murray Printing Co., Westford, Mass.

Library of Congress Cataloging in Publication Data
Thaxton, Ralph, 1944–
  China turned rightside up.
  Includes bibliographical references and index.
  1. Communism—China—History—20th century.
2. China—Politics and government—20th century.
3. Peasant uprisings—China—History—20th century.
I. Title.
HX417.T48 1983   303.6′4′0951   82-40165
ISBN 0-300-02707-9   AACR2

10   9   8   7   6   5   4   3   2   1

To my parents
and other good friends

Contents

Illustrations

Acknowledgments

A book of this nature is not made without accumulating deep intellectual debts to scholars who have been fearless in creating new ideas, conceptions, and paradigms. As a graduate student at the University of Wisconsin I was privileged to study with three intellectual giants: Edward Friedman, James C. Scott, and Maurice Meisner. I have benefited immensely from their teachings and their writings and from our personal exchanges. Without standing on the shoulders of these scholars, I would not have been able to see so clearly the burning issues raised in this work, and the exciting data I have generated would most likely be relegated to the dust bin of social science.

A number of other scholars, including Mark Selden, Frederic Wakeman, Jr., Chalmers Johnson, Jerome Ch'en, G. William Skinner, and Vivienne Shue, offered criticisms of earlier tentative ideas that I was then able to reconsider. Recent correspondence with Samuel L. Popkin, Ronald J. Herring, and Roger Bowen helped me sharpen the focus on several issues in peasant politics and revolutionary economy raised in the early middle chapters, and I thank each for his wisdom. Linda Grove and Phil Billingsley were kind enough to read the manuscript before it underwent one last writing, and I am indebted to them for saving me from committing a number of errors. I owe a great deal to Donald Hindley, who shared his insights with me on questions of state and geopolitics in peasant studies. I also am grateful for the advice and assistance with maps given to me by Robert McColl and Eliza McClennen.

I owe special thanks to my colleagues at the Henan Province History Research Institute in the People's Republic of China. My work at the institute and at Lin county, where in the spring of 1980 I began an investigation of Henan peasant society, enabled me to draw from previously unavailable data on the existential dilemmas of peasants in pre-1949 China. I was also able to evaluate my interpretations of historical evidence presented in Chinese Communist Party documents against some independent recollections of peasant informants. My hosts in Henan opened up the history of the Tianmen *hui*, or Heavenly Gate Society, to me. This book, particularly chapter 3, has been enriched by what I have learned from Mr. Guo Youfan about the history of the Heavenly Gates and from peasants in a former Heavenly Gate village.

The University of Wisconsin at Madison, the Stanford Inter-University Program in Taipei, the Social Science Research Council, the University of California Center for Chinese Studies, the National Endowment for the Humanities, and the Brandeis Sachar International Fellowship Program have underwritten this project. I am extremely grateful for their support. To the librarians of the Bureau of Investigation and the Ministry of Defense in Taiwan, Harvard University, the University of California, the Stanford Hoover Collection, and the Henan Province History Research Institute, I express thanks for patience and assistance.

Last but first there are Janet, Scott, and Jessica. All of them are showered with affection for tolerating someone who tends to self-destruct when it comes to work.

Waltham, Massachusetts

Introduction

The twentieth century has been called the age of peasant revolution, and indeed peasants have become active participants in the dramatic political transformations of our time. The Mexican, Algerian, Vietnamese, and Angolan revolutions all bear this out. At the same time, however, the participation of peasants in such earthshaking political events often seems to represent a defensive reaction to the growth of powerful central states and global market economies. There is, moreover, ample testimony for the thesis that peasant wars to stop these twin processes of modernization have turned out to be losers' wars. Friedrich Engels was correct in surmising from his study of the 1525–26 German Peasants' War that the odds against successful rural revolution are overwhelming, but he was wrong in blaming revolutionary failure on the backwardness of the peasantry.[1] For the most part, the performance of opposition parties, armies, and popular fronts in leading peasants against the state has been poor. This book is about a rare experience. It is about peasants who won. Its emphasis is on the processes whereby Chinese peasants and the Chinese Communist Party (CCP) engineered a revolutionary breakaway from the intensified "taking" of the modern state and the increased pull of global markets in the early twentieth century.

What is to be learned from such a study? First, this study seeks to open up the largely unexplored field of folk politics and culture in the Chinese revolution. It assumes, with John King Fairbank, Harvard's leading China scholar, that in recognizing the People's Republic of China the United States is finally recognizing the reality of the modern Chinese revolution.[2] But what was that reality at the moment of revolutionary triumph? The major premise of this book is that most scholarly works on China mystify the substantive traditions of its modern revolution. To understand this great Asian revolution, we must look at the issues at stake in the combinations of popular culture and action that went into the founding of the People's Republic of China. Yet in the years following the October 1, 1949 Liberation only a handful of Western scholars have focused on the place of peasant history and society in the pre-1949 revolutionary process, and almost no one has asked whether the rural revolution in which the Chinese Communist Party became involved was connected to folk politics and culture. Social scientists by and large relegated the folk themes of the modern Chinese revolution to footnotes and considered the politics and culture of the country folk outside the mainstream of questions on the Chinese Communist movement.

There were two interrelated reasons for this. First, it was easier for the immediate post-World War II generation of Western scholars to study the Chinese revolution in terms of communism. Most scholars had spent the better part of their youth mastering the Marxist and Leninist themes in the writings of Mao Zedong. The corpus of books they produced inevitably contained the Communist Party interpretations of the revolution's meaning. Their writings by and large presented a communist revolution incorporating an invisible, passive rural people whom they coded as the "peasant masses." Second, in the aftermath of World War II American scholars who had fought for the freedoms so deeply cherished in Western democracies found it both natural and necessary to associate the rise of communist parties with the problems posed by totalitarianism. Hence the relationship between the Chinese Communist Party and the peasantry was approached, defined, and analyzed in terms of the party's motivations and capabilities to penetrate, mobilize, and capture peasant society for its own political objectives.

Out of these scholarly pursuits emerged three dominant conceptions of the modern Chinese revolution. In one view the revolution represented an imperial restoration, with October 1, 1949 symbolizing an upswing in a dynastic tradition that had been in decline for a century. Thus the Chinese Communist Party was portrayed in restorationist terms, and the relationship of party to peasantry often resembled that of Marxist cum Confucian benefactor to peasant-client. Leftward-looking Western intellectuals familiar with the radical anti-Confucian heritage imparted to the CCP by the May Fourth Movement of 1919 implicitly took issue with this first conception by tracing the revolutionary success to the emergence of a party charged with a progressive and popularized Chinese Marxist ideology. This conception of the CCP as the major source of ideational inspiration to revolution— vanguard intellectual leadership armed with mobilizational weapons ranging from Comintern organizational secrets to mass nationalism to socialist utopias—assumed that peasants had little to say or do about determining the political course of the revolution in which they participated. Its central premise still colors most studies of the origins of modern China's rural revolution. Finally, a third conception linked the CCP victory to the participation of peasants in warfare. One theoretical formulation of this conception assumed peasants to be citizen volunteers in a modern patriotic war under the leadership of the CCP. Another saw a parallel between the rise of the CCP and the reemergence of a premodern warrior tradition that did not need to appeal to peasant poverty, real or imagined, in order to integrate the countryside into anti-imperialist guerrilla warfare.

To be sure, none of these conceptions denied that the Communist Party's peasant base played an important role in the revolutionary victory. But

Western scholars undertook the search for that role by looking for methods used by the CCP to bring peasant expectations in line with its own ideology and goals. In contrast, I ask whether the CCP in the process of coming to power consciously tried to serve purposes that peasants considered most valuable, or, conversely, whether its cadres defined rural dwellers as backward, petit bourgeois, and hence antimodern and antisocialist. In building a case that demonstrates how peasant values and practices both set limits on and shaped the contours of revolutionary change, I take issue with studies that focus so narrowly on pronouncements from the party or state leadership that they ignore the importance of instructions from the village world. My purpose is not just to correct a variety of misconceptions about the peasantry as a mere receptacle of outside influence, or to help restore a sense of two-way interaction between the CCP and rural people in shaping revolutionary events. What I am suggesting is an entirely different paradigm for explaining the possibilities inherent in the Chinese revolution at the moment of its conception. October 1, 1949, was the climax of peasant initiatives to challenge the fundamental equation of political power and to shatter those images of popular relations with authority passed on to us in the major social science interpretations of pre-1949 China.

I certainly would not go so far as to argue that the Little Tradition* values with which the Chinese Communist Party originally interacted were institutionalized to become the dominant values shaping the order of the PRC state after October 1, 1949. Is it not possible, however, that the conception of folk revolution that characterized pre-1949 CCP relations with the peasantry has survived the intraparty wars over the proper ordering of the post-Liberation PRC state? The PRC today, in the 1980s, is not simply another imperial order, Communist party dictatorship, or warrior regime. Obsessed with the power struggles that riddled the city worlds of Beijing, Wuhan, Shanghai, and Guangzhou (Canton), Western intellectuals did not ask whether an older, more eternal peasant conception of revolutionary change still existed after Liberation, if only in occasional echoes of pre-1949 preferences for order, equity, and justice in the post-Liberation countryside. Is that potent tradition still with us today? If so, what is its relationship to the holders of state power? This seminal problem of peasant society and the order of the post-Liberation state cannot be addressed properly until we have a deeper, clearer comprehension of the perspectives the rural folk brought to both their own and the CCP's involvement in the pre-1949 revolutionary process.[3]

If Chinese peasants did not always see or act in accordance with categories relevant to the Chinese Communist Party, then it is necessary to rescue

---

*By "Little Tradition" I mean peasant subsistence practices carried out separately from the supervision of the dominant classes in the towns and cities and peasant ideas about reality, justice, and authority conceived independently of any sense of belonging to the dominant Confucian state.

folk-conceived political actions from the clutches of orthodox CCP ideology and to resist the temptation of Western scholars to substitute their own intellectual cum party-relevant conceptions of revolution for the standards and sentiments by which the rural people judged and influenced the historical process. In discussing peasant revolution with reference to the rational basis of folk culture, Barrington Moore, Jr., was the first to point out that outside political dissidents have scored few successes in working with peasants whose images of justice and freedom have been slighted.[4] One would think that some work would have been done on the nexus between the revolutionary imagery of China's peasantry and the CCP in the pre-1949 period. Though documentation is available, this work has only just begun. This book will provide a tiny bit of spadework on an understudied topic.

In this "first digging" I have tried to build on Max Weber's belief that even prophets cannot afford to neglect the customary norms of the rural folk if they are to foster followerships for their own purpose.[5] With this starting point in mind, the question inevitably becomes: Could the CCP have rushed victoriously onto the stage of world politics if its erstwhile members had not upheld a number of popular expectations for justice that had been articulated by the peasantry long before the CCP based itself in the countryside in the late 1920s? Christopher Hill's magnificent work on the fermentation of radical ideas among the rural people of seventeenth-century England[6] and Emmanuel Le Roy Ladurie's classic study of antiauthoritarian mentalities among the rural dwellers of fourteenth-century France[7] have shown that self-mobilized protest against real distress and real repression has been an important means of reaffirming a revered way of life for the peasantry. Was the rural world in which the Chinese Communist Party conducted its experiments in revolution and liberation so different?

This is not an easy question to answer, and in addressing it I have had to rely largely on writings sponsored by the CCP itself. The skeptic will remind us, rightly, that much in the revolutionary drama to follow is nothing more than a Chinese Communist Party rendition of folk politics, designed in fact to adjust popular conceptions of the pre-1949 revolution to the changing language of party orthodoxy. I am not unsympathetic to this view. But let us look at it from another angle. If we can learn *even a little bit* about the relationship of folk culture to the modern Chinese revolution from CCP-sponsored publications, is it not also possible that the movements that sprang from the moral imagination of the peasantry had even more to do with the creation of the revolutionary political process than the formal doctrines of the CCP would have us assume?

The history of the Chinese Communist movement in a most important region of its growth is also instructive. The political leaders who now are opening up a China that has been closed to the world for a quarter of a century are the very men and women who worked alongside the peasantry to open up the Chinese Communist Party base area in the borderlands of the provinces of Shanxi, Hebei, Shandong, and Henan during the Anti-Japanese War of Resistance. To this region Chairman Mao Zedong sent commanders Zhu De, Peng Dehuai, and Liu Bocheng—Mao's chief of staff on the Long March and Zhu De's sidekick from Sichuan—to open up the Great Rear Area of the CCP's War of Resistance. This North China border region, which is about the size of France and was populated by about thirty million people in the 1930s,[8] became the nerve center of CCP political processes from 1937 to 1947, the ten great years of Chinese Communist history. Here, in the Taihang Mountains and along the flat plains of the Hebei, Shandong, and Henan border counties, Senior Deputy Vice-Premier Deng Xiaoping served as the political commissar in General Liu Bocheng's 129th Division during the Anti-Japanese War. To this region, which separates the central Hebei plain from the Ordos, the CCP armed forces retreated in 1940, in order to preserve the revolution and prepare for war after the Japanese Imperial Army struck a nearly fatal blow to the central Hebei base area, and again in 1947, when the Guomindang Army overran Yanan. It was here that the Chinese Communists survived and from here that they surged to victory, as Liu Bocheng led the People's Liberation Army to deliver a death blow to the Guomindang Army at the Battle of Huaibei in 1948.

No doubt this region's contribution to the revolution also assigned its leadership a major responsibility in the post-1949 era. The 129th Division led by Liu Bocheng and Deng Xiaoping, for example, played a critical role in promoting land revolution elsewhere in China from 1949 to 1954, and it was this division that restored order in the provinces at the height of Cultural Revolution leftism. The current premier of the PRC, Zhao Ziyang, in 1944 was a little-known CCP official reporting on the peasant movement in Hua county, Henan. Bo Yibo, the deputy director of the Shanxi-based Sacrifice League and the vice-chairman of the Shanxi-Hebei-Shandong-Henan Border Region Government during the Anti-Japanese War, is now vice-premier of the State Council and responsible for monitoring financial aspects of the Four Modernizations.[9] The current first-secretary of Henan Province, Duan Junyi, also played a crucial role in the formation of the Anti-Japanese Resistance coalition and of the Liberation War strategy in the border region. Finally, Ji Dengkui, a recent vice-premier, was instrumental in establishing good CCP relations with the peasant movement in the Hebei-Shandong-Henan area during the Anti-Japanese War. Along with Pan Fusheng, CCP secretary of the Hebei-Shandong-Henan area following the Civil War, Ji Dengkui advocated a development policy in line with peasant preferences for private household production and free market exchange over coerced agricultural collectivization. As we shall see, these preferences had been enforced in a pre-1949 revolutionary process which the Cultural Revolution Left redefined as a "bourgeois rightist tendency."

Since 1976 these men have either held or been close to the reins of state power. Yet in the pages to follow I touch only briefly on their personalities, ideologies, and political styles. They are hardly irrelevant, but my purpose is to transmit an understanding of the situation these men faced when they stood outside modern China's military-state, and when they joined with the desperate classes to end the causes of peasant hunger and national humiliation. These men led peasant China out of social horror and political chaos. How did they achieve this remarkable feat? In a world where Communist parties are usually noted for their left-wing infantilism while out of power, the performance of the Chinese Communist Party might be seen as spectacular. Western scholars of China sometimes forget this. While I am not overly impressed by the PRC record in eradicating poverty after 1949, the indisputable fact of history is that the Chinese Communist movement enhanced the efforts of peasants to impose their own solutions to their pre-1949 problems. By looking at the evolution of CCP practices in this vast hinterland border region during the moments of revolutionary conception I hope to further our understanding of why and how the CCP first assumed responsibility for serving the rural people.

Finally, this book tries to provide an answer to a central question in comparative studies on peasant society and rural revolution. How do revolutionaries create bona fide relations with peasants out of which come the legitimizing processes whereby a political revolution reaches its full development? At the heart of the study is a search for those practices that enabled the Chinese Communists to win the right to rule the countryside. To both Max Weber and Mao Zedong legitimacy was defined principally as the right to exercise force as permitted by the state (in Weber[10]) or the party (in Mao). This insight goes a long way toward explaining the reasons for the CCP victory in rural China. To this wisdom, however, I would add that legitimacy also involves the right to exercise force as prescribed by the peasantry in its quest to order its environment and culture.

In placing the question of legitimacy in comparative perspective, I have neither abandoned the history of the CCP in the region I describe nor allowed the details of my Chinese case to determine my questions—at least not all of them. The posing of theoretical issues and the analysis that proves or disproves the positions I take toward these issues represent an attempt to address the Chinese revolution in terms broader than a case study. I employ this approach so that we do not simply assemble an oxcart of inert Chinese data and so that the theoretical ox that pulls us across the field of agrarian revolution does not drift too far from China. I believe that only simultaneous attention to modern China's rural experience and to Western social science debates over contemporary peasant revolutions will enable us eventually to formulate a plausible interpretation of how the Chinese Communists endeared themselves to the rural folk.

The first chapter tries to explain an intriguing contradiction: peasants historically have not been revolutionaries, and yet traditionally their participation in rebellions to defend the status quo in subsistence relations produced pressures for a fundamental reordering of the Chinese polity. Since peasant revolution was so unlikely in the traditional world, chapter 2 asks why the twentieth-century breakdown of the imperial order created the shockingly *new* conditions that eroded the long-established bases of agrarian political legitimacy and edged peasants toward a revolutionary confrontation with the dominant class. What were those conditions? Did peasants suffer from them? Did they consciously associate their suffering with the politics that engendered those conditions? Next we look at several strategies of peasant protest and find that peasants turned toward anarchism and revolution on their own, without outside Communist party instigation, mainly because revolution was becoming the only act that held out hope for survival. Chapter 4 attempts to ascertain how peasants seized the opportunity presented by the arrival of the CCP's army to regain their most elementary human rights during the Anti-Japanese War. In chapter 5 we look at revolution from the bottom up. A peasant revolt in a remote Taihang Mountain village is placed in the context of some specific social issues affecting peasants in the region and of several long-standing social scientific premises about peasant mobilization and CCP power. Chapter 6 in a sense seeks to reaffirm the arguments of chapter 4 by looking at the relationship between peasant revolution and national resistance. I take war as an intervening independent variable influencing the outcome of a rural revolution that is about to overspill its anti-imperialist embankments, and ask whether the Chinese Communists were entirely successful in cultivating the peasants' commitment to their party's anti-imperialist struggle. The last chapter places the key issues of land revolution and civil war in the context of preceding arguments, and in doing so challenges the claim that the CCP linked the fate of the War of Liberation to all-out class struggle on the land. We shall see that the Chinese Communists won that war to a significant extent by drawing from their Resistance War experiences, even though there were tremendous pressures to carry out national liberation warfare by turning the whole countryside into one big, bloody battlefield. The conclusion places China's experience in the context of some larger theoretical issues implicit in studies of peasantry and comparative revolution.

The source materials I have used are primarily of Chinese origin. They fall into two broad types—conventional and nonconventional. Both reflect the subjective assessments of writers who have been in close touch with the peasantry and just as often with the CCP.

Among the conventional materials are documents published by the various border region committees of the CCP during the Anti-Japanese War of Resistance. The Guomindang captured these documents during its 1946–47 raids on the CCP revolutionary base area and subsequently packed them away in the archives of the Bureau of Investigation and Ministry of National Defense in Taiwan, where I read them in 1973 and 1974. The other conventional sources, rarely consulted by Western scholars, are newspapers and work reports printed by the "traveling presses" of the CCP armed forces during the Wars of Resistance and Liberation. These were produced by commanders, commissars, and common soldiers and were circulated among the regulars and militias as "internal secrets" during the revolution, after which some found their way to the Hoover Library.

As to less conventional sources, I have relied in part on data I collected in the course of several trips to the border region, specifically month-long interviews of peasants, local scribes, and CCP officials in Lin county. Transcripts of these interviews are available in the Brandeis University Library Oral History Files on China.

Finally, I have consulted a number of social histories and popular novels. Most of them were written by local natives during the childhood of the Republic, when inhibitions on writers usually came from inner norms, rather than being imposed by the party or state. I discovered these sources, which had been suspended and suppressed in the Cultural Revolution, during many hours of research in libraries and bookstores in the United States, Hong Kong, and the PRC from 1974 to 1979. There is little doubt that the subjective biases of these sources have influenced, though not determined, the conception and conclusion of this study. Unlike those who have interpreted the Chinese revolution by relying mainly on Japanese sources or the Vietnamese revolution by relying on American sources, I have relied mainly on sources that sprang from the indigenous revolutionary system itself. Of course, the reliability of these sources remains subject to question, and only as China is opened more fully to Western social science research will any independent verification be possible. In the meantime, I believe that the collectivity of sources I present constitutes the closest thing to an accurate compass to the inner culture of China, its revolution, and its Little Tradition.

The pertinent question, therefore, concerns the strengths of the sources at hand. The oral histories provide some genuinely personal accounts of why peasants turned to revolution, told from the perspective of rural people who still have live, if fading, memories of the years between the fall of the Qing dynasty in 1911 and the coming of Liberation in 1949. I have corroborated some of their recollections on the structure of rural class relations and the changing terms of rural livelihood from both CCP and Guomindang-sponsored publications. The CCP documents were written by desperate party cadres looking to solve the social problems of peasant society so they could get on with the urgent business of building a broad anti-imperialist coalition. These documents give us some sense of how CCP cadres saw the issues that were important to the peasants in a rather difficult period of revolutionary mobilization. The little tabloids of the CCP armed forces were usually composed by people who were a bit more certain of their survival, and we owe them thanks for the insights offered on the relationship between guns and the peasant movement. The histories and novels, written by local scribes and native intellectuals, put us in touch with the mood of the popular countryside. Though they were not always from peasant families, these writers carried out their own investigations into the formative encounters of the CCP with China's Little Tradition in cooperation with peasants whose cultures they knew intimately. The explosive peasant language in their works offers a suggestive portal to the dissenting folk eschatology to which the CCP had to relate its plans for revolution and liberation.

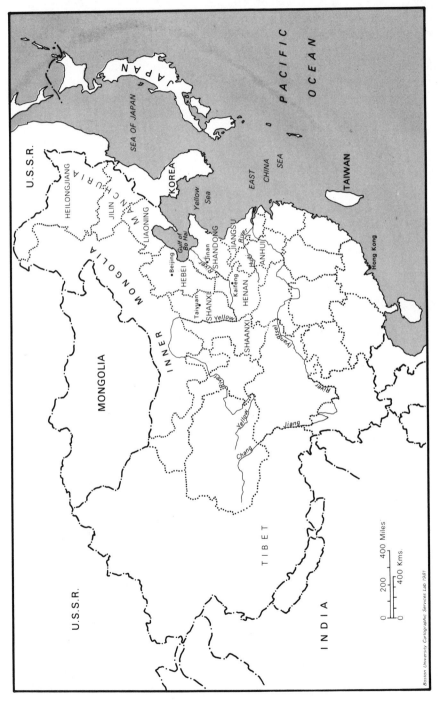

U.S.S.R.

U.S.S.R.

JAPAN

SEA OF JAPAN

PACIFIC

OCEAN

HEILONGJIANG

JILIN

LIAONING

MANCHURIA

KOREA

Yellow
Sea

EAST
CHINA
SEA

TAIWAN

MONGOLIA

INNER

MONGOLIA

•Beijing
Gulf of
Bo Hai

HEBEI

•Jinan

SHANDONG

JIANGSU

Taiyuan

SHANXI

Yellow

Kaifeng

HENAN

Huai River

ANHUI

Yangtze
River

Hong Kong

SHAANXI

Yellow

Jiang
(Yangtse)

Chang

Jiang

TIBET

INDIA

0   200   400 Miles

0   400 Kms

Boston University Cartographic Services Lab 1981

China

1

Subsistence and Subordination
in the Traditional World

Peasants generally have not pursued revolutionary modes of protest. Like tillers elsewhere, the peasants of the North China periphery had historically taken part in various protests to redress local grievances. Their participation in rebellion, however, had seldom gone beyond a defense of land and livelihood to an all-out attack on the imperial Confucian order itself. Paradoxically, the Chinese Communist Party would come to draw popular support for its revolutionary experiment from rural people who, like their Shang ancestors, still engaged in agriculture and sheepherding and who preferred to survive by avoiding a direct clash with the state. If we do not grasp this paradox, we run the risk of deceiving ourselves about why peasants would turn to revolution in post-Qing times or why their revolts would fundamentally change the substance and scope of power relations in rural China.

The peasants' preference for nonadventurous protest notwithstanding, the North China interior traditionally had been a breeding ground for popular rebellion. Here, across the boundless plains of Hebei and Henan and over the stupendous mountains of Shanxi, lay an ancient amphitheater of uprisings that unmistakably expressed antistate overtones.

It was from southern Hebei that Chen Sheng and Wu Guang hoisted the banners of peasant war against the Qing dictatorship in 209 B.C.[1] The peasant rebellions led by Zhu Yuanzhang against the Yuan dynasty had taken place in the Taihang Mountains, and this same area had spawned a massive peasant jacquerie in 1524–25.[2] A century later Li Zicheng threatened to take Beijing from the power base his insurgent army had built up in Shaanxi and then extended to the banks of the Yellow River in Henan. Throughout the Qing dynasty peasants turned to rebellion in times of natural disaster, and as in the Eight Trigrams Rebellion of 1813, they drew on Maitreya Buddhism and its mother goddess deity Guanyin to create their own hopes for the coming of a savior.[3] At the turn of the twentieth century the Yi He Tuan (Boxers) who stormed Beijing took sanctuary in backward villages and towns of the Taihang, and from these localities they led déclassé men armed with cudgels to drive out the Western missionaries.[4] Only two decades later the Red Spear Society drew recruits for its struggles against warlordism from the medieval-looking villages of Hebei, Shandong, and Henan border districts. Peasants, to be sure, took part in these turbulent events. But why did these silent allies of the dynasty sometimes throw their support to insurgents who set out to topple the imperial state?

THE SETTING OF REVOLT

Because participation in rebellion so often led to torture and horrible death, peasants resorted to open rebellion only when they had exhausted other ways of coping with the political pressures on their fragile ecosystem.

The chance for a harvest without hunger was poor. Because of water shortages and short frost-free growing seasons the peasants in Shanxi, and along the Henan-Hebei border,[5] had to stake each year's survival on one major grain crop. Most peasants tilled three to ten one-*mu** plots scattered helter-skelter around their villages. With adequate rainfall the old labor-intensive techniques were conducive to maximum yields, which still proved insufficient. The land usually gave 100 to 150 catties per *mu*, but even a bountiful yield of 300 catties on three to five *mu* was not enough to keep alive a family of five. If the required minimum intake per person was 300 catties,[6] such a family would need at least 1,500 catties just to keep body and soul together, and they most likely needed another 300 to pay for clothes, salt, and repairing implements.

Hence the relentless search for supplementary income. In the Taihang area peasants drew this income from animal husbandry, forestry, and work in coal mines and rock quarries. On the plains to the east they raised yellow oxen and made cotton goods. The only sure way to acquire enough grain for the family, however, was to set up small family businesses, and thousands of peasants were salt makers, blacksmiths, carpenters, and small merchants as well as tillers of the land.

Although tillers in southern Hebei and northern Henan could count on double-cropping, flood waters habitually swept away the standing crop and caused waterlogging, which complicated repeat planting. The dikes erected during the Song dynasty, the reporting stations set up in the Ming, and the silt-laden water-diversion schemes of the Qing expressed a dynastic commitment to harnessing the rivers.[7] In Yuan and Ming times places like Hua county in Henan, which was vulnerable to flooding, did not suffer at all.[8] Still, in the two millennia before 1949 the Yellow River reportedly burst its banks at least once every three years and shifted its course to disrupt the settlements of every third peasant generation.[9] An even more dangerous problem, however, was drought. Rainfall was inadequate to nurture the soil

*One *mu* equals 0.0667 hectares or 0.15 acre of land.

in the dry zone,[10] and the region's peasants were threatened by drought nearly every other year, though obviously given villages suffered less frequently.[11] The fear that gripped villagers in the dry spells before the May–June harvest could easily erupt into rioting. Rather than await relief from landlords or the state, peasants usually sought succor in other ways, including everything from home handicrafts, to local migration networks and patterns,[12] to temporary banditry.

A backwater since the Ming, the North China periphery had a heritage of lawlessness growing out of peasant resistance to the overambitious repre-sentatives of the empire. To be sure, the imperial center sought to integrate peasants into a unified polity by serving the needs of agriculture,[13] but the dynasty seldom did as much for the villages as its Confucian spokesmen proclaimed. Though flood-prevention work on the Yellow River plain was undertaken with direct state intervention, the smaller irrigation works were paid for, directly or indirectly, by the peasantry, as was the case in the Taihang area, where popular initiatives superseded dynastic directives.[14] The Board of Revenue constrained its fiscal claims on the countryside, and officials up and down the hierarchy were told to govern as "parents of the people."[15] The "parent," above all else, was to respect the right of peasants to retain food grains in the villages. The magistrate, for example, was to collect the grain tax in accordance with the peasants' ability to pay, and to stabilize grain prices for peasant consumers by selling or buying grain in the marketplace. The imperial laws of avoidance, whereby a magistrate was prohibited from taking a post in his native locality, were intended to prevent officials from using public office to exploit peasants to a degree that produced organized protest, but officials regarded the backward periphery as a post of exile, and they were quite prepared to rake off the revenues needed to finance a swift exit. By the late Ming period, peasants had come to regard county officials with caution, and, as Pitt-Rivers has documented for Spain's nineteenth-century Andalusia,[16] the village people had developed into a fine art a number of practices for avoiding local authority. These were expressed in the shadow of imperial rule—in the clandestine trade of peasant families and lineages, and in the tax underreportings of whole villages. When the imperial inspectors allowed offending rulers to take too much produce in taxes, peasants mobilized informal networks to resist the encroachment.

Rebel actions to keep unscrupulous power holders at bay were favored by the geopolitical marginality of the border region. The peasants enjoyed the tactical advantage of being relatively far from the main force of political reaction. The long distance from capital-based garrisons removed them from the instant reach of cavalry, while the rivalries between governors over fiscal responsibility for patrolling the seams of provincial power allowed insurgents the time to build up bases from which they might operate against imperial troops for several months or years. As the CCP was to discover during its rise to power, here was a built-in "geopolitical law"[17] that since

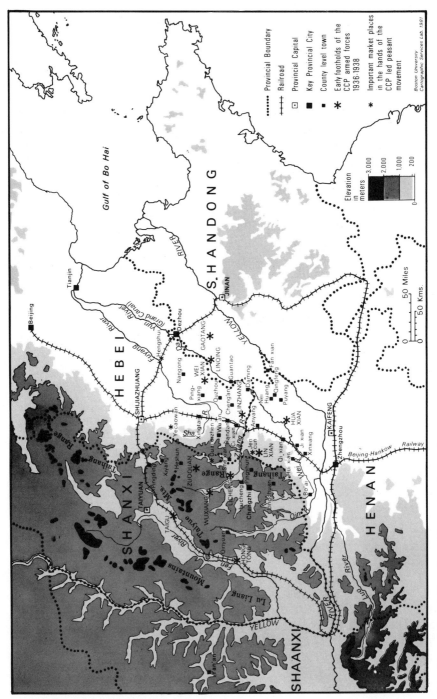

The Shanxi-Hebei-Shandong-Henan border region

ancient times had been invoked by insurgents at war with a distant but sometimes intrusive center. And, like the insurgents of yesteryear, the CCP would persevere against superior government adversaries in part because the North China periphery offered the natural resources (ores, nitrates, and sulfurs) necessary to make swords and spears, gunpowder, and firearms.

Topography also lent itself to rebel growth.[18] In the western half of the North China periphery is the Taihang Mountain range, whose average height is about two thousand meters. The Taihang Mountains rise abruptly from the Henan-Hebei plain above the Zhang River in Lin county. This range, along with the Taiyue and the Luliang Mountains, makes up a natural topography of one thousand peaks and ten thousand deep valleys. The Taihang is not merely hilly and broken land, but rather a fortresslike escarpment with hidden redoubts unreachable even by soldiers on sure-footed horses. Of course, rebel forces also had to cope with the capricious climate, but the mountains were covered with broadleaf forests from which they could draw sustenance and which spared them from the typhoid and cholera epidemics that occasionally plagued the peasant villages on the lowland floodplain to the east and south.

The rebel forces who based themselves in the Taihang followed the major riverways that led down onto the plains of Hebei, Shandong, and Henan— the lowland area that makes up the eastern half of the border region and leads to the North China metropolitan zone. The Qin River, for example, flows from the Taihang Mountains to the Henan border, where it joins with the Wei River to pass up through Hui county in Henan, while the Zhang River rambles along the deep canyons of the Taihang to Lin county in Henan and on to Wei county and Daming in Hebei. In several days a rebel force could follow these river systems out of the Shanxi high country onto the multicrop lands of Henan and then to a series of subregional capitals that were gateways to Beijing and national power. From these points the alluvial fan plains of Hebei and Henan were favorable to regional guerrilla warfare, though the peasants surely resented the duties of war service mandated by competing armies.

The peasants lived in a world without margin for error, and they were hardly ready to rebel at the first sign of an alternative political force. Rebellion was an act of necessity, the last avenue to survival when the state took more of the harvest than they could afford to give up. The long-established Confucian morality held that the imperial patriarch derived the right to rule from a divine mandate; but dynasties that did not heed the peasants' quest for subsistence and security swiftly lost their village followings. The widely recognized peasant claim to a subsistence portion of the harvest, and other family-based income, was sufficient justification for rebellion against local power holders who threatened survival.[19] Paradoxically, when conservative rural dwellers did take a last-ditch stand for survival, their very aversion to the dreadful risks of revolt made them audacious.

The Taihang escarpment in Lin county

The Taihang escarpment in Hui county

PEASANT SOCIETY UNDER THE IMPERIAL STATE: SELF-HELP AND SURVIVAL

The peasants' drive for subsistence was based in their strong desire for self-reliance. They wanted to survive without depending on local power holders whose designs on their land and labor were potentially at odds with their own well-being. Of course, all peasants were part of a larger society and state in which they were at the mercy of overlords and officials,[20] but nearly every peasant family strove to produce its own means of existence, and family self-help was seen as the surest guarantee of survival.

The central concerns, therefore, were to produce a crop sufficient for family consumption and to earn the income to purchase salt, clothing, and medicine and still pay taxes and rent to others. Most peasant families accomplished this through tilling, handicraft, and trading activities in both good years and bad.

When faced with a poor harvest or sickness, peasants usually relied on their own resourcefulness to find root crops and gather medicinal herbs. They formed family protective arrangements, including building windbreaks for the fields, guarding standing crops, and hiding sons from the dreaded *corvée*. Most peasant families called on the local matchmaker for the children, asked friends to witness the purchase of land, and enlisted fellow villagers for funeral services.

According to the Confucian elite, peasants depended on heaven to stabilize their food supply, but clearly they put great reliance in self-help. Their wisdom was hardly different from that of the Irish peasants responsible for the proverb, "Heaven helps those who help themselves." This folk idea, that survival and success were dependent on self-help, would not be missed by the CCP, whose revolutionary deeds would derive in part from the peasants' belief that self-initiated family innovations in food production were a key to successful agriculture.

In addition to their private household pursuits, peasants participated in joint family mutual-aid groups.[21] These informal exchanges among several households included credit associations and small moneymaking schemes, as well as agreements to share labor and livestock for planting and harvesting.[22] In the Taihang area peasant mutual aid sprang from the temporary associations of a few individual heads of households. To the lowland east, where peasants had replaced the digging stick with the plow and expanded their family labor forces, mutual aid had a long history of lineage cooperation. Obviously, in either half of the region peasants with land and livestock were better equipped to initiate mutual aid, and they sometimes used their yellow oxen to turn up the fields of families without livestock, in exchange for their help in gathering the harvest. Or one peasant family might till the land of another to release members of that family for market endeavors outside the village, and the income from sales would be split among the contributing partners. Naturally, harvest failures and high taxes threatened tillers collectively, straining these forms of assistance. The tendency, however, was to rely on cooperative household agriculture before turning to other means of coping with environment and government.

To be sure, village-wide activities did not supersede the peasant household and its mutual-aid arrangements, and few peasants engaged in village endeavors that were not subtended by family and lineage networks spelling out obligations toward friends, marriage partners, and patrons.[23] In many villages peasants also came together in temple-based activities, where they picked up advice from friends on how to till the land or listened to weather observers pass on information about environmental changes through folk proverbs.[24] The temple grounds provided a convenient assembly point for peasants who pitched in to cut timber from the common forests or to tap the underground water of dry river beds. It was customary for the poorest and the oldest inhabitants to cultivate village temple lands.[25] Furthermore, the temple was the meeting ground for concerted action in times of emergency, for example, to defend the village against official-based tax squeeze during food shortages. Though their pursuit of the ideal nonexploited, nondependent village did not take place independent of class and state power, the peasants who struck up these temple-based activities were advancing the idea of survival through collective self-help and self-rule.

The pursuit of independent survival can be seen in peasant marketing initiatives extending beyond the seemingly closed village world. As G. William Skinner has noted, hardly a region of the empire was without its own semiopen marketing system.[26] The economy of the border resembled an amoebalike system with peasants and peddlers coming and going in trading networks that sprawled along the earthen roads of market towns like Guaierzhen in Shanxi, Lin county town, Daokou and Puyang in Henan, and Yangyi, Handan, and Daming in Hebei. Peasants most likely got involved in marketing when the imperial polity was at the peak of its performance in promoting market development and enforcing order and justice in town-centered networks of exchange.[27] But I suspect that peasants carried on much of their buying and selling in district-level markets beyond the tight control of county-based officialdom, and that periodic trade at the subcounty level had a life of its own and lingered on even when the dynasty proved incapable of providing safety, adequate transport facilities, and fairness in town-based trade.

Much of this subcounty agricultural exchange was carried on by peasants with substantial landholdings and without debts to landlord moneylenders, who stood a better chance of surviving the unsettling consequences of the rural market declines traditionally associated with regional turbulence. In contrast, the thousands of minitillers who needed to sell raw cotton or to prosper as tailors, blacksmiths, and transport workers in order to purchase grain and pay taxes were likely to be thrown out of work and left to beg and steal for survival when higher-level county and regional markets were disturbed by natural disaster, by a shortage in the government silver used to underwrite market growth, or by greed and internal war.

There is little doubt that by Qing times most of the regional peasantry was producing for the market, and the imperial state was seeking to control the villages by stimulating and supervising trade in the wealthy Confucian world of the towns. Not surprisingly, therefore, peasants were accustomed to entering into exchanges within trade arenas supervised by the nonofficial gentry and their gentry ally in government—usually the county magistrate.[28] The magistrate and his men sought to regulate the distribution of grain, oil, and salt from market points near the county capital, and since peasants occasionally had to sell a portion of their produce to get the grain or coppers needed to pay the land tax, it was in the interest of government to promote fair and flourishing markets locally.

The important point, though, is that the dynastic attempt to make the village people deliver up a surplus through production did not deter them from consuming, saving, and sometimes profiting from their market involvement.[29] The imperial government's ability to generate revenues in part from its near-monopolies in salt and iron and in part from its own maritime customs and trade meant that peasants did not have to deal with a state whose fiscal stability depended on relentless interventions in popular tilling and trading.[30] Moreover, imperial state controls existed alongside popular pressures for protection and equity in rural trade, and local officials were left to deal with a whole set of Little Tradition defenses against harmful state interference in freely competitive markets.

The peasants of the border region had been growing crops for market exchange since the fourteenth century, and had come to expect, and insist, that power holders run markets on a stable basis with equitable prices. Obviously, the ability of peasants to shape the terms of trade to their favor rested on a number of variables ranging from yearly harvest yields to elasticity of produce demand to the designs of local authority. For example, there were state controls on county-level markets in both grain and salt, and when it came to items such as salt, something peasants could not do without and for which the demand was inelastic, peasants could not easily pressure the market.

Nevertheless, the peasants had several means of holding the line against unfavorable terms in local trade. Reserving land for cereal production helped assure that grain would be made available at tolerable prices—the more land in grain, the more acceptable its price. Similarly, peasants sometimes opened up their own salt fields along the riverways, and they peddled this salt over short periods at prices below those set by the government salt shops.[31] They also had recourse to the petition and the riot, both of which could be aimed at keeping prices fair for buyers and, ideally, favorable for sellers. Although peasants put pressure on local officials to ensure that grain markets would not be monopolized by exporting landlords, big merchants, and gentry, they did not oppose free trade.[32] Simply put, the popular consensus was that government should act to allow competition locally but should not allow the grain needed for survival to be sent out of the county. As late as the last decade of Qing power, peasant crowds in the small market towns of the Taihang area succeeded in pressuring magistrates to fine, and flog, those who violated this principle of local economy.[33] When the magistrate did allow the lower nobility to get away with market dealings that drew off local food supplies, he ran the risk of popular protest.

The popular desire for open and fair markets was not incompatible with peasant attempts to defend the village from the domination of county and district officials who presented the claims of the center. The peasants' determination to preserve local food supplies, or to firm up what James C. Scott has called the "moral economy of localism,"[34] was reflected in their efforts to isolate the village from the larger polity, to create intravillage networks of peasant reciprocity, and to promote the development of the freeholding village.

Above all, peasants attempted to preserve the autonomy of the village by avoiding relations with outside authority. The peasants of Xi Yakou, a Taihang village in She xian, counted among their blessings the fact that "the mountains are high and the Emperor is far away,"[35] and they made every attempt to minimize government interference in matters affecting the material basis of village life, as did their counterparts in other corners of the border region. The peasants' preference for isolation from the imperial state was most vividly apparent in their insistence on resolving disputes over local resources among themselves in order to avoid yamen-based* litigation.

Although the village was hardly an idyllic Rousseauist community with no measure of hierarchy, the dependencies that developed among peasants did not imply exploitation. Their mutual-aid group hierarchies and religious followerships usually amounted to dependency among equals, whose leaders often set standards of equity and fairness against which relations with landlords and local officials might be judged. In an important sense, these peasant dioramas of dependency permitted the peasants to avoid permanent dependence on landlords and gentry who sought to incorporate them into elite-directed hierarchies of unjust exchange and exploitation.

The success with which peasants were able to strengthen village autonomy and avoid dependency relations with landlords and local officials was also contingent on their ability to obtain land. By the late Qing period nearly 70 percent of the peasants in North China were cultivating their own land,[36] and the formation of the freeholding village most likely buttressed peasant localism. In contrast to landless peasants, who made up less than 20 percent

---

*Yamen refers to the county level court system over which the magistrate usually presided.

of the tilling population, peasant landowners did not depend on landlords for their means of existence, and their shared lineage ties gave them considerable leverage in relations with village and district leaders. In a world where landlords had been known to establish dictatorships over the villages in times of dynastic decline, the peasant smallholders kept alive the promise of the self-governed village, and the landless poor were sensitive to this possibility.

The peasants who made the most of market opportunities provided others with additional leverage in their efforts to avoid dependence on landlords. To be sure, their first priority was to replenish their own family resources from their market profits, and they were not averse to pushing the poor off the land and out of the villages. I tend to think, however, that these investing peasants also spread their gains across the village, if only indirectly. They built up dowries for marrying off their children, employed others on their expanded landholdings, and paid a large portion of village taxes. This freed the villages from total dependence on the land and market hierarchies of landlords.

But the question remains: Was the market participation of peasants community or class based? According to one authority, peasants gathered consciously as a community, rather than as a class, in markets under the supervision of the gentry temple managers.[37] Although peasants did in fact approach the market out of some very parochial interests, they seldom participated in the great imperial rituals of Confucian rule, and the festivals and fairs associated with market participation in places like Lin county traditionally fell outside gentry supervision and government control in any strict sense.[38] The local Confucian elite surely monitored these market gatherings, possibly from temple locations, but what was to prevent the peasants who undertook these pilgrimages from experiencing their participation in categories that were congruent with their interest, rather than those belonging to the gentry? The gentry by and large did not have the wherewithal to order peasant participation in small market towns, and they were not able to impose their definition of reality in the markets which focused on village, riverside, and mountain temples.[39] The market fairs of the Little Tradition brought peasants together from the far reaches of a district or county and offered them the opportunity to take collective action to curb the offending practices of landlords and local government. Therefore they were far more appreciated by the country people than were the gentry-managed rituals of Confucian government.

There can be little doubt that peasants lacked the institutional means to keep harvests from landlords and tax officials and that they were no match organizationally for imperial government. Yet the staying power of peasant localism did make for more than a little leverage against the magistrate who had ultimately to represent the imperial polity. The pressures for local subsistence needs to take precedence over the claims of outside authority were real, and village leaders tried very hard to meet popular demands to underreport the harvest and to defend the village rights to local water and wood supply. When taxes were too high peasants threatened to withhold their harvest surpluses and thereby plunge county government into crisis. Sometimes they came together in the towns to insist that the magistrate keep the price of grain and salt tolerable. All these actions served to remind local officials that the dynasty did depend ultimately on tillers to produce a large portion of its revenue and to breathe economic life into the towns and cities of the empire.

PEASANTS AND LOCAL PATRIARCHY: DEPENDENCY, EXCHANGE, AND EXPLOITATION

Though we have been discussing the peasants' self-generating drive for survival and independence, specifically the attempt to avoid elite demands on household production and exchange, there were imperial controls over peasants even in the poorly integrated parts of the empire. The border region peasantry ultimately had to deal with imperial county officials whose revenue demands had a decisive impact on survival possibilities. Just as peasants paid taxes to local officials so they paid rent to landlords, often the allies of the officials. In principle, the emperor stood for peasant welfare, and Confucian officials supported a stable agricultural order. Yet the imperial laws inevitably were mediated by landlord patriarchs who restricted the peasants' subsistence choices, and who from the eighteenth century on were less and less subject to dynastic supervision.

Peasants therefore were left to deal with nonworking landlord members of the gentry who enjoyed relations with the magistrate and who by mid-Qing times were assisting local officials in taxation and in the administration of public works.[40] The capacity of these landowning patriarchs to create peasant followerships in exchange for extending tax protection and for confirming water rights locally was considerable. Although the landlord and gentry figures could not utilize their relations with local power holders to mobilize support for just any of their plans for private gain, they often did skew the distribution of local resources to render peasants dependent on them for goods and services beyond the means of each little family, lineage, and village.

The reality of having to deal with landlord patriarchs in order to supplement family income seriously compromised the peasants' independent quest for survival. In some places peasants affiliated with landlords who could provide them with the means of production in return for labor and loyalty, and they looked upon these landlords as patrons or benefactors *(enren)*.[41] The landlords in the northern Henan, southern Hebei, and western

Shandong area were known to furnish land, implements, and grain loans and to share the harvest with peasants who cultivated their fields and showed them respect. The bonds holding peasants to patrons in this part of China were largely the product of elite sponsorship rather than peasant choice, and they were hardly formed out of an inbred peasant dependency complex. For many peasants, entry into these unequal instrumental dependency relations with landlords was the only alternative to petty theft or homeless migration. To be sure, the overly idealized Confucian picture of reciprocal dependency between peasants and landlords probably never existed, though this does not mean that peasants did not prefer to establish their right to significant elements of reciprocity in relations with landlord patrons. Small measures of mutual reciprocity *(ganqing)* undoubtedly remained at the heart of peasant hopes for humane treatment from the powerful.

The sociologist Barrington Moore, Jr., claims that China's "government and upper classes performed no function that peasants regarded as essential for their way of life."[42] As Moore's view implies, peasants were largely dependent on their own family efforts for survival, and we can be sure that the seminomadic peasant merchants and shepherds of the Taihang area strived for independence from the imperial state and ruling landlord households locally. Yet many of the region's peasants did participate in exchange relations with landlords, and there is some doubt as to whether they experienced all landlords as heartless exploiters pure and simple.[43] Objectively, landlords were exploiters, their dominance of land and property enabling them to draw peasants into unequal exchanges, but peasants often saw the benefits as the product of a mutually binding obligation.

To be sure, peasants most likely preferred self-reliance even to the dependency relations that did benefit them.[44] But the peasants' interpersonal exchanges with landlords often fostered a sense of shared responsibility, so that the tillers related to landlords as partners in agriculture. In some villages patron-client and lineage ties overlapped, so that landlords bearing the surname of peasants could emphasize kinship to deemphasize the class discrimination in unsatisfactory material exchanges. Often peasant-landlord connections went back for several generations in the same families. To landless peasants, such an involuntary relationship offered a strong incentive to stay on the land tilled by their fathers, particularly when the landlord gratified the relationship through his role of godfather. Some landlord patriarchs also sponsored secret societies like the Red Spears to defend the village against outsiders, and the peasants, who shared with them the need to protect crops and households, enlisted in their wars to defend local turf. Even smallholders entered into patron-client relationships with Confucian landlords when family-based strategies of security and survival faltered. For the most part, however, the peasants who were extensively involved in reciprocal dealings with landholding patrons were the landless poor, including tenants and hired hands.[45]

Subsistence Expectations in Traditional
Landlord-Tenant Relations

As far back as the Ming period, tenants in the border region had paid a portion of the harvest in rent to landlords in exchange for a bundle of elementary material necessities. The subsistence expectations that tenants brought to these exchanges were understood by the landlords, who pledged to abide by them.[46] These included steady employment and stability of income.[47] Landlords fulfilled the first by offering three- and five-year leases, with tenants having the option of renewal. Whereas tenants did not enjoy an ironclad guarantee of subsistence income, under customary sharecrop agreements they were entitled to about half the harvest.

In addition to land, the landlords in the Hebei-Shandong-Henan area traditionally supplied tenants with implements, plow oxen, and field silos for drying the main crop. They also sent melons to tenants during summer work breaks and rendered bonus payments to tenants and field hands for the lunar New Year celebration. These landlords took a greater share of production (say, 60 percent instead of half) when they provided more than just the land, but the additional assets usually offset the unequal division of the crop, and the tenant did not find the resulting imbalance threatening.

Landlords frequently honored tenant requests to reduce the crop rent and to provide interest-free grain loans after a poor harvest.[48] It was customary in villages like Wen Xiaoduan and Bai Yilu, located in Henan's Puyang county, for the landlord to fetch the doctor and to help pay medical bills for sick tenants.[49] Gleaning the grain fields was a customary tenant right, and a reliable landlord was expected to honor this right when the harvest was poor.[50]

Tenants also expected landlords to provide some measure of physical protection[51]—head towels and straw hats to protect themselves from sunstroke, and puttees to guard against field snakes. With few exceptions, landlords also took care of the land-tax payment, since the land did not belong to the tenant.

Furthermore, tenants and hired hands expected landlords to help arrange services and goods from the outside. For tenants these included employing field hands to help build up the earth-banks during the busy season or to replenish the windblown topsoil in the slack agricultural months. Many tenants and hired hands were paid a small percentage of the profit derived from marketing livestock they had raised.

Their dependence on landlords for access to their means of production did not make landless peasants rely less on their own labor and ingenuity to get through a normal year. For the most part, the landlords of the border region did not own the huge estates necessary to guarantee endless patronage resources to the landless peasants who toiled in their fields, and they most likely reserved their material contributions for their tenant and hired-hand foremen, or for their "favorites." Thus, by the late Qing, more and more landless peasants had to provide for their families partly by self-help activities that fell outside ordinary tenure and hired-hand agreements. These included year-round subsidiary crop production and small trade in the slack season.

This is not to deny that the landowning elite sponsored patronage to peasants over whom they exercised authority.[52] In addition to sponsoring *yi cang*, or charitable granaries, in the villages, landlords and gentry supported tax-relief and organized irrigation schemes for their villages. They also were active in sponsoring theatrical troupes,[53] which performed in the bigger market villages, where landlords and gentry often resided. The peasants with special ties to the powerful surely got the better part of such benefits, though even marginal peasants without any such connections expressed approval of tax relief or local theater. However, the landlords and gentry were clearly serving their own self-interest in offering these minimal services, which bolstered the stability of local power systems at little cost in moments of crisis while strengthening the ideology of Confucian elite accountability over the long run.

Landlord and Gentry Power and the Great Tradition Version of Peasant Dependency

Certainly the region's landlords saw themselves as more than just landholding rent collectors—they were patrons upon whom tillers could rely to promote their interests out of a shared sense of responsibility. In reducing the crop rent or issuing grain loans, landlords were, in their own minds, acting out of an obligation to the peasants. For their part, the peasants probably felt some obligation to the wealthy landowners who treated them as human beings with social rights and rendered them assistance over the years. Tenants did not object to doing little chores for landlords, for example, because they expected the landlords to do what patrons were supposed to do, such as divide the harvest fairly.

Precisely because the peasant's conception of the judicious patron, or benefactor, was conditioned in part by the landlord's notion of mutual dependency, we must keep in mind that the definition of what the patron stood for—guardianship, kindness, and fairness—was written into the annals of imperial history almost solely by powerful landlords and scholar-officials, not by poor and powerless peasants. The landlords and officials who tried to inculcate these ideas into the peasants did so out of a conviction that the "little folks" ought to respect them as benevolent big men. Naturally, they believed it their duty to contain peasant behavior within psychological and political boundaries so that it would not pose a challenge to patriarchal order, and they dispensed patronage with this goal in mind.[54] Thus, when they gave loans to peasants or redressed peasant tax grievances they were attempting to contain potential deviance from below as well as validate their own status and authority. So it was that much of peasant life was conducted within this agrarian elite definition of exchange and justice, and obviously this definition did not question the legitimacy of its dominant class position.

The language and logic that rationalized landlord relations with the peasantry were drawn from Confucian doctrine. The Confucian ethos to which the agrarian elite subscribed expressed the unshakable conviction that peasants were dependent on its benevolence for their livelihood. The land-owning patriarchs and the officials who drew on this logic as they dispensed goods to the village people quite naturally praised themselves as superior, while relegating peasants to a subordinate species.[55] Of course, peasants sometimes took the elements of noblesse oblige embedded in the Confucian ethic quite literally and reminded their patrons of their right to be treated with benevolence and kindness. To many a Confucian landlord, however, this "right" was rather a privilege that had been bestowed upon the "little people" by their betters. Thus, although an unbridgeable mental universe existed between Confucian elites and peasants, the landed and literate groups acted to maintain the fiction that peasant society was firmly integrated into the larger imperial political order that they stood for locally.

Perhaps because the peasants entertained ideas of justice, community, and power that did not quite correspond with those of the Confucian-thinking power holders, the latter expended a great deal of effort to convince peasants to accept the patriarchal ideology that was to validate the socioeconomic differences between haves and have-nots. Indeed, we cannot ignore the efforts of the Confucian ruling groups to socialize peasants to their own orthodox version of justice, privilege, and power. To take but one example, the operas and plays sponsored by Confucian landowners in border region villages were intended to line up popular culture with elite political beliefs. One of these plays, called *Clapping the Hands Three Times*, was popularized by landlords on the side of imperial state integration. The older peasants from Li Jia village in Lin county, Henan, still can recall the performance of this play in their village before Liberation.[56]

The play began by exalting a young woman from a wealthy family. As it developed, the audience learned that she had rebelled against her father, a prime minister whom she accused of despising the poor and loving the rich, in order to marry a poor beggar for whom she felt benevolence and affection. Now, although marriage alliances sometimes did tie peasants to landlords, interclass conciliation through marriage with upper-crust landlord families was a rare experience for the peasantry. Such plays were designed to convince peasants of the benefits to be gained by prostrating themselves before wealthy, influential landlord benefactors. Plays like this one encouraged some peasants to conduct their daily search for survival out of hopes for prosperity implanted by the landowning Confucian elite, though it seems unlikely that peasants shared the elite's enthusiasm for the system of social stratification that threatened them with subhuman forms of labor.

Just as landlords and gentry magistrates saw their paternalism as *the* source of peasant sustenance, so they believed themselves to be the generic source of the peasants' moral universe. Running through the ideology of Confucianism was a piquant denial that there was a Little Tradition wherein peasants were, by their own independent efforts, supporting themselves and creating their own culture. Believing in the moral superiority of its own rule, the landed and literate elite claimed that what was subjectively just in its own Great Tradition was subjectively just in the Little Tradition of the common folk. Through the long corridors of dynastic time peasants may have internalized this ethic, if only because the vertically tiered imperial polity, being cemented nationally by provisions to agriculture and locally by close relations with landlords and gentry, could make a convincing case that its hierarchical, inegalitarian order permitted tillers to exist.

There is, however, some question as to whether peasants experienced their relations with Confucian power holders so one-dimensionally. To be sure, the rural people recognized the necessity of going along with the idealistic portrayal of underclass life enshrined in Confucianism if they were to fortify their chances for survival. But this accommodation with Confucian land- and power holders by and large was not simply an exchange of deference for paternalism. Although they gave a qualified endorsement of the landlords' normative ordering symbols, the peasants nonetheless attempted to modify the inequities inherent in their relations with local patrons and power holders.[57]

Thus were peasants accustomed to negotiating their own tolerable version of exchange. Their subordination to landlords did not prevent them from adapting the Confucian view of the benevolent landowner to realize their own expectations for social justice, and no doubt they occasionally succeeded in modifying the behavior of landlords to meet the needs of their existence.[58] The tenants of Qiankou village in Henan's Neihuang county, for example, traditionally entreated their landlords in land-rent matters, but their entreatment was articulated out of the expectation that the landlord ought to live up to his obligation to make land available, share the crop on an equitable basis, and reduce the rent after a meager harvest.[59] In denouncing a landlord for failure to meet such expectations, the tenant hoped to arouse opposition to him from within the peasant community and even from the ranks of wealthy landlords.[60] The peasants who insisted on such benevolence from landlords were not subscribing unequivocally to an ethos that confirmed their inferiority, but rather adapting the beliefs of the dominant agrarian class to negotiate their rights to survival.

Clearly, then, whereas the landed Confucian elite extended a helping hand to some peasant survival efforts, the peasants, for their part, had their own standards of equity and justice in agrarian exchange and they evaluated their relations with landlords against those standards.

THE BORDER REGION'S LITTLE TRADITION:
THE HEGEMONY OF THE IMPERIAL STATE AND
THE PERSISTENCE OF FOLK CULTURE

Inevitably, the question becomes: To what extent were the imperial county magistrates and their landlord and gentry allies able to convert the peasants of the border region to their own exalted conception of justice, authority, and power? The way in which we orient ourselves to this question is bound to shape our understanding of the peasants' relationship to revolution, and to the CCP, in the post-Qing period. By raising it at this early point we will be in a better position to ascertain whether the CCP rose to power by reorganizing the views of backward village dwellers so they would fall in line with its own avant-garde ideology or by resonating with a peasant rebel ontology that derived potency for the most part from its own inner strengths.

For several decades mainstream Western social scientists and orthodox Marxists informed us that China's rural people had their perceptions colored by the Confucian ruling groups who subordinated them to their rule. The West, borrowing from Montesquieu's conception of China as a despotic Oriental state, developed the image of a "governed peasantry" whose mental universe was a reflection of the political ethos of the Great Tradition.[61] Marxists stressed conflict rather than harmony and integration, but oddly enough they reinforced the image of "governed peasantry," since their line of reasoning grew out of the premise, developed by Marx and later Gramsci, that the ruling groups who dominated the means of production also shaped the process of underclass thinking and thereby established the hegemony of their upper-crust values in peasant consciousness.[62] The unchallenged dominance of this integrationist logic reinforced a set of a priori assumptions about peasant involvement in revolution. On the one hand, traditional peasant society was said to be integrated and impervious to any change short of a sudden ripping apart of the bonds between peasants and landlord superiors. On the other—Marxist—hand was the conviction that peasants were incapable of knowing their own interest without outside leadership, provided by the gentry in traditional China and by the CCP in modern China. Consequently, most studies of change in pre-1949 China treated peasant culture as a residual variable having no significant impact of its own on the revolutionary process.

The one-dimensional quality of the patron-client and Marxist class models, coupled with the failure of those who applied them to take into account the subjective experience of peasants,[63] bolstered this early conception. What this conception failed to inform us was that in peasant China a popular value system existed alongside, and in competition with, the value system of the ruling Confucian elite.[64] Indeed, there is little evidence that the common folk *(laobaixing)* consistently evaluated their life situation wholly in categories projected by the patriarchs of the Great Tradition. W. F. Wertheim, in writing of the position of the subordinated in any society, makes my point for a nonintegrated peasant China nicely:

> Social class is not an objectively demonstrable entity, but a projection of society in terms of superiority and inferiority in the minds of some people, and . . . we cannot be sure that the evaluation among those who could be said to constitute the society would tend to coincide.[65]

The inability of Confucian groups to convert peasants completely to their philosophy and purpose had more than a little to do with the persistence of independent popular judgments about morality and politics.

Two Orders of Meaning: Elite and Peasant

As marginal participants in a world of extreme power imbalances, China's rural people nonetheless were able to create their own potentially op- positionist countersociety on the fringes of the dominant imperial order. Most peasants had a keen understanding of how rural power relations affected their quest for security. As long as landlords and officials were politically dominant, they operated by and large within the superior Con- fucian value system and deferred to the institutionally based influence of the magistrate. Their involvement in this order of meaning, however, did not rule out the possibility of dissent, if only in restricted fashion, without the stimulus of an outside power change. The same humble tillers who ex- pressed deference in the presence of landholding patrons in their absence often questioned the landlord's claim to moral superiority.

The peasants who adapted their performance in order to secure their means of sustenance from landlords doubtless also held their own counter- vailing interpretations of landlord behavior, which were evidenced tradi- tionally in rudimentary popular beliefs. Some of these beliefs offer clues that peasants participated in exchanges with landlords without endorsing the latter's values. Perhaps they signify much more, for this deviance from local patriarchy is detectable in the consciousness of the popular classes.

Given the benefits peasants derived from landholding benefactors, they naturally interacted with the latter in ways that obverted a strong militant sense of class identity. Nonetheless, peasant families and friends clearly identified with one another through common work groups such as hoeing teams and through common cultural gatherings like village temple fairs. This nascent identity with the shared existential dilemmas of family and village counterparts was broadened and reinforced as peasants increasingly mingled in the extravillage market networks that evolved with the growth of the region's commerce in Ming and Qing times.[66]

Peasants undoubtedly understood that the patron from whom they de- rived assurances of security expected their loyalty in return, and where their survival coincided with the interest of landlords the peasants often displayed sincere allegiance to benefactors. But, peasant loyalties were primarily to the family, to lineage-based friends, and to field companions. Where the latter were not enveloped by strong clan ties or patronage bonds to land-lords, as seems to have been the case in much of the Taihang area, peasants were more given to self-dedication and more capable of renouncing land-lord desires.[67] In this area small groups of peasants and traveling shepherds used to assemble on the side roads and in the hill forests that abutted the fields and temples to call into question the behavior of landlords who were not as righteous as they proclaimed. Criticizing landlords behind their backs was one of the few ways for peasants to cope with the restrictions on expression imposed by the elite.

Even on the periphery of empire, the Confucian ruling groups were fond of pointing out that peasants were affectionately committed to them, and certainly many peasants did admire some of them as patrons. However, since they had no reason to romanticize their relations with superiors, peasants more than likely harbored feelings of social antagonism toward landlords and local authority. Each village had its history of fights and floggings, and this heritage was built into the grim reality of everyday peasant life. The antagonism between peasants and landlord and gentry figures was evidenced partly in a repertory of warnings to tillers. The rope-scarred branch of the lynching tree, the execution scenes in the anti-rebel Confucian operas, and the magistrate's tiger bench stool (a torture designed to break the kneecaps) all impressed upon the peasants' minds the dangers of dissent. These warnings were hardly abstractions. Offered in a political framework that rendered peasants powerless, they served dialec-tically to remind peasants that when nature and the imperial state turned local politics into a zero-sum contest, they would be abandoned into a world in which both sides—peasant and landlord—would make up their own morality as they went along, to justify anything they did, in order to survive.

Nor were peasants without some sense of class awareness. The Confucian land- and officeholders proclaimed that all under heaven were to submit to the benevolent rule and advocated that heavenly ordained hierarchies of high and low should be honored, and such exhortations also alerted peasants to the fact that they were a group apart from landlords and officialdom.[68] If peasants knelt deferentially before their benefactors, they did so chiefly to minimize conflict with landlords who could tamper with their livelihood.[69] Surely these same peasants were aware that such upper-layer people often tended to subjugate the poor, and surely, too, they felt that much of what was given to them by patrons and powerholders was theirs by right.

Nor were the common folk unattuned to the penalties of underclass life. The jokes, wives' tales, proverbs, graffiti, profanity, and clichés of ordinary peasants often signified a shared understanding of the deprivation stemming from their subordination. Peasant jokes reveal the subtle way in which peasants articulated an awareness of the subjugation entailed in working under landlords:

When working for a landlord, Honest Zhang had only spoiled soup and scraps to eat and never anything decent. One day, on the landlord's birthday, he sent Honest Zhang out to buy a big fresh fish in the market. When he had done this, Honest Zhang cut it into three big pieces. The meaty middle piece he cooked up and greatly enjoyed. The remainder, the head and the tail, he wrapped up and took to the master.

The master took one look and asked in astonishment: "What's the meaning of this? There's only the head and the tail. Where's the middle?"

"What's the use of the middle?" said Honest Zhang. "I cut it off and threw it away."

"What! You threw it away?"

"What else should I do with it? It's nearly two years that I've been working for you and I've never eaten the middle part of a fish, so I thought it was only the head and the tail that could be eaten."[70]

The peasants of the border region, like their counterparts in the Dominican village studied by Kenneth Sharpe,[71] did not have a categorical understanding of "class injustice," but they knew that "the big fish always swallows the little fish,"[72] and much of their folklore hinted of the advantages to be had by doing away with Confucian hierarchy and power.

When peasants questioned the values of Confucian-thinking superiors they did so cautiously, out of survival concerns that were not always colored by a preexisting solidaristic counterculture. The discrepancies between peasant and landlord interpretations of social justice sometimes led to pointed disagreements over the same facts. The peasants here, as elsewhere in rural China, often approached these disagreements from religious viewpoints that reaffirmed both their right to sustenance and their opposition to subordination.

Naturally, the integrationist school has focused on the attempts of imperial officialdom to assimilate popular religion[73] and to foster a sense of belonging to the Confucian polity. But the dynasty was never strong enough to effectively impose on the lower classes in the countryside a one-religion empire, ritualized only by Confucianism, and its attempt to do so was contested by the heterodox sects that became the targets of its ideological persecution. A vast assortment of folk religions thrived under the hostile eye of imperial rule, and Confucian doctrine made little impression on the primitive beliefs of their peasant members. The religious outlook of the rural people had its origins outside the imperial state and persisted in Taoist and Buddhist undercurrents independently of official Confucian orthodoxy. It was partly in these subaltern currents of primitive folk religion, which stressed the ultimate leveling of differences between rich and poor and the united actions of the poor to avoid the excessive demands of the Confucian elite, that peasants found the moral strength to dissent.

Peasant religion was in part family based and in part expressive of values carried by the common folk—not just the elite. Take the worship of *zaoshen*, the kitchen god. *Zaoshen* worship was undertaken out of respect for this deity's position as the most lowly client of celestial officials who whispered sweet words on behalf of family survival to the supernatural Jade emperor on the twenty-third day of the twelfth lunar month.[74] In the Taihang area even landlord households recited vows before *zaoshen*, but the peasants took kitchen god worship far more seriously, perhaps because it offered cues to success in planting and harvesting. The guarantor of food grains, the kitchen god stood for family food security before anything else. This was the one popular deity who had not been canonized into the cultism of the Confucian state, and peasant worship of this deity, though symbolically linked to the pantheon of gods, was not the product of integrative social interaction with the custodians of the Confucian order.[75]

The Buddhism of ordinary folk, while permeated by Confucian precepts, hardly made for a unified Confucian-Buddhist opposition to pagan spiritualism. In practice, the peasants turned their backs on official attempts to foist an essentially statist version of Buddhist gospel onto village life and purpose, and they displayed a considerable capacity to bring their own folk conceptions to bear on the messages passed down from landlords and priests and to place Buddhism in the service of their basic needs. The Confucian version of *Guanyin*, the Buddhist goddess of mercy, to take one example, stressed the concern of unapproachable divinities for the sufferings of a quiescent peasantry,[76] whereas peasants looked upon Guanyin as an activist savior who released them from the injustices of the here and now. From time to time, the local Guanyin initiatives of peasants even provided the template for collective protests that were at odds with the orthodox Confucian version of social and political order.

Nor was folk Taoism a Little Tradition "religious support system" for ruling Confucian morality. Taoism was dangerous to Confucianism because of its appeal to the peasant belief that subsistence lay ultimately in solitary retreat from the prevailing requirements of officials, and peasants sometimes drew from Taoist-Buddhist logic to exercise this retreat symbolically. The peasants in the remote Hebei-Shanxi-Henan area had kept alive the midsummer festival of Yulanpen, and over time this ceremony, which landlords and officials only loosely supervised, took on a meaning that did not coincide with the elite attempt to create vertical community in the interest of state integration locally.[77] The local notables attending this festival often sponsored feasts that underscored their obligation to provide for the peasantry. But for the local poor this was also the occasion to celebrate the release of hungry souls into a stateless paradise from the subterranean prisons of Taoist hell. In this sense Yulanpen, or the Festival of the Dead, did not necessarily promote solidarity between peasants and local power holders, because peasants associated it with the time when they would free themselves from the constant state of subordination imposed by the Confucian state, whose officials they equated with the constables of Taoist hell.

The Festival of the Dead signified the coming of a veritable All Souls' Day within the border region's Little Tradition, the chance to break with dynastic time and to hark back to a world that did not require sacrifice to the imperial state.

As long as peasants could fulfill their social needs, the symbolic gaps between them and the caretakers of the Great Tradition remained politically inconsequential. Folk beliefs fundamentally critical of the Confucian *Weltanschauung* began to take on political significance mainly in the moments of openly expressed opposition to the overlords and officials whose violations of Little Tradition morality and justice had moved peasants to rebellion. In these moments, peasants joined with less-rooted members of the local poor to produce a number of criticisms that underscored the illegitimacy of ongoing Confucian hierarchy and power.

Peasant Counterculture and the Temporary Dominance of Folk Values in Traditional Rural Uprisings

Existing side by side with the Confucian ethos was a peasant counterculture that had its roots in some rather loosely articulated folk notions of justice. Insomuch as this culture fell outside the patron-client syndrome cultivated by Confucian landlords and officials, peasants could hardly be said to have been in the thrall of hegemonic elite hierarchy. On the contrary, they preferred to remake society in the image of their own culture rather than accept the one defined as morally fitting by the ruling Confucian groups.

The interesting question is whether the folk counterculture contained the seeds of a fundamentally different sociopolitical order. If we could step back into the quiet villages of the seventeenth century, I doubt that we could outline this counterculture by canvassing the region's peasantry. For one thing, peasants ordinarily did not devote much thought to articulating a coherent revolutionary ideology. For another, peasants usually rebelled within a constraining political framework, and hence they were careful to protest in a deferential manner that fell in line with Confucian ideas of obligation and order. Finally, afraid that their betters might find out, peasants were inclined to be only mildly critical of benefactors to outsiders, regardless of the real situation locally.

With the advantage of hindsight, however, we can detect the emergence of a popular counterorder in those rare moments when the presence of an insurgent army permitted peasants to express the radical ideas they usually kept to themselves. My own feeling is that over the centuries the peasants of the border region had come to experience the arrival of a rebel army as a political catalyst to free them from government oppression and to help them challenge the inegalitarian order of Confucianism and the Great Tradition universe. These moments when the country people openly put forth their own notions of justice, including a set of socioreligious beliefs about subsistence and salvation, were the moments when a customarily conservative peasantry struck out to turn the world downside up, that is, rightside up, and reached out to create a fundamentally different society. That ideal society was a world without interclass paternalism and dependency or political subordination. It was a world in which peasants suspended the ordinary rules of hierarchy and substituted their own versions of justice for the cultural ethos of the imperial Confucian state.

The Late Ming Dynasty Revolt of Li Zicheng

Let us look briefly into the emergence of peasant countervalues in the late Ming dynasty revolt of Li Zicheng, which took place in the same Shaanxi-Shanxi and Henan-Hebei border countries where the CCP would draw popular support in the crisis decades of the twentieth century.[78] An intricate convergence of internal and international changes produced the conditions that gave rise to Li Zicheng's revolt in the 1640s. Nearly two decades of natural disaster and then three straight years of drought and poor harvests without any tax relief set in motion food riots and rent strikes; and the agricultural depression and social unrest of the time are said to have been aggravated by a drop-off in silver imports coming into the Ming treasury from New Spain and Manila.[79] At the outset, many of the peasants who participated in this revolt apparently were aiming only to readjust rents and appeal for tax rebates.[80] There is reason to suspect, however, that what started out as nonradical remedialist protest eventually developed into an all-out peasant attack on the ideas and institutions of Confucian patriarchy, and that peasants attempted to replace the Confucian ethos with their own version of justice and authority as Li Zicheng's army surged toward regional and national power in its brief victories of 1642 to 1644.[81]

We must not underestimate the moral weight of this antistatist explosion. Peasants still associate Li Zicheng's movement with their goal of ending the subordination of society by the state, and the accomplishments of this tradition, kept alive in spoken legend and popular novel, are still recalled in the poor mountain areas that harbored the Chinese Communist movement. Hence we are reminded that when the Li Zicheng army took Henan, peasants there identified its cause with their own. They went beyond appeals for fair rents to drive from the villages the landlords who had not worked the land.[82] Their rebel assemblies stopped paying the rent and taxes that had supported the temples and schools of wealthy Confucian landlords, and they compelled the latter to kneel and pledge allegiance to an "all tiller's world" without distinctions of hierarchy. In redistributing grain, peasants angrily declared that landlords had no right to label them inferior,[83] and they decided it was only just to do away with those who were subjecting the villages to dearth. The folk songs of these peasants called for an end to land usurpation by landlords and for a three-year suspension of taxes imposed by officials.[84]

The peasants involved in this revolt were reacting to defend their rights to subsistence, but at the same time their struggles expressed angry dissent against local patriarchy, reflecting something other than the collective defense of paternalism emphasized in Western accounts of peasant dissent. The rural poor were revolting to remove local power holders, and their revolt no doubt reflected an unflinching struggle against elite-imposed subordination and the local manifestations of imperial misrule.

A Qualification of the Revolutionary Potentiality of the Little Tradition

Nevertheless the imperial order must be understood primarily in terms of the institutional and ideational restraints it placed on the revolutionary potentiality of the Little Tradition, and only secondarily in terms of its own structural weaknesses.[85] The unalterable fact of agrarian Chinese history is that a centralized imperial political system did persist for over two thousand years on a scale even beyond that achieved in Rome and elsewhere, and that the imperial state did manage to keep peasants in a position of subordination and to smash the popular rebellions that rocked its order. Revolution, by which I mean a fundamental sociopolitical reordering of the imperial polity in line with the countervalues of the rural folk, was an impossibility in the traditional world. Without a diamond-clear understanding of the political limitations to peasant-based revolution in that world, we will not be able to appreciate the novel conditions making for revolutionary possibilities in the twentieth century.

To begin with, the imperial state had a long history of knowing how to mobilize its national army for effective, lethal campaigns against the insurgents who sought peasant support in this oldest region of the empire. The centralized, unified command of the imperial court, though slow to react to the seemingly insignificant rebellions on its periphery, enjoyed an overwhelming advantage over the various insurgent armies, with their competing claims to command. The divergent goals and divided opinions in the councils of insurgent generals had the effect of splitting rebel armies, leading to defeat on the battlefield, which in turn lowered morale in the villages located in the heartland of rebel power.

Then, too, the rebel commanders did not do very much to prevent their soldiers from preying on the peasantry. Insurgent army demands for peasants to provision the troops or to participate in combat too often turned into a tug-of-war with tillers, who treasured roots and safety. This built-in tension between rebel forces and peasants whose short-run subsistence needs did not mesh with the battlefield requisites of insurgent armies was a contradiction *within* the revolutionary camp. Even so, relatively immobile tillers could make only limited contributions of time, energy, and property to war, and in the absence of nonpeasant groups who could step in and relieve them from war-related sacrifices insurgent commanders could not hold the country people to their cause. The use of coercion for this purpose often sent peasants scurrying away from rebel armies, perhaps into the camp of contending local landlords and gentry.

The strength of peasant counterculture was another, albeit smaller, problem. In the long periods when Confucian landholders and officials held sway, the peasant counterculture was not fully in place and dominant subjectively, so we cannot assume that peasants in different localities were just waiting for an opportunity to elaborate a set of shared revolutionary ideas once a rebel army set the border region ablaze. The landlords and local magistrates thus enjoyed an advantage in containing conflicts that might have given rise to peasant mobilizations across the region's smaller political and economic arenas. Those who found themselves under attack, for example, would settle grievances with peasants on a one-to-one basis in the confidence of their villages and districts, and every effort would be made to contain local flare-ups within a county. There is little reason to doubt that peasants were willing to participate in procedures to resolve grievances; these, however, limited their access to information that would have facilitated independent linkups with their counterparts elsewhere.[86] Thus, in the absence of national pressures on powerholders in different localities to exploit peasants mercilessly over a long period, the local elite was able to contain the peasant mobilizations that might have led to the fermentation of a unified popular counterculture across the border region.

Finally, the capacity of the rural folk to create an authentic revolutionary ideology by their own efforts, rather than merely reflecting it in a period of openness such as the rare moments of army-led insurgency offered, was somewhat limited. On the one hand, literate Confucian landlords drew from the classics to extoll servility and equate rebellion with sin, part of their manifold effort to keep peasants in darkness. Peasants no doubt grew weary of this skulduggery, but were prone to sliding back to certain ruling group ideas over the course of the revolt. On the other hand, the nonpeasant insurgents who challenged orthodox Confucian power often slipped into the role of ruling patriarchs or established their own war colonies over the villages.[87] Thus the insurgents who promised to recapture a pre-Confucian past without overlords and officials sometimes pursued their goals in an authoritarian style that re-created dependency relations with peasants whose hope initially had been for a world without hierarchy. For these reasons, insurgent armies flying the banner of the region's Little Tradition seldom if ever generated an institution powerful enough to replace the dominant Confucian political culture.

Peasants were willing to work within an imperial system whose officials would not violate the subsistence perimeter they had drawn around production, and for landlords whose contributions softened the harsh reality of underclass life. Of course dependency was not the preferred order of things, and peasants did not consistently evaluate their relations with landlords and local officialdom in the overly idealized categories of Confucian patriarchy. The precarious ecosystem and corruptible officials occasionally combined to drive peasants to defend their rights by protest, but open rebellion was rare. The peasants rose up collectively *against* Confucian hierarchy mainly in the rare, short-lived moments when an insurgent army enabled them to openly voice strong preferences for a world without the state, that is, for a return to the golden era when produce would not be lost to imperial rulers. This in fact was impossible: first, because before the late nineteenth century the imperial state was careful not to allow political conditions to slide into endless chaos; and second, because armed insurgents almost invariably led the country people who aligned with them once again into Confucian history, that is, into relations of political subordination and social hierarchy. Only in the twentieth century, and mainly after the fall of the Qing order, would there emerge the unique set of political circumstances making folk revolution possible through a powerful mass movement. It is to these unprecedented developments in this backward periphery, which until the early twentieth century had been sealed off from catastrophic global influences, that we now turn.

2

New Pressures on
Peasant Livelihood

While traveling through Hebei and Shandong in 1931 R. H. Tawney observed that the position of the peasantry was "that of a man standing permanently up to the neck in water, so that even a ripple is sufficient to drown him."[1] Two years earlier, Colonel Ernest P. Bicknell, the head of an American Red Cross investigatory team, wrote of the dangers in underestimating "how close to starvation these people actually live. Anything, therefore, which disturbs this delicate balance, precipitates tragedy. All they can ever do is keep heads barely above water. Disturb this balance, and they sink."[2] Tawney and Bicknell were to draw the ire of the central government for implying that government itself was a paramount source of peasant impoverishment. The Republican successors of the ancien régime, reversing the lifeguard duties of officialdom, were themselves dragging the drowning victim under.

The stark picture of peasant livelihood drawn by Tawney and Bicknell is directly at odds with the school of thought in Western economic history that argues against the immiserization of the peasantry.[3] The image of rural North China conveyed by the works of J. L. Buck and Ramon Myers is one of minimally exploited, upwardly mobile peasant landowners whose lot often improved with the cultivation of cash crops.[4] Proponents of this school argue that peasant production and peasant living standards did not decline in the post-Qing period. This linear development, according to Myers and others, was interrupted only by the Japanese invasion, which created new claims on peasant harvests and cut off the efforts of local Republican government to update the backward technology of tillers—said to be the key to agricultural progress.[5]

In examining the Buck-Myers position, we begin to draw out the differences between their image and my conception of the peasant economy in the North China interior during the Republican era. Most of the data from which Buck and Myers drew their conclusions was collected from villages skirting the modern roads and railways that linked the North China metropolitan zone with the treaty ports. The villages of the periphery, however, had depended on water transport in late Qing, and few of them benefited from the new lines of transport and trade. Whereas Buck and Myers looked at peasant maximization of profit, defined largely as the absolute level of production and prices received from primary products, my focus is on the changing terms of exchange between peasants and local landlords and officials in competition with them for land, water, harvests, and markets. The border region peasantry was concerned mainly with whether harvest yields and cash income would prove sufficient to meet payments demanded by landlords and Republican government and still provide for family needs. The Western economic history school treats the relationship of peasants to power holders as a secondary, seemingly random variable; my focus is on the ways in which peasant agricultural choices were shaped by power holders at various levels. Finally, although the Buck-Myers school holds correctly that foreigners did not displace landlords and Republican government to develop and directly rule the rural economy, we must still ask whether international influences, passed on indirectly and incompletely, were having an unsettling impact on the region's peasants in the decades before the Japanese invasion.

THE REPUBLICAN COUNTRYSIDE IN LATE QING CONTEXT

An agrarian region where a century before peasant families had been able to survive by labor-intensive techniques, mutual aid and petty trade, and occasional migration was now, between 1911 and 1937, beset with a widespread subsistence crisis. We can begin to comprehend this staggering development by reference to the fiscal crisis of late Qing. This crisis, which involved the loss of imperial treasury to both internal and international contenders for Chinese government revenues, had been building for at least half a century, and continued uninterruptedly into Republican times to complicate the efforts of peasants to survive the usual hardships in their lives.

Internally, the loss of imperial revenues has been traced to the inability of the late Qing to prevent local officials from building informal patronage systems to extort taxes from the peasantry.[6] And the Qing mobilization of militaries to contain popular antitax stirrings doubtlessly increased taxation for provincial and regional army building. Yet it does not appear that either patron-client building or army building broke the imperial treasury, since the Board of Revenue was able to balance the budget as late as 1890 by relying partly on older sources of revenue.[7] Although peasants suffered from late Qing revenue problems, the fiscal crisis of the Chinese state, and its social ramifications in the border region, did not peak until the Republic.

By the late nineteenth century, the Chinese government interest and indemnity payments to various foreign powers was already depleting the revenue on which the Board of Revenue traditionally had relied. With the

1894–95 Sino-Japanese War indemnity and the Boxer indemnity, the Qing was required to pay ever larger sums of money to Japan, Russia, England, the United States, and other global powers.[8] These extortions at gunpoint culminated in the exhaustion of the old sources of imperial state revenue and created pressures for taking more and more peasant income for state debt relief—including the salt tax, the *lijin* (a levy on domestic goods in transit), and a host of surtaxes on production. This crisis in no way abated with the fall of the Qing order. On the one hand, the Western inspectors of the Maritime Customs Service took over the collection of revenue in the provinces and placed the income in non-Chinese banks.[9] On the other, the Beiyang or Northern Warlords waged wars to capture salt supplies and control cash-crop lands, and the winners levied additional salt and land taxes to pay for their personal armies.[10] Thus, despite the centrist preferences of military figures like Yuan Shikai and Jiang Jieshi (Chiang Kaishek), Republican China remained without a central political system strong enough to fully recover the fiscal autonomy lost to warlord cliques and foreign powers.

As the central polity redirected its revenues to pay foreign debts and put down internal revolts the old commitment to river repair, relief grain measures, and resettlement allowances to migrants fell off considerably. The calamities that filled this Qing "giving gap" left millions of peasants hungry and homeless,[11] and the gap only widened after the dynasty gave way to the Republic. In their growing tendency to take from the villages in order to fight internal wars and finance foreign loans Republican militarists soon set aside imperial restraints on state taking and penetrated the defensive perimeter that villagers had drawn against government.[12] Gone was the time when the Board of Revenue regulated central government revenue collection so as not to harm tillers, when provincial officials promoted standards of equity and fairness in taxation, when the county magistrate punished landlords and merchants who purchased grain in good harvest districts in order to sell at speculator's prices in disaster-stricken districts.[13] This new taking process had been moving the region's villages toward a social breaking point in the two decades preceding the perpetual hunger of the 1930s.

Four Theories of Peasant Hunger

The Western economic history school dismisses the twentieth-century "immiserization" of the peasantry as mostly a self-serving deception perpetuated by the CCP. This way of looking at rural China, however, avoids the central question of why the central government never gained a popular mandate to rule the countryside, and insinuates that the central government under Jiang Jieshi did not contribute to the subsistence dilemmas of rural dwellers. The Western economic school drew support from a number of theories that rested on this latter questionable assumption.

According to one theory, the inability of the central government to penetrate the countryside prevented Jiang Jieshi, and the Guomindang, from collecting revenue and promoting rural prosperity,[14] and of course rampant provincial warlordism did constitute a considerable obstacle to central government attempts to tax the towns and villages. The fact that military governors like Feng Yuxiang in Henan and Yan Xishan in Shanxi accepted payments and/or took up posts in the Central Committee of the Guomindang after 1927 ought not to be ignored, however, because such warlord alliances with the central government did contribute significantly to peasant hunger. Revenue officials in Shanxi were not assigned directly by the central government, and so the drawing of taxes out of its villages by warlord-gentry cliques was probably not officially sanctioned. But in Henan province, where governor Liu Zhi was handpicked by Jiang Jieshi,[15] the military-gentry cliques took taxes in the name of the Guomindang after 1930.[16] Neither situation placed any real political limitations on tapping and spending of village resources. All in all, the new taxes of the imperfectly united Praetorian Republic further depleted the food supply of the already marginal peasantry.[17]

Another theory pointed to the central government alignment with the conservative gentry spokesmen of the ancien regime, and thus questioned whether peasant poverty was a handicap imposed by seemingly pacifist and paternalistic local power brokers. Officially the central government emphasized it was not the agent of class injustice while the gentry denied any wanton exploitation, but the landlord gentry figures who took up Guomindang district posts and served in Guomindang army commands were no longer committed to past obligations. They by and large used their Guomindang connections to enrich themselves at the expense of the peasantry, and their nonpaternalist dominance contributed substantially to peasant immiserization and class tension in the countryside.

A third theory (which owed its origins to the attempt of United States congressman Joseph McCarthy to redefine the Chinese revolution mainly in reference to international Communist influence) declared the CCP to be subverting the Guomindang on behalf of the Stalinist Comintern. Proponents of this view accused the Chinese Communists of radicalizing the peasantry in the late 1920s, and thereby making it impossible for Jiang Jieshi's party to carry out moderate agrarian reform. The problem with this interpretation is that the Jiang Jieshi military rose to power by cannibalizing the Guomindang in the decades before the Chinese Communists entered this region with force. The militarization of the Guomindang and the replacement of party government with a nonreformist military[18] was a blow to the Guomindang politicians who might have relieved the hunger of the rural people. On the one hand, during the Northern Revolutionary Expedition Jiang Jieshi cashiered the reform-minded left-wing Guomindang under Wang Jingwei for its talk of rent reduction and tax cuts. On the other, after 1931 Jiang even alienated the Western Hills right-wing faction under Hu

Hanmin, with its plan for patron-client party rule at the county level.[19] With these developments accomplished, Jiang Jieshi established a personal patron-client network over the shaky warlord coalition he had formed from the civil war of 1929–30, and these nonparty militarists plundered peasant households and village granaries until the middle years of the war with Japan.

A fourth theory held that hunger got out of hand primarily because of problems created by the Japanese invasion of 1937. The wartime inflation, said to have been triggered by the Japanese sweep into North China, presumably destabilized the new Republic of China.[20] The Republic, though ruled by a corrupt officer corps, was assumed to be on the road to recovery under Generalissimo Jiang Jieshi. The problem with this position, which was assumed by American financial advisers to the central government, is that inflation in the North China interior was induced in part by Jiang Jieshi's military entourage in the years leading to invasion, and that the War with Japan provided these militarists with yet another reason for intensifying an inflation that had been dogging the peasantry for several years, if not decades.[21]

The mounting subsistence crisis under the central government is best understood against the backdrop of late Qing and early Republican development.[22] By the 1860s the Qing dynasty had begun to neglect the Yellow River Water Works,[23] and from 1875 on the peasants in the lowlands of the North China periphery were at the mercy of the floods that rushed down from the Taihang Mountains nearly every spring. Hardly a cent of the millions of dollars raised from the villages went to repairing the Yellow River dikes, and provincial militarists shelved plans to dredge the Fen, Zhang, and Wei rivers. In southern Hebei, the Hua-Puyang area, and western Shandong, yearly floods battered down the old dikes under the Nationalist government after 1927.[24] From 1929 to 1939 the land in southern Hebei was repeatedly immersed in fifteen feet of water, plow animals were drowned, and homes were swept away on the Fuyang River. There was a folk song about the family sorrows wrought by these floods:

> The flood waters crest to the heavens
> For nine of ten years there have been drowning floods
> Sons are sold in exchange for a handful of millet
> Daughters are sold to pay taxes
> The oxen have starved, the dogs have been slaughtered
> It's time to swing a bag and go wandering for food[25]

The precursor of death was drought. Three rainless years had ushered in the Great Famine of 1876 to 1879 and the North China Famine of 1920 and 1921. Death rates had been so high that in the late 1920s the first signs of dryness created panic among even the better-off peasants. With just one harvest failure grain prices would soar and every family would be left to get by on husks, stalk, bark, and shriveled vegetation.

Refugees from the 1901 Shanxi famine

Natural Disasters, Famine Conditions, and Social Consequences
in North China 1875–1942*

1876–79
The Great Famine Stalks Shanxi, Hebei, Shandong, and Henan.
Three Years of Drought Lead to Successive Crop Failures. Ten
Million Peasants Starve to Death. Death Rates Range from
60–90 percent of Village Inhabitants in Shandong, Henan,
and Shanxi.

1887–89
The Henan Floods. Followed by Famines. No Crops to Harvest.
Two Million Lives Lost to Starvation and Drowning.

1896–1906
Yellow River Floods Rage across Shandong and Hebei. 1898
Major Flood Disasters in Hebei, Shandong, Anhui, and Jiangsu.
Two Hundred Thousand Refugees from Yellow River Flood;
Five Million from Huai River Floods.

1901
Famine in Shanxi.

1918–19
Terrible Drought in northern Henan and southern Hebei.

*For sources of data see note 22.

1920–21   The North China Famine Grips the Area of the Great Famine. Three Years of No Rain Lead to Crop Failures in Shanxi, Hebei, and Shandong. Approximately Two Million Peasants Perish. Death Rates from 3–50 percent of Village Populations in southern Hebei and western Shandong.

1924–25   Flash Floods in central Hebei and western Shandong. Thousands of Refugees on the Run, Disastrous Floods Now Occurring Every Other Year on the Fen, Sha, and Zhang Rivers.

1926–29   Impending Famine in Hebei, Shandong, and Henan. Droughts of 1923, 1926, and 1927 Lead to 50–80 percent Autumn Grain Crop Losses in 1926, 27, 28. Death Rates 10–20 percent. Reports of 80–90 percent of Shandong-Hebei Border Region Village Inhabitants Below the Normal Subsistence Level.

1928–34   The Great Northwest Famine Hits Shanxi, Shaanxi, and Gansu. Henan Seriously Afflicted Too. Droughts in the Summer of 1929 and 1930 Reduce Crops. American Red Cross Reports Scope and Severity of Famine Much Greater than 1920–21 North China Famine.

1932–33   Drought and Famine on the Taiyuan Plain and in the Qin River Valley.

1929–39   Fuyang River Flooding in Hebei.

1942   The Henan Famine Follows Three Years of Murderous Droughts in Hebei, Shanxi, and Henan. Five Million Tillers Perish.

Relief from drought was harder to come by in the Nationalist decade than in late Qing, though it was grossly inadequate in both eras. Qing dynasty granaries had been depleted by fiscal debts, and, owing partly to county-

A peasant family confronting death in the developing order
of Guomindang warlordism, in the 1942 Henan famine

level corruption and partly to poor provincial roads, the grain that arrived in the famine-afflicted districts of Shanxi and Henan was too little, too late.[26] In late Qing the gentry in these provinces reportedly issued grain from their charitable granaries *(yi cang)* without interest, but after the dynasty fell such loans were made on high-interest terms.[27] The regional militarists not only pillaged village granaries, they also seized the grain peasants had saved for seeding or for family relief. The grain was stored in private railcars, and the fear of interception by rivals prevented military governors from moving it into famine zones only a few hundred *li* up or down the rail lines.[28] And during the awful droughts of 1928 to 1934 and 1942 the Guomindang made no attempt to disseminate the drought-resistant sorghum seeds that had been developed for the arid provinces or to dispense relief grain.[29]

Locust swarms followed the famines of 1876–79, 1920–21, and 1942. Ravaging the crops that had withstood the drought, locusts invariably damaged the lands from which any village hoped to draw relief and recovery. Yet at no time did either the Beiyang Warlords or the Guomindang armies that drew sustenance from these croplands assist tillers in their struggles to beat back the locust attacks.

The Western economic history school has treated these natural disasters as "random disturbances,"[30] but in the interior these disasters surely were exacerbated by the warlord pillage that had shifted much of the burden of indemnity payments and taxes for army building onto the peasantry. Of course peasants did not readily understand the interlinkage between imperialism, warlord plunder, and their own distress, but as the disasters repeatedly broke down village defenses against famine the country people came to equate disaster with a hungry wolf in the clothing of Republican government.[31] This reaction persisted through the 1920s, so that peasants took the fact that the Guomindang accepted flood and famine without struggle as evidence of illegitimate government, and not just fate alone.

Though each of the Northern Warlords professed intentions to integrate the villages into a unified central polity, their development programs defied the imperial dynastic practices that had kept peasants secure and seemingly loyal. All of them were intent on acquiring grain for their troops, or so they said. The problem was that they invariably taxed the peasantry without paying sufficient attention to the amount of cereals left on hand after the harvest disasters. And the central government never altered this new practice. Pillage was so thoroughly institutionalized in Jiang Jieshi's praetorian regime that Henan peasants called the Guomindang Warlords the "calamity troops" and included General Dang Enbo among the plagues of the province.[32] To make matters worse, the landed gentry were inclined to align with the aristocratic-minded warlord officers in command of this calamity, and with the Republican officials who paid little attention to the old principle of avoidance. When Jiang Jieshi's Guomindang Army penetrated the region after 1928, the bigger landlords often drew into their patronage networks Guomindang officers who carpetbagged from district to district, squeezing as much as possible in the shortest time from peasant communities to whom they felt no obligation.[33]

No Republican government, including the Guomindang, overcame the traditional geopolitical obstacles to ruling this interior region. The central government commands went after the cities of the inner core of the North China Plain—Beijing, Tianjin, Shijiazhuang, Anyang, and Xinxiang. Here the land was fertile, roads and railways were less costly to construct, and cash cropping prevailed,[34] all to the advantage of Guomindang revenue agents. The central government did little to improve highways and install telegraphs beyond the Beijing-Hankou Railway stops of Xingdai, Handan, Anyang, and Xinxiang, and the little county-level capitals leading up into the Taihang Range remained days and weeks away from the garrison forces that had to enforce the claims of local Republican powerholders. The circumstantial evidence suggests that the central government had to rely on bandits like Sun Dianying to take over the main-line towns like Handan and Anyang, which had been under attack by popular forces through the 1920s,[35] and its commanders undoubtedly relied on military rogues to patrol the county-level capitals of the Taihang—which in any event were thought to be strategically unimportant. In addition, floods impeded the travels of Guomindang foot soldiers and cavalry, so that peasants often had time to get their protest movements beyond the take-off stage before outside forces arrived to repress them.

With the Qing dynasty gone and power in the hands of Jiang Jieshi and the provincial militarists, landlord and gentry figures were free to exploit the peasantry without fear of reprimand. Many landlords entertained visions of becoming magistrates, warlord army captains, and chamber of commerce heads, and they relied on these new sources of power and money to abuse Republican government in ways that intensified inequities. Simultaneously, militarization placed its own pressure on landlords to reduce contributions to peasants. For example, the Shanxi landlord who was faced with paying the transient tax imposed on his crops by Yan Xishan's *lijin* collectors passed on his losses to peasants by either raising the rent or withdrawing pay for carting crops to market. As landlords shifted their interest from mutuality to money—a shift engendered by the perpetual attraction to cash-crop profits and nurtured by greed—they pressed tillers to give more produce, labor, and time for less pay. As these changes settled into the foundations of Republican local politics and society, landlords abandoned the social and ceremonial acts that once allowed them to pass as patrons.[36]

The Emergence of Immoral Landlordism

The early years of the Republic saw an impersonal *rentier* replace the landlord with whom peasants had interacted on the basis of mutuality. An outlook of immoral landlordism, or landlordism without obligations to tillers, best describes the new landlord mentality which prevailed in Yao village in northern Henan and in Si Beichia village in southern Hebei.[37] By the 1920s the only responsibility the landlord felt toward those who tilled the land was to collect the rent or the interest, reflecting a drastically altered belief about what ought to be contributed to land and labor. Disturbed and baffled by changes in tenure, loans, and wages, peasants often expressed their incredulity that landlords had gone so far in violating the old terms of work life.

This break with tradition was reflected in many landlords' refusal to deal personally with the peasants they were exploiting. Where fixed rent prevailed landlords began relying on a middleman to arrange rental agreements with peasants who formerly were friends as well as neighbors and relatives.[38] This enabled them to get the better of the bargain in crop rent and to take back the land when the harvest was poor without the "trouble" of the older contracts. Perhaps as a study of Ten Mile Inn in Wuan *xian* suggests, lineage ties between peasants and landlord still made for a close interpersonal bond[39] even as landlords respected past obligations less and less, so that tenants bearing the same surname as the landlord retained the right to renew the lease, and so on. Most of the poor peasants who did not share their landlords' lineage, however, were stripped of a number of traditional rights. The tenants of Bai Yilu village in Puyang *xian*, for example, were forbidden to face the members of the landlord's family while serving food to them.[40] The tenants of San San village in Lin *xian* were not consulted when the landlord decided to sell the tenancy they tilled, and the land was sold out from under them even though they had established the right of first purchase.[41]

Generational experience was important too. By the late 1920s, the adolescent peasant had come to know the kind of landlord who had broken many promises to his father and grandfather, regardless of their work performance, and not a few of these rural youths will reappear in later pages as members of the CCP in the border region. Another indication of the widening social gap between landlords and peasants was the erosion of fictive bonds. Many a landowning patriarch who in the past had acted as a godfather to his tenant's children now consented to issue loans or renew lease only on condition that he might dictate the marriage of a daughter or the labor duties of a son. It is difficult to express the sense of betrayal felt by the victims of such schemes, but the heated arguments over quotidian issues frequently gave rise to physical clashes of one kind or another.[42] The secret-society bonds which brought peasants and landowning patrons together were equally strained.

Terms of Exchange: Tenants, Freeholders, and Rich Peasants

The issue of tenancy and exchange shares would be irrelevant if land tenure percentages in the North China interior were as low as 7 to 15 percent,[43] or if the negative correlation between debilitating land-tenure developments and the subsequent rise of the CCP in this region were firmly established. These Western economic school claims appear questionable, however, when juxtaposed with the changed nature of the peasant economy in various parts of the region.

Take the northern Henan quadrant as an example. A small peasant economy had existed before 1911, with peasant landowners making up approximately 70 to 80 percent and tenants constituting about 10 to 15 percent of the tilling population.[44] Not long after the Qing dynasty fell, however, there were counties, such as Hua *xian*, wherein 36 percent of the tillers were said to be tenants,[45] and the incidence of tenancy was as high as 40 percent in some of the richer market villages and towns of the Hebei-Shanxi-Henan area, with landlords and gentry holding hundreds and even thousands of *mu*.[46]

The incidence of tenancy, however, does not tell us much about the work life problems of landless tillers. Let us examine the terms of exchange between landlord and tenant in specific rental systems. Landlord contributions to tenants probably had fallen off in late Qing, but in early Republican times landlords began overturning old tenure agreements and placing the major burden of agricultural risk on tenants.

In the past, landlords had dismissed tenants for a variety of reasons, including incompetence and dishonesty, as J. L. Buck has emphasized.[47] After the death of Yuan Shikai, however, even competent, honest tenants could no longer count on the security of employment. Many landlords, seeing the long-term tenant as a liability in thin times, reduced the security of tenure from five years to one,[48] often involving a nonreturnable pre-rent deposit.[49] (These deposits existed throughout the Taihang area—the tenants of She county in Hebei knew them as *xian ba mao*, or "first pluck a hair."[50]) The shift to one-year contracts made it virtually impossible for tenants to produce for their family security. They could not be certain of their location from one year to the next, and much of their income had to go toward the cost of annual moves. Such a change was made possible in part by demographic overflow on the plains above the Yellow River, where keen competition for land among tillers who had little choice but to exchange their labor for a hand-to-mouth existence worked to the landlords' advantage. In Hebei, Shandong, and Henan many landlords revoked permanent tenure pacts, denying the original tenant the customary right to invalidate any subletting or selling of land so that they could dismiss him and then rent to an outsider who would work the land for less pay.[51]

The most startling change, however, was carried out by landlords who favored fixed-rent contracts over the old practice of sharing the harvest on a 50-50 basis.[52] Both rental systems, share and fixed, persisted into the late 1920s, but with the coming of the Republic the replacement of share-cropping with fixed rent occurred at an accelerated pace throughout the border region and much of China. Tenants with fixed-rent contracts had to guarantee the landlord a given amount of grain no matter whether the harvest was good or bad.[53] Those in Qiankou village in Neihuang referred to this fixed-rent system as "iron rent," or rent without any flexibility.[54]

When the harvest was abundant, of course, tenants paying fixed rent stood to make a greater profit than sharecroppers, but if the rent due surpassed the total harvest yield the tenant not only was left without any crop income, but had to make up the difference, in either grain or cash. Few landlords made exceptions to this rule. This, among other things, explains why tenants in northern Henan expressed a strong preference for share rent when natural disasters threatened the crop, and why there were demands for a return to share rent during the pronounced harvest crises that occurred ever more frequently beginning with the long drought of 1918.[55] This tendency anticipated the development of tenant struggles under the protection of the CCP and its popular army several decades later, but it did not markedly reverse the progress made by landlords in bringing about the fixed-rent system during the 1920s.

Even in northern Henan, where tenants managed to stave off a total landlord transformation of share rent, landlords still called on them to share the crop according to a grossly inequitable formula.[56] The tenants of Lin, Hua, and Xinxiang, for example, were required to pay 70 to 80 percent of the crop, and landlords increasingly collected this rent without concern for changes in the harvest.[57] The tenants of Hu village in Henan's Puyang *xian* and of Liang village in Shandong's Fan *xian* felt that seven or eight parts of the harvest was an unfair payment:[58] it caused them worry, anxiety, and frustration when harvest time neared. Like their counterparts in Dazi and Luoer villages, both in Hua county, these tillers also suffered from landlord cutbacks in autumn harvest dinners and New Year bonus pay.[59]

Few landlords would reduce the rent when the harvest was poor or give peck-for-peck grain loans when the crops failed.[60] The lending of grain by pecks smaller than the customary standard and the collecting of rent on grossly inequitable scales became hallmarks of landlordism in the Taihang during Republican years.[61] The ancient fallback practice of gleaning the straw and stalk from the wheat and sorghum fields, which Buck called the tenants' "inalienable right through a custom of centuries,"[62] was increasingly defined as a criminal act.[63]

Old forms of protection also were falling by the wayside. The landlords of Hua *xian* no longer supplied the puttees that tenants had used to protect themselves from leeches and snakes or the straw hats and head towels field hands wore for protection from sunstroke.[64] Far worse, landlords now required the tenant to pay the land tax as a precondition for tenure renewal.[65] In addition to paying taxes on each *mu* of rental land, tenants in Hua *xian* and Ren Bing *xian* had to pay half of the miscellaneous surcharges levied by the warlord faction of the moment.[66] Not content with withdrawing customary supplies, landlords increasingly demanded that tenants contribute more assets to the altered sharecrop relationship. The tenants in Hua *xian* now had to provide their own implements and meals, and pay hired hands out of their 20 to 30 percent of the harvest.[67] In Puyang *xian* tenants had to feed the cattle, fill in the land where it had thinned out, and drive their landlords' horsecarts to the market towns for social visits and business calls, without pay.[68] All these assignments left tenants less time and energy to devote to their subsidiary crops in summer and to their small trade in winter.

There is little doubt that peasant landowners remained the village-dwelling majority in the border region in Republican times. But by emphasizing the central role of "peasant-as-the-freestanding-owner-cultivator" the Western economic school has diverted attention from the new hardships suffered by landowning peasants in post-Qing years. The downswings in grain harvests and handicrafts in the 1920s forced smallholders who had less than ten *mu* to borrow money and to rent extra land from landlords in order to survive. These solutions, however, had dire social consequences, as the experience of Yaocun, a market village at the edge of the Taihang Mountains in Lin county, Henan, demonstrates.[69] In early Republican years some 77 percent of the peasants in Yao village owned their own land, but after 1914 they found themselves in sharp competition for land. Zhang Zuoren, a former poor peasant, explains how landlords took advantage of smallholder debts incurred to cope with parched fields and family illness to acquire their land:

> Before Liberation there were seven people in my family. We had only two *mu* of land. My father was a blacksmith. The two *mu* and his blacksmith business was enough to meet our daily needs. But in 1921, a year of drought, my father fell ill. He was unable to work the family field. We therefore borrowed 100 *yuan* [dollars] from landlord Wei Xiaoguang. After three years Wei demanded the 100 dollars plus another 100 in interest. Thus we had to sell our land in 1924. This was our land, but now landlord Wei had it. After this my mother turned to cooking for people outside of Yao village. My brothers and I worked in other villages as blacksmiths and carpenters.[70]

By 1930 eleven landlords and fifteen rich peasants held 1,095 *mu* out of a total 1,794, including the best-irrigated, most fertile 700 *mu*, on which they charged fixed rent. Yao village had only thirty-five secure landowning peasant families, who together held about 338 *mu*, or about nine *mu* per household. This left 263 land-hungry smallholders trying to wrest livings from only 361 *mu* of poorly irrigated fields. The overwhelming majority of these minitillers, who in other analyses have been hidden in the provincial and county percentages on the landowning peasantry, were trying to feed families of five, six, and more on one or two *mu* of the least arable land.

These "freestanding tillers" had become a poor micropeasantry made up of part smallholders and part tenants who were scurrying to compensate for increased landlord demands on income formerly slated for family survival. In previous years few of these peasants had entered into loan or rental agreements with landlords; most had earned enough income from family harvests and family businesses like carpentry and blacksmith work to support themselves. But the diminished availability of water, along with family illness, drove them to resort to land rent as well as cash loans.

By drilling deep wells, the landlords in Yao village captured the water supply and the land-hungry smallholders found it increasingly necessary to rent tiny strips of the better-irrigated emerald-green fields. When the harvest was plentiful they were able to pay two hundred catties of fixed rent and still make a profit, but when drought reduced the harvest they were in trouble because landlords still pressed them for the rent. Many were obliged to dip into their family-based income to pay. When these poor smallholders were unable to generate enough income to pay the fixed rent the landlords charged interest on the back rent. To pay these debts they often had to sell family land cheap to the landlords who maintained the fixed-rent system. Few of them could make up the setbacks incurred from this landlord rent offensive, and by the early 1930s 101 of the 263 smallholder households had turned to begging and migration.

For landlords to manipulate problems of repayment in order to usurp land was not peculiar to Yao village or to Lin county. By 1930 it was a widespread practice in the border region.[71] Landlords who had issued peck-for-peck grain loans in Qing times were demanding repayment of one and five-sixteenth pecks, and some doubled and tripled their monthly interest rates. The shrewd landlords did not tamper with the old loan rates; they simply refused to defer interest payments in a poor harvest year, and thereby acquired the mortgaged land of the indebted family. By re-leasing this same land to its original peasant owner landlords turned smallholders into tenants, who now paid rent and taxes on land that yesterday had been theirs. Other usurers bribed Republican officials to accept false landownership papers they had drawn up on the unregistered lands of indebted peasant smallholders. Marriage alliances and patronage relationships with power holders in Republican local government[72] helped landlords to turn the screws of usury ever tighter when the new military tax machines and the world depression gripped the border region in the early 1930s.

In parts of the border region the rich peasant economy remained intact until the late 1920s, when there was a decline in the fortunes of many tillers who in the previous century had some grain to sell in markets. Hui county in northern Henan, for example, had sported a strong rich peasant economy, but the number of rich peasant households in four key villages diminished by 2 to 20 percent between 1928 and 1933.[73] By then, the average rich peasant landholding had declined from fifty-eight to forty-eight *mu*, and total harvest yields had declined accordingly. This decline in land and harvests was not the product of *fenjia*, the family division of inheritance to offspring— *fenjia* influence on rich peasant households was not all that significant. The decline was related to other factors. As Guomindang military taxes raised the risks of investing income in managerial cum market agriculture many rich peasants turned toward rentier landlordism, giving up their long-distance trade-and-transport businesses. Others, to avoid taking out loans after harvest failures, sold their land piece by piece to town-dwelling landlords. In the end, the rich peasants who could not survive by renting or selling family lands tumbled into the world of a micropeasantry threatened by land subdivision, poor harvests, and landlord usury within the village and by mounting warlord taxes from without. Their search for prosperity gave way to a struggle to keep from going under with the rest of the rural poor.

The development of immoral landlordism threatened the shared resources of whole villages. Following the fall of the dynasty, the bigger landlords in the Taihang, Taiyue, and Lu Liang mountains attempted to capture village water resources, forests, and coal mines.[74] By the late 1920s these landlords also were usurping public temple facilities for their own use.[75]

By aligning with the small-time bandits and militarists in Republican local government, these landlords managed to carry their encroachment on village resources to an extreme.[76] Peasants now had to pay a fee for water drawn from village wells, a tax on wood and fish taken from local forests and streams, and a tax on the coal they mined, collected in the form of a wage deduction. Since peasants previously had been able to use or sell the wood, the fish, and the coal, the new claims meant a major loss in fallback income when the grain crop failed. These same landlords often pocketed the temple tithes which had been used to help villagers facing real hardship, and they rented out the temple lands formerly used by the really destitute members of the local poor. All of these losses came at a time when all peasants were jockeying harder for village resources, so the chances that the weak, the sick, and the aged peasants could rely on the old sources of village welfare were diminished substantially.

The landlords who fostered these changes in customs of exchange and justice nonetheless claimed to be Confucian benefactors of the poor. Not only did they declare they were governing their domains with benevolence, they also demanded that peasants participate in ceremonies praising them for their paternalistic services. Many of these nouveau riche landlords apparently had only the dimmest recollection of the benevolent practices that had induced tillers to pay respect to their households.

The worsening crisis in peasant subsistence reached its zenith under Jiang Jieshi after 1931–32. Jiang's officers engineered their military takeovers in the towns of the border region without challenging the landlord and gentry figures who were squeezing the peasantry. They neither made the privileged landlords and gentry uphold their old obligations to peasantry, nor promoted reforms to restore land to the tiller, nor established new vertical alliances with peasants by performing services such as nullifying evictions or obtaining land titles, as do many patron-client parties in today's world.[77] This meant that things would get worse, and they did.

Precisely when Jiang Jieshi was threatening to punish landlords who did not act as Confucian benefactors, landlords were dictating terms that spelled disaster for tenants. The Taihang landlord who leased scraggly hillslope land to landless peasants repossessed the field the first season after the tenant had invested family labor and capital for improvement, then re-leased it to anyone who could pay a higher rent.[78] Landlords defined a customary *mu* as seven *fen* (instead of ten) and computed the untillable edge of the field and the thin woodland as regular land.[79] Thus tenants signed rental contracts on shrinking fields and paid rent on untillable lands. As late as 1936 landlords were collecting rent when the crop was lost to flood, and threatening to evict tenants who could not pay.[80] Many tenants now had to give up their natural fertilizer as well as that of their oxen to landlords, and cover the costs of transporting landlord crops to market.[81] Certainly some of these changes had occurred before the Guomindang military rode into the region, but neither Marshal Yan Xishan nor First Army Commander Liu Zhi did anything after 1930 to make landlords abide by the customary terms of tenure.

By leaving peasant landowners in the clutches of usurers the central government clearly broke Sun Yatsen's promise of land to the tiller, and thereby identified itself with the ruin of thrifty freeholders. Neither its officials nor officers amortized debts or arrested usury in the border region. After 1931 landlords raised monthly interest rates from 1 to 5 percent, so that peasants had to pay 60 percent interest on loans for which there had been a ceiling of 12.[82] Within a few short years indebted peasant families made up 80 to 95 percent of the population in villages like Suojing in Ci county and Sha Luo in Wuan county.[83]

It was the changing terms of credit, rather than the absolute level of interest per se, that drove smallholders into bankruptcy. Traditionally, peasants had paid back loans when their harvest fortunes permitted, and they paid interest only on the original loan. Now, however, landlord money-lenders set a fixed time of payment for the original interest payment plus an interest charge for any period beyond the deadline. Furthermore, lenders often verbally demanded a seasonal payment on loans that were written only for one month. By this procedure, they swindled land from the peasant who defaulted on a loan, then still collected interest from that same peasant at a later harvest date. None of these new loan terms were challenged effectively on behalf of landholding peasants by the magistrates who were accepted or appointed by Jiang Jieshi's commanders.

Three kinds of landlord usury stuck like a thorn in the flesh of small-holders in late Republican years.[84] One the peasants called *ri ye mang*, or day and night interest, because the lender counted one day as beginning at sundown and ending at sunup and another day beginning at sunup and ending at sunset, and thereby doubled the interest on old monthly loans. Rolling donkey interest *(lu da gun)* was widespread in Shanxi, Hebei, and Shandong villages, and peasants in remote Shanxi hamlets like Yun Zhou-xi and Sha Hukou still recall its harshness.[85] In the past, lenders had calculated rates on a steady monthly basis. With rolling donkey interest, rather than unchanging monthly payments, the longer the time, the higher the rate, and rates rolled to 100 to 200 percent from Shandong to the Taihang Mountains. Another form of usury was the preloan interest deduction, or *xin kuo li*. On a loan of ten dollars, for example, the lender would write the contract for ten dollars but deduct three as an advance payment of interest, leaving tillers to pay back ten dollars for seven received.

Throughout the region usurers went right on luring smallholders to pledge their lands as security on a loan and yet secretly, without peasant consent, writing the contract as a permanent land sale in the event of a default.[86] For the Jiang Jieshi military to go along with these usury processes did not make sound political sense; only the most corrupt of Republican county level officials could have let landlords engage in usury in order to lay claim to peasant lands on which they paid no taxes. And only a central government whose military clients were nonreformist to the core would allow usurers to ruin the very peasants who had ultimately to pay the bulk of land taxes to feed its armies.

A few rich peasant families managed to survive by emphasizing the exploitative relations they had established with tenants and hired hands, and by bribing local powerholders not to pressgang family members into the Guomindang army.[87] The central government failure to abolish the multifarious taxes, however, severely reduced rich peasant chances to remain at subsistence level and many had to worry constantly about plunging into the world of the hungry poor.

The most socially vulnerable member of the working peasantry may have been the permanent hired hand. This category, which had embraced job security and subsistence wages, was disappearing in late Republican years, when landlords were switching to short-term hired hands and day laborers and slashing wages. The hired hands of Bai Zhuang village in northern Henan no longer received meal money for market fairs, a set of clothes for raising livestock, medical assistance, or time off for Tomb Sweeping Day.[88] Short-term hired hands often went from job to job as agricultural day laborers. Many of these semiemployed drifters were young people whose families had died of hunger in the early 1930s. Their plight was akin to that of Lao Man from Upper Felicity village in northern Henan:

> At 14 I had to look after myself. When the Japanese invaded China I was 20 years old. There was a big flood that year, and I fled to Shanxi with a lot of other villagers. For the next seven years I worked as a laborer for one landlord after another. I worked for anyone who would give me food to eat. I didn't even ask for wages. And still I was constantly humiliated by them. They treated me like dirt, worse than their cattle. If I could get a bowl of porridge to eat twice a day I felt I was lucky. But I wasn't able to get even this for my work. Sometimes in winter I was just thrown out of doors when there was no more work to do.[89]

Relentless Insecurity under the Surtax Party

Landlord violations played an important part in arousing peasants to rebel over land and harvest issues, but class exploitation can provide only a half-baked explanation of the new pressures that moved the rural poor to defend their interests. The violent intrusions of rival militaries in search of resources for running their war machines also generated terrific pressures. Pursuing a line of analysis taken by Charles Tilly in his writings on peasant rebellion in seventeenth-century France, let us look at the effects of militarist state-makers promoting their interests by forcibly extracting from the countryside resources needed for war.[90] The interventions of warlord armies, whose officers were to become generals in the Guomindang warlord regime, helped to create the conditions for popular revolt throughout much of the border region.

Whereas the old regime had by and large adjusted its tax claims in accordance with harvest changes, the Beiyang warlords levied fixed taxes on the villages. The pre-Jieshi warlords in Hebei, Shandong, Henan, and Shanxi—particularly Henan militarist Wu Peifu—had overturned everything peasants considered fair: that taxes should be pared or postponed after a poor harvest; that tax collectors should tolerate village under-reporting; and that wealthy landowners should pay the lion's share of tax grains, in proportion to the actual yields on their more fertile lands. Although nothing about the central government's extractive practices alarmed peasants more than its tax campaigns, the Western economic school has said little about the worsening of the peasants' tax dilemma with Jiang Jieshi's 1930 triumph.[91]

The nature and number of taxes, the terms of collection, and the externally influenced rates left tillers without the slightest possibility of keeping needed cereals in the villages. The fixed-charge taxes posed a real threat to tillers whose life chances rose and fell with variable harvest income, and a number of them created want in good and bad years alike.[92]

One of these taxes was a special assessment on the harvest of each peasant household.[93] This tax, taken in silver, treated all villagers as equal, so that the poorest tiller had to pay the same tax as the wealthiest landowner. It was not a graduated tax on income—the burden fell heavily on small-holders—particularly in villages where landlords made peasants make up for the taxes they themselves avoided through underreporting.

With the coming of the Republic the old Qing *di shui*, or tax on amount of land owned, was commuted into silver, and the Beiyang Warlords and the Jiang Jieshi military piled upon it an endless string of surcharges.[94] These additional field taxes sometimes surpassed the regular land tax, with its customary limit of 30 percent on the actual harvest yield, tenfold and more. The tax collectors took this surtax almost solely from peasant landowners—most of them already indebted to usurers in an economy increasingly afflicted by inflation. This tax bore little relationship to the quality of the soil, the number of persons per household, or harvest yield—the wealthy landlord who owned one hundred *mu* paid about the same proportion of his harvest as the peasant who owned only nine or ten *mu*. And the militarists pressed for payment one, two, and even three years in advance of the annual collection dates.

The Guomindang became known as the "surtax party" to the common people, as throughout the border region its officials continued the warlord-gentry tax innovations that had stirred peasant anger since late Qing. To the autumn harvest tax, the vegetable tax, and the homemade wine tax—all independent of the land tax—were added a host of taxes to fund Qing and Republican local government. The reason peasants cultivated an eggplant garden, or raised a pig, or brewed persimmon wine was to keep from going under in lean years; but now when the main crop failed, these multiple surtaxes turned into a terrifying charge on any such fallback products.

The Guomindang authorities must have known they were playing with fire with these surtaxes.[95] In 1903, when Qing officials in Yongyi imposed a tax on persimmon wine, which by tradition was untaxed, in order to meet the foreign demand to pay indemnity reparations *(tanpai peikuan)*, several thousand people demonstrated in the county seat and destroyed the *yamen* quarters. Such antisurtax outbursts punctuated the next two decades of border region politics, and when the Guomindang entered the scene in the late 1920s antisurtax notices, warning the gentry *mintuan* and the Republican tax agents of the dire consequences of enforcement, covered the walls and trees of counties like Neihuang and Hui *xian* in Henan.[96]

But with the coming of the Guomindang warlords a far bigger tax wave was about to roll over peasants in the eastern half of the region. Following his anti-Communist coup d'etat of April 12–13, 1927 and his victory in the 1929–30 interwarlord wars, Jiang Jieshi secured an alliance with Marshal Yan Xishan against the Fengtien military clique and obtained support from several Beiyang militarists, including Pang Bingxun.[97] These two great achievements enabled him to take over the county seats on a line running south from Shijiazhuang to Xinxiang and west from Hua county through Anyang and on to Lin county.[98] The consequences of this last development, which was accomplished roughly by 1932 through anti-Communist extermination campaigns, were considerable for the villages occupied by the Guomindang. With the takeover came more and more soldiers and, inevitably, the pillaging of granaries, pressganging of peasants, and a new wave of taxes for temporary troop support.[99] The levy for 1930 on Baiquan village in Hui county perhaps typified requisition at the village level[100]—twenty-six troop-support taxes, including a wheat tax for the troops, a tax to pay for currency notes being printed by the Guomindang, a tax for war service porters, and a tax to put down peasant rebellions elsewhere in the county. (The list does not include the war service taxes and duties imposed by the Guomindang for the War with Japan some years later.)

Tax pillage, therefore, had been going on for years before the Japanese entered the region, and the grain tax for troop support alone sometimes exceeded the entire crop.[101] Never supporting themselves by their own labor—never even lessening the military tax burden when the crops were poor—the Guomindang subcommands were predators in the guise of warrior patriots.

The central government, and its plundering armies, left the tax-collection process in the hands of landlords and the gentry.[102] The priority of Jiang's junta was to build up grain reserves to stave off urban food shortages and to feed regional armies whose loyalty appeared secure, and linkups were made with bigger landlords around the richer wheat-growing market towns and villages to reach this goal. As the Guomindang military established its presence the landlord tax supervisors completely abandoned their efforts to help skirt taxes, and strove to please officers by pressing the peasants to pay taxes. After 1932 many of the landlord tax supervisors in Lin county, for instance, utilized their district posts to make peasants pay the land and harvest taxes, even though they themselves possessed the biggest and best lands.[103]

The uncertain timing, mode, and methods of collection made the weight of these new tax claims unbearable for peasants and increasingly for small merchants. Everyone knew the *tanpai* was coming, but no one could prepare for this frequent levy that Republican county and district power holders took at irregular intervals in order to supplement their income.[104] Though tillers had been paying land taxes in silver taels since the last days of Qing rule, it was mainly in late Republican years, when the worth of silver in China was tied to the world market, that the country people were pressed to pay taxes based on silver conversion rates that threatened to ruin them. Few tillers could produce the additional grains needed to keep pace with the rising silver rates, and the "silver hooks," as peasants called the tax collectors, left scores of villages without subsistence grain.[105] The *tanpai* alone increased fivefold in the northern Henan counties of Ji, Qi, and Hua from 1928 to 1933, and after 1928 Republican tax officials could not collect *tanpai* or any other tax without the escort of beefed-up county police forces.[106]

The Market and Additional Insecurity under the Central Government

The unfolding of cash-crop arrangements within the overtaxed villages of the North China periphery further threatened, then ruined, peasants in the Republican period. The tilling of cotton had been popular since Ming times, and New World crops like peanuts had been introduced during the Qing. Many peasants found it desirable to cultivate cash crops before World War I, when externally influenced market prices were favorable.[107] Shortly after the war, however, tillers were turning to money crops more and more to make up family shortages in food, salt, and clothing. The shortages originally stemmed from crop disasters and debts, but as the Republic wore on individual household taxes and taxes for exemption from conscription provided further incentive for growing cotton, peanuts, tobacco, and opium. By the late 1920s this incentive had become institutionalized. In many parts of the border region, landlords pressed tillers to grow cash crops in place of subsistence cereals, and they often enforced this conversion with the backing of warlord governors like Yan Xishan.[108] At first Governor Yan had attempted to stimulate cotton production in Shanxi by offering rewards, but by the early 1930s he was penalizing the counties where tillers failed to plant a given number of *mu* with cotton. Just as the landowning peasants who produced these cash crops still had to worry about paying cumulative interest to usurers, so tenants found themselves paying higher crop rents to rentiers who were out to get their money regardless of changes in crop yield.[109]

Increasingly, peasant income from cash crops lagged behind the price of basic commodities—specifically grain and salt. What good was a bumper crop of cotton, peanuts, or opium when the price it brought proved insufficient to purchase subsistence goods in local markets? No good at all, which is why peasants in the coerced cash crop zones of the border region spoke in panic about rising food prices.[110] In worsening terms of rent, interest, and wages, landlords passed on their losses from world price declines to peasants in order to steady their own profits, or, as was the case in some Shanxi villages, to keep themselves from going under. And meanwhile droughts were reducing grain crops by one-half, under a military junta that chose not to use its power to stabilize commodity prices in local markets.

Throughout the border region landlords in league with Republican officials were hoarding and speculating in grain. The price of grain swung upward with the onset of cash cropping, but the officials did nothing to prevent grain-dealing landlords from evicting tenants or foreclosing on smallholders when poor grain harvests or falling cash crop prices made paying of rent and debts impossible. With officials no longer underselling the "grain-dealing minority" food-grain prices inevitably turned against peasants in late spring before the November crop could relieve hunger. These same officials failed to prevent landlords, big merchants, and militarists from exporting grain, acquired by rock bottom purchases or by requisitioning, to the cities, where the price was no longer related to popular conceptions of fairness.[111]

The rising price of grain was accompanied by a permanent disaster in popular salt consumption—the hated *yan zai* or salt famine.[112] The origins of the *yan zai* lay partly in the Boxer indemnity and partly in the 1913 Reorganization Loan Agreement. The latter agreement was imposed on the Chinese Republic by the British, who relied on Yuan Shikai and his warlord successors to generate additional salt revenues to make indemnity payments and foreign loan payments. The efficiency of central government salt revenue collection was improved from 1915 to 1937, partly by raising the gabelle and partly by imposing new taxes on the salt sold by smugglers at prices below those of the gabelle. The push for salt-related revenue was felt throughout the border region, for the peasants in outlying districts of the Taihang were unable to obtain salt at an affordable price unless they purchased it from the smugglers operating out of the salt trade networks along the Hebei-Henan border.[113]

But by the 1920s there was pressure to purchase "official salt," that is, salt from warlord government shops. All through the decade the rural people had to cope with the salt controls of provincial warlords like Yan Xishan and Feng Yuxiang. These warlords sold salt through salt shops farmed out to landlord and gentry figures, who fixed its price at a nonnegotiable sum and added their own taxes.[114] In Shanxi, where Yan Xishan's army attempted to prohibit the popular production and sale of local earth salt,[115] the gentry who took over the salt shops refused to sell it to peddlers for retail in the villages. This new pressure mounted at a time when the older border region salt markets, which during the Qing had been reached by earthern roads and riverways, were losing to the growing traffic in salt on the Beijing-Hankou and Longhai railways.[116] By the late 1920s Hua county town, previously a major salt distribution point, had been bypassed by the Beijing-Hankou railway. The trade of its salt merchants had fallen off drastically,[117] after nearly a decade of "popular disturbances" over rising salt taxes and prices.

Next came the intrusion of "sea salt" from the Hebei coast. By 1931 this salt was controlled by the Jiang Jieshi military, and its entry brought efforts by Nationalist salt-tax officials to stamp out salt production and smuggling by peasants along the Hebei-Henan border. These peasant saltmakers peddled their salt in the markets of Daming and Handan at prices well below those of the sea salt, and by 1932–1933 they were under attack from the salt-tax police.[118] In April of 1933 thousands of these hungry "salt people" in the southern Hebei counties of Julu, Pingxian, Jize, and Quzhou joined together to go to Handan to protest the imposition of the new government controls.[119] The central government did not take these protests lightly, because much of the capital for government road-building and railway development was to be derived from the sale of its competing sea salt.[120]

Owing to these developments, peasants in the remote counties of the Taihang sometimes went for a year without salt.[121] Many of them were the victims of goiter even before the cash-crop price drops of the World Depression put salt beyond their means. The peasants of Xi Banyan still bear psychological scars of hyperthyroidism.[122]

The central government was said to have transformed *lijin* into a consolidated tax that was earmarked for its coffers after 1928. *Lijin*, however, lingered on under various provincial militarists, and it posed an ever-present problem for peasants who were fortunate enough to have grain, cloth, and timber to take to markets.

The interventions of the imperfectly integrated Central Army in popular markets increased the insecurity of rural life. The high-ranking Guomindang officers did not afford protection to peasants traveling the market roads, and officers like Sun Dianying were wont to raid the spots where peasants exchanged raw goods and purchased prepared foods.[123] Furthermore, the poorly provisioned Guominjun troops incorporated into the Central Army seized grain and tobacco without paying at all so that local markets through which they traveled were prone to panic and closure. Finally, the Guomindang officers captured local public monies and properties to engage in army trading for their private benefit, and their takeovers were followed by campaigns to stamp out competition in the rural civilian transport sector.

Then came the World Depression. The Depression spared no social class, and it dealt a severe jolt to much of the region's peasantry. The sharp dive in the world price of peanuts (1929–33) and cotton (1930–32) placed the price of food, clothing, and salt outside the income of tillers just when the terms of work life were turning decisively against them.[124] The overall impact of the U.S. Price Support Act of 1933 was to lower the price of peanuts to producers in India, Senegal, and China, and by 1934 the peanut-growing villages in Neihuang and Puyang were beset with bankruptcy.[125]

Inflation followed depression. The prewar inflation often has been portrayed as a logical fiscal measure undertaken by the Nationalist government to prevent an economic tailspin, but the process, engendered in part by the Jiang Jieshi junta and in part by the world powers, set in motion a topless inflation that produced its own form of depression in the North China hinterland.

The international monetary activities of the great powers opened the possibility that peasant China would suffer unbridled inflation.[126] Under the 1934 U.S. Silver Purchase Act the United States had begun making massive silver purchases on the London market, and the United States, England, and Japan subsequently carried out a series of currency devaluations. These international currency transactions seriously jeopardized the foreign-exchange position the central government had enjoyed vis-à-vis the world powers, and led to the loss of larger and larger sums of money in foreign-exchange trading. As international silver dealings tied changes in internal Chinese prices to world silver prices, walloping sales of Chinese silver began to seriously destabilize the currency of the Republic of China, and the agricultural depression in the border region steadily worsened.

The resulting impoverishment of the peasantry was exacerbated by the fact that it was no longer possible to stem losses from silver outflow by the importation of Japanese or Mexican silver. By 1905 indemnity payments made in metals to the Japanese had replaced the shipments of silver bullion the Chinese had sought in trade with Japan, and for the next three decades the Japanese conspired to capture the gold mines of Manchuria and silver mines of North China in order to finance their conquest and trade. To add to Republican China's troubles, the Mexican Revolution and the American financial domination of the Mexican mining industry slowed down silver production and dislocated the older trade outlets from 1910 to 1917, and the 1920–21 and 1927–28 downturns in world silver quotations further depressed Mexican silver production.[127] These international economic constraints made it all the more difficult for the Nationalist government to offset economic decline in the North China interior by bringing specie *into* China (and doubtless helped set the stage for the central government collaboration in the American silver purchase scheme, which further shook public confidence in the government).

The fiscal crisis that had restrained each military junta with plans to establish itself as the central government of the Republic of China culminated in a disaster during the Nationalist decade. Not only was the hyperinflation not resolved by the central government and the monetary policies of its Western fiscal advisors, as the Western economic history school assumes,[128] but Jiang Jieshi's junta actually *intensified* this development.

Nearly three years after the central government nationalized it, enormous sums of silver still were flowing out of the country and the exchange rate of the *yuan* was steadily falling.[129] The internal causes concern us less here than the effects on the country people. Now everyone wanted silver. It was the landlord who acquired it, however, by jacking up crop rents; by substituting husks for crop payments so he could sell grain for silver; by issuing his own paper currency so he could dictate the silver-to-paper exchange rates by which peasants paid rent and interest or purchased grain locally.[130]

In 1935, the Guomindang banking clique, at the behest of generalissimo Jiang Jieshi, abandoned the silver standard and began issuing *fabi*, notes that were not convertible into silver coinage, in order to make up for its own deficit. The resulting inflation further eroded peasant purchasing power. This prewar inflation was bound to worsen for the rural people as the generalissimo's men turned to the printing press for war-related expenditures after 1937. Both peasants and landlords strongly preferred grain over *fabi*, but farm hands, carters, and coal miners were paid in inflated currency that bore no relationship to the worth of old grain wages.[131] Inflation set off a collapse of local banks, particularly in Shanxi, shrinking the already-scarce credit and employment opportunities for peasant families, lineages, and villages in rural trading and mining ventures.[132] That the warlords and bandits who were linking up with the Central Army often administered inflation to their exclusive interest further exacerbated the social dilemma of the rural people.[133] Thus a peasantry that had been living by its wits for some time, and that had been hurt badly by World Depression now had to find some way to survive a runaway inflation brought on by a militarized Guomindang whose leadership was committed to expanding by plunder.

Militarism, Uprooting, and Statelessness

The failure of the central government to restabilize the living environments of village dwellers and to reintegrate uprooted peasants into schemes to preserve its protoexpansionist system of extraction and control was a critical factor—perhaps as critical as class exploitation or the Japanese invasion—in creating the conditions that brought on rebellion, then revolution, in the border region. That the central government did not develop these strategies was related both to the failure of its junta to resolve the fiscal crisis of the state and to the failure of any one major colonial power to develop a unified client state in Republican times. Japan took initiatives in this direction, but did not succeed, owing to the divisive splits among its ruling factions and to the shortage of capital available for the development of North China. Thus no foreign champion emerged capable of forcing its schemes for state growth onto a dominant Chinese warlord contender, and the statelessness associated with the militarist wars over revenue collection and expenditure persisted.

If the central government had fostered a framework for indigenous commercial development, many peasants might have found a niche in village implement shops and dye plants, in coal mines, or in town-based textile mills, factories, and foundries—all of which had a start in several border region rail towns *before* the Guomindang warlord takeover and the world depression. This course of development promised a real pay-off for the central government, for its peasant beneficiaries would have produced the resources and revenues needed for government administrative units and armies. Because the Jiang Jieshi military feared the reemergence of competing power blocs in the domains of former warlord adversaries, however, the Guomindang backed away from commerce-rejuvenating reforms. Instead, the ongoing Guomindang plunder prevailed. The Guomindang occupation of roads and railways that were in fact adequate for trade impaired regional trade and transport opportunities for peasants, small merchants, and peddlers. And the Guomindang support of the landlord and gentry elements who had the worst record in investing surplus capital and the weakest commitment to subsistence-wage guarantees further inhibited the development of milling and mining networks. In all of these ways, the Guomindang failed to help create the conditions for a capitalist course of agricultural cum industrial development, and thereby reduced the employment opportunities that existed in the primitive mines and mills of the border region and its provincial capitals.[134]

Although a few international relief committees made available funds to assist the peasantry, the central government developed no comprehensive system for providing relief to the hungry. There were no state famine-relief programs, no poorhouses or public-works projects, no welfare assistance tied to wage-labor workshops. The Jiang Jieshi defeat of the provincial militarists who were withholding famine-relief grain and withdrawing famine-relief funds for their personal armies still brought no help.[135] When the bottom fell out, therefore, hundreds of thousands of peasants turned to petty theft, banditry, and migration, taking to the trails leading from Hebei and Henan to the Taihang Mountains. Had the Guomindang filled the gaps in Republican welfare after 1927 the Chinese Communists would not have had this constant pool of impoverished recruits from which to draw for revolution, nor would the Japanese have found peasants so ready for alternative government.

Since the 1650s the Qing dynasty had been sponsoring migration and resettlement of landless and destitute peasants from the Taihang into the plains of Henan and Hebei and to a lesser extent from the North China Plain into Manchuria, rebalancing land/population ratios while returning new tax revenues to the treasury. During the Nationalist decade, however, peasants became the victims of a frontier closing-off process, and the pivotal role the state had played in the North China interior was lost.[136]

The central government abandoned the reserve army of peasant frontier settlers from the Taihang Mountains and the North China Plain. No aid, either by way of government grants or tax exemptions, was given peasant migrants for the initial resettlement years. Seldom, if ever, did the migrants receive any protection from Guomindang troops, and those who migrated at their own risk—which would have helped the Guomindang defuse the demographic powderkeg in the border region—often were intimidated and injured by the parasitic practices of the militarists who were aligning with Jiang Jieshi.

The Japanese attack on Manchuria in 1931 and the subsequent Guomindang acceptance of Manzhouguo[137] engendered a dramatic reversal in the terms of Manchurian migration for Hebei and Shandong peasants. The Japanese army placed the Chinese-owned railways under the supervision of the South Manchurian Railway, then canceled the third-class train fares that had made possible the massive overland migrations in the 1920s.[138] Then, in September of 1933, the Daito Company, a Japanese labor contract agency, began restricting the numbers of new migrant workers and curtailing their right to remit earnings to their villages. Precisely in the years of Guomindang appeasement, 1931 to 1936, there set in a sharp decline in over-land migration to Manchuria, while interregional railway construction was peaking and superceding sea transport to the Northeast.[139] The Guomindang failure to keep open the frontier played into the hands of a Japanese migration policy that exacerbated problems of employment and survival in the border region.

Another crucial state means for coping with the potentially volatile peasant response to insecurity and loss of local roots had been the penitentiary system, and certainly the central government was committed to incarcerating the peasant victims of its taking practices. But the warlord government arrangements for incarceration proved grossly inadequate for holding tax evaders, crop thieves, and bandits, and there is little evidence that this institutional gap was filled by the Guomindang after 1931–32.[140] Throughout the Republican era the makeshift prisons of the border region were ripe for hunger riots and revolts leading to massive breakouts, and the incarcerated peasants often challenged the controls of these penal institutions in the years before the CCP and the Japanese posed their own challenge to the Guomindang militarists who maintained them.

Political scientist Eric Nordlinger has shown that many military governments, though not given to improving rural society through economic progress, manage to persist in power through praetorian practices that are not necessarily conducive to national integration.[141] Against this insight, it is baffling why Jiang Jieshi, whose First Group Army was determined to take over the troops of its former warlord opponents, was unable to build up a unified national army from interventions in the border region. This failure is all the more intriguing when we recall that, as in the Warring States period, this region was a recruiting ground for renegade armies, and that by the 1930s hundreds of thousands of unemployed, hungry, and uprooted rural people were the potential rank and file for any army that would assure them a bare existence.

The high-ranking Guomindang officers from landlord and lower gentry backgrounds looked down on the rank and file who came from impoverished peasant families. The mistrust and animosity that characterized relations between Yuan Shikai's officers and the miserable uprooted peasants and vagabonds who were drawn to army life[142] seems to have complicated the task of army building for Jiang Jieshi and his provincial warlord coalition, and the Guomindang made no headway in combatting the root cause of this dangerous cleavage.

The most powerful factor contributing to the disintegration of Guomindang field forces north of the Yellow River, however, was the failure of the Jiang Jieshi Central Army to serve its soldiery from sound fiscal practices. The problem, again, was that the high-ranking officers treated the army as a revenue-producing agency for personal gain, regardless of the consequences for the wretched foot-soldier.

These fiscal malpractices were institutionalized before the CCP and the Japanese inserted themselves to influence Central Army fortunes[143] in the border region, so that all through the 1930s the rural people thought twice about joining or staying with the Guomindang army. In northern Henan, where the Guomindang general Pang Bingxun replicated the pressgang practices of his patron Wu Peifu, the only way the Guomindang could get young peasants to serve was to capture them in raids on temple fairs. Throughout the region peasants were used as underpaid military coolies, and thousands perished in forced marches because the Guomindang did not provide them with any war relief services (resting quarters and medical attention). Moreover, the provincial commands were not insulated from the inflation that was ruining the civilian sector, so the ordinary Guomindang "recruit" still faced insecurity. Finally, the Guomindang officers felt no obligation to feed the empty stomachs of the soldiers, and reduced and withheld troop pay at the same time they granted themselves higher salaries and secretly embezzled funds. The logical result of all this was dissension in the ranks and desertion at the division level where the fighting was to be done. The trickle of defections of 1931−36 turned into a deluge once the Guomindang army faced competition from the CCP armed forces and the Japanese army.

Not all responsibility for these central government failures can be placed on the Jiang Jieshi junta. Much of the crisis was in the works from late Qing and, along with the destructive power of imperialism, set limits on Republican state development. What mattered, though, was that even marginal and stern reforms, for which there was ample room within a truly conservative Confucian tradition, could have spared the central government from attempts at revolutionary change from below. Yet the Guomindang militarists did not get on with the state-making schemes that would have moved peasants off the land and into endeavors more directly under their political supervision. The reason for this failure lay in the realm of values as well as the brittle military coalition over which Jiang Jieshi presided after 1930.

The Failure of the Central Government to
Establish Its Hegemony over the Peasantry

The overwhelming concern of peasants was hunger; but their misery did not prevent them from developing some common-sense notions of how landlordism, warlord-gentry plunder, and the Nationalist inflation were ruining them. The new political developments in Republican China, anticipated by neither Marx nor Gramsci in their assessments of peasant revolutionary potential, allowed peasants to associate Jiang Jieshi's Bonapartist regime with their ruin, and neither Jiang Jieshi nor the warlords in his camp were able to inspire a peasant belief in the legitimacy of their rule. Guomindang power grew out of the barrel of a gun, but popular obedience to its "authority" did not. There were several reasons for the failure of Guomindang military leadership to develop the kind of shared value system that would have made it acceptable to peasants in the ways implied by the Western economic history school.

In the first place, the Central Army was letting landlords have a field day. Their ruthless acts drew peasants together to contest injustice, and in some respects the resulting contentious judgments of the injured poor approached class consciousness.[144] Most tenants shared a number of pressing problems (crop rents and labor duties) that obviously were the making of landlords. No longer able to count on landlords to treat them as reliable individuals with human needs, tenants related less and less to them as personal benefactors. The tenants and hired hands who shuffled from rentier to rentier, sharing the uncertainty of short-term work and poor wages, began to see nearly all landlords as impersonal rent collectors, and a rudimentary consensus emerged that the landlord was the black crow who stole the crop or the vampire who drained their energy.[145]

With this distancing, a stronger sense of class allegiance began to develop among tenants. They were less willing to perform routine favors and rituals of loyalty, and they increasingly complained to the landlord's face about the new terms of work life. By the late 1920s tenants in the Taihang area were being hauled into jails and courts and paraded in bondage around the streets of county level capitals by local power holders. Such ordeals, designed to induce quiescence, brought together tenants from various villages to share feelings about common sufferings.[146]

Both the new division of the crop and the decline in real wages intensified the tenants' and hired hands' sense of antagonism. Many expressed their anger in mental categories actively at odds with the landlord version of agrarian change and legitimacy. This symbolic reworking involved nonverbal, spoken, and written counterinterpretations of the behavior of immoral landlords.[147]

The tenants of Qiankou village in Henan had looked upon the landlord, Liu Yaobin, as someone with whom they had shared an obligation toward agriculture, but when Liu refused to postpone the rent for a year following a flood disaster they began to rethink their previous acceptance of his Confucian standards of fairness.[148] These standards, written on tablets overhanging the Liu household doors, spoke of mutual loyalty and kindness. But the tenants thereafter saw them as testimony to the landlord's hypocritical behavior. The tenants of Taiping village in Shandong, to take another example, had addressed landlord Wang Hongyin by his preferred family name—"Wang the Magnificent."[149] But when Wang began working them to death they nicknamed him Zi Zhoubei, the "thoroughly discredited flesheater." Perhaps, as social scientist Peter Lupsha suggests,[150] these undercurrents of peasant indignation over specific, recognized social rights betrayed the deeper motives that would fuel peasant actions against landlords in the late 1920s, and then again when the CCP brought its revolutionary army into the region.

In redefining tenure relations landlords often conjoined the experiences of tenants. Some tenants had to pay a fixed crop rent to a landlord plus another rent in cash to a second, and sometimes even third, rentier who had purchased the subsoil rights from the original landlord.[151] Tenants involved in short-term chain tenancy arrangements could see that they were the victims of as many as a dozen different landlords. Nor were they surprised when the landlord who denied them the old harvest share or seed grain still found a way to send grain to dealers outside the village. When famine made tenants desperate, landlords often moved into the relative comfort and safety of the big market villages and county towns. Finally, through their trips to the county level capitals (on the landlord's errands), tenants and farm hands observed first hand the relations between landlords from surrounding districts and between local landlords and Republican military rulers.[152]

Increasingly, smallholders who took up work as part-time tenants encountered the problems of rental peasants. Even more important, smallholders, tenants, and hired hands found themselves in a similar situation when it came to the usurious grain and cash loans that were so essential to survival. By the late 1920s many peasants who previously had negotiated loans individually with usurers had come to realize that they were ensnared in the same grinding credit-dependency as their counterparts. Landlords helped create this realization. First, they required peasants to put up the land and property of a guarantor as a security deposit for a loan. Taihang peasants called this riding the double-headed horse *(shuangtou ma)*, because when they defaulted the lender confiscated the belongings of both the debtor and the guarantor, usually a relative or friend.[153] Second, they issued the usurious *yi cang* loan on terms that were strikingly similar for tenants, small-holders, and hired hands. Thus, the name *dai longtou*, translated as "the muzzlers" or "the basket carriers," was soon given to usurers by peasants.[154] This term symbolized the notion that landlord usurers were snatching everyone's grain basket, and that the destiny of all tillers hung on the same ruinous relationship.

Ranking high on the list of changes that endangered the material well-being of most peasants were the insufficient payments for cash crops and the insatiable salt gabelle. These two changes constituted the cutting edge of the truly harmful market and political influences in peasant lives. Yet what affected the exchange position of the whole peasantry, enveloping villages with different land and water resources and peasant households with different survival capabilities, was the addition of inflation to the cost of grain and salt. Peasants were crushed as consumers. As the Central Army and its half-reorganized warlord subcommands spread inflationary notes into border region market towns, the *fabi* became the bête noire of peasants in some of the remotest market points of the region, including those in the Taihang.

This is not to say that the region's peasants automatically responded to the loss of livelihood by stressing their class bonds. In some instances, lineage, village, and patron-client relationships proved to be more practical, and perhaps more humane, when it came to striking up a relationship that would instantly relieve hunger. Then there were instances in which class feelings remained sharp but were overriden by communal rivalries that were hardly in the interest of the survival of the peasantry as a class. In the Taihang county of Pingchuan, for example, the tenants of Zhao village and Tian hamlet were restless over the raising of old rents, but in 1932 these same tenants followed rival landlords from their respective villages into hand-to-hand combat over competing claims to an irrigation channel that originally had been constructed on the basis of mutuality.[155]

Still another development favored the growth of popular consciousness about new pressures on livelihood. This was the failure of the traditional landholding elite to reconstitute itself, either by the efforts of its benevolent or bourgeois members, as a class of and for itself.

Marx believed that peasants were incapable of comprehending their own class interest as long as they remained the clients of paternalist landlords. Most of the region's poor tillers did not have to be reminded that few interclass ties of patronage remained between them and landlords, however.

By the 1920s a local elite composed of nouveau riche landlords and lower gentry had begun to dominate the affairs of village and county politics exclusively in their own illegal interest. These *tuhao lieshen*, or local tyrants and evil gentry, no longer honored traditional intravillage procedures for resolving disputes with peasants over rights to land and water, and they increasingly entered local society as hated gangsters who occasionally even violated the interest of other landlord households. The few fair and decent landlords were never honored or held to be in the right by the military rulers of the region. This encouraged the criminal landlords to behave more blatantly, rationalizing their offensive behavior by haughty Confucian commentaries and ceremonies that alienated and angered hungry villagers all the more.

If the central government or its army had stepped in to persuade the landlord and gentry elements to promote a commercial process with relatively safe risks and sure returns for peasants, wealthy landowners might have gained the respect and status they sought by pointing to the resources, knowledge, and accomplishments they gave to agriculture. This, however, was not done, and peasants continued to see rich landlords as jackals who fattened themselves through ties to the militarists preying on the monetization of agriculture. Thus, in an important sense, the region's peasants remained suspended between an immoral landlordism and an illegitimate Republican militarism, and it was in this gap in ruling-class hegemony that many of the country people developed a clear and critical understanding of the relationship between their awful social dilemmas and the taking practices of landlords and Republican power holders.

Finally, the nature of the central government presence in the border region further contributed to the growth of peasant consciousness. On the one hand, the institutions of the central government—the Guomindang itself, its courts, and propaganda corps—did not penetrate the villages to effectively reorganize the life of the peasantry after 1927. The *Sanqing tuan*, the Guomindang Youth Corps, did not begin to operate around the administrative villages in northern Henan until about 1938, and even then its negative anti-Communist message made little impression on peasants in need of utilitarian advice for survival.[156] On the other hand, the coercive apparatus of the central government invariably accentuated the growing symbolic gap between peasants and its own raison d'être. The tool of the Guomindang's anti-Communist fanaticism, the Sun Yatsen Society fostered a militant antifolk orientation among the Central Army officers who were occupying the county towns and requisitioning the market villages leading to the Taihang Mountains in Henan, Shanxi, and Hebei before 1937.[157] By catering to the Confucian homilies of wicked landlords and by whitewashing the village wall graffiti that detailed popular defiance of Republican county government Jiang Jieshi's officers etched themselves out as the guardians of the illegitimate district and county rulers they were linking up with after mid-1927.

Here, then, was an extraordinary political development: the central government was as ineffective in remaking peasant culture as the Central Army was effective in defaming it. Here was a hinterland region where peasants had not had their own conceptions of justice and power effectively converted by the old regime or significantly remolded by a strong new state, and it was in this symbolic space that peasants found it possible to continuously create their own criticism of the performance of the militarized Guomindang. It should not be surprising, therefore, that what was right in peasant thinking—that Republican government ought not to interfere with the initiatives of tillers to stay free of hunger—would come to the fore as peasants began struggling to regain the world they were losing.

The new pressures on peasant livelihood owed their origins mainly to the fiscal crisis induced by the world powers. The Western economic history school has diverted attention from this phenomenon and its consequences in the countryside. By the 1910s and 1920s nouveau riche landlords and gentry were overturning the old terms of agrarian exchange, making it more difficult for peasant families and villages to survive. These nouveau riche elements were not the genuinely upright Confucian gentlemen of the past. They made a mockery of the older notions of Confucian noblesse oblige and compounded the moral dilemma of the peasantry by cooperating with the warlords. In a border region with an ecosystem as precarious as this one, the warlord command that peasants engage in cash crop production so it could be taxed for army building was nothing short of systematic pillage. This pillage became more intense, and perhaps more systematic, as Jiang Jieshi's generals cannibalized party government and imposed new troop support taxes. Far from helping the peasants relieve their hunger by commercial endeavors, resettlement, and army service, the Guomindang warlords abandoned them to deal as best they could with drought and the dangerous price drops of the World Depression. Though the central government under Jiang maintained the fiction of being "centrist," this junta, like so many military dictatorships, remained faithful only to its own army-building efforts, which lacked any popular support. It fostered a topless inflation without significantly improving China's credit with the world powers, then let its warlord allies shift the burden of this bald government theft onto the peasantry. The irony was that despite the Guomindang's offensive mobilization of peasant resources, no stable Republican state emerged to establish its ideological supremacy over the angry poor, who, in these same stateless times, were beginning to take matters into their own hands.

3

Revolt, Repression, and Retreat

The peasant revolts of the North China interior were born of desperation. The peasants did not want trouble from landlords or gentry, and they did not set out to overthrow Republican government. Trouble, however, there would be, and peasants would learn that nonradical protest could not resolve the problems of livelihood. Until they turned against local power holders and their warlord supporters, hundreds of thousands would go hungry. Those who wished to survive would have to do so through protest strategies forged outside the militarized Republic. Ironically, in sacrificing themselves in revolts against the warlord-gentry regimes that had replaced the imperial order peasants were preparing the ground in which the Chinese Communist Party would grow.

STRATEGIES OF SURVIVAL

The peasants north of the Yellow River pursued three strategies of survival.[1] One was retreatist self-help, from largely self-reliant, family-centered initiatives. Another was remedialist protest wherein they attempted to reestablish a tolerable relationship with landlords and local government. The third was a baldly oppositionist stance. No one strategy necessarily excluded the others and two strategies sometimes developed together. Naturally, the growth or decline of any one survival strategy was conditioned by government reaction, as well as the peasants' capacity to sustain it. Insofar as peasant self-help and remedialist protest *initially* reflected nonradical attempts to regain the minimum decencies of life, the will and capacity of Republican officials to accommodate them would play a critical part in moving the rural people toward contentious protest and violent opposition.

Self-Help

Self-help seemed the surest way to guarantee that no one would go hungry. From 1900 on self-help included peasant reliance on the global market, with many households adapting their crops and cultivation techniques to earn income through the increasingly monetized agricultural economy. Accord-ing to Popkin, the peasant shift to commercial agriculture during the early twentieth century often represented a voluntary pursuit of a new opportu-nity to maximize profits rather than another cautious experiment in main-taining a marginal existence.[2] But does this theory of the optimizing peasantry, free to reap the rewards of unrestricted market investment, accord with the cash-crop experiences of peasants in the North China hinterland? Shortly after World War I tillers in the Hebei-Shandong-Henan area began switching from customary grains to sweet potatoes, maize, and root crops in order to release more land to cash crops such as cotton, opium, tobacco, and peanuts linked to Tianjin and its overseas markets.[3] In Puyang county in Henan, for example, wheat was grown on one-half the arable land surface prior to 1920. With the conversion to peanuts (whose oil had become an export around 1911), the wheat land under cultivation was reduced by 50 percent in less than a decade. Peasants who switched to cash crops could sell their new produce to purchase more food for family consumption than they could grow on their tiny plots.[4] Tobacco, opium, and cotton took two to four times as much labor, water, and capital as customary wheat,[5] however, and the caloric supply from sweet potatoes and root crops seldom made up for the additional expenditure of energy. Many peasants got by on only dande-lions and other wild greens in summer, pumpkin in autumn, and bran and bark in winter. By the 1920s whole villages were consuming some of the poorest foods possible to achieve minimal protein efficiency.[6]

The market price declines of the Great Depression, which occurred in the middle of the murderous Northwestern droughts, saw many tillers retreating from cash crops back to subsistence agriculture.[7] As the 1920s wore on, peasants in poverty-stricken Shanxi reemphasized subsistence cereals over cash cotton.[8] The peasants on the southern Hebei plain had shifted from millet to cotton as cotton prices rose from 1910 to 1930, but after 1930 they renewed their grain production to offset unaffordable food prices.[9] Similar-ly, though peasants in Henan had begun to plant the poppy on poorer soils for twice the market value of food grains, it remained their *choice* only as long as the high prices and relatively low taxes of the early 1920s prevailed.[10]

Peasants often combined their retreat to grain production with a diversi-fied approach to agriculture designed to resist cash monocropping. This strategy was easier and less risky in the traditional agricultural sector, which included the more remote villages on a line leading west from Anyang in northern Henan toward the Taihang Range and beyond. Being relatively free to resist the efforts of warlords to stimulate cash-crop production for markets fostered from abroad, peasants here fought to continue their an-cient combinations of millet, sorghum, beans, eggplant, spinach, and cu-cumbers over the monocropped cotton, peanuts, opium, and tobacco with which landlords and warlords often were involved. The path back to diversi-fied multicropping was not always smooth, but these peasants' chances of survival were greater than those of their counterparts who were caught up in cash monocultures and the ambuscade of warlord government on the plains.

A more drastic self-help measure was the attempt to squeeze a livelihood from family endeavors that could not possibly sustain parents and children in any state short of constant hunger.[11] Throughout the border region tillers made tremendous sacrifices to avoid breaking up the family and leaving ancestral ground, stretching their household economies to the point of overexhaustion.[12]

This stark scenario involved sharing the thin offerings that could be wrung from shrinking supplies of food, cloth, and fuel. Following the famines of 1876−79 and 1920−21 the peasants adapted themselves to hunger both by cutting back their family food consumption and gleaning unpalatable poverty foods from the barren countryside.[13] In stretches of the Hebei, Shandong, and Henan interior peasants felt lucky if they could scavenge the foods for which their famished ancestors had searched in time of famine over the centuries—sweet potato vines, ground leaves, thistle, and watergrass made up their menus.

With cotton production for home handicraft work tapering off, many tillers could no longer afford new clothing. In some Shanxi and Hebei villages couples had to take turns wearing the "family pair of pants" in order to search for food and fuel.[14] The peasants in several Taihang villages, unable to afford even tattered bedsheets, nestled together under heated sand to keep from freezing to death in winter.[15]

With much of the Taihang timberlands having been denuded over several centuries, peasants faced near insurmountable problems in obtaining firewood during the last years of the Qing dynasty.[16] The felling of Shanxi pine and cedar forests by peasants seeking land and fuel reached a frenzy in early Republican years. By these deforestation practices peasants exploited the ecology to the point where it could not reproduce the resources to sustain their own demographic explosions. The warlord tendency to curry favor with gentry forest monopolists rather than foster commercial forest management made it still harder for peasants to obtain fuel after 1916−17. The warlords also let the rivers ravage the soil base that was vital for tree replenishment. By the 1920s even solvent peasants in hundreds of Hebei and Shandong villages were selling precious timbers from their homes, either for food or money, in order to get through the hard times.

Not long after the Qing dynasty fell peasant families began to search for alternative sources of income by separating into extravillage labor forces.[17] With landlords claiming more income from peasant-owned plots, the men began working on the croplands of wealthy landlords in the big market villages and in small coal mines. Peasant women stayed at home to till family plots so their menfolk could pursue these wage-earning activities,[18] which probably served their purpose until the drought-related harvest failures of 1919−20 and the spate of mine shutdowns at the end of World War I—shutdowns linked to the lessened Japanese production of the pig iron needed to supply the Allies with steel.

Parents facing shrinking income sent their sons and daughters to the cities in search of temporary factory work, in the hope that the children could send back enough income to tide father-and-mother through the spring hunger. Even this modest hope met with disappointment. The uneven distribution of Western economic investment in China had left this border region without any urban industrial workshops to speak of, and the cities that rimmed the region—Shijiazhuang, Jinan, Zhengzhou, and Taiyuan—offered employment to only a handful of jobless rural people.[19] Moreover, the young people usually looked for factory work in the North and Northeast, the two most underdeveloped industrial zones of metropolitan China. The tolerable wages they derived from the boom in clothmaking, brick tile plants, and oil-processing operations near Zhengzhou, Jinan, and Tianjin did not last through the postwar decade.[20] These enterprises, underfinanced by banks and overtaxed by militarists, were also run by foremen who did not deal fairly in matters of wages and illness.[21] By 1922–23, when there was a significant depreciation in currency,[22] the laboring poor began to retreat from the cities to the fields and mines of the interior. The subsequent Guomindang-inspired purges of former peasants who fought alongside the Chinese Communist party in the factory struggles of this period sped up the flight back to the countryside.

The logical alternative to either starving in the villages or breaking up the family was migration. The landless and jobless peasants initially sought short-term seasonal work around their home villages, but many became long-term wage laborers in far-off fields.[23] From 1890 until 1920 a steady stream of migrant workers went from places like Lin *xian* in Henan to Pingshun *xian* in Shanxi.[24] Such a pattern could hold as long as the Taihang held out the promise of abundant hillslope land and limited government.

Of course the main systemic migration pattern was out of the Taihang Mountains onto the plains of Henan, Shandong, and Hebei,[25] and the Great Famine of 1876–79 reinforced this pattern. By the late 1920s, however, many of the peasants from the Taihang area had abandoned their older, local trails of relief and joined in the migrations of Hebei and Shandong peasants to Manchuria.[26] The Qing preference had been to preserve the northeastern frontier with its surplus of cultivatable land for pure-blood Manchus, but the first year of the Great Famine sent over one million half-starved Han peasants to Manchuria against the wishes of Emperor Guangxu,[27] and the dynasty officially removed its restrictions on immigration in 1878, the peak of the Great Famine. For the next fifty years these massive Manchurian migrations became fairly constant.

For a time migration held out the hope of freedom from hunger and landlord exploitation. The preference for subsistence agriculture over cash-cropping was encouraged in the early twentieth century by lands available

Homeless migrants pouring through a passage in the
Taihang Mountains, in the 1930s

for either rental or ownership in upland Shanxi and Jilin,[28] and the promise
of small profits was kept alive in the burgeoning trade in timber and herbal
crops to be harvested from forests located deep in the Taihang, Luliang, and
Changbai mountains. In the Taihang, the peasant mountaineers were infamous among landlords for their dogged efforts to survive by private household tilling and trading schemes that smacked of competitive commerce.
They started cedar tree, jujube, and charcoal production on patches of land
in the highland wilderness obtained by squatter's rights or outright purchase, and they traded their products in the market villages and towns of the
foothills, valleys, and plains. Many migrants, moreover, augmented their
household incomes by harvesting timber from the public forests to which
they had established de facto ownership by group cultivation, so that their
search for food and fuel took on a collective dimension.[29]

The peasant migrants to the Taihang Mountains endured extremely low
standards of living.[30] Owing to poor soil and primitive technology,[31] they
seldom achieved total self-sufficiency in the production of basic food grains
(corn, millet, and buckwheat usually replaced wheat here). Even in a
normal year the harvest had to be supplemented with income derived from

small trade or smuggling of a sort, and many migrants did not make it through the pandemic drought that stalked the border region from 1920–21 on through the World Depression.

In some respects, however, the rural people who pioneered highland villages such as Sha Hukou and Xikou in the Taihang Range were less subject to oppression, and perhaps in a better position overall to survive.[32] To be sure, many of these quasi-peasants also had to pay rent, but their landlords often lived ten to thirty *li* away in market towns like Xinliangkou in the Taihang.[33] These absentee landlords did not always return to the upland villages to supervise rent collection, and they did not possess the strong *mintuan* forces needed to consistently enforce their claims. Moreover, the migrants and mountain peasants were less subject to the tax directives of Guomindang warlord district level administrations, which were located in or near villages having a historical reputation for rich yields and flourishing markets. Quite often, therefore, they were able to survive by combining smallholding and sharecropping with hunting and fur trading, whiskey distilling, and salt-smuggling networks.

It seems that many peasants initially looked upon migration as a semipermanent means of tapping the resources of frontier economies. The peasants who worked, robbed, and begged their way from Henan across the Taihang Mountains into Shanxi initially did not intend to emigrate to the mountain hamlets they began settling in the 1910s and 1920s.[34] For the migrants to Manchuria too the goal was to return to their Hebei, Shandong, and Henan roots, and to their native villages in the Taihang, rather than become a permanent surplus labor force either for the Chinese warlord or for Japanese development of this crucial agricultural export enclave.[35] The peasant migrants to Manchuria usually left their villages right after the spring harvest and returned in time for the autumn harvest, or the lunar New Year. During half a century many began to trade the insecurity of North China work life for a more permanent settlement in the Northeast, but rare was the migrant who did not try to save enough either to return home to die on village soil or to have his ashes sent back to the family burial ground.[36]

Family and village histories make clear that migration was often a form of flight by frightened peasants who had engaged in violent fights with landlords.[37] Some landlords, unwilling to return to the traditional terms of exchange and justice, responded to peasant survival issues by outright brutality. Many of the peasants who fled from Lin, Anyang, and Hua counties in Henan into the Taihang Mountains and on beyond the Great Wall into Shaanxi were smallholders and sharecroppers who had quarreled with landlords over long-standing family rights to remain on the land and receive regular wages.[38] Similarly, among the landless Shandong peasants who fled north of the Great Wall many felt a deep enmity for landlords who had taken too much of the harvest or purchased herbal crops at prices arrived at by coercion.[39]

Thousands of landless tillers turned to petty theft and banditry. These peasants usually took the crops of those who seemed relatively secure, often consciously drawing on widespread popular support for the right of the poor to pilfer crops of wealthy landlords. Threatened smallholders became just as irate as landlords when their crops were tampered with, but they did not readily mobilize village pressure to punish those who stole the needs of their existence from the fields of the better off.[40]

Because attempts to squelch it were dangerous without the firm backing of *mintuan* and garrison commands, crop pilfering was a more feasible means of self-help for the peasants in the imperfectly patrolled Taihang Mountain area.[41] At the edge of the North China Plain, where landlords could better patrol the process of peasant production for global markets, petty theft became an extraordinarily painful means of hanging on. Many tillers who pilfered only a few seeds from cash-crop peanut fields in Henan and Shandong were beaten black and blue, fined, and banished from their villages.[42]

It was a short step from petty theft to the banditry that had been building in the border region since the fall of the Qing.[43] The turn to banditry represented a more active peasant response to the extractive pressures of landlordism and Republican local government. The experience of Lin county in the early 1920s illustrates this response.[44] In 1919–20, the year of the "Big Dryness" in folk memory, the Lin *xian* government insisted on collecting the grain tax. The peasants who were unable to meet its tax demands began leaving their villages to go begging in Shanxi. In the central and eastern part of the county, however, men began to form bandit leagues that embraced as many as seventeen villages. These peasant bandits roamed from the West River to the Zhang River on the Hebei-Shanxi-Henan border. They carried off the crops, oxen, and money of a few wealthy landlords, but focused their major attacks on the Lin county government finance bureau, which held the grain and money taken from their villages. As long as these peasants could sustain their antigovernment activity they could avoid pillaging the village people, because the gains of their banditry brought them food, clothing, and cash with which to purchase medicine.[45] These peasant bandit leagues were not active throughout the entire year, nor did they sell protection; they were offering stability and protection to peasant communities whose experience with government tax collectors paralleled their own.

The multiplication of mutual loan societies, joint land reclamation projects, and burial associations was typical of another type of self-help in the twenties and thirties. In the Taihang, the peasant tendency at this time was to participate in short-term mutual aid only for immediate needs,[46] but many tillers were extending some of their emergency efforts to supplement solitary household self-help strategies on a more permanent basis.

The various mutual-survival pacts conceived by peasants in the cash-crop villages along the Hebei-Shandong-Henan border and along the Luo River, where Shanxi meets Henan, were a response to population pressures and to the absence of credit for plow-animal purchases.[47] Most of these arrangements featured smallholder loans of oxen to propertyless relatives and friends who, in return, helped feed oxen and clear fields. In some instances, tenants started up collective land-rental projects which featured strictly labor exchanges. Such property- and labor-based mutual aid would provide the social grid for the small-scale cooperative peasant endeavors that the CCP would aim at ensuring peasant livelihood and expanding village production during the next decade.

In the Taihang Mountains these peasant adaptations also gave birth to a limited range of mutual-relief activities.[48] Some peasant families lived together in huts and caves in order to save house rent, engaged in substitute tilling when sickness struck, and tilled subsidiary tenancies on a rotating basis. Others loaned barren lands to relatives and shared their watereddown bran soup with those who were returning home after years of unsuccessfully scavenging the extravillage economy of the warlord Republic. The growth of burial associations, with several families chipping in the money needed to obtain burial garments and arrange funeral services, was another important aspect of these mutual-aid initiatives.

Most peasants still stood watch over their own family fields before the harvest,[49] but a growing number of mutual crop-watch associations sprang forth in response to banditry and the decline of protection from local patriarchs.[50] Many families also found it advantageous to join together to dispute with landlords over property rights and harvest shares, which sometimes led to pooling income to sue landlords in the lower courts.[51]

Many of the peasants who migrated from Henan into the Taihang arranged tenancy jobs, provided temporary shelter, and even paid the initial rent for their families and friends.[52] Not all of the migrants had the strength to traverse the dangerously jagged and narrow trails of the Taihang Mountains, or to fight off the wolves in the highlands, but mutual-aid efforts enabled many of those who fled their home villages in Lin and Hua counties to survive in the years spanning the World Depression.

As peasants left the land, losing touch with their family and village resources, they probably lost much of their capacity to hold onto their older mutual-aid relationships. Yet the semirooted and rootless poor did manage to re-create some rudimentary joint self-help arrangements among themselves. The peasant women who became the hired hands and kitchen help of landlords smuggled food to ragged vagabonds who solicited help, and helped some of them obtain menial jobs in the few landlord households known to treat their workers fairly.[53] The homeless ex-peasants who turned to begging, and who took up residence in the old roadside temples, often shared food with peasants who were fleeing landlords, taught them rules for begging, and told them of employment possibilities amid the fugitive communities that had formed in the coal mines of Shanxi, Henan, and Shandong.[54] Because neither gentry-paid mine foremen nor the county police were inclined to descend into these dangerous and unhealthy coal pits, the miners were left alone there to create work-share arrangements and forge little communities of resistance.

The joint self-help of peasants on the land included exchanging scarce resources and giving small gifts. To be sure, such sharing and charitable activities petered out when the weather and warlords depleted local resources, but through them the peasants were reinforcing horizontal bonds and creating class cooperation and leadership that did not depend on ruling landlord-gentry patriarchs for survival. Moreover, the development of absentee landlordism in predominantly smallholder and tenant villages left these little peasant groups to deal with only a few smallfry landlords, especially, though not exclusively, the case in the Taihang area. The peasants in these villages started their efforts to prevent landlords from usurping village resources out of joint family mutual-aid initiatives they had conceived without any outside advice or assistance, and they would play an important part in later village struggles aided by the CCP.

Remedialist Protest

Next to self-help, the safest survival strategy was to try to persuade power holders to return to the traditional terms of justice. This remedialist thrust colored disputes over landlord wrongdoings, and the peasant grievances expressed to Republican officials. The rural people who initiated this remedialist style of protest sought to renegotiate a tolerable relationship with county, provincial, and national power holders. Remedialist protest seemed the way to avoid a direct and dangerous confrontation with Republican government, and many peasants took it up in the hope that landlords and magistrates would redress grievances within a framework of paternalistic accountability. Quite often, then, the peasants' remedialist protests amounted to little more than a demand for Republican power holders to honor the dynastic commitment to provision the countryside and protect the villages from rapacious landlords, gentry, and officials.

Throughout the border region, particularly in northern Henan, tenants entreated landlords to reinstate long-term leases and to return to sharecrop agreements that had promised equity and survival. The share tenants of Lin xian pleaded with landlords to reduce the crop rent after poor harvests, and to postpone it during drought.[55] In Hua xian tenants demanded landlord protection against warlord taxes.[56] Their counterparts in Puyang xian said that landlords should reassume the cost of, among other things, feeding the livestock and running market errands.[57]

That these small tenant protests occasionally were accompanied by violence, such as the torching of a courtyard when the rent was collected forcibly, did not make the demands any more radical. Few tenants were crying out for the land or demanding a permanent cancellation of rent.

Personal appeals before landlords reflected a felt right to receive the piece-meal tenure benefits produced by the tenants' own efforts, rather than a belief that landlords owed them a whole package of patronage services.[58] The migrant tenants in the Taihang counties of Pingshun and Changzhi were merely trying to preserve the threadbare existence they could wring from tenure pacts that had never been invested with firm promises of landlord patronage for difficult times. They often had to entreat landlords just to allow them to get through the first harvest, to stop rent increases on poorly graded plots, and to delay the repossession of land they were improving.[59]

The peasant landowners focused their protests on landlords who had threatened their family security either by usury or foreclosures and forgeries. At the outset, before indebtedness and land losses led to ruin, these peasants did little more than importune landlords to recognize their right to harvests produced from tiny patches of family land.[60] Many of them tried to regain lost land by persuading relatives to plead their case before the landlord or by saving the cash they earned from working outside the village to pay the cost of resecuring land through litigation.[61] The stormiest disputes over landownership were pressed by peasants whose forebears had been landless refugees to the freeholding villages of Hebei, Shanxi, and Henan.[62] The fact that several generations had sacrificed themselves to pioneer this land added a volatile element to these confrontations. Still, the tillers' simple goal was to modify the harsh terms of usury and to make clear their continuing record of ownership. They were not challenging the right of landlords to profit by tolerable interest charges or to acquire land by long-accepted means of competition.

What aroused tenants, smallholders, and hired hands to pursue remedialist protest collectively was the landlord hoarding of grain, especially the refusal to release relief grain during the spring hunger.[63] Few peasants initially set out to seize these hoarded grains. Those who could no longer bear their hunger elected small, five-person delegations to solicit interest-free loans. When landlords denied them this old practice of borrowing, they pawned and sold property to purchase the grain. But by the late 1920s landlords preferred to send the grain outside the villages to market towns, where prices were higher, and some therefore refused to loan grain even at raised interest rates. Peasants found they had little choice but to seize the grain. The confessions of those who were caught indicate that they intended to repay the seized grain with the next good harvest[64] (though surely anyone in the hands of the police would say this).

Peasants made protests before landlords and gentry in hopes of re-establishing older rights to local water supplies, village forests and fishing grounds, and the fruits of labor in the local mines. The peasants of Xiyan village along the Fen River in Shanxi protested the closing of irrigation gates designed to carry water to their downstream fields during the dry season.[65] Only after their requests to reopen the gates were denied did they fight with gentry retainers. Similarly, the peasants of Xiaobeiwu, a village in the Taihang, protested taxes levied on fish caught out of their customary fishing waters along the Yutai River, but only after gentry-hired ruffians tried to enforce these new claims by confiscating the catch did a physical clash take place.[66] The rural people who labored in the coal mines around Gu Mountain in Hebei and Fenghuang Mountain in Shanxi entreated mine bosses not to cut wages, and resorted to fisticuffs only when the police were called to silence them.[67]

What turned these protests into incipient local class wars was the staunch refusal of the nouveau riche big men to right their wrongdoings. This refusal enraged peasants, especially in villages, districts, and counties where the new men of wealth were treading on long-standing rights. Now, in the 1920s, the streams and forests may have been renamed after some Great Tradition benefactor, but the peasants insisted that the water and woods always had belonged to everyone, not just a few immoral powerful men.

These remedialist protests proliferated in the years approaching the seizure of power by the Guomindang warlord regime. These were years when peasants were determined to bring Republican government to sanction their struggles to defend themselves against the aggressive claims of landlords, gentry, and militarists. Little groups of peasant neighbors spent desperately needed income to involve landlords in lower-court litigations over land rights, peasant delegations petitioned the magistrate to suspend the grain tax, and peasant crowds converged on government salt shops to protest rising prices.[68] The rural people who initiated these protests were not challenging the right of Republican officials to pass judgments or issue edicts. All they were asking was that things be set right again, and seldom was their demand originally put forth in a militantly aggressive manner. This nonradical strategy of protest was being pursued by peasants who supposedly never had placed any real faith in the Republic of China.

Oppositionist Revolt: From the Red Spears to the Heavenly Gates

The peasants pursued an oppositionist strategy of survival largely through their participation in secret societies to which they had looked for protection in the past. The major secret society in the Shanxi-Hebei-Shandong-Henan border region was the Hongqiang hui, or Red Spear Society, and peasant participation in this *hui* grew in response to banditry and warlordism. Paradoxically, the Red Spear movement was riddled with self-help and remedialist themes of protest, and its members oscillated from quietist pullbacks to village autonomy to militant outbursts against the warlords attempting to capture the region, particularly the Henan warlord Wu Peifu and the Manchurian warlord Zhang Zuolin.

The political thrust of the Red Spear Society was not originally toward oppositionist revolt. The society apparently was sponsored by landholding patriarchs seeking to reaffirm their authority over district and county domains threatened by the warlord competition for the North China Plain, Manchuria, and the Huai River area after 1916–17. The Red Spears in the Hebei-Shandong-Henan area developed out of the subcounty militia system wherein conservative-minded notables selectively dispensed patronage to recruit peasants to defend local territory against the endemic banditry and warlordism that followed on the death of Yuan Shikai.[69] The leaders of these *hui* were gentry, landlords, merchants, and rich peasants. These local big men convened the Red Spear assemblies, covering the costs of tea, lamp oil, and firearms used by the peasant membership. In the beginning the peasant landowners, far more than those without land, played a pivotal role in Red Spear village defense systems, since they welcomed gentry assistance in protecting family labor forces and in guarding village lands from warlords.[70]

Chesneaux points out that although the Red Spears gained popularity by recruiting from the rural poor, this relationship led the peasant membership to depend on gentry and landlords, "whose intrigues they frequently served."[71] The Red Spears, he goes on, did not fight against gentry and landlords. Their opposition to official pillage was said to be protest *within* the prerevolutionary polity.[72] The goal of the Red Spear gentry was to mobilize peasants for the defense of their local domains, making certain they did not organize along class lines to challenge their wealth and power. This goal was underpinned by gentry measures taken to restrain peasants and nonpeasants who filled the Red Spear associations.[73] The Red Spear patriarchs used patronage to separate, rather than unite, the village self-defense groups, and thereby controlled their potential for collective action locally. At the same time, they tried to prevent the Red Spear military commanders, many of whom had risen from the ranks, from mingling with ordinary peasants, so that they might prevent them from recruiting their own rebel units independently.

Perry contends that there was little chance of revolution coming from the Red Spear Society in the Huai River area because the gentry leadership, by virtue of its vertical bonds and common residential ties with the settled villagers, could mobilize tillers against outsiders[74]—a line of analysis that follows naturally from Chesneaux. To be sure, the Red Spear leaders did not want to drive peasants to starvation and real oppositionist revolt, and the early thrust of Red Spear activity in the border region, which was the heartland of the Red Spears, seems to support the Chesneaux-Perry thesis. But the evolving Red Spear revolts, and their accompanying social and political realignments, encourage a rethinking of the nature and limits of secret-society revolt in the most chaotic years of the Republic.

As the warlord era wore on, the relationship between the Red Spear patriarchs and the peasantry produced some ugly confrontations, and the patriarchs found it decidedly more difficult to integrate the defensive mobilizations of peasants with their own interests. By the mid-1920s a number of the gentry were beginning to transform the Red Spears into their own private *mintuan*,[75] and in response to this change peasants increasingly regrouped into alternative Red Spear units.[76] The baffling question is why and how this realignment came about.

The growing tendency of the Red Spear gentry to align with warlords flew in the face of peasant attempts to avoid the growing military requisition.[77] Throughout the postwar period the warlords who rode into the border region had badgered the Red Spear gentry to help them establish *lianzhuang hui* in the villages. The *lianzhuang hui* was the instrument of extraction and control, and above all the arm of militarist tax machinery. When faced with the choice between protecting the resources of the peasantry and carrying out the goals of the *lianzhuang hui*, some of the Red Spear patriarchs chose to let the tillers suffer. By the late 1920s they were complying with warlords to collect the land tax from self-employed smallholders, to register the weapons owned by each peasant household, and to arrest the unemployed peasants involved in crop theft.[78] Since the Red Spear patriarchs often resided in big market villages, if not the county towns, they attempted to shift much of this warlord tax claim to poor and peripheral villages, and this shift doubtlessly made them even more the instrument of requisition to the local peasantry.[79]

The oppositionist Red Spear mobilizations of the 1920s grew out of the peasants' failed attempt to avoid a clash with the intrusive arm of the tax Republic. No doubt these mobilizations retained their defensive impetus. But as they grew to thirty, fifty, and eighty thousand[80] the illegitimate Red Spear gentry lost control of recruitment, and some of the Red Spear military commanders began to form independent units with the capacity of organizing guerrilla-style countermobilizations. By the mid-1920s there were some two million men in Red Spear commands within the thirty counties situated at the crossroads of the Hebei-Shandong-Henan border area.[81] From 1916 to 1921 Red Spear gentry in these counties had been able to stabilize the situation, but after 1921 the society grew large and disorderly, as discharged soldiers, vagabonds, and bandits joined it.[82] Thus the Red Spears grew larger month by month, and as the character of membership changed, the local gentry could no longer control them. In the end, the Red Spear elite defined the activities of these Red Spear spinoffs as criminal *(fei)*, and this definition was synonymous with that of the militarists who were taking over the Republic of China.

As in Mexico just prior to the Cristero Rebellion of the 1920s, the attempt of militarists to draw powerful local bosses into their own extractive schemes was coupled with a religious inquisition in the border region, and the effect of this on the relationship between Red Spear patriarchs and the village communities whose religious practices were being threatened proved acidic.[83] In effect, warlords like Yan Xishan and Wu Peifu left the Red Spear gentry to either stand with the heterodox religious mobilizations of the country people or to side with the attempts of their armed tax agents to eliminate these popular sects by war. From the moment the local Red Spear gentry accepted the assumptions of the militarists, they deepened the line of conflict between themselves and the wretched Red Spear rebels whose religion was already under attack from warlord armies. By 1927–28, the Red Spear rebels were flying the flag of the Eight Trigrams and openly proclaiming their pursuit of a Buddhist-inspired antigovernment apocalypse. And they did not hesitate to depose the Red Spear patriarchs who made peace with the Beiyang and Guomindang warlords.[84]

By the time Jiang Jieshi co-opted the region's warlord governors, the Red Spear rebels had become a force to be reckoned with. Let us look at a few examples. During the 1923 midautumn festival, the Red Spears attacked the Linqu *xian* government in Shandong. They killed the guards and police, burned the *yamen* records, and released peasants who had been imprisoned for contesting taxes after a harvest failure. On March 3, 1927, the Red Spears in Hebei's Chengan *xian* rioted against irregular troop taxes, disarmed the public security corps, and replaced the government with a committee for conducting hearings on popular grievances. In June and July of 1927, the Red Spears of Hua county in Henan, disguised as the regular militia, disarmed the police and overwhelmed the garrisons at Laoan and Sangcun, then broke into the finance bureau and seized the government salt shop.[85]

Of course some of the Red Spear commanders were seeking merely to take over the county revenue collection process so they could cement their rebel followerships, but many of their practices suggest that their legitimacy was based on more than a takeover of local agencies of extraction. To begin with, the Red Spears addressed the tax relief issue first by abolishing the slate of warlord surtaxes, and second by collecting only the customary Qing dynasty land tax from peasants who could afford to pay.[86] Increasing numbers of tax collectors were kidnaped and killed in these Red Spear revolts, and the more coordinated attacks on the towns were joined by merchants threatened by warlord taxes on salt and kerosene and warlord drives to float multimillion-dollar bonds underwritten by Shanxi and Henan banks that were in fact bankrupt.[87] No doubt some of these merchants had lost out to the growing rail traffic in salt during the first decade of militarism. The Red Spears also called for an end to turning cereal lands into opium fields and to warlord interference in the buying and selling routines of peasant market-goers.[88] By these practices, as by their attempt to replace the *mintuan* that had become the instrument of abusive gentry rule, the Red Spears were seeking to substitute their own system of martial law for military lawlessness.

Still, it is not easy to determine whether the oppositionist Red Spears stood for the interest of the peasantry per se or spoke as leaders of patron-client machines with substantial peasant followership. Certainly the Red Spear rebels seldom abandoned the subsistence issues that in peasant minds gave legitimacy to their bold initiatives. By the same token, however, they were willing to negotiate a return to the status quo with county, provincial, and national authority. Even as the Red Spears captured finances and sponsored development projects they remained open to retaining former Republican magistrates, aligning with the enemies of their warlord enemies, and becoming the county-level hunger-prevention force of the central government.[89] The Red Spears were looking for a strong center to back up their daring maneuvers for restoring the rural peace.

Perhaps only a minority of Red Spear groups made the great leap from gentry-sponsored rebellion to revolt aimed at replacing gentry, magistrates, and warlords with a political order that put power in the hands of poor folk. By the late 1920s, however, a growing number of peasants and quasi-peasants in the North China interior had begun to form secret-society networks of their own, by and large opposed to the unlawful Red Spear gentry and to warlord politicians. The Red Spear Society in Neihuang *xian* and the Tianmen *hui* or Heavenly Gate Society in Lin *xian* exemplified this ultraoppositionist secret-society approach to politics.

These peasant movements sprang up in two of northern Henan's poorest counties, neither of which was situated along the major railways by which warlords so often traveled to put down the protests of the poor. Both occurred after 1925, when peasant involvement in oppositionist insurrection had begun to rival self-help and remedialist survival initiatives. By looking at these independent mass mobilizations we can see how the peasants' efforts to survive evolved into revolutionary confrontations involving a violent rejection of Republican rule.

The Red Spears in Neihuang County

The peasant Red Spears of Neihuang's Qiankou village had been losing income to landlords since the end of the Qing, and their location on the Hebei-Henan border exposed them to militarist taxation.[90] Liu Yaobin, the major landlord in Qiankou, had studied the Confucian classics, but by 1924 he was no longer seen as a benefactor. The owner of a pawnshop, Liu was a notorious usurer, and his diligent attention to debts owed him was matched only by his persistence in pressing for fixed rent. By the mid-1920s Liu had joined with other landlords in Neihuang to collect the peanut crops of peasants in lieu of interest and rent, which enabled him to manipulate the price of peanuts sold to Daming, Daokou, and Tianjin from where the peanut oil was shipped to overseas markets. This cut deeply into the income of Qiankou's tillers, so that each year when the new grain crop was still in the blade and the old one had been consumed they faced serious food shortages.

Nonetheless, Qiankou peasants were comparatively fortunate. Situated near the Xiao River, they had access to riverbank lands which their grandfathers had shown them how to develop for salt-field production. They produced salt by the old natural solar baking process and traded it in surrounding villages and in the markets of Daming, Nangong, and Handan in Hebei. The practice of reclaiming riverbank land for salt production hidden from the state was an old strategy of self-help here. By 1925 it had become the only way Qiankou peasants could earn enough income to purchase subsistence grain.

In 1926 Liu Yaobin managed to establish title deeds for the riverbank land that supported the salt production. The peasants did not recognize his claim, but Liu forced the issue by calling in the *mintuan*, and several salt producers were beaten and jailed. Following this, one hundred peasants declared their intention to recover the salt fields, and they defeated Liu and his local retainers in a skirmish at Wenxinggu market village.

This victory curtailed landlord interference in Qiankou's principal self-help strategy for 1926–27, but soon another new threat arose. This was the new wave of miscellaneous taxes taken by county-level gentry-sponsored *mintuan*, which required peasants to pay more and more of their income from salt sales. This threat prompted peasant saltmakers and young students from Qiankou, Wenxinggu, Chai, and Maji to join with people in surrounding villages in anti-miscellaneous-tax resistance.

The students were from the Daming Seventh Normal School, in Hebei, which had been closed by the Jiang Jieshi Guomindang after the coup d'état of April 12–13, 1927. Some of these students were members of the Chinese Communist Party, and upon returning to Neihuang a few of them became involved in the peasants' antitax protests in the market places of Qingdian and Wenxinggu.

These antitax activities were led by peasant Red Spears. But they were turned back by Liu Yaobin and several hundred *mintuan* from the Neihuang-Puyang-Hua *xian* triangle on January 6, 1928. Red Spear peasants from nearly thirty villages had come to Wenxinggu temple to call for the end of the new surtaxes, but the *mintuan* opened fire to disperse the demonstrators. A number of the rebels, including members of the CCP, were shot or imprisoned, and the peasant movement beat a hasty retreat.

In the next year, 1928–29, the CCP students who had escaped this attack secretly established ties with peasants in Qiankou and other villages to carry on an underground anti-miscellaneous-tax struggle from the back reaches of the Xiao River. They captured the leader of the *mintuan* in Hua village, got hold of twelve guns, and proceeded to wage a protracted antitax campaign which drove the local tax agents from the villages. Within months several thousand peasants were celebrating an antitax victory at Wenxinggu.

By the spring of 1929 the peasants of Qiankou had won back their right to work the salt fields. They formed village transport teams which carried salt by wagon to Daming and Handan where it was sold for local consumption, or taken on by river to Tianjin. As we have seen, this local salt sold at a far cheaper price than the "sea salt" that was an important source of warlord revenue, depriving warlord salt monopolists of their revenues. Accordingly, around 1930 new Guomindang tax police from Tianjin rode into the Xiao River area with orders to close the salt fields. When the saltmakers did not comply, the tax police attempted to fill in the salt ponds with dirt, and a new round of peasant resistance began.

The tax police retreated to Puyang city, where they offered to receive a peasant delegation from the Xiao River saltmaking villages. The peasants' delegation, however, was imprisoned, and the tax police refused to negotiate the restoration of the salt fields to the local people. At this point the peasants, with the support of the returned CCP students, decided to rush Puyang to drive out the tax police, who, again, were an arm of the Guomindang.

In preparation for the assault on the Puyang county government the Xiao River Red Spears contacted saltmakers and salt merchants around Puyang city to ask them to join the struggle. They agreed, and with the plan of attack set, some four thousand people, including a hundred-person vanguard from Qiankou, rushed the Puyang tax police headquarters and captured the Tianjin police while other rebel units disarmed the *mintuan*. These events paved the way for the development of an alternative order of power in Neihuang, perhaps akin to that being established in Hua, Lin, and other Henan "red" counties before the Guomindang closed this possibility after 1932.

The Heavenly Gates in Lin County

The Tianmen *hui*, or Heavenly Gate Society, uprisings of 1926–27 grew out of peasant attempts to avoid Republican taxes and predatory banditry.[91] Its heartland was in Lin *xian*, where the movement emerged in 1925. Its membership was made up of poor peasants, quarry workers, and coal miners in the Hebei-Shanxi-Henan border counties where the Taihang Mountains begin.

We already have linked the rise of peasant bandit leagues in Lin *xian* to the efforts of peasants to resist rigid Republican county government taxation during the intensive droughts of 1919–22. In October of 1922 the Lin *xian* officials charged the head of the Lin county *mintuan*, Zhang Yushan, with the task of exterminating the peasant bandit leagues. Zhang betrayed them, and turned over his weapons to the bandits in return for cash. From 1922 on the Lin *xian* government had no way of controlling its own territory. The militia was underpaid and prone to desertion in the face of bandit attacks. If the government was to collect taxes and contain popular banditry then force had to be brought in from the outside. The landlords, gentry, and officials therefore invited bandits from neighboring Anyang county to patrol Lin *xian* and put down the popular bandit leagues, which had come under the leadership of Zhang Yushan. In the daytime these Anyang bandits served as soldiers in the pay of Lin county government, but at nightfall they donned masks and robbed the villagers. The Tianmen *hui* uprising of 1926–27 was a direct response to this predatory banditry and to government tax plunder. In August of 1926 the Lin county officials announced a surtax on the already burdensome land tax and autumn harvest tax.[92] In response, thousands of peasants joined in an antitax revolt under the banner of the Heavenly Gate Society.

The Heavenly Gate Society was led by Han Yuming, a stonecutter from Dongyou village in south central Lin *xian*.[93] In 1925 Han Yuming had clashed with the Anyang bandit troops in the wake of a raid on the village where his in-laws resided, and by late 1926 he had raised the banner of the Heavenly Gates against the Lin *xian* government. In less than one year a hundred thousand peasants swelled the ranks of the Tianmen *hui*, and the society had branches in more than twenty border counties, including Linzhang, Anyang, Shian, Hui, Hua, and Qingfeng in Henan, and She, Wuan, Ci, Handan, Chengan, Wei, Yongnian, Quzhou and Xingdai in Hebei. A Nationalist government operative reported the Heavenly Gates spreading like wildfire along the Henan-Hebei border.[94]

Some of the early activities of the Tianmen *hui* reflected the remedialist tendencies in the peasant movement.[95] Within Lin county the Heavenly Gate groups launched a campaign to combat government-backed banditry, and drove the predatory bandits back to Anyang and points east. Peasants and merchants in Lin *xian* did not have to worry about unjust taxes and highway banditry for nearly a year. Along the Lin county-Ci county border, the Tianmen *hui* was joined by Red Spear peasants who had defected from the Ci *xian* Red Spear chief, Zhu Yufu, and Han Yuming led them to demand that Zhu stop laying off miners at Yili and refrain from taking over the Zonghe coal mine, which employed hundreds of land-short peasants from the area.[96] With the Tianmen *hui* victory here in the summer of 1927 the Heavenly Gate peasants and miners received an indemnity payment, and a truce was made.

By the spring of 1927, however, the Tianmen *hui* had seen a number of its attempts to negotiate a return to peace and order undercut by the ploys of Lin *xian* officials, by the intrigues of the Red Spear gentry, and by attacks from the Fengtien warlord clique. Increasingly, the Heavenly Gates dealt with this elite intolerance by protest acts that directly challenged local Republican power holders. The Heavenly Gates in Lin *xian* put to death some of the landlords who had sided with the warlord tax requisition, destroyed the county *mintuan*, and compelled landlords and gentry to pay for the guns to be used by the village self-defense units. The magistrate, Liu Wanyan, was driven out of the county; and peasants subsequently declared their intention to eliminate Lin county town and move the capital to the countryside, back to its mythical pagan origins.[97]

Like some of the Red Spear spinoffs, such as the Black Flags in Shandong and the Yellow Sands in Henan, the Heavenly Gate Society had a streak of millenarianism running through its cry for folk justice.[98] As the movement reached high tide, Han Yuming and his lieutenants declared they were going to deliver the peasants into the protection of the Ming dynasty, and Han wore a crown that symbolized loyalty to the Ming. Before the Heavenly Gates lost out to pro-Guomindang militarists fearful of its autonomy its membership reached three hundred thousand in the border region. Its religious commitment to relieve peasant misery by returning to a Ming world without the existing Republican military order doubtlessly boosted its phenomenal growth in 1926–27.

Within Lin *xian* a peasant counterorder was in the making, and its local leadership was in the process of giving it a regional focus. In late 1926 Han Yuming persuaded the Heavenly Gates of twenty counties to put aside their factional differences to defeat warlord Zhang Zuolin's Fengtien cavalry, which Heavenly Gate forces annihilated in March of 1927.[99] This victory drove the militarists back to the major stations of the Beijing-Hankou Railway, and it put the Hebei-Shanxi-Henan area in the hands of the Heavenly Gates until Jiang Jieshi and the region's warlords colluded to demobilize this massive peasant movement after the coup d'état of April 12–13.

By mid-1927 peasant-armed self-protection associations were evident nearly everywhere in the border region. Their struggles threatened to cut the warlords off from village food grains and the iron ores of the interior. Li Dazhao, the populist theoretician of the CCP, hailed them as the harbinger of a struggle to end the age of warlordism. There was, however, only minimal CCP involvement in the Red Spear revolts and none in the Heavenly Gate uprising, and in neither did the presence of the party create the bridge from rebellion to revolution. When it came to the Red Spears, the CCP was throwing its support to overtaxed peasants and salt peddlers whose struggles, to use Tilly's term, had begun as "defensive mobilizations"[100] to fight off the new militarists. But this party support was not what mothered the popular revolt. On the one hand, the intransigence of Republican tax rule was turning the peasants' essentially defensive mobilizations toward oppositionist revolt, involving attempts to create alternative orders of power. On the other hand, the weakness of repression at the level of Republican county government signaled a choice between survival cum revolution and death via increasingly impotent self-help and remedialist acts of protest. To be sure, this choice was about to be threatened by the coming of the Guomindang warlords. But through their intermittent victories of 1925 to 1932 the peasants, and the CCP, were discovering that Republican local government alone was not powerful enough to repress them. Like the Red Spears in Neihuang and the Heavenly Gates in Lin *xian*, thousands upon thousands could move to openly challenge local power holders.

THE LIMITS OF PEASANT REVOLT:
REPRESSION AND DEPRESSION

Jiang Jieshi's coup d'état put new limits on the peasant movements in the North China interior. In the process of leading the Northern Revolutionary

Expedition Jiang Jieshi had transformed the Guomindang into a military order made up of multiple cliques of generals and gentry. This transformation had repercussions throughout the border region.[101] Regional gunmen and their gentry allies took the show of strength by Jiang Jieshi as the signal to suppress the peasant movements. In the tenuous alliances struck by Jiang with the warlords the task of reordering the rebellious countryside was left to the ruthless power wielders who had been the object of peasant wrath. Without the backing of Jiang, the landlords, gentry, and warlords could not have clamped down as they did on the rebellions of the poor. The peasant movements in the Hebei-Shanxi-Henan area fought off the weakened gentry *mintuan* until the pro-Guomindang warlord governors sent their troops to exterminate the "criminal societies." In the central-government-inspired anti-Communist rioting campaign that followed, thousands of peasant rebels were put to death. If the Guomindang officers did not always directly back this repression, neither did they do anything to stop it. The progress of those who pushed forward with renewed military repression, plus the World Depression, seriously eroded the leverage rural people had built up through revolt.

Self-Help

To be sure, progress in cash-crop yields was reported in southern Hebei and western Shandong districts unafflicted by disaster just prior to the Great Depression. In the dozen villages along the Hebei-Shandong border where Guanping meets Guantao, however, tillers were in trouble even in the years of banner cotton yields.[102] In 1928 the price of cotton had gone up 180 percent, but with less land devoted to cereal production and half of the fall food crop lost, the price of scarce grains proved prohibitive. Cash-cropping had become an intolerable form of self-exploitation:

1. *Beisitou village*: Of five hundred families two hundred had left. Eighty to 90 percent of the people were existing on chaff and cotton seed. Begging was common. Many had died of hunger. Women and children were being sold for traveling expenses for the men going to Shanxi or Manchuria.

2. *Fangerjia*: A market village of three hundred families. About fifteen families had left. Between 80 and 90 percent were living on chaff. Local officials reported half the village to be near death. Many children were being sold.

3. *Beiguaichu*: A nonmarket hamlet of 140 families. Half had left. Ninety percent were eating cotton seeds. More than thirty persons had starved. The children were being sold.

4. *Xinzhuang*: A 150-family village in a prosperous cotton-growing district. Very few persons had left. Half were existing on chaff and seed, but no starvation. The village had been hurt badly by unaffordable grain prices.

5. *Luzhuang*: Of five hundred families two hundred had migrated to Shanxi or Manchuria. Eighty to 90 percent were getting by on chaff. Starva-

tion was common. Children were being sold constantly.

6. *Beixiabu*: 130 families. Eighty persons had migrated. Eighty to 90 percent eating chaff. Seventy-five persons died of hunger. More than one hundred children sold.

The generalissimo's alliance with the region's warlords did little to improve the position of peasants in the cash sector. As a rule, the Guomindang capture of a county was followed by orders from the central government to induce peasants to take up cash-cropping, with cotton, tobacco, and peanuts receiving high priority. During the Depression the landlords in southeast Shanxi and northern Henan, with the backing of warlord guns, compelled peasants who wanted to switch back to cereals to keep tilling cash cotton, peanuts, and opium.[103] The Western observers who reported throngs of rural producers transporting these crops to the markets seldom mentioned the dilemma cash-cropping posed for each peasant household: peasants could not market enough of their raw cash crops to obtain the cash they needed to pay the new military-gentry taxes locally and still have enough income left over to purchase basic food-grains and salt.[104] The revolts of 1925–32 had been aiming to resolve this problem, which after April of 1927 again presented itself increasingly. By this time peasants in western Shandong were sticking their land deeds on their doors and fleeing because they could not pay the official land taxes[105]—even before the world price of cotton and peanuts crashed.

Many of the makeshift family self-help schemes were all but exhausted during the Depression. Belt-tightening had moved on to begging. The peasants of Xiyang county still recall their days of begging in the Taihang:

> At that time there were many beggars. When you would go to one family, they might give you a little, but never enough to fill your stomach. In one day you had to go to many, many families, many, many villages and you still couldn't get enough to eat.[106]

The peasants of Lucheng fought among themselves over the leaves and bark of elm, while their counterparts in Xiyang, Boai, and Lin *xian* were reduced to eating the corpses of people who had died from hunger.[107]

Nor did the wages derived from short-term outwork automatically benefit peasant family budgets. Highwaymen and landlord usurers were determined to make this income theirs. In Lin *xian*, for example, over 17 percent of the peasants were going outside the county to find jobs as short-term agricultural day laborers, and yet they were surrendering two-thirds of their earnings to usurers.[108]

By the early 1930s sending women and children out of the villages to supplement family income had become a losing proposition too. Landlords not only grossly underpaid the women and children who worked for them, they also confiscated the cash peasant youths brought back to their indebted families. Clashes over the right to retain these wages always occurred around the lunar New Year when peasant offspring returned home from the small factories of the towns and cities.

Many peasant women had to turn to temporary prostitution. According to one source nearly half of the peasant women in a dozen villages in the Taihang counties of Licheng, Taigu, Yu, Heshun, and Zuoquan were involved in permanent prostitution by the early 1930s, even though this course no longer held out the hope of supplementing household income or even keeping the children alive.[109] A few fortunate prostitutes survived by catering to the merchants in big market towns or by becoming concubines to the gentry in the treaty port world,[110] but the wretched prostitutes in the poor towns and villages of the periphery had to stake their existence on peddling sex to bankrupt petty merchants and soldiers unaccustomed to paying for anything.

Migration too had become an extremely risky ordeal. From 1911 on the Taihang migrants to the Yellow River plain were exposed to typhoid epidemics, and migrants to Manchuria endured at least two major outbreaks of bubonic plague. They became carriers of this dreadful disease as they jammed into rat-infested steamships on the oceanic route or trapped the marmot whose valuable furs and *pasterella pestis* they took onto the railcars to the Manchurian countryside.[111]

Survival was threatened even more severely by the drastic downward swing in the pattern of migration to the North China heartland, and most significantly to Manchuria.[112] During the early twentieth century this spill-back began to take on fantastic dimensions, and was exacerbated by landlords and warlords indifferent to the requirements of migrant survival. As emphasized in the previous chapter, the militarized Guomindang contributed to this horrible development. By the early 1930s, the social crisis confronting peasants caught up in a historic reversal of a migration pattern that had held since the fourteenth century was compounded tenfold.

With the central government failure to restabilize rural class relations, the peasant families who had migrated up into the Taihang area in search of food and fuel in the 1920s found landlords more difficult to reason with. As deforestation worsened and the search for subsistence moved higher and higher, many an absentee landlord, eager to squeeze the most from valley and lower hillslope land, usurped the land and taxed the forest products of the migrants. These landlords also took back rental land and abandoned all aid to the migrant peasants who could not meet rent or mortgage payments. By the late 1920s, thousands of disinherited Taihang migrants had begun drifting back to their home villages in Hebei and Henan.[113]

Nor did the Jiang Jieshi warlord regime promote peasant initiatives to stay on in Manchuria. Absentee rentiers in the Northeast began raising rents just as migrant tenants were suffering losses from a decline in the price for cash export crops, stimulating the backward flow of migrants in the early stage of the World Depression.[114] Beginning in 1927, the third successive year of poor grain harvests and peasant revolt in Hebei, Shandong, and Henan, the number of migrants to Manchuria jumped from five hundred thousand to over one million per year.[115] Of approximately one million migrants annually over the next three years, however, 33, 43, and 59 percent returned in 1927, 1928, and 1929 respectively. Tragically, the peasants who fled to Manchuria from the famine-ridden cash-crop zones of Shanxi and Shaanxi from 1928 to 1931 posed yet another threat to the border region migrants who preferred to wait out these harsh years in the Northeast, for they often adapted to the insecurity of migrant life by banditry. On top of this came the Japanese army. Acting partly out of fear that Jiang Jieshi's officer corps was spreading Bolshevism and banditry over the Great Wall, the Japanese invaded and occupied Manchuria. Japan's conquest stemmed the tide of Han peasant migration to the Northeast, and the subsequent Guomindang army retreat into North China proper left the migrants to Manchuria to be exploited by landlords in collusion with the Japanese. Many of the Taihang migrants to Manchuria actually had to fight their way back to their native Shanxi villages after the Mukden Incident in September of 1931.[116]

The migrants who were thrown back to their home villages with the close of the frontiers and the collapse of the world economy had to face the despotic landlords from whom their families had fled. Those who returned home to Henan's Lin *xian* from the Taihang received a violent welcome,[117] as did their Manchurian counterparts who were pouring back to Shandong's Fan *xian*.[118] The migrants who returned from Manchuria to the Taihang after 1931,[119] rumored to be dangerous outsiders involved in Communist brigandage and rioting, were banished or incarcerated.

With militarists in the patronage of Jiang Jieshi penetrating the towns of the border region the big landlords began cracking down on petty theft and social banditry. This was done in part by bandaging up the *mintuan* and bringing back the *baojia* system.* The Taihang Mountain hamlets being settled anew by migrant and refugee families from Shanxi, Hebei, Shandong, and Henan did not readily lend themselves to these controls, which took hold mainly in market villages with close links to district and county administration.[120] These villages were constantly patrolled by landlord retainers and county police, who sometimes put even the small crop thieves to death before firing squads. The police often were assisted by semiprofessional bounty hunters who stood to collect silver dollars by turning in anyone they could pass off as a "Communist rioter," and thousands of peasants, carpenters, and broom sellers ended up on their execution rolls during the anti-Communist rioting campaigns in the Hebei-Shanxi-Henan area during the 1930s.

---

*An institution of state control, the *baojia* was imposed by the Guomindang warlords in collaboration with landlords in an effort to police the countryside.

The relationship of the Jiang Jieshi military to prewar banditry further shrank the survival choices of the poor. With the arrival of the Guomindang army commanders along the Henan-Shanxi-Hebei border after 1928 the predatory banditry that had flourished in the pre-Heavenly Gate period once again found an alliance with government. In the very counties where the oppositionist peasant movement had evicted night bandits and eliminated pressures to produce cash crops, the Guomindang commander Pang Bingxun enlisted bandits from Anyang and elsewhere to improve on Republican government taxation after 1932.[121] At the same time, the bandit Sun Dianying, who so conveniently identified with the cause of Jiang Jieshi after 1927, pillaged border region towns and villages throughout the Nationalist decade, just as he had done prior to 1925.[122] Keep in mind, too, that the small bands of hungry peasants involved in seasonal pilfering and raids on the finance bureaus often lost out to the Guomindang officers who were protecting and profiting from predatory banditry here.

The Jiang Jieshi officer corps would not tolerate the existence of popular banditry. As a competitor for the spoils of the cash-crop zones of Hebei, Shandong, and Henan and the protection to be sold to the merchants and smugglers traveling the caravan trails linking the Taihang with southern Hebei and western Shandong, the Guomindang army was prepared to use force to eliminate banditry. For the peasant bandit leagues, therefore, survival meant fighting to remain free from the warlordism of the Nationalist government.[123]

After the April 1927 coup, some of the peasants' small group survival options were declared to be in violation of the anti-Communist rioting laws, which held the meeting of more than several persons to constitute a conspiracy. Of course the central government may not have had the seemingly harmless mutual-aid activities of peasants as its target, but criminal landlords saw in these anti-Communist regulations the opportunity to demobilize peasant adaptations that ran counter to their interest. They confiscated the lands that peasant squatters were reclaiming by joint effort, and they refused to allow peasant relatives and friends to act as witnesses in disputes.[124] The Guomindang officers in cooperation with the county police rounded up and shot little groups of migrants who were crossing from northern Henan into the Taihang Mountains,[125] and they drove the beggars, whose activities were declared illegal in 1931, out of the market towns back toward the hinterland.

Remedialist Protest

With the central government militarists penetrating the border region landlords and gentry responded to the peasants' remedialist protests by measures as brutal as those used in medieval China. In localities where landlords could enlist the Guomindang militarists, peasants were made to pay a pound of flesh, and more, for their humble pleas and petitions, as the landlord reign of terror against tenants illustrates. In Lucheng *xian* tenants pleading for rent reduction were tied to trees for a winter's night, and many tenants who could not pay crop rents died in landlord jails and pigsties.[126] The landlords of Puyang are said to have kicked tenants who solicited hunger loans, and to have beaten those who entreated them to pay for extracontractual labor services.[127] Droit du seigneur, the feudal landlord privilege of deflowering tenant brides, was revived in parts of the border region,[128] and tenants who openly decried it were driven from their villages.

The police arrested, and sometimes killed, peasants who challenged the landlord attempt to take over village water resources, to regulate access to nearby forests and fishing waters, and to withhold coal mine wages—which were diverted to pay taxes for supporting the official troops stationed near the mines.[129] Landlords also urged the Guomindang officers to draft peasants who would not work for them on their terms into the army.[130] These police attacks and forced drafts were carried out without objection from local Republican magistrates or central government authority.

Of course a great deal of central government reform was undertaken on paper, but in practice the militarized Guomindang neither appreciated nor accommodated the remedialist protests of the peasantry. The Guomindang handled the peasants' litigations, petitions for tax relief, and demonstrations for price justice in ways that overrode their survival concerns and raised the level of conflict in the countryside.

Although no thorough study exists of how the Republican courts handled peasant lawsuits against landlords who violated land rights and embezzled village funds, it appears that the Guomindang judicial officials allowed landlords to win these litigations.[131] Certainly this was so in Henan localities, where peasants approached the district officials with petitions to sue landlords who had falsified deeds to family lands. The officials broke their promise to investigate peasant claims, leaving peasant families little choice but to pursue the litigations up through the county and prefectural courts, where they ran up against a string of nondecisions.[132] The judges suspended the cases and invariably sent them back to the court of origin, allowing landlords to continue their lawless exploitation. This breach of peasant faith in the lower courts helped shape the popular belief that the new Republic was at odds with the rights of poor folk.

If the Guomindang response to the peasants' remedialist tax protests is a reliable indicator of its performance, it did little to stop local power wielders from forcibly taking peasant food grains. In northern Henan the Guomindang officers placed the district level posts in the hands of landlords, who in turn collected taxes for themselves and the Guomindang army.[133] Peasant petitions for grain-tax relief resulted in raised taxes and beefed-up governmental tax forces.[134] As for the warlords who temporarily became the tax forces of the Jiang Jieshi Guomindang, we already know they turned their backs on the poor. High-ranking Guomindang officers were seen rebuking peasant delegations petitioning for grain-tax relief during the 1942 Henan famine, even though the peasants were promising to pay when the harvest permitted.[135] These same Guomindang warlords refused to negotiate with the leaders of popular demonstrations for lower salt prices, and aligned themselves with the gentry against the antigabelle rebels in the rural towns.

Oppositionist Revolt

Following the April 1927 coup, Jiang Jieshi struck an alliance with the former Beiyang warlords and predatory bandits in the Shaanxi-Henan area. The militarists who made up this so-called Official Army threw their weight to the county-level power holders under attack from the Red Spear and Heavenly Gate groups. As Jiang Jieshi began to gain the upper hand in the struggle with provincial warlords, his new allies prepared the ground for a violent demobilization of the peasant movements on the plains to the east of the Taihang Mountains.

The central government's prewar success in demobilizing oppositionist revolt was dependent in part on its ambiguous relationship to border-region militarists and secret-society big men. By looking into this relationship we can better comprehend how the Guomindang military smashed the peasant movement after 1927, and why the rural people would join the CCP in opposition to the Guomindang during the Anti-Japanese War. The way in which the national events set in motion by the Jiang Jieshi coup impinged on the Heavenly Gate revolt in Lin *xian* sheds some light on this development.

The Guomindang demobilization was accomplished through both force and patronage. Without the force of newfound warlord allies the Guomindang warlord regime could not have struck so quickly. Two developments were crucial here. One was the temporary support given to Jiang Jieshi by Marshal Yan Xishan. Yan did not want to be cut off from Hebei by either the Fengtien army or the Heavenly Gates, so he sent his Shanxi army to Shijiazhuang and Handan in support of Jiang.[136] As early as the winter of 1927–28 Yan had begun to execute scores of "criminal elements" each day to quell the Red Spears and Yellow Sands in Handan and Wuan *xian*. The second development was the defection of Pang Bingxun, formerly of Wu Peifu's clique, into Jiang Jieshi's camp after 1928.[137] Only months after this defection a five-thousand-man Guomindang army unit under Pang arrived in Lin county to put down the revolt of the Heavenly Gate Society, which outnumbered it twenty to one.

The Heavenly Gates withstood the first round of Guomindang repression, and over the next two years organized underground resistance from the Taihang Mountains. Han Yuming's Heavenly Gates survived in the interstices of warlord strife, as they arranged a temporary alliance with warlord Zhang Xueliang, then a major enemy of the Jiang clique.[138] The Guomindang officers thus had to change their approach; by 1930 they had begun to employ patronage as a means of ending the Heavenly Gate revolt.

First of all, the Guomindang warlords offered patronage to the Red Spear gentry at war with Heavenly Gates and Red Spear spinoffs. Officers like Li

Zhongzheng in southern Hebei and Liu Zhenhua in northern Henan arranged for Red Spear chiefs to become advisers to the Central Army. These arrangements were consummated secretly by the Guomindang militarists as preparation for their campaign to rout the Heavenly Gates, who now were reported to be Communist.[139]

Following this, the Heavenly Gate leadership was offered a truce by the Guomindang, which promised to support Han Yuming's antibandit campaign in Lin county. The Heavenly Gate leadership agreed to an offer of arms, and even allowed the Guomindang to train the Heavenly Gate militia in Lin *xian*. The rumor was that Han Yuming would accept a post as a commander in the Guomindang Bandit Suppression Army of Liu Zhenhua—Jiang Jieshi's client in the Shaanxi-Shanxi-Henan border area.

The negotiated truce with the Guomindang proved fatal. The Heavenly Gate leadership was betrayed once Jiang won his wars with other militarists, tripled his troop strength, and established liaisons with the tainted Red Spear gentry.[140] In 1930 Jiang sent commander Liu Zhenhua from Xinxiang county in northern Henan to organize a plot against the Heavenly Gate Society in Lin county. On the day of a big banquet sponsored by the Lin *xian* Guomindang in honor of the Heavenly Gate Society, Liu Zhenhua and Liu Huixin captured Han Yuming and his lieutenants and took them to Xinxiang, where they were executed and beheaded. This betrayal was coupled with a strike against the Heavenly Gates being trained by the Guomindang in western Lin *xian*, and by a rash of executions of Heavenly Gate leaders

Pillars of the Guomindang warlord regime: *(left to right)*
Yan Xishan, Feng Yuxiang, Jiang Jieshi, Li Zongren

from 1930 to 1932. Most of the Heavenly Gate rebels fled into the Taihang Mountains, where from 1932 on they turned to small-scale guerrilla warfare against Guomindang officer Pang Bingxun. These Heavenly Gate guerrillas occasionally touched base with their former village strongholds along the Hebei-Shanxi-Henan border. For the most part, however, after 1932 the Lin county villages that had given birth to the Heavenly Gates felt the heavy hand of the Jiang Jieshi warlord counterrevolution.

If the Guomindang enjoyed no preexisting popular support in the towns and villages and could not automatically count on the cooperation of rival warlords, then what external factors allowed its recently arrived troops to assert their will against a massive peasant insurrection that only months before had defended itself against government butchery? Feuds between the secret societies and between the North China warlords played a part, and so did meddling by foreign powers. From the moment Jiang Jieshi staged the coup of April 12–13, 1927, the Soviet Union and the United States began to see in him their hopes for an anti-Japanese strongman capable of setting up a respectively pro-Russian, pro-American central government. Between 1925 and 1932 Jiang Jieshi became Stalin's man in China, and Stalin and the Comintern promoted the generalissimo's interest by refusing to assist the CCP attempt to create a peasant movement independent of Guomindang power. This of course strengthened Jiang's hand when it came to combatting the CCP members who were involved in the mobilizations of the Red Spears. In the same period, with the Hoover administration still in power, Jiang Jieshi received an American loan of $50 million for the purpose of quelling warlord revolts in North and Northeast China.[141] The generalissimo used this money to reward the militarists who helped him capture border-region rail depots and carry out repression in the nearby countryside. By 1931 he had been strengthened enough to allow the Japanese to delimit Zhang Xueliang's sphere of influence in Manchuria, and with this move undercut the power base of the one warlord who had offered the Heavenly Gates a potential counterweight to the Guomindang in the border region.

As the Guomindang militarists bore down on the peasant movement, peasants resorted to resistance, including various forms of retreat. The rebellious land-hungry peasants who had welcomed the Red Spears and Heavenly Gates were known to seek shelter in tiny Taihang Mountain hamlets and in back-river hovels along the Hebei-Henan border after 1930. With one foot in the world of beggary and banditry, these poor migrant peasants consciously removed themselves from worsening relations with landlords and Guomindang warlords in the lowlands.

The poor itinerant Taihang uplanders, in particular, were able to pursue this survival-oriented retreat and carry on resistance for several reasons. First of all, they were able to take advantage of topography in organizing their resistance. Not all of their hamlets found their way onto Republican maps, and, in any event, the upland peasants remained confident that Guomindang warlord officers would not risk tracking their rebellious activities into dangerous mountainous terrain, especially since the warlords had to rely on weak landlord and *mintuan* forces locally. In the second place, landlord dominance was relatively weak in the backward hamlets of the highlands. Few landlords were inclined to sink personal investments in the poor soils, let alone directly supervise the tough upland peasants. Most preferred to become squires in the safer lowland market towns, or better yet, to become officers in the privileged Guomindang warlord regime, with its base in the garrisoned city world. Third, and finally, the highland poor faced landlords and local officials who did not have the continuous backing of a consolidated Central Army, and the low strategic priority assigned to the mountainous periphery meant that a good deal of hidden food production, smuggling, and reprisal protest could be pursued from hamlets and villages in the interstices of Republican power.

To be sure, in the low-lying towns and market villages the Guomindang military presence often was sufficient to subordinate peasants to landlordism, predatory banditry, and taxation. The peasants in these localities had to swallow their bitterness in silence rather than relieve it through revolt in the years of Guomindang rule. In the political gaps that developed out of the statelessness of Republican times, however, many peasants were able to retaliate against the extractions of landlords and the depredations of looting bandits and Guomindang tax men. The peasants of Sanjiadian, a village in Shanxi's Jincheng *xian*, rushed into the fields to recover their crops from landlords whose retainers attempted to confiscate the harvest for back interest and taxes, and these landlords "could not do anything about it because they were outnumbered by the angry poor."[142] The Hua county migrants who settled in Jiku village in Shaanxi's Fubing *xian* crippled the oxen of landlords who tried forcibly to take their lands, and then compelled them to reconsider wage cuts.[143] Thus, many peasants who had taken to the Taihang and beyond, and who had to live in poor mountain huts and hill caves, were carrying on their retreat by violent nonconformity. To be sure, they were not taking power through this retreat, but they were keeping their flesh on their bones and keeping alive a set of values that sanctioned the contentious little protests they undertook outside the sphere of Guomindang military power.

REVOLT AND RETREAT FROM THE POLITICAL HEGEMONY OF REPUBLICAN WARLORDISM: RELIGIOUS PROFANATION IN THE PEASANT PULLBACK

Prior to the Guomindang repression, the rural people conducted their search for survival in consonance with their religious understandings of self-help, remedialist protest, and emancipation.[144] In some villages peasants called on *Zaoshen*, the hearth deity, to bless their family plans for self-help. Their remedialist protests for relief grain and lower taxes often were enacted before the Buddhist goddess of mercy, while their armed oppositionist revolts sometimes were quartered in Guandi, or war god, temples. No doubt the reactionary Red Spear gentry tried to draw on articles of Buddhism and Taoism to solidify their tenuous hold on secret-society followings, but they seldom could stop an antistate, and by association anti-Confucian, folklore from fermenting among the peasantry. Just as the Red Spear rebels espoused religious codes that upheld their right to save themselves by taking up arms, so the Heavenly Gates kept secrecy and maintained discipline by Buddhist scriptures. These secret societies also launched their attacks on Republican county government with seditious religious assertions.

Precisely because the region's peasant revolts showed signs of heterodoxy, they were suppressed ruthlessly where the Guomindang clampdown prevailed.[145] The nonbenevolent landlords and officials wanted to silence these religious uproars forever. In the wake of takeovers by Guomindang cavalry, they destroyed peasant idols, including the "useless" hearth god and earth deities. The Guanyin temples were desecrated, and many of the Guandi temples were converted into the Bandit Suppression Headquarters of the Guomindang army. Increasingly after 1927 Republican county officials imposed strict regulations on the temple fairs where large peasant crowds gathered to initiate protests, and they helped the Guomindang warlords seize the heterodox peasant rebels who led these protests. This, then, was the decade when Jiang Jieshi's antifolk military came to signify the total sacrifice the country people were being told to make for an attenuated Republic, with its rituals of Confucian and Catholic respectability.

The militarized Guomindang and the Chinese Communist Party offered different criticisms of these heterodox peasant movements. To the cadres of the Guomindang New Life Movement, the "evil religion" of the Red Spears and Heavenly Gates reflected a radical sectarian anarchy that stood in the way of national unity. To the CCP activists of the May Fourth Movement, the millenarian conceptions embedded in the Red Spear and Heavenly Gate movements were not sufficiently class oriented for proletarian revolution.

But just as the peasant Red Spears revolted against the Guomindang because its cadres did not sufficiently combat the profane acts of landlords and gentry, so they responded coldly to the CCP cadres who offered them liberation without respecting their religious codes for justice and salvation.[146] Fortunately for the CCP, however, the late 1920s saw its cadres giving serious attention to the peasants' attempt to pull back from all outside authority and to define their own liberation without outside moral domination by militarists or parties.

This pullback was an important factor in making for revolutionary possibilities a decade later. Peasants and quasi-peasants in the weakly dominated localities of the border region were left to themselves to articulate some

cutting symbolic criticisms of landlords, government-bandits, and militarists. Their folklore projected a popular counterconception of what Republican politics was and ought to be.

Peasants expressed much of their opposition through folk songs, festivals,
theater, and cults. The peasants of the Taihang, like those in the Red Hills of
Shaanxi, declared the landlords who had usurped their lands to be living
Kings of Hell.[147] In Xiwu, a Taihang village in southwest Shanxi, peasants
associated their enserfment by landlords with eternal damnation, and their
protests to escape servitude reflected a firm rejection of the idea of hell as
everlasting punishment. Within the Taihang area the peasants' Guanyin
cults took on a libertarian tone that expressed anything but harmony with
landlord hierarchy. The Guanyin cults were associated with the egalitarian
and redistributive temple fraternities of the upland poor who, like their
counterparts in the highlands of South China, drew from them to justify
various acts of protest.[148] Since Guomindang warlord domination was not
total in the Taihang these peasants could organize concerted protests against
grain-hoarding landlords and grain-seeking local governments during the
March 3 and July 15 festivals, the latter being the occasion when they freed
hungry folk from the jails and feasted together in a carnivallike atmosphere.[149] This rebellious folk eschatology could not be expressed collectively or continuously in the face of the growing Guomindang warlord
repression, of course, but it was far from dead, and it was given constant
invigoration by the Boxer, Red Spear, and Heavenly Gate fugitives who
brought their antilandlord and antiwarlord bitterness into the Taihang area
from 1900 to 1930.

Here, then, were rural people who were actively charting a symbolic
rejection of the Guomindang warlord regime based largely on their own
conceptions of justice and liberty. In much of the border region they stood
ready, mentally if not physically, to make their own history in the gaps of
central government power.

The limits of self-help and remedialist protest drew peasants to confrontation and oppositionist revolt. The peasant movement clearly was not
the product of later Japanese invasion. Rather, the uneven development
and the deep militarist divisions of Republican times allowed peasants to
mount a significant challenge to the catastrophic increases in food prices,
taxes, and poverty. This challenge, which peaked in the years 1925 to 1932,
doubtlessly flourished in the more backward counties of the border region.
Huang Xuanwen, writing of the prewar Xiao River area, recalls:

> The Southern Revolution was like a broken wave, but because the conditions
> and geography are different the form of revolutionary development took on a
> special meaning in the Xiao River base area. It lies at the boundary of three
> counties where the transportation is inconvenient and the political control of
> counterrevolutionary power is weaker. Moreover, the party leadership and the

base of mass participation is comparatively better. All these things favor the development of the peasants' armed struggle.[150]

Thus it was possible for the popular Red Spears and Heavenly Gates to compel bad landlords, corrupt Republican officials, and plunderous warlords to back off from their claims until the Guomindang warlord regime set things wrong again.[151] To be sure, the post-1927 central government remained a house that was only artificially pieced together, and beneath the appearance of unity there persisted a number of divisive political tendencies—interpersonal rivalries, violent clashes over territorial tax bases, the officer corps' embezzlement of finances needed to consolidate a national army, and secret liaisons with the Japanese to assure maintenance of personal assets in the event of a Nationalist government collapse. But when Jiang Jieshi gained the upper hand these same warlords were able to achieve a temporary consensus on the necessity of combining to put down the revolts of the poor—the Guomindang warlords *were* in command of many of the region's county-level capitals by 1932. By and by, however, these militarists were sitting on top of a retreatist countryside. They were unable to effectively co-opt peasant rebel leaders by patronage or to integrate the retreating peasantry into their tax regimes. Their anti-Communist rioting campaigns only made peasants more angry and strengthened popular resolve to avoid the grasping hand of central government "armies."

To be sure, the Guomindang warlords repressed the rising tide of peasant revolutionary mobilization. It is tempting to conclude that if it had not been for the CCP reorganization of the peasant movement after its Long March into Shaanxi, or for the Japanese invasion splitting the reformist Wang Jingwei and the nonreformist Jiang Jieshi factions once and for all, and thereby finalizing the destabilization of Guomindang power, the regional peasantry would have been left to conduct its incipient socioreligious wars in the undertow of Guomindang militarism. All of this of course begs the question as to whether there was a real possibility of revolution from below without outside CCP organization or an outside power shift, as occurred with the Japanese invasion.

If peasants had begun to forge the forms of revolt needed to resist and relieve the new pressures on them, they were not empowered to eliminate these pressures. What they lacked was not simply a Communist party or a foreign invasion, but an army that would permit them to go beyond the stalemated revolts of 1925 to 1927 and to break the repression of the Guomindang militarists. The impossible in 1930 became possible in 1936–37 when the army of Mao Zedong and Zhu De[152] came riding from Shaanxi into the Taihang Mountains ahead of the first significant Japanese advance into the North China interior.

The question then was: Where would it all lead? To the restoration of an inegalitarian patron-client polity and the self-serving ideology of a Communist party? To the destructive mobilization of peasants for the Anti-

Japanese War? To a politics based on a revolution the rural people wanted? All of these possibilities were alive and real, but the revolution was to be grounded in a Little Tradition whose rebel leadership would point the CCP toward what was socially and politically desirable in the years ahead.

4

The Revolutionary Return
to Traditional Morality

The spring of 1936 saw CCP commanders Zhu De and Liu Bocheng fording the Yellow River, bringing their insurgent army into the Taihang Mountains, then down onto the grain-growing counties of Henan and Hebei.[1] This was nearly two years before the Japanese divisions occupying Handan and the Beijing-Hankou Railway began the offensive to seize the wheat-producing counties of the northern Henan panhandle. If the Jiang Jieshi military had taught the rural people the dangers of open confrontation with landlords and Republican local government, the coming of the Mao-Zhu army rekindled peasant hopes for a more powerful revolutionary mobilization against landlords and power holders. Once the CCP armed forces made an appearance in the border region, the party was expected to put a stop to coerced cash-cropping and military taxation, and its cadres began to root their political process in peasant strategies for survival. For the country people, revolution was to be a return to the moral arrangements that had traditionally characterized the subsistence ethic. Of course the CCP did not simply restore peasant relations with past authority. The peasants were seizing the opportunity to overthrow landlord, gentry, and government figures who had delegitimized themselves in the post-Qing decades.

The Chinese Communist Party and Countryside

The Chinese Communists recruited their local party leaders from the thousands of hungry peasants who were being forced off the land and who, even when able to eke out an existence on the land, were nearing the end of their rope. These rural people became the main social force behind the revolutionary village and market processes in the border region. Rural exploitation and household bankruptcy, not Communist party appeals or the Japanese invasion, produced the pool of desperate militants who led the return to family roots, land, and power.

Many of the local CCP leaders were from families with one foot in and one foot out of the village world. They had been the target of the militarist repression that cooled the revolts of the 1920s. Generally speaking, they passed into the CCP out of four strategies of survival.

One was migration. Impoverished peasant migrants became the stalwarts of the CCP in the border region.[2] By the time the War of Resistance broke out tremendous numbers of landless and homeless people were wandering through the countryside in search of employment, and thousands were living in deserted, run-down village temples. Many of these peasant migrants were barely hanging on in the Taihang villages they had begun to homestead in the late 1920s or were drifting back from Manchuria to their native villages on the plains of Hebei, Shandong, and Henan, where they now faced underemployment and unfavorable wages. Once the CCP armed forces entered the border region they were able to recapture their local means of survival, and more. The Henan migrant family of Yang Dayong, for example, had made do on their family fields before usury and natural disaster forced them to mortgage their land and migrate to the Taihang Mountains in 1937–38. The coming of the CCP army enabled them to return home, abolish their debts, and recover their land. By 1941 the Yangs were sending their sons to study in the CCP anti-Japanese middle schools and to manage the public grain bureaus of the CCP-influenced Shanxi-Hebei-Shandong-Henan border region government.[3]

The offspring of peasants who after 1910 had pulled up roots to work in the sweatshops of Taiyuan, Zhengzhou, and Tianjin also found themselves returning home to lead the revolution.[4] These uprooted peasant youths had seen their fathers seized from their shanty homes in the dead of night by the Nationalist officials who crushed the CCP labor unions in North China cities in 1926–27. A number of them had joined the underground CCP around 1931, probably in response to the Japanese invasion of Manchuria as well as out of revenge for their fathers. From 1931 on they were running from the Guomindang's anti-Communist rioting campaigns, which had closed the city-based workshops. Once back in the countryside they found safety only by working in mines and out-of-the-way market towns. During the complicated, uneasy peace of the CCP-Guomindang Second United Front they emerged as members of the Sacrifice League, a patriotic organization through which they called on landlords to stop exploiting peasants and urged local magistrates to check the repressive gentry so that they could foster interclass cooperation for the Anti-Japanese War.

From the moment the CCP armed forces rushed in, poor desperate peasants renewed their struggles against landlords and local power wielders, secretly dispatching small groups of friends to find the Liu-Deng army and invite its commanders to their villages to settle blood debts with landlords and stop Guomindang plunder.[5] Though a number of Western social scientists theorize that the secure landowning "middle peasants" were the militant element in the Chinese revolution,[6] the peasants who asserted themselves in the border region were the comparatively insecure landless tenants and hired hands. In Lin county, Hua county, and elsewhere they moved in and out of local villages and forests to arrange strikes involving ten to fifteen thousand people against landlord rentiers, grain hoarders, and tax officials.[7] Ji Dengkui's investigation of the peasant movement in Hua county emphasized their leading role:

> It is important that tenants and hired hands lead the peasant movement, thoroughly implement rent reduction, and strike down the semi-feudalists. Some persons advocate we should believe in the old peasants. This is too vague, and it allows the leadership to fall into the hands of the middle peasants. As a result the movement does not do well.[8]

From 1938 through 1943 the landless peasants joined with hard-pressed migrants and poor smallholders to eliminate landlord-imposed hunger rents and indebtedness, and to reestablish communities of landowning tillers in control of village food-producing resources.

Finally, there were youths who came to the CCP from a tradition of normal school protest. They had gone to school on the shoestring savings of a relative or the loan of a godfather. But they were not pursuing education for education's sake—they were seeking positions of power so that they could move against gentry and government figures who had ruined their families. Like the returned students from the Daming Seventh Normal School in Hebei, they had been involved in antitax protests for nearly a decade before they carried the CCP's anti-Japanese cause to the peasants coming to the market towns of their native counties.[9] Or like the normal-school students from Wei county, also in Hebei, they hailed from peasant families whose fathers had been put to death in the anti-Communist rioting campaigns of the late 1920s, and they survived the first flush of the Japanese invasion by joining the CCP anti-Japanese training schools in Nangong.[10] Their nationalism was conditioned by a strong obsession to punish local power holders.

The CCP, like the Guomindang, faced a seemingly insurmountable ecological crisis between 1937 and 1945.[11] According to Qi Wu, so devastating was this crisis during the War of Resistance that the CCP had to take river reconstruction and famine relief as the premise for both its social revolution and national resistance work in the countryside.[12] The 1939 southern Hebei floods swept away hundreds of villages and towns, and then turned Qinghe, Rcn, Zaoqiang, Guantao, and thirty other counties into the swampy reservoir of the Fuyang River. Thousands upon thousands of tillable *mu* tumbled into the Yellow River, and more than three million peasants fled their home fields. The droughts of 1939–40 and 1942 blistered northern Henan and southern Hebei, leaving lowland peasants without harvests and seeds. The massive locust swarms of 1942–43 damaged 17.1 percent of the cultivatable land in the CCP Taihang districts. By 1941 typhoid fever and bubonic plague had eliminated virtually all signs of life in vast stretches of western Hebei. Even survivors of the Red Army's Long March were filled with horror when they encountered blackened peasant corpses in the ghost villages dotting the rat-covered hills along the Hebei-Shanxi border.

The CCP *had* to summon its armed forces and all its cadres to deal with the deepening crisis of the border region ecosystem before proceeding to the politics of revolution and war. The CCP Red Army (now renamed the Eighth Route Army) could begin to resolve this crisis mainly because the floods, locusts, and epidemics did not climb up from the Yellow River Flood Plain to totally decimate its rehabilitationist projects in the Taihang Mountains.

By 1939–40 the CCP had formed the Taihang-Southern Hebei Public Relief Bureau, which replicated some of the river conservancy work of yesteryear.[13] In 1941 the Southern Hebei Irrigation Committee organized thousands of refugees to repair riverbanks, dredge riverbeds, and develop irrigation facilities along the Fuyang, Wei, and Dayun rivers. In the Taihang the revolutionary army was opening tunnels and chiseling peaks to create canal systems that fed down from the highlands to the richer valley bottomlands. The taming of the rivers proceeded smoothly on the Hebei-Henan plain, until the Japanese interrupted the process in July of 1939. From 1942 to 1944 in the Taihang counties of Pingshun and Licheng the CCP also set up the Agricultural Forestry Department *(nonglinbu)*, whose tree-planting campaigns began to correct, in small measure, the deforestation and soil depletion of the late Qing and early Republican decades.[14]

Relief from drought was the top priority. Under Liu Bocheng, the 129th Division of the Eighth Route Army spent much of its time transporting water to dry villages, developing river branches to feed into village streams, and helping peasants with autumn planting.[15] But the droughts continued, and only after the winter of 1944 were Taihang peasants able to reap back-to-back bumper harvests. Meanwhile, relief and resettlement campaigns started up in the famished counties above the Yellow River in northern Henan. Song Qingling, the chairwoman of the nonpartisan China Defense League, documented the effectiveness of CCP-led relief teams in setting up shelters, food kitchens, and employment registries throughout the border region, but her report was censored by the central government.[16]

Getting rid of the locusts posed complications. Peasants, superstitious about destroying these "immortal insects," stuck flags in the fields to solicit assistance from Liu Mengjiang, the legendary locust-slaying general.[17] Moreover, the liquid poison customarily used to kill the larvae was unavailable; at first the CCP Forest Department relied on ineffective Western remedies. In the end, Liu Bocheng's troops led peasants in a series of antilocust campaigns in the Taihang. Peasants were encouraged to place flags in infested fields to help the soldiers, and sticks and hoes were distributed to the villagers. The peasants who helped dig were awarded millet, and they organized countywide contests with rewards going to the village rather than family or clan. By 1944 peasants working along with the CCP army had reduced locust damage to less than 10 percent of the croplands in the CCP Taihang districts.

Clearly the CCP was doing far more than simply reinstating the government services that had been missing since late Qing. What really legitimated the CCP in peasant eyes, however, was that the party cadres respected the wisdom of not imposing political restrictions on peasant efforts to return to the tilling and trading routines that made life possible. The CCP gained a foothold in the border region by placing itself at the service of peasants who had come to equate hopes for survival with their own anarchist version of self-help and self-rule. In this sense, the early phase of peasant revolutionary mobilization was not simply the product of the CCP's own institutional presence or its own institutionally sponsored material offerings to the peasantry.

An early school of political mobilization, with its origins in the 1950s Rand Studies of Bolshevik strategies and tactics, held that peasants could not mobilize for revolution without outside organizational direction because they lacked the resources needed to take action against authority.[18] During the War of Resistance CCP organization would become an important aspect of revolutionary politics in the border region. But the mobilization of the peasantry cannot be attributed solely to the presence, programs, and performance of only a few thousand CCP members who repeatedly were compelled to take sick leave for gastric ulcers, neurasthenia, and pernicious anemia and who had to spend much of their time traveling to and from spontaneous mass meetings and Eighth Route Army outposts.

Prior to the arrival of the Liu-Deng 129th Division CCP presence in the border region was exceedingly weak. Many of the CCP affiliates in Shanxi had been suppressed by Yan Xishan's so-called Public Justice Corps during the height of Guomindang warlord terror, so that in places like Anze, Qinyuan, and Qin *xian* only a few party members remained.[19] Furthermore, the North China Bureau under Liu Shaoqi had few more than eight hundred members in Shijiazhuang as late as 1936–37, and they often had to get the assistance of the revolutionary army before they could establish viable party branches locally. Rather than assume that the preexisting strength of the Communist party turned peasants toward revolution, therefore, one must ask why and how in Taihang counties like Pingshun, with its dearth of organizational weaponry, more than ten thousand peasants formed peasant associations, while yet another seventeen hundred joined the people's militia at the first sight of the revolutionary army.[20] In the Taihang Mountains, and much of the northern Henan panhandle, the resurgence of peasant mobilization, inspired by the coming of the Liu-Deng army and initiated by the rural poor, opened the door to fruitful CCP interaction with the village world.

Comrade Zhao Ziyang's October 1944 report on "How the Masses of Hua County Rose Up" made clear that the success of the CCP was due to the fact that the mass meetings of the Anti-Japanese War period were convened by the peasants themselves, and that the party cadres recognized the independence of the mass movement and respected the tenant and hired-hand activists who carried out the resolutions of the mass meetings which addressed their immediate material interests. "The movement of tenants and hired hands," wrote Zhao, "is an independent movement. If we want to fully mobilize the tenants and hired hands we must give a free hand to their struggles to form their own independent movement."[21] Clearly, to Zhao Ziyang, the issue was not one of Communist party mobilization, but rather CCP responsibility for giving human invigoration to the renewed mobilizations of the poor to recover their means of survival.

Yet the assumption that the CCP achieved political legitimacy by imposing its own preconceived program for local problems led Western scholars to minimize the impact of peasant initiatives on the course of revolutionary events in the countryside. Oddly enough, the initial CCP border region leadership approach to the matter of peasant mobilization tended to reinforce this impression. Many CCP cadres saw themselves as the vanguard of peasant liberation from landlord exploitation and imperialist plunder, and they invariably expressed their purpose in writings about the "problem" of managing peasant initiatives within the set policy framework of the party.

The peasantry, however, was not a blank slate on which the CCP could inscribe its conditions for revolution. The Chinese Communists had to heed a set of social concerns posed by the poorest peasants if they were to be accepted, and the growth of party competence was dependent on its ability to embrace the popular notions of obligation and justice underlying these concerns. Throughout the border region the CCP cadres formulated demands posed by the country folk into practical guidelines that were to serve as the basis for obedience to local party-led government during the revolution. These guidelines often reflected the party's endorsement of peasant democratic outpourings that were by no means originally embraced by its county and regional leadership.

Thus, much of what appeared as a nonradical platform of CCP-managed agrarian reform, beginning around 1941–42, reflected what became possible only after party cadres acted in consonance with the peasants' vociferous struggles for survival and justice. The peasants left the stamp of their own convictions on CCP policy, and gave it a uniquely popular twist. We can see this Little Tradition imprint in the realm of redistribution and adjudication.

During the Second United Front, the CCP conceived a policy that called for landlords to share the harvest and reduce the rent by 25 percent when the crop was poor. The purpose was to reduce class tensions that impeded both peasant survival initiatives and the party's efforts to stitch together a multi-class anti-Japanese coalition. Existing alongside this CCP policy, however, was the determination of tenants to take back the land or to seize the entire wheat harvest.[22] Local CCP officials quite often discovered that the way to influence the rent-reduction process was to go along instantly with redressing these and other peasant grievances, regardless of whether some political committee approved or disapproved.

Similarly, local CCP officials were apprehensive when peasants insisted their rights ought to prevail in the process of formulating legal doctrines and handling court cases. But, border region government edicts that did not directly address peasant problems proved extraordinarily difficult to implement, and tainted CCP leaders with suspicion. The effectiveness with which the country people insinuated their interests into CCP legal policy is reflected in the reports of party members who investigated peasant complaints over litigations. Here is one example from Hua county:

> There was a landlord Guo in Gong village. The peasants there launched a struggle against him, and then set forth three demands: that he should be fined two hundred thousand dollars, that he should be brought before an accounts settling meeting, and that he should be tried in the local courts. As it turned out, the county authorities fined Guo one hundred thousand dollars, and arbitrarily said the case was closed. The masses felt this was handled wrongly. Despite the intervention of one of our county level mediators, the peasants came out in a protest march to condemn the way this matter had been handled. On this occasion, we proved to be on the wrong side of the masses.[23]

District-level CCP judicial officers employed various procedures to placate the peasants, but in the end they went along with what peasants wanted by way of litigation practices during the War of Resistance. To Huang Wen, a member of the CCP Hebei-Shandong-Henan District Committee, the essence of the party's position was that "the government's land and labor laws should come from the tenants and hired hands' own regulations, and the latter in turn are to implement these laws through struggle."[24] The Rand theory was predicated on the Leninist assumption that the CCP mobilized peasants because of its unique institutional capacity to manipulate power resources and manage agriculture in ways that served the ends of its emergent revolutionary protostate.[25] Indeed, some CCP leaders did initially set out to mobilize peasants, and consolidate their control over the peasant movement, by offering patronage and protection in exchange for peasant compliance with county and regional tax directives and labor duties. By 1942, however, the limits of this formulation had become apparent.

The CCP could not exert organizational dominance over the peasantry via patronage during the first five years of its presence because both politics and the ecosystem severely restricted the grain and goods to be gathered up and redistributed to poor villagers. Once the party took bigger market towns like Changzhi, Anyang, and Shijiazhuang and gained a firmer grip on both river and rail transportation networks in the years following the War of Resistance, peasant mobilization via patronage became a real possibility. In the early and middle phase of the War of Resistance (roughly 1937–42), however, the CCP was inheriting the bankrupt treasuries of small county-level capitals and starting its revenue building from scratch in an extremely poor area where tillers could do little more than produce the food needed for survival.

The Liu Bocheng-Deng Xiaoping leadership was unusually sensitive to the dangers of party building via extractions from the village people. The Guomindang had depended on Russian arms and peasant resources, but the CCP was committed to allowing peasants to regain their means of livelihood without the intervention of a selfish, corruptible party. Its cadres won peasant support initially by identifying themselves with the promise of a world without the state, a world in which neither landlords nor officials intervened in peasant attempts to keep precious food grains in the villages. The right to conceal as much grain as was needed to hedge against hunger was not challenged, and the party largely abandoned revenue-collection practices that posed a threat to subsistence requirements. The CCP thus came to govern the border region by going along with the unyielding attempts of peasants to conduct their quest for survival independent of its own local claims and national purpose. This course obligated cadres to practice self-sacrifice and ruthless honesty when it came to dealing with the immediate self-interest of peasants.

By the spring of 1938 the border region was convulsed by peasant struggles which owed their origins as much to a spirit of *l'anarchie spontanée* as to the presence, policy, and performance of the CCP. The local insurrections that lent support to the CCP in the years 1937–40 were fueled by the audacious struggles of poor villagers who set out to secure full autonomy from the town-based Republican warlord-landlord regimes.[26] In the Taihang Mountains these rural people, acting independent of the CCP's North China Bureau, stopped paying rent, seized grain from landlord bins, and attacked the tax officials in district- and county-level Republican government. Banks were burned and trade was wrenched away from market towns occupied by warlord forces. Here, in the opening moments of revolution, CCP commanders Zhu De and Liu Bocheng were catering to the peasants' anarchist challenge to the power of landlords and Republican militarists. The CCP's popular army, much like the legions of the legendary Li Zicheng, was linking up with the spontaneous efforts of poor peasants who were determined to strike out violently against landlords and the Guomindang gangster-state. Far from subordinating or sacrificing the rural people for its own plans for power, the CCP's armed vanguard yielded to explosive peasant expressions for freedom from hunger and death-bearing domination—that is, to the right of poor folk to assert their own interest through independent, revolutionary action.

Operating from ungoverned hamlets in the impenetrable Taihang Massif, the CCP army prepared for its struggle against Guomindang militarists and the Japanese Imperial Army. The central government failure to run modern communication and transport networks into the western highlands gave Zhu

The people storm Ji county town in Shanxi just prior to
the outbreak of the Anti-Japanese War of Resistance

The Zhang River rambling down into Lin county from the Taihang Mountains
The high country served as a backcourt of the Eighth Route Army and a
debouchment of the 129th Division during the Anti-Japanese War of Resistance

De and Liu Bocheng the time and tactical freedom to concentrate their troops in support of peasant revolts in the Taihang and then disperse them among the villages along the Hebei-Henan border, and on into western Shandong. Since southern Hebei and northern Henan produced nearly half of the region's cotton and the northern Henan panhandle was its bread-basket, the CCP army strategy was to hike down to the plains and to ferry along the Zhang and Wei rivers to liberate peasant villages in the lowlands, freeing peasants in the plains to produce certain products for trade with the people of the Taihang. It was possible to retreat to the Taihang Mountains when the Anti-Japanese War took its toll, as happened on the Hebei flank of the northern Taihang Range around 1940. Thus from their mile-high Taihang redoubt in the years 1937–40, roughly the hiatus between the Guomindang flight away from the border region's small county towns in 1938 and the all-out Japanese attack on the Taihang-Taiyue area in 1941–42, the CCP began to formulate the geopolitical strategy that would lay the stepping stones to revolutionary power. As Liu Bocheng emphasized in "On Guerrilla Warfare," this strategy was carried out in combination with peasant actions and was to favor mountains and forests over plains, under-developed zones over main lines of transport, villages where the mass movement was already in motion over those where it was not, and areas with less Japanese strength over areas with more.[27] The CCP-led rural revolution was to flourish in the power gaps of the failing warlord Republic and imperialism.

The World Regained: The CCP and the Recovery of Basic Social Rights

These political changes did not instantly do away with all of the awful dilemmas in peasant lives, but they did make it possible to recapture customary social rights, and more. Following the anarchist outburst of 1936–40, the CCP continuously addressed the issues that had aroused the passions of the rural people. The landlord offensive in rent, interest, and wages was brought to a halt, and the CCP spoke to each of these specific, salient issues in governing the countryside. On these issues, the CCP resurrected the moral economy of the mobilizing peasantry.

Official CCP policy toward peasant and landlord during the Anti-Japanese War of Resistance was to lighten class exploitation through reducing rent and interest payments rather than eliminate the system of landlordism per se. The CCP was looking for ways to mitigate class tensions so as to persuade peasants to cooperate with landlords and intermediate classes in its multiclass, anti-imperialist resistance movement. For example, tenants were asked to pay crop rent and landlords, in turn, were asked to reduce the land rent and increase the amount of rental land to the tenant. Was there not, however, a sharp contradiction between the peasants' goals of sweeping away rent and interest and striking down landed power holders and the CCP attempt to reestablish mutually beneficial terms of exchange between peasants and landlord via rent and interest reduction?

Indeed, if the poorest rural people had become so militantly antiauthority, then why once they had the backing of the CCP armed forces did they agree to return to some of the older reciprocities with landlords? One explanation might be that peasants who were frightened by the decline of reliable dependency relations with landed patrons were fighting alongside the CCP to make landlords behave once again as trustworthy benefactors. Or, perhaps the repeated violations of mutuality had convinced most peasants that relations with landlords were barely worth salvaging, so that peasants wanted the party cadres to guarantee them an important role in determining what constituted a reasonable exchange with a landlord. Yet another explanation might be that peasants were utterly fed up with landlords and that the desperate poor had no intention of accommodating landlord interests without securing from the CCP the promise that there would be an abrupt end to landlordism and interclass accommodation with revolutionary progress in the Anti-Japanese War of Resistance.

The first and second explanations are logical enough, but neither was the norm for the tenant and hired-hand leaders of the mass movement, for there was nothing but deep bitterness between them and landlords. For the most part, these semi-rooted landless peasants were bent on extirpating the cruel landlords from their villages. Moreover, when they spoke out and sought revenge against landlord superiors they were not in the least concerned with the anti-Japanese nationalist program of the CCP. A Wang Ming contingent of the CCP said that the violence of the peasants' struggle was opposed to the United Front and should be stopped, but this line did not prevail in the border region. Zhao Ziyang's 1944 report on Hua *xian* pointed out that the violent mobilizations of the peasants were necessary to replace the order of landlord domination, and that the cadres should not be surprised if peasants resorted to violence to establish their own revolutionary village orders. Of course the leftism of the masses was a real danger, and CCP cadres were to seek out radical peasant elements and patiently draw them away from extremism. But an even greater danger presented itself in the thinking of cadres who were so afraid of leftism, and so preoccupied with its impact on national resistance work, that they restrained peasants from building up a revolutionary order that served the needs of livelihood. The peasants who took up CCP banners would settle for nothing less than a return to a balanced subsistence exchange with landlords and a decisive power shift from landlords to poor folk locally, and cadres had to respect that fact.

The Improved Terms of Exchange: Tenants, Freeholders, Rich Peasants, and Hired Hands

It was in this changed sociopolitical context that the CCP formed iron bonds of trust and friendship with tenants in the border region.[28] Many tenants often stopped paying rent when the Liu-Deng army rushed in. But to the extent that tenants were concerned with recapturing older rights and reestablishing the basic elements of justice in exchange relations with landlords, one can speak of the CCP standing by their struggles to regain the world they had lost. This was an important theme in the CCP-led rent-reduction movement of 1942–44.

Land being the key to sustenance, the CCP supported tenant strikes to make landlords honor the old five-year and lifelong land leases.[29] Pre-rent deposits, chain repossessions, and subleasings to secondary landlords were abolished, so that the original cultivator recovered the right to stay on the land or to sublease it.[30] Peasants with inherited tenancies reclaimed their irrevocable right to till the land as long as they paid the original rent to the landlord.

A major feature of the rent-reduction movement was the return to share rent.[31] The CCP—and the tenants who participated in its village branches—made significant headway in reestablishing the old, flexible sharecrop system in place of the fixed-rent system of the post-Qing years.[32] Fixed rent had been eliminated in the majority of border region villages by late 1944.

The CCP's tenant cadres also were determined to redress the new injustices that had been built into share rent by the immoral landlords of the Republic. A fiery discussion led by the chairman of a tenant meeting in Hua county made no bones about this:

> Let's first discuss the share that landlords take. We and they do the same work, but then they can take up to 70 percent of everything while the most we can hope for is 50 percent. So they end up with more food than we do. Does anyone think this way of sharing is right? The meeting set forth a resounding "No!" If it's not right, then what shall we do about it? "Abolish it!" was the cry of the whole. From this moment on, then, such a way of sharing is abolished! That is what we all will do when we get back to our villages![33]

By 1942–43 the old 50-50 share contract was back in vogue, and in villages like Qinlaozhuang tenants stressed relations in which "both sides benefit."[34] Along the Hebei-Shandong border several variants of the share contract received CCP attention and approval.[35] One was "rental plow land," under which the landlord supplied oxen, tools, seeds, and fertilizer, and tenant and landlord shared the harvest on a 50-50 or a 40-60 basis. Under the "share plow land" contract the tenants supplied the oxen, tools, seeds, and fertilizer, and the harvest split was 50-50. A third variant was "small plow," under which the tenant only plowed and harvested the landlord's field in return for about 20 percent of the harvest.

CCP policy initially was to promote fixed-rent divisions, because the profit boost to tenants in bumper crop years was considered "progressive." In 1942–44, however, most tenants insisted on the less risky sharecrop agreement, and this agreement became the hallmark of landlord-tenant relations in the border region. Rather than shoot for windfall profits, tenants were out to restabilize their incomes by making landlords share the risk of harvest fluctuations.

Most interestingly, tenants sometimes followed up on this pull back to the security of share rent with a push to transform share relations to their advantage. In 1943 the CCP share-tenant leadership in Yao village decided that they should receive 70 and the landlord 30 percent of the harvest, reversing the crop division formula that landlords had imposed in the 1920s.[36] By 1944–45 the CCP cadres in Qinlaozhuang were substituting crop-division formulas that guaranteed tenants at least 62.5 percent of the harvest, or rewarded tenants according to labor expended plus harvest yield per *mu*.[37] We do not know how widespread such practices were, but they had more than the weight of the CCP behind them.

Tenants also made landlords resume contributions to their welfare, including the customary provisions for harvest festivals and market fair holidays.[38] In Hua county's Luoer and Liang villages, for example, landlords reinstated steamed bread loaves and tobacco supplies for the three annual fairs and the dumpling and wine dinner on Autumn Harvest Day. CCP officials were suspicious of such provisions, because landlords might present them as patronage and reassume the role of sweet-talking benefactors. To tenants, however, these provisions were bound up with the joyous celebrations of work life, and did not signify patronage. CCP officials such as Ji Dengkui therefore treated the issue as a matter of recovering cultural incentives to production, that is, as an integral component of rent reduction.

The CCP's tenant leadership required landlords to reduce the crop rent by the traditional 25 percent when the harvest was poor and to cancel it during drought.[39] The tenant demand for remissions was also realized—landlords were to offer interest-free grain loans to tide tillers through the spring hunger.[40] In Puyang county's Wenxiaoduan, Baiyilu, Minglou, and Ting villages, landlords once again had to fetch a doctor and pay medical fees when tenants became sick.[41] Gleaning rights also were recovered, so that the landlord could no longer confiscate the stalk and straw that tillers had gathered after the autumn harvest.[42]

Landlords were forbidden to evict tenants who did not pay the rent on time or who pressed them to return back rent. Again they had to provide head towels and puttees to tenants and field hands.[43] More important, they were not allowed to shift the land tax to tenants, and the days of worry over paying this tax as a precondition for lease renewal ended.[44]

By 1942 the tenant refusals to feed the cattle, carry the topsoil, and drive the horsecarts to the county markets for landlords without pay were resounding from village to village.[45] Now landlords again had to perform a good many brokerage services for tenants, and the hiring of farm hands to help with spring planting and carters to help with summer and autumn harvesting headed the list.

The CCP did not carry out rent reduction in the same way from locality to

Table 1. Tenant Harvest Shares from the 1942–44 Chinese Communist Party Rent-Reduction Movement in the Shanxi-Hebei-Shandong-Henan Base Area

	Good Harvest	*Normal Harvest*	*Poor Harvest*
	Traditional 50-50 Sharecrop Contract (Pre-1911)		
Crop Total	120	100	50
Landlord Rent	60	50	25
Tenant's Share	60	50	25
	Modern Rent Fixed at 200 Catties of the Crop (Post-1911 Republican Period)		
Crop Total	400	300	200
Landlord Rent	200	200	200
Tenant's Share	200	100	0
		Loss to the tenant of traditional income stability and expectation of rent reduction in poor harvests	
	CCP Return to Traditional 50-50 Sharecropping (1942–44)		
Crop Total	120	100	50
Landlord Rent	60	50	25
Tenant's Share	60	50	25
		Restabilization of tenant income with reduced rent for poor harvests	
	CCP 37.5 percent Rent Ceiling (1942–44)		
Crop Total	120	100	50
Landlord Rent	45	37.5	18.75
Tenant's Share	75	62.5	31.25
		Recovery of old subsistence cushion plus a slightly larger slice of the harvest to the tenant in good and poor years	

locality. But the regional CCP leadership did pursue three general objectives, and party officials patented a small number of practical methods that broadened revolutionary participation.

To begin with, the CCP isolated the "bad landlords" and tried to win over those who were willing to treat tenants fairly.[46] The methods for persuading landlords to reduce rent and issue hunger loans ran the gamut from threats, to praise, to rewards. The CCP made sure that landlords could see the Eighth Route Army standing by to enforce rent reduction. Landlords were assured their grain loans would be repaid, but CCP cadres also let it be known that tenants and hired hands were free to cut and eat the standing crops should the loans not be forthcoming. Landlords who pared rent and issued loans were praised as "good landlords"; CCP magistrates even wrote them thank-you letters. Clearly, the CCP goal was class conciliation, not class war. When CCP officials discovered that some landlords had collected rent in violation of the 1942–44 rent-reduction regulations, they even permitted the offending landlords an income-tax reduction equivalent to the amount of rent returned to tenants.

CCP cadres resorted to sterner measures with stubborn landlords. They called on hundreds of tenants and hired hands from neighboring villages to support demonstrations and sit-ins against the offending landlord, and had the wife and children of the wronged tenant sit inside his household until he agreed to redress the grievances. And, they publicized any landlord effort to undercut rent reduction, whether through bribery, blackmail, or threats.

The CCP also was aiming to unite tenants and hired hands with small-holders and rich peasants. The goal was to foster countywide peasant movements under the leadership of pro-CCP peasant activists.[47] Lineage and friendship relations facilitated these broad peasant class mobilizations, but intraclass cleavages produced a number of contradictions. The small-holders, for example, often joined in the tenant and hired hand struggles to compel the criminal landlords to sell land to them. Though the CCP tried to see that the landless peasants had first chance to purchase the land sold by landlords, tenants often lost out in the competition with smallholders for this land, as happened in Puyang. Worse yet, rich peasants who leased to tenants the land they had rented from landlords were considered exploiters, and CCP cadres had to quickly call in special mediation committees for such cases.

After drawing together peasants from each stratum, the CCP encouraged the landless leaders of the rent reduction struggles to form joint assemblies of tenants and hired hands and poor peasant congresses, which combined to form peasant unions—the forerunners of the peasant associations that would help prepare the villages for participation in the Anti-Japanese War.[48] The tenant and hired hand leaders established ties with their counterparts in other villages and extended their campaigns into the market fairs.

The rent- and interest-reduction movements appealed as strongly to peasants who had lost family lands to landlords as to tenants and hired hands. These former freeholders saw their chance to release themselves from the clutches of usurers, and to regain their land. They became the backbone of the CCP peasant movement in the border region.

The CCP's interest-reduction policy did not call for peasants to engage in radical land redistribution, but the early interest-reduction practices of indebted land-hungry smallholders signaled the more radical pattern of politics to come in the land revolution. Once the Liu-Deng army gained the upper hand in the Taihang District, the peasant freeholders took back the land that was theirs, then reinstated the interest-free seasonal grain loans of the past. These peasants had little idea of how CCP interest reduction was to work. What they did understand was that the original cultivator had a right to the land, and that the army provided them with the miraculous power to drive out of the villages the disreputable landlord usurers who had driven them to risky and ruinous undertakings.[49]

The regional CCP leadership feared the political drawbacks of the small-holders' spontaneous acts, for the party was desperate to boost production and secure territory. For one thing, the peasant insistence on abolishing all interest payments prompted landlords to curtail credit to tillers who needed it, and the CCP simply could not afford to let the already scarce supply of private credit sources in this impoverished region dry up. For another, to push landlords into drastic interest-reduction measures was to risk driving them out of the richer market villages inside the emerging base area toward the Japanese-occupied towns and cities, where they would invest their capital in business undertakings that might produce the goods and foreign exchange with which the Japanese army could strengthen its position against the CCP.

Thus, by 1941–42 the CCP was instructing its county, district, and village cadres to concentrate on arresting the development of landlord usury and amortizing peasant debts.[50] True to its smallholder constituency, however, the CCP went along with the popular demand to abolish the usury that had ruined peasant landowners under the Guomindang. Landlord usurers were not banished, but their compound interest schemes were abolished. Day and night interest, rolling donkey interest, and preloan interest deductions all were prohibited. The peasants who had suffered from these usury arrangements were free to stop payments immediately, take back their family lands, and keep their family-generated income.

Seeking to stimulate credit sources, the CCP permitted landlords to profit on low-interest cash loans. If peasants did take out such loans,[51] interest was reduced to 10 percent, which was about the most they had paid traditionally, and there were safeguards. First, peasants paid interest only on the original loan. If lenders doubled the interest on the principal, the peasant debtor paid back only the principal. If the interest on the principal more than doubled, the recipient could stop payment on both principal and interest— which in practice abolished rather than reduced interest. Second, the CCP encouraged lenders and borrowers to draw up contracts on the basis of the old three-to-five-month loan period. If the debt was not called after five months, the peasants could invalidate the contract automatically; but if the debt was called and the peasant was unable to pay then payment could be postponed for one year. Third, the CCP cut by 15 percent the interest rate on all loans made before the inception of the Anti-Japanese War of Resistance. Since the local CCP cadres simply refused to guarantee landlord creditors the interest due them unless they honored the cut, peasants who demanded the 15 percent reduction did not hesitate to warn landlords that the penalty for not honoring it was nonpayment.

The abolition and amortization of debts enabled peasants to resecure their lands in increasing numbers. In the southern Taihang districts, where the CCP 129th Division was operating, the percentage of peasant households owning at least ten *mu* jumped from 37 in 1940 to 55 in 1944,[52] and the northern Taihang districts, under the protection of the CCP 115th Division, saw a similar development.[53] By the end of the War of Resistance in 1945 these middle peasants stood at 64.8 of the entire peasantry.[54] When the poor peasants who held one to two *mu* are added in, the percentage of owner-cultivators was leaping to 80 and 90 percent in the CCP's model Taihang villages.

The CCP was reconstituting peasant society in the image of the older freestanding smallholder community, without the landlord exploitation that had existed under Guomindang warlord rule. Indeed, most of the peasants who now regained land had been reduced by the previous regimes of landlord rent and usury into part-owners and part-tenants. Now they were demanding to divide the land, and so the CCP had to press landlords to transfer land back to them while taking every precaution not to precipitate a landlord counterrevolt. The CCP emphasis thus was on transfers through sales and mortgages. The landlords were guaranteed a profit on land sales as well as loans, and they were not taxed on the land mortgages they turned back to peasants—a wise measure, since peasants insisted that landlords pay taxes on lands held in tenancy and on mortgage arrangements.[55]

The fear of losing family land through defaults on loans or falsified ownership papers was gone, but the arid plots peasants recovered were nearly worthless without the constellation of resources needed for cultivating them. Most peasants still lacked both water and capital with which to bring back the days of the good harvest.

The rent- and interest-reduction movements fulfilled the first need by guaranteeing peasants, including tenants, their right to local water. In Pang village there was a popular uproar over landlord charges for well water,[56] and these charges were discontinued there and elsewhere.

For capital, at first the CCP coaxed landlords to provide low-interest loans for seeds, implements, and livestock. This hardly reassured peasant landowners that they could survive, and eventually prosper, without depending on untrustworthy landlord enemies, however. Consequently, the CCP cadres attempted to supplement the landlord loans by arranging loans through peasant associations and village loan co-ops at interest rates on a par with rates in the private sector, or only slightly higher. These loan arrangements were riddled with corruption and constant bickering.[57] And in any event, because of the chronic shortage of capital available locally, they brought little benefit to peasant families in any given village.

This problem began to resolve itself when the CCP sent its Taihang-South

Hebei bank cadres into the villages to provide direct interest-free loans for peasants who needed capital and property to reinvigorate family fields and resume home handicrafts. The major beneficiaries of the CCP's loan programs were the peasants with land and oxen.[58] They got almost all of the loans, even though they sometimes had two and three times as much capital as tenants and hired hands. By 1941–42 the revival of smallholding village economies was well under way, and the wheat- and cotton-growing villages of northern Henan and southern Hebei were beginning to make a comeback. Interestingly, the bank cadres were far more successful in making loans when they dealt directly with women, because the male village heads, fearing a default, often failed to announce the availability of loans.[59] In subsequent years the older peasant women in Dongfenghua village, Wuzhi county, took out loans to refurbish their old spinning wheels, so they could make the cloth they had lacked for many years.

But why did the landowning peasants, rather than the landless, become the primary recipients of the CCP's early loans? To begin with, smallholders made up the village majority, and through the peasant associations they exerted strong pressure on the CCP's leadership for loans. Also, the CCP was trying to re-create a sturdy landowning peasantry that would pay taxes to its popular revolutionary army. Finally, from the standpoint of regional CCP officials, it seemed only logical to give loan priority to the landowning small producers. The CCP was not about to send its own scarce funds to tenants and hired hands who were producing in part for landlords and who, under the rent-and-interest-reduction program, could secure loans from these landlords.

To be sure, the calculus of CCP politics focused on the *Realpolitik* of war-related taxes. The CCP, however, did not win the support of conservative owner-cultivators by appealing to any imagined peasant proclivity to produce for the patriotic Anti-Japanese War. The rebirth of the landowning peasantry was anchored in the CCP's rather cautious respect for the strong tradition of anarchism manifested among the poor landowning peasants of the border region, specifically their determination to avoid land taxes. In the early years the CCP took very little from these recently bankrupted small peasants, and few if any of them paid any taxes to the CCP-led county-level governments from 1937 to 1940.[60]

By sponsoring loans and suspending taxes, the CCP enabled the landowning peasants to reconstitute the family mutual-aid relationships that allowed them to eke out a living on their own.[61] Although at first the CCP tried to get tillers to produce greater harvests by collective cultivation and by imposing its own cooperatives, the mutual-aid experiments that provided the social grid for the Great Production Movement of 1944–45 grew up mainly from the voluntary endeavors of peasant landowners whose lineage ties facilitated pooling of energies for both production and politics. Relatively free from landlords, they increasingly aligned with the CCP's landless-peasant leadership to oppose landlords and rich peasants who tried to usurp village relief grain through usury or to shun the village tax process. By 1943 they had assumed leading positions in the peasant associations, and they were involved heavily in the struggle for self-government at the village level. The peasant landholders put into practice the ageless idea of the free village. Their participation began to re-create the basis for collective action, giving the CCP a far greater capacity to organize the villages in support of the revolutionary struggle for survival.

By 1942 the CCP members of the Shanxi-Hebei-Shandong-Henan border region government had recognized that the rich peasants were the carriers of the seeds of capitalism in the countryside. Rich peasants, or the "petty bourgeoisie," were said to be the cornerstone of the New Democracy proclaimed by Mao Zedong. Henceforth the CCP looked to these peasants to stimulate production within the villages and to inspire trade within the markets of the anti-Japanese base.[62]

By 1944 CCP cadres had begun to revive the rich peasant economy in Hui and Xiuwu counties along the Wei River in Henan, and peasants there were expanding their landholdings and profiting from commercial pursuits. In contrast to the years of Guomindang rule, the rich peasants were undertaking trade and transport ventures that were independent of labor-repressive land-rent and money-lending schemes. To be sure, the rich peasants were out primarily to help their own families, but their gains were no longer necessarily the losses of the poor. Their profits were not automatically redistributed, but those who were successful provided fair jobs for formerly underemployed hired hands and paid a substantial part of village taxes.

Nevertheless, a web of complexity seems to have slowed the development of the rich-peasant economy in the border region. The basic obstacle was the deep poverty of the Taihang Subregion. When this is coupled with the fact that the CCP did not firmly establish commercial exchanges with the plains villages until the middle of the Resistance War, it becomes easy to understand why the percentage of rich peasants remained around 4−5 until 1945.[63]

There were other problems. One was leftism. Because the CCP had its base in poor landless and poor landowning peasants, it was not easy to convince the rich peasants they would be safe from the embittered poor: land had to be protected, profits ensured, and family labor forces freed from war-related obligations. Clearly, the CCP was dropping the anti-rich-peasant line that had alienated the rich peasants in the early Jiangxi Soviet,[64] but the cadres were slow in modifying the mistreatment of rich peasants and small merchants. Only after 1943−44 were the rich peasants reassured about keeping what they earned and making investments.

Another problem was rightism: landlord attempts to draw rich peasants into their intrigues against the village poor.[65] This danger cropped up again and again in 1944−45, when it became clear the CCP was going to win the Resistance War and it became possible for landlords to worm their way into village government. The CCP minimized this development by tightening up the controls of the tenants' and hired hands' unions and by accepting rich peasants as members of the "middle peasantry," enabling them to carry on commerce under the umbrella of the peasant associations.

The CCP addressed the needs of hired hands by passing labor laws that sanctioned wage raises, but the hired hands insisted that salary adjustments begin with contract security.[66] In Puyang the hired hands of Dingzhuang, Zhu, and Wuzhuang commenced negotiations of their contracts during the Qingming Festival, making certain that landlord and rich peasant employers were prohibited from dismissing employees without the consent of all hired hands. The hired hands' struggle for wage justice included landlord responsibility for meal payments and warm clothing (quilted jackets, waist bands, and cotton shoes). If workers fell ill, the landlord was made to pay the doctor's fee and to continue paying wages. Hired hands now were paid at least 1 percent of the total sale price for the calves and colts they bred, and they were reimbursed when they made trips to market. The hired hands in Baiyilu village made landlords resume the old practice of giving burial money and paying six months' salary to the family of anyone who died on the job. These gains were not great, but they made all the difference to rural people who had been living like slaves under labor-repressive landlords.

The extension of CCP might, and the downfall of local power holders, allowed peasants to press their claims for community resources recently denied them. In 1943 the CCP in Lin *xian* led peasants to recover temple lands and local forests,[67] and by 1944–45 CCP cadres joined with peasants and students in Nangong to convert the courtyard lands of the Wenyi temples into vegetable fields for experimental seed production.[68]

Taxes and Traditional Morality under the CCP

Some Western social scientists hold that the CCP was able to win in North China rather than South China because its revolutionary army could tap the abundant grain supplies of villages on the plains of Hebei, Shandong, and Henan. The CCP-peasant relationship on the issue of taxation reminds us, however, that the party did not gain a foothold in the pre-1940 period by taking from the country people. Rather, the Zhu De-Liu Bocheng army was fulfilling the old promise, kept alive by past armies of the poor, that peasants would receive a three-year reprieve from government taxation.[69] In this respect, the CCP followed the tradition of the Ming dynasty revolt led by Li Zicheng.

Beyond this, the CCP rectified the tax injustices of local Republican government by taxing harvests in accordance with the peasants' ability to pay. In sharp contrast to the Guomindang warlords' fixed tax claims, taxes were pared in lean years, and were taken mainly from those whose harvest created surpluses beyond subsistence needs. Thus, before the War of Resistance brought the issue of taxes to a head, the CCP was respecting the peasants' long-standing demand to keep cereals in the villages rather than give them up to government.

By 1940 the CCP had abolished the household assessments of the Nationalist era.[70] Later on when the CCP cadres did collect taxes they treated peasants equitably, not equally, with a graduated tax that took into consideration changes in crop yields. The poorest peasant families paid no more than 2 percent of their income in taxes, considerably less than the landlord or rich peasant household paid. Peasants were no longer dealing with a government that stabilized its own revenues by fixed charges on their family income.

To make the land tax less threatening, the CCP land appraisal cadres calculated it by amount of land, quality of soil, and the number of persons per family.[71] The most significant feature of the process was that land was appraised according to the actual harvest yield minus a per capita grain-consumption quota.[72] If the annual per capita consumption requirement was 300 catties, the CCP starting point for land-tax assessments was 301 catties. There was no tax on less than 300 catties. This "subsistence-first" emphasis was a return to the moral starting point in the extractive practices that peasants had expected under the dynasty. But at first tax officials who had to depend on peasants to report grain harvests still could not collect the grain they needed. The *Border Region Government News (Bianqu zhengbao)* made clear that peasants often underreported landholdings and handed in false harvest figures, cooperating with CCP tax cadres only after they judged the appraisal methods to be in accordance with what they felt was right.[73] The peasants of Pingshun county even demanded that CCP tax cadres ease up on families who increased yields by increasing fertilizer, and by 1944–45 the party had acceded to this demand.[74]

The CCP swept away the surtaxes of the warlord Republic.[75] Peasants could cultivate vegetable crops, raise pigs, and make persimmon wine for small profits in good harvest years, and they could depend on these tax-free side occupations in poor years, or in years when the war compelled the party to ask for grain taxes.[76] In any event, the absence of surcharges on subsidiary production spelled the difference between subsistence and pressing hunger.

To claim that the CCP, unlike the Guomindang, did not requisition the villages would be false. Of course the CCP army carried on "voluntary" campaigns to levy extra-grain taxes to finance its armed struggles throughout the revolution, but the commands of Zhu De and Liu Bocheng by and large did this without mandating that peasants meet rigid quotas. And the party cadres who carried out tax orders were peasants rather than high-ranking CCP tax officials.[77]

Rarely was the CCP army able to establish stable county-level governments that had both the personnel and the time to estimate complex graduated tax quotas for each village. Instead, it reactivated the village assemblies through which peasants themselves decided who would contribute how much grain to the insurgent army.[78] In the Taihang Mountain stronghold of Liu Bocheng's 129th Division, peasants themselves took the taxes for the troops on the basis of their ageless claims for a reasonable tax burden *(heli fudan)*,[79] a 30-70 tax-share formula, which required landlords to pay 70 percent of the tax levy. Although this formula did not fall far short of soaking rich landlords, peasants still pressed the CCP leaders of the peasant associations for landlords to pay all of the grain levy demanded by the revolutionary army. In northern Shandong the one or two wealthiest landlords within a given county paid it. Meanwhile, the people's militias were enforcing regular army requisition directives by squeezing the landlords who had taxed the villages to death under the Guomindang.

Though the CCP taxed far more equitably than the Guomindang warlords, there still were tensions between peasants and the party on the tax issue. What ultimately alleviated the tax pressure on the rooted peasants were the agricultural production campaigns pursued by the 129th Division. The Taihang area contained stretches of virgin land in which the soldiers could plant food-crops to supply themselves. In the Henan and Shandong localities, where the 905th Regiment was operating, the troops began a number of small joint-production activities on land they rented from peasants.[80] By 1943 teams of five soldiers were achieving year-round self-sufficiency in vegetable and cotton production, and the Liu-Deng army was making a modest but significant start toward self-sufficiency in food grains, with about four months' supply per soldier.[81] Some of the army's larger collective side occupations, such as the twenty-man-battalion bean curd and pig-breeding cooperatives, produced profits, which were shared on the basis of individual work performance.[82] With the Japanese army threatening after 1938 the CCP armed forces encountered a major challenge to their attempt to provision themselves. But in the Taihang, where the 129th Division production campaigns blossomed forth into full-scale land-reclamation projects, peasants could reap their harvests without being constantly bombarded by fixed military taxes, and the Eighth Routers could even trade their surpluses in the popular markets they were traveling through.

All these tax reliefs served to minimize peasant food-grain losses. But the CCP tax bureau leaders often pushed for tax measures that would be less threatening to other social classes. At the heart of their proposals was the uniform progressive income tax which they tried to institute during 1941–45.[83] This tax spoke to the peasant fear of poor harvests and the landlord fear of grain requisitioning. It had the potential of expanding the CCP's tax base, and of spreading the burden of taxation across the richer grain-growing villages in Henan and on into western and central Shandong. Perhaps more important, it permitted the CCP to persuade wealthy landlords and prosperous peasants that the border region government was not out to break them.

The uniform progressive income-tax formula called for a fair and simple tax. Within the Taihang Subregion this was to be a tax on the harvest income of the working peasantry, taken on direct land income, with peasants paying about one peck in taxes for every sixty pecks of millet they harvested from each *mu* of land.

Additionally, the CCP cadres taxed one peck of every ten the peasants marketed for income. The tax per peck was calculated according to the current market price of grain, fluctuating with the movement of prices the peasants received. Marginal smallholders who did not have any grain to sell when prices shot up did not benefit, but then this tax only applied to the grain actually sold. In practice, then, the CCP was providing a tax shelter for peasants who had poor yields and a profit incentive for those who produced grain surpluses for local markets.

The progressive income tax spoke to the basic peasant demand that the rich pay more than the poor, but at the same time eased landlord fear of having to shoulder the whole tax burden. Moreover, this tax was an incentive for landlords to profit. Although the CCP offered few income-tax exemptions to landlords who rented out land, landlords could deduct the wages they paid to hired laborers. This tax break induced many landlords to invest more capital in agriculture, thereby opening up employment opportunities to hired hands. At the same time, the CCP lured landlords into transferring their capital from nonproductive labor-repressive dealings into beneficial enterprises by offering tax exemptions on income from investments in commercial light industries.

Despite these readjustments, for much of the war the CCP had to rely on grain taxes for three-quarters of its treasury income, and these taxes weighed heavily on the peasantry. Recurring harvest failures, as well as the outside threat to border region security, proved a continuing menace to the development of fair and simple taxation in the base area.[84] The only thing that made taxes tolerable was the timing, mode, and method of tax collection in the secure counties of the CCP's Taihang Subregion. There the Chinese Communists took the land tax regularly after the May-June harvest, so that peasants could predict when it was coming. It was paid in kind, which meant that peasants no longer suffered from the unfavorable exchange rates built into the silver taxes. The CCP recruited its tax-appraisal cadres from peasant association activists and its tax collectors from the leaders of joint-family mutual-aid groups. These peasants, who often turned out to be smallholders, were free to collect taxes on the basis of mutual-aid group harvests and to postpone tax payments when the crops failed.[85] In the final analysis, the CCP Border Region government affirmed the power of ordinary folk to carry out tax directives without neglecting local consumption norms.

The Reopening of Markets and the Renewal of Free Trade

Once the October 1917 Revolution spilled over into the Russian countryside the Bolsheviks penalized the peasants most likely to produce a marketable surplus and replaced trade with government requisitioning.[86] The CCP

border region government was not unaware of this development.[87] The
Liu-Deng leadership, however, seems to have been determined to prevent
the War of Resistance from degenerating into the kind of "war communism"
that could have created the pretext for the party curtailment of competitive
free trade. Although the CCP had enabled peasants to recapture their
means of existence in the years 1937–42, its cadres still had to combine
peasant struggles for survival in separate villages with a workable plan to
win back markets if it was to construct a sound political economy in the
border region. The pressures of necessity, as well as the CCP commitment to
serve the civilian peasantry, impelled the border region government to
re-create a rural market economy involving tens of thousands of peasants,
peddlers, and artisans.

During the War of Resistance the CCP emphasized free trade *(ziyou
maoyi)* and free competition *(ziyou jingzheng)*.[88] But why did the CCP
welcome the free market in such a famished peasant society? In part
because, as Jeffery Paige has implied in *Agrarian Revolution*, free markets
and production for profit could work to remove the landlord restraints on
small producers inside the villages, and release peasants to create their own
networks of profitable exchange in the countryside.[89] The revival of the free
market was also interwoven with the CCP's strategy of national resistance,
since the CCP army was fighting to keep markets out of Japanese hands. A
source on the CCP-led peasant economy made this point nicely:

> Our economy is unlike that of the Soviet Union. We want to allow the beneficial
> flow of peasant goods into lanes of rural commerce. This is how we will defeat
> the imperialists. This—the economy of the New Democracy—is the corner-
> stone of our policies in the liberated areas. The democratic government will
> protect this economy.[90]

One political barrier still had to be removed in order to develop a true free
trade economy: the parasitic Guomindang warlord order. This the Liu-
Deng leadership did by defeating the Guomindang officers who were cut off
from crack Central Army units in 1939–42,[91] and by drawing into the border
region government the defecting prefect officials who could no longer
stomach the squeeze associated with the tax-collection machinery of Jiang
Jieshi's gangster regime.[92] Rong Wusheng, a leading official in Yan Xishan's
Opium Bureau in 1937, defected to the CCP in the Taihang Mountains
shortly after the war broke out and was elected vice-chairman of the border
region government around 1940. Rong became a celebrity in the border
region because he, and the few officials who followed him, brought over
hundreds of thousands of silver dollars from Yan Xishan's opium treasury to
help create a capital reserve for the South Hebei People's Bank, and the
border region government relied on this reserve to finance some of the
infrastructure needed to facilitate market development.

Shortly thereafter the CCP formed the United Taihang-South Hebei

Bank and the Bureau of Industry and Commerce. Judging from the leadership debates that took place at Licheng in southeast Shanxi, the CCP initially underestimated the task of reopening rural markets within the border region. This task had received urgent priority by 1942, but still there were problems. Commerce within the border region was slumping badly, and the Japanese army was beginning to disrupt markets that were inside the emergent revolutionary base. Another difficulty was that the CCP army had no real expertise in promoting and protecting rural marketing. The problem that seems to have preoccupied the CCP leadership, however, was the outlook of its own financial cadres, and their approach to rural economy.

At first the CCP Trade Bureau officials were notoriously anti-free trade. They tried to reinstitute markets solely through their own Trade Bureau stock companies and cooperatives, but they lacked sufficient capital, merchandising experience, and simple market sense, not to mention personnel. They seemed oblivious to the fact that since village economies were scattered peasant capital was scattered too, and they blindly dispersed and concentrated capital without careful regard for local conditions.[93] All too often they made plans for production and trade before peasant markets had matured, and became upset when the market did not develop in accordance with their bureaucratic plans. As in the Taihang Subregion, they eventually learned that in a world of small peasant markets, where the interchanges of goods were not of great scale, supply was uncertain, and transport roads were primitive, it was not possible to have planned production from the outset. By 1944 the CCP had begun to build a market economy up from the isolated villages, but even then the Trade Bureau cadres could not effectively introduce plans for production among the dispersed peasants. The market was coming back, but the comeback was being determined more by the interests of peasants than the plans of the CCP.

To facilitate merchandising, Trade Bureau officials linked up with two thousand chambers of commerce *(shanglian hui)*, and by 1941 they had at least one contact in every market town in the Taihang Subregion.[94] Through the *shanglian hui* the CCP recruited peddlers and traveling merchants who had been hurt badly by grain usury and the gabelle. The CCP sought to help these rural people make a living by extending their trade and transport businesses into the depressed villages and towns of the Taihang area, and so the Trade Bureau cadres were reprimanded for behaving as if they did not need private business management in areas where their cooperatives had developed, and for not recognizing that the private exchanges of the small merchants was of great benefit in getting trade going within a scattered economy where capital was extremely scarce.[95]

Furthermore, the CCP had to stop its Trade Bureau cadres from bleeding the villages.[96] At first the bureau replicated the Guomindang practices of charging road tolls, depending heavily on trade from the towns, and drawing grain out of the villages without returning certain basic commodities to the peasantry. Worse yet, the Trade Bureau cadres who were responsible for eliminating the *yahang* (a middleman who took a commission on goods exchanged between local market participants) merely substituted a new government *yahang* in place of the old private ones, and this made it more difficult for peasants to decide market standards among themselves.[97] Such tendencies lingered on throughout the revolution, but the CCP repeatedly cashiered its cadres for such self-serving practices and pounded home their obligation to serve peasants and merchants in border region markets.

The Return to a Stable Market Economy with Survival Guarantees

The CCP banned the production of nonessential cash crops, such as opium, enabling tillers to cultivate subsistence cereals whenever harvest fluctuations, capital shortages, and price swings increased the risk of cash-cropping. The CCP had little choice but to side with peasants who preferred this order of market participation. Although peasants were attentive to making profit, they had been badly burned by coerced cash-cropping, and they were determined to enter only markets that did not entrap them.

To develop flourishing markets in the border region the CCP had to stablilize the commodity prices which had proved so damaging to the peasantry. A persistently perplexing problem was the sharp price swing occurring with the entry of the Central Army and its *fabi* or of the Japanese army. In response to these changes, peasants and merchants frantically stored up commodities, with the consequence that prices skyrocketed and trade skidded to a standstill.

The CCP used several measures to stabilize prices in the free trade markets of the Taihang Subregion before the Japanese stormed the base area around 1941−42. The core of CCP practice was to allow free trade and free competition to stimulate commodity prices, so that price movement was associated closely with the changing supply and demand being created by peasants in their dual role as producers and consumers. Wherever possible, the CCP tipped the scales of supply and demand slightly toward supply by encouraging the rural people to increase their production of marketable products, the goal being to stabilize prices at levels affordable to buyers but profitable to sellers.

In keeping with the policy of free trade, the CCP Trade Bureau cadres generally sold the grain purchased by their small grain work teams according to the ongoing free market price. To keep grain prices from soaring suddenly, however, as happened when the supply of crops was insufficient, the cadres sold grain at slightly below the competitive market price. Their purpose was not to fix prices, but to set for sellers a standard for tolerable market prices in periods of dearth, as the dynasty had traditionally done in response to popular demand for fair prices.[98]

The CCP combined its promotions of native grain, cloth, and salt with careful purchases of essential imports that could be absorbed at favorable prices, and all exporting was undertaken with an eye toward gaining an upper hand in foreign exchange. This was a key to price stabilization, but as late as 1941 the CCP still was striving for it. The rural people did not yet have confidence in the guerrilla currency. In 1941−42 the southern Hebei and western Shandong branches of the Taihang-South Hebei Bank printed currencies that were tied to small reserves in grain, cotton, and silver, and peasants inside the base area increasingly gained confidence in these currencies in comparison to the Guomindang *fabi*. As the CCP Taihang-South Hebei Bank began to win its currency wars with the Guomindang price stabilization proceeded more smoothly, and by 1942 the struggle to stabilize currency was mainly with the Japanese, who in March of 1938 had begun to extend their own economic influence into the border region by their purchases of central government *fabi*.[99] The CCP bettered its foreign-exchange position even further when its Tax Bureau cadres placed a protective tariff on commodities coming from the Guomindang and Japanese-occupied counties into party-held counties. Finally, the Trade Bureau activists worked alongside the chambers of commerce to prohibit landlords from hoarding grain locally, and to penalize landlords and merchants for smuggling Guomindang bank notes into the base area.

Certainly, the CCP did not eliminate all government involvement in price making, but even when it came to salt the party was committed to abolishing military price fixes and gentry taxes. In the Taihang Subregion the CCP pursued a two-pronged approach to salt market development.[100] The CCP Trade Bureau cadres set up sixteen regional salt shops, from which they dispensed salt to peasants and peddlers at the free market price. When the free market price proved intolerably high, however, they lowered the price. In this way, peasants living in the vicinity of the salt shops were able to purchase salt for family consumption, and those in distant hamlets could purchase it from peddlers who bought from the border government shops. On the other hand, however, the CCP made known its support for the "salt people" who had clashed with Nationalist tax agents, and by 1943 the salt makers and salt merchants from southern Hebei were selling in the markets leading to the Sha River district and the Taihang.

The minimization of transport fees was yet another facet of CCP efforts to reopen markets for the peasantry. With the CCP armed forces affording market road protection and with the party supporting a competitive price system, peasants were naturally inclined to trade grain and other goods in the market towns. The risks of transportation, however, still reduced the ability of the CCP to introduce poor isolated villages to flourishing markets. By abolishing the infamous *lijin*,[101] the party hoped peddlers and merchants would assume the risk of taking their trade into villages with primitive transport links. The small traders swiftly reopened the lanes of intraregional commerce, but the primitive dirt roads slowed the extension of beneficial trade to the poorest villages to a snail's pace.

Reviving the Traditional Markets

The goal of the CCP was to revive trade in the basic level markets of the border region. Toward this end, the CCP centered its efforts on the frequent trade fairs of the traditional market villages in the counties under its control.[102] In Ren village in Lin county and Yangyi village in Boai these efforts preceded the coming of the Japanese army. The CCP Trade Bureau activists working in these settings provided straight cash loans to peasants who traded their crops and crafts in the market fairs, and they purchased oxen in great numbers to loan to peasants at plow and harvest time, through the peasant associations.

The CCP sought to link its efforts to renew popular market participation with the social crisis relief programs sponsored by the border region government. Rather than rely solely on public works funds to compensate relief workers, the CCP encouraged peasant refugees from disaster-stricken villages to earn income by transporting grain from the big market villages to their home villages. They were paid in wheat or millet, and they were free to earn additional income for transporting commodities on their return trips to the marketplace.

By 1943 the CCP 129th Division had established a protective umbrella for the peasants and merchants involved in these market endeavors. Commander Liu Bocheng's troops teamed up with the people's militias to keep open the market roads, escort the trade caravans, and guard the market fairs. The 129th Division officers not only conceived a system of equitable compensation for troop damage to peasant fields and village forests, they also persuaded the foot soldiers to pay for commodities according to the free market price. Many of these soldiers had served under warlord officers who had permitted them to badger peasants and peddlers for lower prices, so that CCP commanders had to correct such predatory habits in the markets near their changing encampments. The newspaper of the CCP's 129th Division, *The People's Troops*, was devoted to convincing soldiers that they should respect the free trade rights of the country people:

> One day in the village street a new Eighth Route Army recruit used half a catty of salt to exchange for a pack of cigarettes. The ongoing market price of one pack of cigarettes was thirty *yuan*, whereas a half catty of salt was worth only fifteen *yuan*. The cigarette peddler naturally was unwilling to exchange with the soldier. This new recruit took the pack of cigarettes anyway. Although the cigarette peddler was very upset, he did not dare say anything. Just as the transaction was being made, Commander Ning Jianning stepped to the front of the two and said to the cigarette peddler: "He is a new comrade and still does not understand thoroughly the rules of our army. Try to forgive him. I will give

you the fifteen *yuan* difference and let's forget about it." Commander Ning then took fifteen *yuan* from his pocket and gave it to the cigarette peddler. When Ning returned to the regiment encampment he sought the new recruit and explained: "Our Eighth Route Army troops are not the same as the reactionary troops. We buy equitably and sell equitably. We may not use pressure to purchase or force to sell. From now on, you must be sure to show more respect for the market rules of the masses. I returned the fifteen *yuan* to the peddler for you."[103]

The Eighth Route commanders were prohibited from using public capital to engage in private business, and those who did use public funds, carts, and oxen to profiteer were reprimanded and lambasted in the pages of *The People's Troops*.[104]

Peasants and merchants no longer had to fear being pilfered on their way to market, forced to sell at lower prices, or put in unfair competition with government-backed army enterprises—all of which had happened under the Central Army warlords.

The CCP Trade Bureau cadres were market brokers of a sort. They introduced products for purchase and sale to the peasants coming to their cooperatives and shops in the big market villages, and conferred with peasants in poor nonmarket villages on how they might best serve them.[105] They sometimes arranged basic commodity exchanges for peasants in different markets, so that peasants in hemp-glutted markets, for instance, could trade their products to people in localities which lacked ropes and baskets made of hemp. Most interestingly, the cadres established commercial service posts from which they provided drinking water, price information, commercial maps, and even small sums of travel money for peasants, peddlers, and merchants who were on the way to the big village markets and town-based markets.

The epicenter of prewar peasant revolt had been the village temple, and the temple-based assemblies became powerful under the CCP also. The temple fairs in the market villages and towns drew together thousands of peasants and provided a focal point from which the CCP could propagandize the processes of local redistribution, regional trade, and national resistance. Although the temple fairs are scarcely visible in formal CCP documentation, the cadres clearly addressed themselves to the social dilemmas of peasants attending these fairs.[106] A short list of CCP temple fair services looked like this:

1. Millet soup at an affordable cost
2. Medical clinics including doctors and a pharmacy cooperative with:
   a. smallpox vaccinations for children
   b. filmstrips illustrating precautions to be taken against typhoid fever and cholera
3. Protection and patriotic news from the CCP Sacrifice League

   a. Skits and plays on how peasants in different villages had been harmed
      by warlord Yan Xishan, and how the Liu-Deng 129th Division was
      linking up with the people's militias to defend the autumn harvest
      from the gentry-led *mintuan*
   b. Blackboard maps indicating successes scored by the CCP armed
      forces, and the changing field position of the Japanese army
4. Exhibition tents wherein peasants could witness modern technology,
   such as sewing machines compared to hand looms

The temple fairs provided the CCP with a customary platform for com-
municating novel ideas, for strengthening the collective thrust of peasant
movements in the context of the Second United Front, and for building up
the political economy of the border region.

To begin with, the peasants who facilitated party work in the temple fairs
involved people from surrounding villages in a network of exchanges about
experiments designed to stabilize and improve their livelihood. It was from
the fairs, for example, that the party was better able to stimulate and spread
the mutual aid movement. To do this, the cadres celebrated the achievements of individual peasant entrepreneurs from outstanding mutual-aid
teams, and then called on them to explain their successes to their counterparts who came to the fairs from afar. A publication about this aspect of the
peasant movement in the Hebei-Shandong-Henan Subregion made clear
that the creation of a network of productive mutual aid partnerships was
based far more on emotive peasant exchanges than the manipulative techniques of high party officials:[107]

> In Houshangu village Qian Rugui often went from the door of a friend or
> relative to discuss mutual aid. When he went to the county market fairs, he
> rubbed shoulders with peasants from other villages and roused their interest in
> mutual aid. His power to persuade and convince the masses was much more
> effective than the propaganda efforts of our county and district party cadres. In
> contrast to our people, Qian Rugui knew how to patiently enact vivacious and
> vivid demonstrations. Through their exchanges with Qian Rugui in the market
> fairs, the peasants in several of the villages near Houshangu voluntarily began
> to get organized. . . . Several villages extended special invitations to Qian
> Rugui to come to their villages for mutual aid discussions and demonstrations.[108]

The peasants aligned with the CCP were thus providing the leadership to
the popular mobilizations taking place around the temple fairs, and these
respected local people quite often turned the temple fairgrounds into
rallying points for collective struggles which drew nonpeasant groups including miners and college students to their cause. In southeast Shanxi and
northern Henan the temple fairs became the occasion for popular demonstrations to deal with the landlords who had transgressed traditional understandings about land rent and water rights, and for petitions to remove the
magistrates who had gone along with the Guomindang repression. The fairs

still were local affairs, but with the CCP broadcasting rent, interest, and wage changes and the CCP army spreading the news of its support for peasant mobilization, the temple fair participants began to acquire a shared understanding of the political changes occurring throughout the border region.

The temple fairs were still district and county level happenings, but they favored the growth of a stable and unified border region economy. Here was where the CCP carried on its currency exchange work, so that in the fairs around Yangyi temple in Boai county we find party cadres calling on peasants to gather up and turn in central government *fabi* in return for border region government currency.[109] Moreover, the small merchants who traveled the temple-fair circuits spread the news of the CCP's trade and banking successes to the remote corners of the border region, and eventually to the still unliberated counties of the larger North China region as a whole. By 1944−45 the *Magazine of the Plains* was recording turnouts in the fairs of Linnan, in Hebei, of nearly 150,000 people for some twenty-one fairs per year.[110] In any case, if peasant participation in the fairs had fallen under the Guomindang, it shot up significantly after the arrival of the Liu-Deng army in 1937−38.

Peasants, Markets, and Survival: Popular Impulses and CCP Controls

Our understanding of peasants and markets is often based on the Marxist assumption that peasants have been subjugated to the goals of the protostate forces giving form to the market. Clearly this was the case in mid-seventeenth-century England, where the dominant capitalist class, with its political base in Parliament, instituted labor markets by dispossessing the peasantry.[111] Just as Barrington Moore, Jr., has reminded us that this dispossession was not carried out without the use of force,[112] so we have seen that the twentieth-century warlord attempt to drag China's peasants into markets that lacked any standards of fairness provoked a violent popular reaction.

Once the CCP and its revolutionary army entered the border region these same peasants led the fight to restore disrupted markets and to remove the rigged price system. These peasants were bent on making capitalism real and democratic, and it was their insistence on a return to open markets and just prices that placed this decisive matter on the CCP's agenda for rural revolution. In responding to this demand, the CCP was nurturing capitalism from below on behalf of village-based free traders. Peasant survival was the first order of the border region government, and peasant market rights ran a close second. The CCP was thus improving on its image as an antifeudal and a national liberation vanguard by lending its armed support for peasant interest in reviving trade.

The reason why many of the same peasants who only a decade before had been victimized by monetized agriculture expressed an interest in free marketing is not hard to find: the risk was far smaller than that imposed by global market development and the central government. Once the CCP responded positively to the peasants' market preferences, increasing numbers of rural people entered the market, insisting on fair and favorable terms.

The CCP allowed each peasant family to sell on the free market any of the grain that exceeded family consumption needs, as determined by voluntary harvest reports. Peasants could enter and exit from local markets when they chose, therefore, and they could keep harvest surpluses as a hedge against hunger or sell them and make investment decisions for assisting their children or acquiring livestock. The CCP commitment to realize this principle prompted peasants to view market income as a relatively safe means of rebuilding their family household economies and climbing up from poverty, and there is little evidence that poverty per se posed a mental obstacle to market pursuits.

To be sure, the proclivity to produce for survival first and profit second persisted among peasants even after the CCP embraced the popular impulse to open markets.[113] But inside the CCP base area tillers were pressured less and less to produce for imperfect markets. With the CCP freeing peasants from labor-repressive landlords, and with the Liu-Deng army removing the warlords who had imposed taxes, cash crops, and inflation, peasants could pursue markets with far less risk than previously.

The CCP minimized risk in several ways. The first was to reemphasize the diversified multicrop approaches which peasants had been denied during the warlord cash-crop years, so that they now could produce for the market without becoming dependent on one nonfood crop. The second was to reintroduce cash crops only where the soil was suitable, and where peasants could use them for household benefit and market gain. Let us consider the contribution of Song Youyou, a fifty-year-old skilled cotton producer in Zhang village in the Taihang.[114] Song had fled from a famine in Henan, in which his wife had died. By 1942 Song and his daughter had been given land by the border region government, and in 1943–44 when the government called on people to plant cotton Song took it up. The land was suitable and the government was offering capital and seed loans, but many peasants still feared that planting cotton was not as safe as corn. Only after Song's abundant cotton harvest brought over three times the value of corn did other peasants begin producing for the market. By 1945 Song had become the village cotton director, and Zhang village was receiving orders from private and public buyers in advance of production. With the CCP reassuring peasants in villages like this one that they would not be locked into cash markets and would not be compelled to produce for a huge standing army, fears about market participation began to subside. Indeed, for much of the peasantry, the CCP base area was treasured for the protection it afforded their efforts to link family production to nonthreatening market involvement.

Or was the CCP filling the interstices of the Guomindang failure to develop independent capitalist enterprises only for the purpose of forging new "taking links" with the villages, and making underhanded preparations to procure the surpluses that peasants preferred to keep for their families?[115] Certainly the CCP did tax peasant trade, and when possible popular trade within the border region was carried on within the scope of party controls. The basic point, however, is that the market infrastructure being formed by the CCP enabled peasants to enhance their family-based food-producing economies during the Anti-Japanese War, and still engage in market pursuits that raised levels of both protein consumption and penny savings. Greater market participation was an important means whereby peasants could begin to reverse the processes of uprooting, dependency, and powerlessness that had been dehumanizing the villages for decades, and by 1942–43 they were progressing toward this goal.

The expansion of commerce made it possible for tens of thousands of uprooted peasants to return home to start household enterprises such as oil presses, coal stations, and herbal drug stores during the revolution.[116] The income earned from these undertakings at first barely balanced family budgets, but it was enough to bring families together again. In the Taihang peasant daughters who had turned to prostitution began returning home to work in hemp- and cotton-making enterprises and peasant sons who had turned to day laboring now began cultivating family lands and producing charcoal in local forests.

The anthropologist familiar with cutthroat peasant competition in environments of scarcity might suspect that competitive marketing, reinforcing peasant preferences for family household production and profit, would prompt families to view the gains of other households as their loss. The idea that the cultural handcuffs of a poverty-stricken environment can immobilize peasants who would otherwise cooperate for shared gains and other-regarding community goals is advanced by Edward Banfield in *The Moral Basis of a Backward Society*,[117] and his findings on southern Italy may yet turn out to be relevant for peasant China. Had the reopening of markets prompted a peasant individualism that obviated other-regarding community norms, however, surely the CCP would have encountered great difficulty in promoting mutual aid among the village folk. To be sure, competition was intense, and the CCP did not dare interfere with peasant family production and profit. But by removing the political forces that both froze villages in constant scarcity and kept peasants out of free markets, the CCP enabled peasants to extend their joint family labor and property exchanges into mutually beneficial activities.

The Great Production Movement, begun in the base area in 1944, inspired peasant mutual-aid groups to join in profit-earning side occupations and trading ventures.[118] Peasants not only obtained what they reaped from joint family production on the land, they also released some of their members for trade and transport during the busy season. The CCP promoted these collective market pursuits by counterchecking the very factors which for Banfield explained the origins and persistence of noncooperation among the peasants of southern Italy: the poverty of the region and the absence of a supportive extended family. In the Hebei-Shandong-Henan area party cadres gave priority to material assets and the extended family. The Great Production Movement flourished ultimately in villages where peasant landowners owned plow animals and the plow—the critical material component of production, and of beneficial mutual aid. These plains settlements also were the locus of lineage-based mutual-aid groups involving three, ten, and fourteen families who joined together to form larger, but still family-based, village consumer and sales cooperatives. In the 1,211 mutual-aid groups involving 180 villages (nearly 80 percent of the population) in Guancheng in western Shandong,[119] for example, plow-owning peasants and their property-poor lineage members combined to conceive side occupations linked to commerce (see table 2). These peasants were entering the market together rather than as atomized little families in a zero-sum competition. Members of their extended kinship groups stood to derive mutual benefits from the gains that would add a flour shop or a well to village resources, and these additions undoubtedly strengthened the capacity of peasant families to reroot in a stable community setting.

The CCP was fostering popular commerce to break away not only from the harmful relations with militarists and the world market, but also the dole of the party's own relief programs. When party cadres issued loans to refugees in Taihang villages like Qingta and Chaiguan to start up disaster-relief cooperatives, they urged the refugees to produce for the market "in order to raise the consumption power of poverty-stricken families and overcome the dependency psychology of 'relying on economic relief for subsistence.' "[120]

Rural commerce engendered greater self-reliance in several respects. To begin with, peasants were regaining control over the lifelines of their economies. Through family farm operations, mutual aid, and light industries like dye plants and coal mines peasants were producing grain, cloth, and fuel for their own consumption and sale, and slowly but surely these endeavors began to reshape the internal market.

For the first time in half a century peasants were able to maintain the initiative in production and trade. They could produce grain reserves and use their surpluses to trade for items deemed essential to family survival and prosperity. The circulation of local products, specifically grains, was crucial to the development of a self-supporting internal market economy, especially since the border region government itself had to build up grain reserves in order to improve its foreign-exchange position in the currency wars being waged against it by the Guomindang and the Japanese.

Finally, by promoting trade among peasants in different counties the CCP was reducing the pressures on peasants to deal in markets that were subject

Table 2. Peasant Mutual Aid in Guancheng, 1944–45

| | | Class Divisions | | | | Distribution of Plow Oxen Ownership | | | | | Side Occupations —Marketing, bean curd & rice flour | Stocks | Profits in Yuan |
| | | | Peasants | | | | Peasants | | | | | | |
Leadership	Number of Households*	Landlords	Rich	Middle	Poor	Landlords	Rich	Middle	Poor	Carts			
Middle Peasants	17			9	8			12	3	5	yes		$6,000
Poor Peasants	19	2	1	3	13	1	2	4	10	6	yes	400 catties of beans	$12,000
Poor Peasants	17	1		9	7			11	4	5	yes		$5,000
Poor Peasants	17			8	9			10	4	6	yes		
Poor Peasants	20			10	10			9	4	5	yes	1,200 catties of beans	
Poor Peasants	17	1		8	8		2	9	2	7	yes	660 catties of beans 350 catties of sorghum	$10,000
Poor Peasants	9			7	2			7	2	2	yes	Profits used to start up village rice flour shops	
Middle Peasants	13			9	4			9	1	4	yes	Same as above	

to Guomindang inflation and Japanese blockade and harrassment. It anchored its textile movement, for instance, in the old cotton belt of Wei county in southern Hebei, and then extended it via a loan of 800,000 *yuan* for spinning into the Taihang Mountain counties of Pingshun, Licheng, Yushe, and Zuoquan.[121] By 1944 peasants in Wei county were reaping profits by selling cotton in the underdeveloped textile counties of the Taihang, and the formerly unemployed peasant women in these counties began to profit from household cotton-handicraft work. This popular trade, which began to receive militia escorts into the Taihang in 1942−43,[122] permitted tens of thousands of refugees to settle down in jobs, and it permitted the CCP to run the blockade imposed on cotton goods by the Japanese Army.

In *The Rational Peasant*, Popkin stresses the pivotal role played by political leadership in developing a market economy conducive to peasant involvement in revolution.[123] This point is crucial for understanding the CCP practices that allowed the border region peasantry to take full advantage of markets. An impressive array of popular networks stood guardian over the emergent revolutionary economy with its enhancing market processes. These networks, however, cannot accurately be called the ancillary arm of a market economy, for the CCP was not reorganizing peasant society to follow the market but, on the contrary, enabling peasants to *reorganize* the market to serve themselves in their social milieu. Put another way, the CCP was raising a market economy from peasant efforts to enlist capital to the cause of their own needs, associations, and values, so that the commercial process did not produce the dehumanization and powerlessness which according to Karl Polanyi occurred in England when a capitalist elite rearranged the forms of village life to fit with its own labor markets.[124]

The so-called auxiliary political arrangements of the market actually sprang from the peasants and the CCP border region government. They were aimed at ensuring the integrity of peasant efforts to recapture the minimum decencies of life, and this included taming the market to ensure that the exchange of land and labor, taking of taxes, and distribution of scarcity and surplus did not plunge the poorest rural people below the danger line. By founding its traveling courts in informal village mediation committees the CCP invited peasants to take legal action against landlords who collected rent by illegal scales or carried on illegal trade.[125] By decentralizing grain-tax collection into the hands of mutual aid group conferences the CCP encouraged peasants to transform the villages into self-regulating tax agencies.[126] The CCP grain arbitration committees were also under peasant leadership, and this meant that adjustments in village relief-grain and village grain exports were in the hands of peasants who were pledged to the survival of the whole village.[127] In backing these local organizations, the CCP was not denying peasants the right to profit, but it certainly was determined to stand by the poor peasant demand that the villages not become arenas for market dealings that endangered survival.

Watching over these efforts were the peasant associations, which the CCP renamed peasant national salvation associations to inspire peasants to welcome the participation of teachers, merchants, and landlords with an interest in national resistance work. In the Taihang Subregion the distribution of class participation in the associations reflected the political ascendancy of landless peasants (40 percent) and smallholders (40 percent) over landlords (20 percent) who once held sway.[128] The Second United Front, therefore, saw a shift in power to formerly powerless peasants, while honest landlords were encouraged to take part in village politics and join the border government coalition.

What guaranteed the resiliency of the peasant associations, however, was the commitment of the Mao-Zhu army commanders to arm the village self-defense teams and conjoin them into county-level people's militias. The experience of Mao Zedong, Zhu De, and Liu Bocheng was that without arming peasants who would work the will of the peasant associations the gains of rent reduction, land repossession, and market reopenings would be lost. They understood that in a peasant world where plunderous warlord armies used deadly force the CCP counterforce would not have to impose arms on the country people. The peasants doubtlessly welcomed the chance to take up arms to stop landlords and warlords from violating their social rights, and there is no evidence to suggest they suffered for their sanity in doing so.[129]

The Hegemony of Peasant Values under the CCP
and Its Revolutionary Army

If the CCP gained a mandate to rule by backing the peasants' independent efforts to regain their sources of livelihood, how did its cadres promote a peasant belief in their cause? They had several options. One was to enter peasant life as old-style benefactors. Another was to provide the Communist party ideology peasants supposedly needed to gain a clear and critical understanding of their interest. Still another was to serve the efforts of peasants to articulate their own folk ideas about what was just. Given the chaos of the countryside and the dilemmas of coordinating social revolution with national resistance, the Chinese Communists most likely drew from each of these options depending on the issues they faced in specific local situations. What triumphed in the border region, however, was the political projection of peasant countervalues.

The possibility that party leaders would reestablish personal dependency ties with peasants and re-create party clienteles among the rural poor was real. This top-down patron-client approach to peasant mobilization had settled in the CCP by 1942. By then many party leaders at the county level were presenting flood relief grain, helping with rent reduction, and promoting village mutual aid as services sponsored by benefactors. The peasants, in turn, sometimes took such behavior as a cue to accept CCP services as patronage dispensed to grateful clients. The more these vertical relationships of dependency and deference took hold in CCP relations with peasants, however, the more the party undermined its quest to inspire the rural people to continue re-creating their shattered economies by their own self-reliant endeavors.

It was during the Thought Rectifications of 1942–44 that the leadership of the CCP Shanxi-Hebei-Shandong-Henan revolutionary base area began to veer away from dependency and patronage. In these years, the CCP moved toward revolution by rectifying the tendencies in its own ranks to slide back to elite values and work styles that kept peasants divided and dependent on sagelike superiors. In order to avoid slipping into patron-client relations, the CCP began critical interparty discussions on the dangers of clientelism and dependency. A report by Lai Ruoyu on the 1942–44 rent-reduction movement pointed out that the rectifications were related directly to the question of *how* the CCP aligned itself with peasant subsistence goals, and claimed that party leaders, many of whom were literate persons from the towns, were overcoming the hierarchical mental style that stood in the way of independent peasant mobilization:

> Speaking in terms of the cadres' thought and work style, a monopolist patron-client work style seriously existed in the 1942 mass movement. Therefore, although the masses gained substantial subsistence benefits, their consciousness actually was not heightened.
>
> After we went through the last two years of the rectification movement, the thought and work style of the party cadres was transformed. In the production movement of the last two years we clearly witnessed the growth of a new work style. In the rent reduction movement of this year the new work style was even more accurate and more self-conscious. Thus the peasants took the initiative. If it were not for this condition, then it would be difficult for us to overcome the benefactor work style. This is the bountiful harvest of our rectification campaign. It is a change of a *fundamental* nature.[130]

The CCP campaign to create a political work style in harmony with peasant conceptions of a nonhierarchical order also took hold in the revolutionary army, in both soldier-commander and soldier-peasant relations. Once Liu Bocheng implemented thought rectification in the 129th Division the poor foot-soldiers criticized their commanders for behaving like patriarchs atop a new political hierarchy.[131] At the company level, Liu's commanders were reprimanded for looking down on common soldiers, and they were obliged to rise early with their troops to till the fields alongside peasants rather than sleep past sunup as was their preference. Similarly, the subofficers who took advantage of their special relations with commanders to molest peasant daughters or make off with peasant crops were brought to shame and severely punished.

Continued peasant militancy, in this sense, was not dependent upon the CCP transforming the mentality of the common folk. A patron-client mode of rule was reappearing from *within the CCP*—from *above* rather than below. By transforming its own approach to peasant mobilization the CCP strengthened the independent struggles of the peasantry, and dignified itself in peasant eyes.

There was of course the continuing danger that the CCP would gel into a benevolent but hegemonic dictatorship. After traveling through CCP territory in 1944, however, U.S. Foreign Service Officer John Service observed that "the Communists are not even actively preaching Communism."[132] And nearly two decades later Franz Schurmann noted that Mao Zedong never claimed that the revolutionary *Weltanschauung* was created either by him or the CCP.[133] While it is widely assumed that the CCP established the hegemony of its political thought over the peasantry,[134] and hence became the bearer of revolutionary consciousness for illiterate folk, Service and Schurmann make the point that CCP cadres did not bother to introduce peasants to an ideological dialogue on the wonders of Marxism or Leninism. Instead, the CCP derived its legitimacy among peasants largely by harmonizing with the widely treasured folk values that stood in opposition to Confucian high culture, and by simultaneously rectifying the tendency of its cadres to replace the hegemony of the defunct "Confucian shop" with their own Communist *Weltanschauung*, stamped onto the villages through courts, schools, and dramatic performances.

Though the CCP, unlike the Guomindang, entered the villages and markets to help organize the subsistence struggles of the rural poor, what enabled its cadres to cultivate a revolutionary partnership with the peasantry was the success they enjoyed in strengthening the collective consciousness of poor folk.

CCP success in sustaining peasant mobilization stemmed in part from the reinforcement of a shared class identity among the local poor. No doubt local CCP leaders faced conflicts between peasants and landlord clansmen, between peasants in villages where class struggle was advanced and in those where there was no active struggle, and between peasants and party cadres who put on the airs of abusive officials, so that struggles involving rent and wages, land ownership, and the redistribution of local privilege were sometimes at odds with the CCP attempt to get peasants to identify their survival with the collective strength of the Little Tradition. Some progress was made with the establishment of the peasant associations which, when functioning properly, served as a collective *peasant* body made up of militant poor people who upheld the right of any peasant to present a grievance to the association and mobilized a popular majority in support of decisions taken to right injustices. The rhythm of the vanguard villages was not imposed on peasants in villages where class tensions were relatively mild. Starting from the poorest villages, where landlord domination was weak, the CCP cadres encouraged tenants and hired-hand leaders to invite peasants from several neighboring villages to attend "allied village meetings" for the purpose of examining and celebrating their successes. A growing number of the "guests" were inspired to think about the virtues of collective action. Important too was the willingness of the CCP to work with local storytellers, writers, and singers whose short stories, novelettes, and music embodied the language, humor, and religious beliefs of the peasantry. The success of border region writers like Zhao Shuli, who hailed from a peasant family background conditioned by Buddhist and Taoist beliefs, had more than a little to do with the fact that their simple writings centered on the revival of the village as a self-governing folk society whose identity formed around the independent redemptive acts of its poorest members.[135]

The CCP also built on a sense of peasant class allegiance by mitigating conflicts over harvest shares among tenants and over wages between hired hands and rich peasants, and by encouraging peasants to criticize party cadres who ran village government on behalf of landlords who used patronage to distort the democracy of the poor. The slogan of the CCP village and district branches was to become "all peasants under Heaven are one family" *(tianxia nongmin shi yi jia)*.[136] This slogan solidified, symbolically, the process that brought together hundreds and thousands of peasants demonstrating in both their home villages and the temple fairs to settle common grievances against local rulers.

The sense of antagonism peasants felt toward nouveau riche landlords was expressed openly once they had the backing of the CCP and its armed forces. Older peasants, often grandmothers who knew of the subtle landlord maneuverings that had impoverished their husbands and children, voiced their indignation from the temple platforms, and their denunciations captivated the whole village. The temple also became the place where peasants vented their anger against landlords who still ruled the roost and declared the poor had no right to speak. In 1943, for instance, the peasants of Liang Zhai village in northern Henan decided they had had enough of Liang Liangui, a rich landlord who had usurped lands, embezzled monies, and refused hunger loans. They itemized his transgressions in song and posted the lyrics in the temple, so that peasants from other places could read and hear the lyrics sung during the lunar New Year celebrations. A look at the lyrics gives some idea of the bitter class feelings of poor folk during the Anti-Japanese War:

Part 1
   Liang Liangui is doing extremely well.
   He not only is blessed with talent, but also has
received an excellent education.
   It is no surprise that he is in charge of the village
accounts.
   With the help of the Japanese forces, he rules unchallenged
over his domain.
   You might as well forget about asking him for credit; he

will give you a beating with his cudgel if you are a bit late
with your payment.

He always gets what he wants, and he needs to tell no one
what he spends his money on.

He harasses the poor families much more than the wealthy.

Many families have lost everything, and some have even
been forced to leave the village to go begging for food.

When the cow-herder was captured and detained by the traitorous collaborators, Liang went so far so to make everyone pay for a part of the ransom.

Some were made to pay three dollars, others four, and
some as much as six.

He took money when he could, and if someone could not pay
in cash, then he would seize their ox.

In this way, he forced many people to sell their oxen to
him at outrageously low prices.

He has received large amounts of money through corruption
and he is even in the service of the Japanese.

He owns many *mu* of land outside the village, and many
people old and young are in his employ.

He is wealthy, powerful, and the foreigners are his friends.
His power is such that nobody dares to stand in his way.

Part 2

Since you asked me, I will tell you where Master Liang lives.

Enter by the south gate and then walk toward the west.

There you will see a large mansion with extensions on
either side and a wide gate facing south.

Inside, you will find numerous sets of lacquered furniture,
as well as vases and decorative fans laid out on the tables.

The clocks and watches tick noisily away.

Nobody understands anything about the ancient inscriptions
and paintings on the wall.

Who knows what is hidden away in the cupboards and trunks?

I for one cannot tell you as I have never looked inside them.

Where does Master Liang get all his power from?

His wealth comes from the accounts he controls.

He is also skilled in directing his troops, and he commands
many guns in the village.

But the bad weather will give way sooner or later to the sun.

Let's see how long his dynasty will last!

Part 3

There are over fifty persons in the Liang gang, and their
influence reaches as far as the west gate.

Liang Liangui is in charge of the village accounts, and
he is determined to get as much as he can from the village.

Each month when payment is due, he dons his tiger-skin,
grabs hold of his cudgel, and together with his henchmen, goes
plundering through the village.

Into the baskets carried by his henchmen goes everything
he wants.
He not only wants steamed buns but even the unfilled dough.
There are always two basketfuls of pork and beef.
There are ginger, spring onions, oil, dried shrimps, savories,
noodles, rice, pepper, spices, cotton threads and matches too.
Then too he wants dried meat, wood combs, nets, handkerchiefs,
soap, vases, cosmetics, stationery, tins, plates, cooking utensils,
bowls and even chamber pots.
He takes everything which can be carried away.
If there's anything he wants which cannot be taken away, he
will make the owner sign over the ownership to him.
There is no part of the village which he does not plunder;
he does not even miss the little sour pears.
Of course he claims that everything he takes will be for
the use of everyone, but then everything soon disappears without
a trace.
Like the dumplings which he seizes, they soon go to fill his
wife's stomach.
You rule supreme now Master Liang, but sooner or later your
power will come to an end.[137]

Of course the CCP could not always play to such antagonism and still control the popular class struggles that churned beneath the multiclass alliance of the Second United Front. In practice, as Mao Zedong emphasized, the peasants' initiatives to defend their elemental social rights could not be surrendered to cooperation with diehard landlords and warlords.[138] To the recently arrived party cadre, the real challenge was to persuade embittered peasants to accept the landlords who were willing to abide by share rent, tax leveling, and free trade as enlightened, patriotic supporters of the anti-Japanese government.

Lastly, the CCP spoke to the heightened sense of class interest among the formerly powerless rural people. Shi Liqun's *Talking about Chinese History*, first issued in 1941 by New China Youth, recalls that peasant and landlord struggles over labor and capital had been going on in the Hebei-Shandong-Henan area since the Spring and Autumn period.[139] One of its feature stories, "The Big Fish Swallows the Little Fish," was written to inform CCP cadres that peasants were aware of the ageless landlord tendency to concentrate property and power at the expense of poor folk, and it invited the cadres to establish close bonds with peasants who were rising to resist this tendency.

We also discover CCP commanders cultivating a growing sense of popular class awareness both among their soldiers and the peasants they were to protect. A little newspaper called *The Militia* carried an account of Liu Bocheng's encounter with a landlord bearing a gift during the rent-reduction movement in the Taihang, to underline just this point:

One day a landlord sent Liu Bocheng a large melon. Liu was unwilling to eat food taken from the peasants and food for which he had not paid. He summoned a guard to return the melon to the landlord. The landlord, however, sent it back again. This time, however, the landlord sent a relative to present the melon. Liu Bocheng was puzzled by this. He felt there was some sort of a problem and that he should conduct a personal investigation to see what was occurring at the landlord's household. After returning he said the village was in the midst of reducing rent and interest and the thrust of the movement had reached the landlord's household. Thereupon General Liu requested the landlord to come and see him. He made the landlord take the melon and personally carry it back to the village. Furthermore, Liu bluntly told him, "Whoever says the government promulgation of reduction of rent and interest is a good law, whoever respects it, should also realize the Eighth Route Army also agrees with this law." As the landlord listened, he knew the words were genuine and hurriedly picked up the melon and left. Liu Bocheng then said, "The method of this landlord is the method of candy and melons used by the Kitchen Range God of the twenty-third day of the twelfth lunar month. When the Kitchen God eats candy offered from a person's household he must, in return, speak favorably to the Jade Emperor on behalf of the household." Liu Bocheng's class position and class awareness was this sensitive.[140]

This refusal to accept the melon showed reverence for the subsistence needs of peasant families, and contempt for landlords who tried to manipulate peasant religion via patronage. Liu was validating the hearth god as the symbolic guarantor of peasant family security while rekindling the peasant hope for a world without subjugation by landlords, warriors, and bureaucrats. At the same time, he was exposing landlords seeking to reenact the mystification that had passed them off as benefactors of the peasantry. In little ways like this, the CCP army let the country people know that it stood with them against the immoral landlords responsible for their common subjugation.

The CCP thus came to embody what was truly just by enabling the country people to establish their own standards of justice in politics. The Guomindang caricature of a "Red Bandit" army born of "predatory raiding" and the Western stereotype of a CCP applying its own Marxist-Leninist predefinition of what was best for the peasantry have overshadowed the emergence of a popular conception of revolution inside base areas like the one before us. The CCP had first learned the importance of going along with popular struggles against the warlord-state in the anti-Confucian May Fourth Movement of 1919. This lesson had been driven home by the party's sorry attempt to organize the popular jacquerie of 1925–27 within the limits of the Comintern-supported alliance with Guomindang. In turning to the countryside for sanctuary from the Guomindang warlord counterrevolution, the CCP was linking up with peasants whose antistate ideas had come to the fore in the previous decade of survival protests. Equally important, the CCP was linking up with peasants in an extremely famished ecosystem located in the interstices of Republican warlord rule, so that its power and legitimacy rested more on enhancing the struggles of peasants to solve their own problems than on direct control of either real property or office-based patronage. Lastly, the weakness of the CCP armed forces in relation to the superior Guomindang and Japanese militaries meant that the CCP had to stake its survival largely on accommodating the goals of peasants in revolution. In this political context, the inciting counterelements in the border region's Little Tradition would burst forth in struggles of semirooted peasants to settle scores with landlords and officials who had violently debased their families and driven their villages to hunger.

The rise of the CCP must be understood in terms of peasant choices between two political forces whose approaches to a depleted dry-zone agricultural system offered two distinctively different outcomes: the Guomindang's taxation and repression permitted landlords to render peasants impotent to resolve increased protein deficiencies; the CCP-backed revolution offered peasants a means of escape from an enfeebling eco-political crunch via redistributive practices that resolved fatal protein shortages and rearranged the order of sacrifice locally.[141]

Although past scholarship has emphasized the role of the vanguard CCP in bringing peasants into revolution, peasants clearly influenced the revolutionary process by their independent acts. The CCP enabled the local poor to return to customary exchanges with enlightened landlords, but this return did not involve the restoration of an idealized lost relationship between lord and peasant. The mass movement to reduce rent and interest placed limits on landlord exploitation, and in the process of participating in this movement peasants moved to transform exchange shares and the very equation of village power. The return to traditional morality was revolutionary because it occurred on the crest of anarchist outbursts through which peasants began, and then continued, to transfer political power from the hands of landlords and local power wielders to their own collective associations.

In defeating the Guomindang warlords, the CCP and its revolutionary army were creating the *political* conditions that allowed peasants to blend their indigenous moral economy with low-risk market initiatives. With the CCP standing for the right to trade openly and competitively, and with the revolutionary army enforcing that right, peasants began to participate in free markets. Now they were able to avoid the debilitating terms of trade that landlords, gentry, and warlords had molded from the monetized global market networks of Republican decades, and to reestablish rooted families, lineages, and villages in command of enhancing capital investments.

Finally, the CCP was orchestrating all of these endeavors outside of a failing Republican order. Filling the fissures of an aborted Guomindang socialization process were the instructions of rebelling peasants in little Taihang Mountain villages that remained largely free from the vertical administration of the CCP's regional and county-level leadership. Let us now reconstruct the emergence of revolutionary order in one of these Taihang villages.

5

The Revolutionary Instructions
from Below

The hearts of landlords are as cruel as wolves
Like maneaters, they suck our blood and devour
our hair and skin
The waters of Qilipu flow swiftly
Yet the bitterness of blood and tears is so deep,
it will never be forgotten

Then a clap of thunder sounded
The current of social morality changed
The winds and clouds slowly encircled Motian Ling
and Red Flags sprouted throughout the Taihang.

The novel from which this poem comes, Liu Jiang's *Taihang Storm*,[1] is, in one sense, a morality play written to emphasize the superhuman capacities and the superior virtues of the CCP compared to those of its domestic and international foes. Much of its style and symbol must be taken with a grain of salt, as typical of the claims that celebrate any victory of the oppressed. Nevertheless, by studying popular novels like this one, we can inform ourselves about the place of folk culture in the pre−1949 revolutionary process.[2]

The grievances that move tillers and quasi-tillers in the village of Qilipu, one of several hamlets near Phoenix Mountain in the Taihang range, to revolt are the same exorbitant salt prices and usurious loans that plagued other border region communities.[3] Many of the Guomindang and CCP actors who enter this little drama were undoubtedly historical figures. The Eighth Route Army raised its flag on Phoenix Mountain around 1940−41, and afterwards this area became a springboard to the battlefields of Hebei, Shandong, and Henan.[4]

The Taihang Storm offers a fresh look at the peasants' struggle and calls into question the Western version of the CCP as an elite mobilizing a quiescent peasantry. Based on a conception of peasants mobilizing themselves for survival long before the appearance of outside political organization, it explains that by the 1920s peasant revolt was the only restraint on exploitation in many of China's villages, and it encourages us to look at the reordering of the countryside in terms of the peasants' revolutionary instructions rather than party ideology. Thus it qualifies the theory, first put forth by Benjamin I. Schwartz in *Chinese Communism and the Rise of Mao*, that the CCP imposed its own exclusive single-party hegemony over a peasant base, with the definition of revolutionary order being created by the party rather than the country people.[5] The success of the CCP lay mainly in going along with the struggles of semirooted peasants who were capable of unbelievable defiance and deception, and Qilipu's history reminds us that the party was obliged to give play to the peasants' ideas about morality and justice, creating revolutionary order out of its interaction with the popular struggle.

Nor was party legitimacy linked, simplistically, to its capacity to restore good Confucian government, for the cadres did not succeed in the village world by catering either to peasant nostalgia for the Confucian past or to peasant needs for patronage. The passions of Qilipu peasants reveal a world where Great Tradition modes of thought had not taken a pervasive hold among ordinary peasant families, and where there was a shared anti-Confucian universe among the underclass carriers of an emergent counter-tradition of popular protest. The success of the CCP in Qilipu sprang more from its ability to harmonize with the anti-Confucian sentiments already radiating from the village than its ability to substitute a Marxist cum Confucian mode of rule for peasant conceptions of order and justice.

What specific factors account for the swiftness and staying power of peasant mobilization in villages like Qilipu? In 1952 Father Ramon de Jaegher, a Belgian Catholic missionary in the border region during the Anti-Japanese War, attempted to answer this question in *The Enemy Within*.[6] Refusing to associate the CCP with salvation, Father de Jaegher argued that the Chinese Communists had won by attacking the peasant family and the popular Buddhist theism that supposedly taught passive compliance and the suppression of grievances. Implicit in this interpretation was the assumption that popular religion and class struggle were incompatible in rural China.[7] Historically speaking, this interpretation is not hard to understand. The Roman Catholic Church came out of the French Revolution profoundly conservative. The Catholic missionaries who came to rural China were escaping from a traumatic confrontation with popular movements in Europe, and were opposed to peasant outbursts against perceived order. The missionaries in the North China interior naturally sought the security of Republican government, and men like de Jaegher had personal ties with the Guomindang commanders occupying the towns along the caravan trails that led into the Taihang Mountains. They lacked the moral enlightenment that has come to Catholic priests through their post-Vatican II experience with repressive military regimes in Latin America. In China, the Church had not taken the moral stand that the ruling military junta should restrain its security forces from murderous assaults on poor villagers. Missionaries like de Jaegher thus wound up arguing that peasants preferred the Guomindang, Western missionaries, and even the Japanese army to the presumedly godless protostate goals of the CCP. Their conservative theology was, however, rivaled by the consciousness of peasants in Taihang villages like Qilipu, and it was actively condemned by the CCP cadres who came to the defense of the village folk.

The Bitter Heritage: The Unforgivable Past

Qilipu, an extremely poor village, is located along the Taihang boundary of Shanxi and Henan, only ten *li* from the county seat and seven from the government salt shop. The peasants called their village Qilipu (Seven Mile Village) because it is only seven miles from the Motian Ling peaks of the Taihang Range in southeast Shanxi. As they left the village and climbed the Motian hills in search of livelihood the road forked, one trail leading down to northern Henan, the other to southern Hebei. Work and women being scarce in Qilipu, peasant men traveled these trails to seek both in villages on the plains. Even before the Great Depression, only a few peasants could scratch out a living in Qilipu. And only a few women from surrounding villages were willing to marry Qilipu men. They had heard how horrible life had become for many of the families there.

The peasants' anger was aimed mainly at landlords, particularly the Lis, who had been powerful landowners in Qilipu since the Ming dynasty. In many cases, three peasant generations had worked under the Li household, including the family of Guan Yinbao, a hired hand for Li Baotai. By 1927, the sixteenth year of the Republic of China, the heritage of Guan Yinbao's family had embittered almost every peasant in Qilipu.

During the Great Famine of 1876−79, when the peasants were driven to the verge of cannibalism, Guan Yinbao's grandfather, Zaitian, had agreed to work for Li Hongyuan, Li Baotai's grandfather, in return for shelter, wages, and medical care. Li Hongyuan, however, broke this agreement and dismissed Zaitian, leaving him to die in the temple.

Long before his death Zaitian had repeatedly warned his son, Mandun, against working for the Li household, but at the age of seventeen, having no other way of surviving, the boy went to work for Li Hongyuan. There were disappointing harvests and Mandun and his companions lived in constant fear of hunger. In the North China famine of 1920−21 several villagers had starved, and some were so weak they could not even help each other bury their dead. The stench of rotting corpses filled Qilipu streets and homes— except one. The Li family shut the doors of its huge brick house, and enjoyed tea, meat, and steamed bread.

In 1926−27 Li Hongyuan grew apprehensive about rumors in the county seat. The rebel Heavenly Gate Society and the Red Spear Society[8] were said to be on their way from the North China Plain to the Taihang to take from the rich to help the poor. Li Hongyuan therefore brought An Qing, a *gongfu* teacher, to Qilipu to teach martial arts to the villagers so they could help defend his domain.

Instead of preparing for the defense of their benefactor, however, Mandun and some other hired hands took the *gongfu* training in order to resist Li himself. Landlord Li did not realize how deeply his broken promises to Zaitian had injured Mandun, or how deeply his violations of village cultural practices had offended other peasants.

The peasants were upset by Li Hongyuan's interventions in their community temple fair. Qilipu's Goddess of Mercy Temple Hall *(Guanyin tang)* was a public temple open to all peasants to worship without any mandatory payment. Its mid-summer temple fair was the highlight of annual festivities, and peasants came from 90 *li* to take part in the fair. Along about 1919–20, however, Li stationed armed retainers around the temple and made the peasants pay to enter and worship. Later he began using the fair to promote *gongfu* contests so he could select the most promising warriors for fighting the Heavenly Gates and Red Spears.

Not long after winning one of these matches, Mandun married Lianxiang. In the same summer, typhoid fever struck the village, killing Lianxiang's mother. To repay the loan they took from landlord Li for their mother's funeral, Lianxiang and her brother, Zhuxiang, sold their home and land, and rented nine *mu* of sandy hill slope land from Li. To help them, Mandun worked for additional income in surrounding villages, and he and Zhuxiang worked together in spring planting. Lianxiang transplanted seedlings and prepared meals for the three of them.

During these hard years (1919 to 1921) Lianxiang gave birth to Guan Yinbao, and she wandered through the countryside in search of work, sleeping in makeshift shelters. By the time Guan Yinbao was seven, Mandun had told him about his grandfather's suffering under the Li household and had taught him *gongfu*.

In the spring of 1927, peasants in Qilipu heard about the birth of the Communist party. They had heard rumors that the party was against warlords like Yan Xishan and Zhang Zuolin, and some said it would help the poor. Li Hongyuan, fearful that such talk would give rise to rebellion, summoned Li Jinhuai, a relative who served as a troubleshooter, to help discredit the rumors, which circulated in the Guanyin temple. Li Jinhuai had helped landlord Li swindle land and silence dissent in the past. These ingratiating achievements, which had earned him the reputation of an "ass-licker," were on peasant minds when, from the temple platform, Li yelled, "When I was in the city, I heard the Communist party is the same as the long-haired bandit rebels of the past;[9] they are a gang of wild ghosts neither accepted by Heaven nor appreciated on earth."

By 1927 most of Qilipu's peasants had come to see Li Hongyuan as a scourge. That year, for instance, the crops had failed, and Li Hongyuan had called in the debt of his tenant Zhou Xiaowu. Even after paying all of his harvest to Li, Zhou still owed him six pecks of grain, so Li had Zhou and his sons locked out of their house. When one of the sons cursed the Lis, Li had him beaten. In despair, Zhou hanged himself. Two nights later, Li Hongyuan's front courtyard compound burned to the ground. A few weeks later, during the Lantern Festival, the peasants around Qilipu were buying firecrackers for celebrating the burning, and Sanhai, who had torched the house, was living as a fugitive.

In the same year, the peasants in Qilipu were planning for their March Third rites to the Buddhist goddess of mercy, Guanyin, to whom they turned for protection and relief in hard times—drought was threatening the Taihang. Attempting to upstage the Bodhisattva, however, landlord Li told a village temple gathering that his household would prepare food for the occasion. As Li left the temple, Mandun angrily threw his bowl of soup in the direction of Li's back and kicked the ground in disgust:

> All you do is bad! You pray from the Buddhist scriptures to trick the poor; you slaughter our pigs and sheep to prepare the livestock for a contribution to the gods; and the salt shop you and your relatives have opened in the city under the hidden hand of the officials sells salt at outrageous prices. For long years we've worked for you and yet we still eat this kind of poor food!

Popular resentment of Li's hypocritical "Buddhist protection" was so widespread that the peasants from the surrounding villages began streaming into Qilipu on March Second to avoid paying homage to him. The peasants who came to pray at the Guanyin tang were seeking relief from the drought, but Li Hongyuan ordered Li Jinhuai to collect cash for the incense and joss paper money they burned before the goddess of mercy. As peasants entered the temple hall they put the steamed bread loaves they had brought for their family offerings into twelve big baskets belonging to landlord Li, but, in symbolic protest, not one of them took the food offerings prepared by the Li household.

Not long afterward, an ode to the transformation of the Buddhist goddess of mercy spread from Qilipu through the surrounding villages:

> The stove of old mother Guanyin is upsidedown
> Someone has used her name to change the oil cake
> The incense lamp is similar to the shakable money tree
> The bamboo candle stick is like the assassin's knife

In a few days, a similar ode came back into Qilipu from sister villages:

> Old mother Guanyin, by all means
> You should not take our bread and also demand
>   our money and property
> Next year, when March Third comes
> You can bet we will not dare return again

This popular symbolic dissent owed its origins to a "centrifugal Buddhism" which called for instant, practical solutions to pressing social dilemmas, and which seems to have departed significantly from the escapist
conception of salvation embedded in orthodox Buddhist scriptures.[10] Landlords like Li Hongyuan counseled patience, humility, and subordination.
The moral tone of the peasants' Guanyin odes, however, heralded the
immediacy of subsistence needs and the inefficacy of humility, and declared
landlord hierarchy to be the destroyer of their Guanyin, the deliverer from
hunger and oppression. The potent allegories in the Guanyin folk songs
imply a symbolic rejection of a world wherein the Bodhisattva kept peasant
property; incense took the few coins in their tattered trousers; and bamboo
candlesticks were the instruments of landlord repression. Peasants were
bolstering their budding protest with folk reasoning that was in direct
opposition to the rationale of Confucian landlords. Qilipu's peasants did not
return to the temple to worship Guanyin in the image of Li's beliefs, and
their interpretation of Guanyin was expressed in their growing challenge to
landlord and warlord rule.

March 3 was also the day of the Southern Seas temple fair in the county
seat. Along with thousands of other peasants, Mandun always had attended
this fair to buy tools and salt. However, the price of salt was skyrocketing,
because the only salt shop in the entire county had fallen into the hands of Li
Hongyuan and Liang Jinbang, a gentry figure who lived in Wohuzhuan. In
1909, just before the fall of the Qing dynasty, these two men had taken over
the distribution, sale, and taxation of salt for the whole county. Now, under
warlord Yan Xishan, they still retained their hold on retail salt by virtue of
their influence over local officials. As the price of salt rose, peasants were
pressed to pay with "official currency," as opposed to customary coppers.
Throughout the 1920s popular protests to restore the fairness of salt prices
were a feature of the Southern Seas temple fairs. At the 1927 fair, Mandun
led an angry crowd of peasants to break down the doors of the salt shop
and distribute two-hundred-pound salt bags to rioters from across the
fairgrounds.

Mandun then led hundreds of peasants to petition Qian Xianren, the
county magistrate, to get rid of the unfair salt-shop operators. The peti-
tioners urged Qian to write an order to eliminate the unfair practices of the
salt shop, and to announce that salt would be bought and sold fairly. Upon
receiving his promise, the peasants returned to their villages. No one
guessed the magistrate had sent a report to the provincial government.

But late one evening some two weeks later, a detachment of provincial
troops arrived. The next morning Qian Xianren, city officials, and Liang
Jinbang told the commander that "the poor devils" had plundered the salt
shop, and enlisted his troops to repress the rebels in return for two thousand
yuan.

That same evening the troops surrounded Qilipu. They shot Mandun in the leg, and dragged him and several other peasants to the county jail. A few days later, Mandun was nailed alive to the wall over the main gate to the county seat, as a warning to others. The peasants coming to the city to take part in fairs or to buy salt had to pass through these gates, and from several miles away they could see Mandun's body stretched across the wall. It was said that Mandun was so full of anger he did not close his eyes in death, and that the officials were afraid to look into his eyes. Few peasants walked under these walls without remembering that this was where Mandun had led the attack on the salt shop.

To refute the peasant need for protection against salt shop operators like Liang Jinbang was to radicalize modest pleas for customary justice. When the Republican magistrates responded to petitions for salt at a tolerable price with repression, they made peasants like Mandun into beloved martyrs. Long before the Communist party came to Motian Ling, Mandun's death came to symbolize the struggle of the poor all across the county.

The Fight for Survival and Fantasies about Revolt: Landlord Exploitation and Peasant Resistance

After Mandun was murdered, Zhuxiang died in jail, leaving Guan Yinbao and his mother in increasingly precarious circumstances. Hunger was not their only problem. Lianxiang was raped by An Qing, the *gongfu* teacher, and she and her son fled Qilipu. For the next ten years Lianxiang prepared meals for landlord families and Guan Yinbao worked as a cowherd for one landlord and as a hired hand for another. Their combined pay, however, was barely enough to survive. Like many other desperate migrants, Guan Yinbao and his mother returned to their old village roots, around 1935 or 1936.

During their ten years away, Li Hongyuan had died. An Qing and his mistress, Yu Shiwa, Li Hongyuan's wife, had become managers of the Li estate. Following in the footsteps of Li Hongyuan, the pair transgressed important customary rights of the hired help. They refused to arrange medical attention for kitchen hands who had hurt themselves doing chores, and dismissed hired hands without severance payments. Yu Xin, the aged Li household foreman, repeatedly came to the defense of the workers, and in doing so clashed with Yu Shiwa. Li Baotai, who peasants whispered was An Qing and Yu Shiwa's bastard, had grown up to become the most notorious landlord in Qilipu. During the World Depression many landlords around Motian Ling went bankrupt and Li Baotai bought most of their better lands, thereby acquiring a string of tenancy and mortgage arrangements that extended miles beyond his land rentals in Qilipu to the villages of Tuerzhai, Danan Shan, and Qianzhai. Now, during the years of terrible drought, Li supplemented his profits from grain loan interest by foreclosing on land mortgages.

Li Baotai acquired his reputation in part from his palanquin racket.

According to custom, the bride's family had to provide a palanquin for the marriage ceremony. But Li had acquired both of the palanquins in Qilipu, and the cost of getting a palanquin through his rental agency was three dollars. No one could remember such harsh terms under any dynasty. Everyone referred to palanquin rental as a Wart on Life.

Along with An Qing and Yu Shiwa, Li Baotai became the major shareholder in the Phoenix Mountain Coal Mine. Peasants could recall the time when the mine was a village-run enterprise from which they earned a living in the slack agricultural season. After the 1911 Revolution, however, the local Republican government increased the mine taxes every year, and the mine was sold to the highest bidders—the principal owners of the salt shop.

Even before Li Baotai became the mine boss, An Qing and Yu Shiwa had cut back so much on pay and left the mine so unsafe that the miners had struck. There were fights with the mine police. Some of the miners entreated the Li household for higher wages, and when they were refused they attempted to beat An Qing to death. After this attack, An Qing was afraid to return to Qilipu, and Li Baotai temporarily moved in with his uncle Liang Guangzhao, the son of Liang Jinbang, who arranged for Li's police protection in Qilipu.

Li Baotai's kinship and business ties with Liang Guangzhao made him one of the most powerful landholders in the county. Together they were the two richest persons in the entire county. Liang was both the principal of the normal school and the head of the chamber of commerce, which gave him an official share of livestock and grain taxes. Under Liang's protection, Li Baotai took over the Qilipu village office, collected taxes on any pretext, and ordered his armed retainers to brutalize anyone who objected.

During Guan Yinbao and his mother's absence Li had confiscated their family house and turned it into livestock quarters. The peasants all knew the property belonged to Lianxiang, but her brother, who had purchased the house from landlord Zhao Zhuzai, had died without leaving any written proof of ownership. During the preceding decade Dong Shouchang, the village sheriff and Li Baotai's bodyguard, had written a false record of sale between Mandun and Li, and bribed the land office to stamp the deed with its official seal.

When Dong confronted Guan Yinbao with a trespassing charge, therefore, Guan Yinbao and his friend Ma Zhaiguai beat the sheriff severely. But Li Baotai and his retainers arrested Guan and Ma. The false deed claimed that not only had Mandun sold the property, but he still owed a debt of forty dollars, to be paid with three years of work as a hired hand, which Li collected from Guan Yinbao.

To punish Ma Zhaiguai, Sheriff Dong tied him on a wide pole, whipped him with a soaked hemp rope, and left him tied on the pole for a winter evening. Li Baotai threatened to send Ma to prison if he did not pay the village office thirty foreign silver dollars. Ma's friends secured his release by promising that he would work for the village office under Li Baotai for two winters, but during this period Ma died. When Ma's friends brought his body into Qilipu, Li kicked the corpse and cursed them. From that day forth, Li Baotai prohibited the peasants from bringing the corpses of their families into the village, thereby transgressing the peasants' customary right to rest a body in the home for three days of preburial ceremonies. The peasants sent a delegation to plead with Li to allow them to place Ma's body in the five doctrines temple on the village boundary, but before Li could consent or refuse, a group of village youths had carried the corpse into the lonely temple.

Guan Yinbao, Xiao Wu, and several other peasants stayed with Ma's wife through the night, the naked corpse before them. All night they turned over ways to rid the village of Li Baotai. If they burned down the Li house, Xiao Wu exclaimed, landlord Li would make them rebuild it. If they cut Li's crops at night, he would make up his losses in higher rents. If they assassinated Li and fled the village, they would be risking their lives. As Guan Yinbao pointed out, "The magistrates will post wanted-posters everywhere and the sky will become a big cage and the earth will become the Taoist demon's invisible net." To strike alone would make it too easy for Li and the officials to kill the rebels one by one.

Guan Yinbao wanted to overturn Heaven. But Xiao Wu insisted that even Mandun's son was like a big ox tied to the wheat grinder *(zhuan zaicao tou)* of the Li household, powerless to change anything. As the first rays of dawn brightened the temple, Guan Yinbao thought of his beloved father, and then fantasized himself leading a temple fair uprising involving hundreds of poor folk. In the temple revolt fantasy, all landlords were swept from earth and the peasants were left in a world without suffering.

As Guan Yinbao's three years of serfdom drew to a close, Li attempted to prolong his debt bondage and to prevent him from marrying a peasant girl by the name of Yuanying. Li felt there would be no safety for his family if Guan Yinbao were to escape bondage and marry. Yuanying had been purchased as a child bride by a poor miner on a sixty-dollar loan from Li, and the miner had died in an accident several days after the marriage, leaving his debt unpaid. Li rewrote Guan Yinbao's three-year contract to put Yuanying's debt in his name, thereby requiring him to pay sixty dollars plus 5 percent interest per month for the three years he had worked for Li. Suspecting that Li Baotai was trying to keep Mandun's son from marrying, Yu Xin and several other aged peasants secretly arranged a rapid marriage for the young couple. Li was furious, but he decided against collecting the debt because he did not want a direct confrontation with the villagers.

Peasants and the CCP before the Revolution

The peasants of Qilipu first met the people who would help them realize their political fantasies in the Motian Ling forest and the Phoenix Mountain mines. It was in the nearby forest that Yu Xin met Fang Zhengkui, a mine worker who knew about the CCP. A native of the Motian Ling-Phoenix Mountain area, Fang had been press-ganged by Yan Xishan's army around 1930, only to escape to the Motian hills shortly after Yan's troops were defeated by Zhang Xueliang. Having no living relatives in his home village, Fang wandered in and out of other villages, striking up relations with older peasants like Yu Xin and telling stories to peasant children.

Guan Yinbao's first contact with the CCP came during a trip to the mine to fetch coal for Li Baotai. Stranded at the mine by a flash flood, which lasted five days and swept away the bridge to Qilipu, Guan Yinbao sought shelter there. Guan Yinbao boasted he was the mine boss's hired hand in hopes of winning the heart of some miner who would shelter him through the storm. But the miners did not offer shelter because, ironically, they were not in the least fond of Li Baotai.

Finally, a man called Zheng Hongzhuan, who had come from the foothills to the coal mine to keep accounts for Li Baotai, offered Guan Yinbao food and shelter in his cave home. Zheng Hongzhuan treated the miners with respect, and his wife, Su Hua, told Guan Yinbao "they were all brothers." Guan Yinbao was suspicious of these people because he had never been treated equally by anyone with ties to the landlord mine bosses, and he did not comprehend all of the terms used by Zheng and Su Hua. After dinner, Guan Yinbao told the pair his family history, and his host declared a day would come when the poor would take up arms against landlords. Still, Guan Yinbao hesitated to talk openly. An old lesson came to mind: "People often say it's easy to draw a dragon or a tiger, but it's hard to draw their bones. It's easy to know a person and recognize his face, but it's hard to know his feelings." "Who knows about such matters?" he told his host. "It's all predetermined by fate."

Zheng Hongzhuan said it was not so:

The landlords control everything, including the coal mine, the land, and the property. They harm the poor. We are left without even a little grain, and after we die there isn't even an inch of earth for a grave. The rich eat the best food and wear the best clothing, even though they do not need to work. We poor are poor from one generation to the next, yet we work under intolerable misery. Just what is reasonable about this?

Answering his own question, Zheng continued:

What kind of world is this? The hotter a person feels the more he sweats, the colder a person feels the more he trembles. When there is drought the weather brings too much rain and flooding! The landlords have money and power. Above them are magistrates and below them are dog's legs runners supporting them. If you oppose them, they will send the government troops to massacre and eliminate your whole family and clan, and when they catch you they will put iron chains on your hands and legs and imprison you. Just like your father.

> Wasn't this the way it was? They nailed him alive on the city wall. So if we poor
> are to have a good life . . . we must pull out the whole head of the onion and the
> garlic by the roots.

Zheng explained that the poor and the rich were two classes, and the poor
should rise up in revolution. But Guan Yinbao, like most peasants of the
backwoods, was unfamiliar with the terms "class" and "revolution." Moreover, he wanted to know why they could not make revolution instantly.
Zheng gave this explanation:

> You can't swallow and digest hot bread. When there is a drama, there must be
> an opening scene. When we make a revolution it's even more important to take
> it step by step. It's like a person cutting down a big tree. We must dig out the
> root and cut off the branches. If you want to sweep away Li Baotai, then we
> have to bring down the government magistrates; but the government magis-
> trates and the big warlords are hooked in with the imperialist foreign devils. So
> for the time being we first have to fight the foreign devils. If these guys are able
> to firmly occupy China, then they can rely on the landlords, magistrates, and
> warlords. If we look at the landlords and the imperialist foreign devils, these
> two heads, you can say either is a root or a branch tip. If we look at it this way,
> then at the same time we fight against the imperialists we also take some time to
> fight Li Baotai. We want to teach this kind of tyrant a lesson, to whittle down his
> sharp point. Then we can keep the interest of the poor. Once the masses knock
> down Li Baotai, then slowly but surely the power of the poor will grow day by
> day. When that day comes do you think we still will need to worry why we poor
> folk cannot take power in this world?

This evening with Zheng started Guan Yinbao thinking about the relationship between the officials, his father, and revolution. His mother had
told him the officials who had nailed his father to the wall had said he was a
Communist party rebel. Was this the same as making a revolution? "It's just
so," replied Zheng Hongzhuan. "The Communist Party is precisely for
leading the poor in rebellion, and the rebellion of the poor is what makes
revolution."

Returning by donkey to Qilipu, Guan Yinbao reflected on Zheng's advice
about "getting the poor together to protect the interest of the poor." Water
raged across the fields, carrying the land away in its currents. Refugees
passed in shock over the flooded land, telling of the ruined sorghum and
Indian corn for miles around. In Qianzhai the crops lay hailbeaten and
withered.

Guan Yinbao began to doubt the old idea that poor folk were dependent
on Heaven and Li Baotai for their survival. Where, after all, did the grain in
Li's bin come from? In the good crop years Li stripped the poor and piled up
grain. If no one were to pay rent or interest, then everyone would be able to
pass through calamities like the one before them.

As he arrived in Qilipu, Guan's mind turned to the forty *piculs* of millet
in the *yi cang*, the village granary—under the control of landlord Li. Most of

the peasants had gathered at the goddess of mercy temple hall to ponder how they might survive the spring hunger. Quite a few were willing to listen to Guan Yinbao and his young companions talk about eating the grain in the *yi cang*.

The Yi Cang Revolt: Peasant Indignation and Landlord Panic during the Revolution

The *yi cang* was established by Li Hongyuan around 1915, when famine threatened Qilipu and the surrounding villages. Li Hongyuan persuaded the neighborhood heads to approve his proposal to deposit forty *piculs* of grain in a village granary under his patronage, and to do so with government approval.

In the next twenty years hundreds of Qilipu's peasants had come to Li Hongyuan's courtyard to plead for grain loans from the *yi cang*, agreeing to · repay the loans within one year to qualify for future loans. In the past, Li had loaned grain to be paid back at tolerable interest rates, but with the establishment of the *yi cang*, he charged "4/6 interest." Under this arrangement, if a family borrowed six pecks it paid back six pecks plus four. A family placed its property as a deposit, and forfeited half if they defaulted.

To inaugurate the *yi cang*, Li enlisted a stonecutter from Lin county in Henan to erect a seven-foot-high tablet at the goddess of mercy temple bearing the message:

> In the autumn of one year my village encountered misfortune. Hail did serious damage to the harvest. The next year there was drought. Because of the drought all four corners of the land were left barren and starved corpses were left on the roads. But the Duke of Li immediately served the public out of his righteousness. He unbuttoned his pocket and gave grain to the poor. He established the grain bank to save the poor. The virtue of his actions truly benefited them. The villagers paid tribute and homage to the Duke of Li for his deep kindness. The grain bank will last for ten thousand years. Henceforth, no matter who comes to borrow grain from the grain bank, they will obey the regulations of 4/6 interest. I place this rock tablet here as evidence to clearly show future generations the righteousness of my regulation.

Li Hongyuan thought he would be wealthy forever. The peasants would pay him interest on the grain loans and at the same time protect his grain from outsiders. Several years later, however, the peasants in Qilipu made up their own saying about the *yi cang*:

> In Qilipu the giving of grain is a devilish design
> Li Hongyuan monopolizes all of the grain bins
> The village officials earn benefits from pigs' legs and bellies
> If the poor want millet they must pay 4/6 interest

Precisely this sense of injustice made Guan Yinbao and his companion Hai Sheng want to break the shackles of the *yi cang* under Li Baotai twenty years later, during the spring hunger of 1936. Almost everyone in Qilipu had borrowed grain from the *yi cang*, and most of the debtors felt they had been cheated by Li Hongyuan and Li Baotai. The widespread indignation over the grain loan interest allowed Guan Yinbao and his companions to investigate how many persons had borrowed grain, how many felt they had been cheated, and how many were willing to come together to make Li Baotai abolish the 4/6 interest. They decided to put the matter to everyone during a meeting near the temple hall.

What encouraged these youths to openly challenge landlord Li over the *yi cang* was a rumor from the Phoenix Mountain Mine. According to the rumor, the Communist party was bringing its Red Army into Shanxi. If the Red Army forded the Yellow River and came straight ahead, people were saying, it would arrive in Qilipu in ten days. Within several weeks Liu Bocheng brought the 129th Division into the Taihang Mountains, and headed toward southeast Shanxi via the counties along the Zhang River.[11] The news was like distant thunder rumbling across the sky. The telephones in the market towns buzzed with rumors about the oncoming Red Terror. On the temple fair grapevines, however, the news was that the army of the poor was coming. Throughout the Taihang peasants were saying, "The Red Army soldiers are the commanders and troops from Heaven. Their special mission is to fight the local despots and kill the landlords, to kill the rich and help the poor." In Qilipu, Li Baotai and his ilk were growing extremely anxious. At twilight they boarded up their houses and chanted all night as they hid their riches. Guan Yinbao and his friends determined to arouse everyone against Li Baotai and his *yi cang* loans.

The initial morning temple meeting aroused instant anger. Xiao Wu, whose father had died under Li Baotai's ancestors, reckoned that the Li household had taken over one hundred pecks of grain in interest since the grain bank had been established in 1915. "When we eat the grain in the *yi cang*, we are eating our grain!" Everyone agreed with Xiao Wu. The general sentiment was for abolishing this injustice.

But the peasants were not without opposition within their own ranks, mainly from Old Zhuan, the father of Hai Sheng and a longtime hired hand of Li Hongyuan and Li Baotai. The memory of Mandun and threats from Li Baotai made Old Zhuan extremely fearful for his son's safety. Upon hearing him threaten to smash Li Hongyuan's temple tablet, Zhuan cautioned against open defiance, insisting that only robbers would take grain from the *yi cang*. This was turning logic wrongside up, Guan Yinbao and Xiao Wu argued:

> Uncle Zhuan, think it over: we work for Li Baotai from dawn to dusk. We have tolerated this our whole life. Although you work hard you still can't earn your daily meals for your own family. Are toilers like us really destined to this dog's life from birth? What is it they depend on to be able to lay under the shade of trees and enjoy such a good life and order us to wait on them?

Old Zhuan's opposition permitted landlord Li to stymie the swelling protest. Li Baotai, alerted to the trouble by Sheriff Dong, came to the temple to confront the peasants. The *yi cang* regulation wasn't made by him, Li insisted, but by three generations of village ancestors. Wasn't this the will of the whole village? Li's ancestors had contributed grain to save the village from famine, and now they dared to do this!

Old Zhuan, arriving with the sheriff, beat his son in front of everyone, and landlord Li quickly seized on the peasants' shame to scold his hired hand for not disciplining his rebel son. Leaving the temple, Li reaffirmed his triumph by shouting, "Whoever opposes me is just a Communist!"

The day after the news of the *yi cang* protest spread to the Phoenix Mountain Mine, Zheng Hongzhuan came into Qilipu. To cover up the real purpose of his call, Zheng told Li Baotai he had come to check on the mine debts, as the previous bookkeeper had done.

From Guan Yinbao Zheng learned there were several schools of opinion among the peasants. Some said the 4/6 interest regulation should be obeyed; others said if Li didn't change the regulation they would smash the tablet. Still others said they should determine how much grain Li had gotten from the *yi cang* in interest over the past twenty years. This third course of action, discussed by Zheng and Guan Yinbao, offered the key to uniting the whole village. The "smashing the rock" viewpoint could not build class consciousness, Zheng emphasized. The better course would be to organize only those peasants who had borrowed grain from the *yi cang* and concentrate on calculating what they had lost through the 4/6 interest regulation.

At this point, Zheng Hongzhuan revealed that he was a member of the CCP and that the party had approved Guan Yinbao as a member. Here, in the Taihang highlands, we can begin to see how the CCP was recruiting the most wretched of second-generation peasant rebels to help develop a practical course of popular revolution from below.[12]

Within Qilipu the *yi cang* protest continued to build. Old Zhuan, chastised by the community for slapping his son, experienced a change of heart, and the rebel youths welcomed him to their cause. Zhuan had access to the old *yi cang* debt books in the rear house of Li's courtyard, and smuggled two of them to Guan Yinbao, who shuttled them to Jin Shan, a semiliterate peasant who knew how to count. According to their calculation, the Li household had taken a total of 264 *piculs*, 4 pecks, and 8 pints of millet from the *yi cang*.

The *yi cang* interest was counted during the spring hunger. One morning, when peasants were bringing their bowls to the temple for breakfast, they discovered a long list stuck on the temple wall, showing in red which family had borrowed how much grain, who had paid how much interest to landlord Li, and Li's total withdrawals from the grain bank over twenty years. Every person who could read the list told ten and every ten told a hundred, and before long the whole village was assembled on the temple grounds.

Many peasants confirmed the temple list calculations by counting with pebbles on the ground. They were enraged even more because now they could see clearly that landlord Li could have helped them make it through the hunger without jeopardizing his own livelihood. At this point, the younger rebels led the whole village to Li Baotai's courtyard to make him account for his *yi cang* withdrawals. They found the landlord torching the remaining debt books, and he watched in horror as they put out the flames.

The peasants insisted that the private burning of public debt books was a crime, and they demanded that Li promise to get rid of the 4/6 interest regulation. Still seeing the tablet as proof the Li household had established the grain bank to save the poor, however, Li Baotai suggested that the matter be put before the county magistrate, with a few villagers acting as plaintiff and Li as the defendant. This suggestion silenced the crowd in the courtyard. Li Baotai had close contacts with the magistrate through Liang Guangzhao. Furthermore, Li Baolong, landlord Li's brother, was a member of the Guomindang, and held a high position in the district administration. To go to the county court would require money, and it surely would result in trouble. The peasants insisted on settling the matter immediately, and they pressured Li Baotai to admit that the *yi cang* belonged to everyone in Qilipu.

Li Baotai, however, refused to admit his debt to the *yi cang*. When Guan Yinbao accused the Li family of taking grain from the *yi cang* without registering their property or paying interest, Li retorted that the benevolence of his ancestors had been forgotten. This defense of false benevolence so enraged the peasants that they compelled Li to proclaim they were their own benefactors. If Guan Yinbao had not intervened, they would have beaten the landlord to death. They made Li write a mortgage on his house, declare his debt of 264 *piculs*, 4 pecks, 8 pints, and set a time limit for payment of the *yi cang* loan, including a one-year interest charge of 370 *piculs*, 2 pecks, 7 pints. At noon on the day Li Baotai promised on paper to right his wrongs several peasants smashed the temple rock tablet.

Qilipu in the United Front: Peasant and Elite Struggles during the Resistance War

The Roman Catholic priests who were thrown out of their Taihang mission villages during the Anti-Japanese War later wrote that the Red Army commanders there had formed the Second United Front with the Jiang Jieshi Guomindang for the overall purpose of covering up their subversion of Republican local government rather than defeating the Japanese.[13] A close look at why and how the peasants, miners, and students in the Motian Ling-Phoenix Mountain area aligned with the CCP Eighth Route Army, however, provides us with a very different, entirely plausible, explanation for the CCP stance toward local power holders.

In Qilipu Li Baotai and Li Baolong turned the *yi cang* incident into a bloody struggle during the War of Resistance. On hearing of the oncoming

Red Army, Li constantly asked his wife, "Is the world really going to change?" But, before she could respond, he would answer,

> It's impossible! From the ancient period, a world without rich and poor is not a real world. If all of us ride the palanquin, who will carry it? If someone rides the palanquin, then certainly someone must carry the palanquin.

"If the poor don't depend on the rich, then they cannot make a living," Li repeatedly reassured himself. By this time, however, the peasants were convinced they could better survive without Li's benevolence, and they frequently dunned him to pay his *yi cang* debt on time.

With only a few months to pay back the debt, Li Baotai wrote a letter to Li Baolong in Taiyuan, asking him for assistance. When Li Baolong received the letter, however, he burned it with all the other secret letters that he feared could implicate him in dealings with his landlords. Li Baolong, like many Guomindang officials in Taiyuan, was in a panic because the Red Army was on the outskirts of the city and Yan Xishan had temporarily called a halt to his anti-Communist activity.

Li Baolong did not dare act against the rebels in Qilipu until four months later, when the CCP-Guomindang Anti-Japanese Front signaled that the Red Army would be moving to meet the Japanese. Li Baolong was a Guomindang district chief. But since the provincial Guomindang was losing its grip on local politics, Li was unable to count on his party superiors for direct assistance. Li therefore wrote a report to the Shanxi Guomindang headquarters, asking permission to "go directly into the tiger's cave" to find the Communist party in his native area. Headquarters sent this report to the Bureau of Investigation and Statistics, a police informant network within the Military Council of the Guomindang. The investigation bureau later turned the case over to the police department which, in turn, gave Li full authority to handle the matter.

With this mandate, Li Baolong arranged for Wang Manxi, a police deputy who had murdered hundreds of peasants for the anti-Communist bounty paid by the government from 1931 to 1936, to take a posse armed with foreign carbines into Qilipu. The posse took Guan Yinbao, Old Zhuan, his son, Jin Shan, and Xiao Wu—the five principal *yi cang* rebels—to the county seat, where they locked them up in the fire god temple.

An atmosphere of doom pervaded the temple quarters. The room contained a broken table the police had used in interrogations, several instruments of torture such as the tiger bench *(laohu dong)* and the bamboo pressure pole *(ya ganzi dagan)*, and ropes for hanging prisoners. The peasants were terrified. When the Guomindang police chief Han Hu and his lieutenant tortured Old Zhuan to reveal who stole the debt books from landlord Li, Zhuan spit in the lieutenant's face and delivered a deadly *gongfu* kick to his groin. Han looked on in disbelief, shouting that they were all bad eggs. But Guan Yinbao set him straight:

> If there really are bad eggs and sons of turtles on this earth, it is no one other than you guys! All of you live in the yamen, but everything, including your food, drink, clothes, and expenses, comes from the people. According to what is just, you should work for the people. The landlords only know how to use big pecks and make loans at outrageous interest rates. But you officials won't govern it. Instead, you use your twelve-foot tongues to lick the asses of landlords! So you just tell me where I can find any eggs worse than you officials!

At this point, the police hanged Old Zhuan and beat Guan Yinbao and his companions, forcing them to sign previously composed confessions that the *yi cang* rebels were Communists.

Word about the posse captives spread to the CCP members at the Phoenix Mountain Mine. Liu Bingqian, a local youth who had joined the CCP partly because his mother had been brutalized by her gentry employer Liang Jinbang, took the news to the county seat, where Zheng Hongzhuan was working with Sacrifice League students and teachers from Beijing and Tianjin who were establishing national salvation centers inside the temples.[14] The CCP members in the Sacrifice League called a meeting to organize a demonstration against the Guomindang. Within less than forty-eight hours the CCP brought 2,700 peasants from Chen and Zhundu villages, 700 workers from the Phoenix Mountain Coal Mine, and 400 students from the nearby middle school to its headquarters in the temple for the tutelary god of the city. Zheng had brushed four main conditions on the protest banner:

Strike Down the Corrupt County Magistrate, Bai Zhifan
Strike Down the Police Chief Han Hu Who Murders People without
    Batting an Eye
Strike Down the Rotten Eggs Who Break the Solidarity of the National
    War of Resistance
Release All Political Prisoners Immediately

Bai Zhifan assured the Sacrifice League that he did not know about the five prisoners from Qilipu, and that he cherished the peasants as if he were their father:

> The love for one's parents is extended to mercy for the people. When we show mercy for the people, we treat their material well-being with care. This is the way of love in the world. If an official seizes people without purpose, this is an injustice.

The impatient CCP members led the crowd to surround the police department. Zheng Hongzhuan searched Li Baolong's room and found three falsified Communist papers, a little black book containing a list of Li's enemies, and a police report on the killing of Old Zhuan.

Upon making the police reveal the whereabouts of the prisoners, Zheng Hongzhuan led a small group to the fire god temple. Guan Yinbao and his companions were beaten so badly that they were unrecognizable. Zheng and Liu Bingqian were so enraged they broke into tears. Liu yelled for his comrades to:

Bring the bastard county magistrate in here and make him witness the crimes these poor masters have suffered! Just who after all has violated the Royal decrees! If the official doesn't want to serve the people, we'll cut off his penis! When the people stick a knife up his ass, he shouldn't think it's so far from his heart! Turn this rightside up and look at it another way. If the landlords were faced with this matter, then we could see his true inner feelings. He would cry out loud to his grandfather and the God of Heaven, and become a great filial piety son!

Several peasants carried the *yi cang* rebels to the tutelary temple, where Zheng Hongzhuan told the peasants and the miners everything about the behavior of the Guomindang district chief and the police chief, reading aloud the names in Li Baolong's little black book. At the urging of the crowd, Liu Bingqian proposed that the Guomindang uphold three conditions of indemnity: payment for the funeral services, including the hiring of cymbal players and singers and providing a four-inch-thick wooden coffin; a periodic subsistence payment to Old Zhuan's family for the rest of their lives; payment for the medical fees for the wounded persons. Zheng Hongzhuan then led the peasants as they carried Zhuan's corpse through the streets to the magistrate's office, where they remained until the government made an indemnity payment. Then, and only then, did they return to their villages.

Not long after this, in the autumn of 1941, Liu Bocheng brought the 129th Division to Phoenix Mountain, and the CCP there established a Fourth District government with headquarters at Qianzhai. The villages around Qianzhai began coming over to the CCP by the hundreds.

In Qilipu Guan Yinbao and his companions organized a village self-defense team and set up a peasant association, with headquarters in the goddess of mercy temple. From this time on, the peasants made the regulations governing village affairs, and the world of Li Baotai began falling apart. The peasants elected one of the *yi cang* rebels as village chief, replacing Li Baotai by a vote of 736 to 7. They sent Sheriff Dong to a labor reform team for disrupting the village electoral process. And they brought strong pressure for Li Baotai and another powerful landlord to pay the entire sum of grain requested by the Eighth Route Army to fight the Japanese around Motian Ling.

The peasants made the grain tax for the Anti-Japanese War a key issue in village politics. Guan Yinbao originally proposed that the village pay 30 percent and the two landlords 70, the CCP formula to make the rich share the grain tax for the troops and thereby win the poor to the national struggle—but the peasants in Qilipu demanded that the landlords pay it all. They had no way of predicting the future demand for grain supplies for the troops. If the war were to worsen, they reasoned, the landlords might try to hold them to this 30/70 precedent.

But Guan Yinbao knew it would be very hard to make the two landlords pay the 230 *piculs* and 600 dollars the Anti-Japanese government was asking. It had been exceedingly difficult to make Li Baotai pay his *yi cang* debt and to lend a mere 30 *piculs* of unhulled cereals for a small detachment of the Eighth Route Army. Recalling the success of their *yi cang* protest, Guan Yinbao and the peasant association representatives presented the 30/70 payment plan to everyone at the goddess of mercy temple, and encouraged the peasants to deliberate and debate the proposal.

The landlords agreed to pay grain for fighting the Japanese, but they insisted the peasants share the tax burden on the basis of the number of family members and of land acreage. Li Baotai was against the 30/70 split with its rich-poor distinctions:

> How can we even talk about whether there are rich landlords here in our poor mountain village. All of us have only half-a-year of grain and then we must get by on bran and vegetables. You can distinguish only two kinds of people here—the "big poor" and the "little poor." I always support the Anti-Japanese government. From the outset, I knew our government would handle matters equitably. The ancients often said "justice to the masses is not without principle." When handling affairs I always depend on conscience.

The peasants were infuriated by Li's Confucian logic because, in their minds, Li Baotai was saying "a just tax wasn't for those who had money to give money or for those who had grain to give grain" and that "if we want him to give a little more, then no one in our village has a conscience!" Many still insisted that the two landlords pay the entire tax. The majority begrudgingly agreed to share the tax on a 30/70 basis, but only after Guan Yinbao assured them the landlords would pay seven-tenths of the grain tax.

Li Baotai, although maddened by these decisions, was willing to bend to peasant opinion because he was counting on Bai Zhifan and Li Baolong, who were in touch with the gentry and the Guomindang, to repress the peasants and the anti-Japanese activities of the CCP Fourth District government. These local power holders arranged to draw Zeng Hongnan, a Guomindang officer from Hebei, into their patronage network to smash the rebels. Li Baolong then established a secret liaison with the Japanese. Not long after the Japanese attacked the Fourth District, the Guomindang police chief, Han Hu, became a Japanese civil defense captain, Wang Manxi joined a mixed Japanese regiment, and Zeng Hongnan became commander of yet another mixed Japanese unit.

Originally Wang Manxi's Anti-Communist Corps, Han Hu's police gang, and Zeng Hongnan's troops were scattered regional "security forces" who struck terror into the hearts of broom makers from Wuan and brick makers from Lin *xian*. Now, with the Japanese army organizing them, these armed security forces launched a counterrevolution against the peasant movement around Phoenix Mountain, where they murdered many of the CCP members and Eighth Route Army war service workers.

At this point, the CCP response to rural repression and the CCP Anti-Japanese War of Resistance converged. Liu Bingqian and Fang Zhengkui organized the people's militias in the Fourth District into a broad network of basic cadre teams, which they coordinated with the Phoenix Mountain mine workers' anti-Japanese self-defense team. Along with Liu and Fang, Guan Yinbao led these teams to defend their home villages and the CCP headquarters at Qianzhai. The people's militias teamed up with the Eighth Route Army to capture 700 prisoners, kill 200 persons, including Li Baolong, and surround Zeng Hongnan's one hundred ragtag soldiers. This victory put the Fourth District of the Taihang in CCP hands for the remainder of the Resistance War, and thereby consolidated the revolts of peasants in Qilipu and surrounding villages.

Perhaps the potential for landlords to act in an exploitative manner existed in the weak vertical bonds that supposedly characterized relations between landlord and peasant prior to the twentieth century, as Barrington Moore, Jr. has argued.[15] But the peasants in Qilipu were revolting against worsening exploitation that seems to have had its origins in changes in local politics and society, stemming ultimately, as I already suggested, from the fiscal crisis of the Republic. Revolts to lower salt prices and regain relief grain grew out of peasant efforts to stop local power holders from starving them. The collective thrust of these protests should not obscure the fact that revolt began and sustained itself with the acts of individual peasant families to regain their rights to harvest and home. When peasants like Guan Yinbao joined the CCP they were fulfilling a promise to parents and grandparents to right the wrongs of the past, a past that predated the 1921 birth of the Communist party itself. The CCP derived its legitimacy from supporting the independently gestated revolts of these semirooted peasants.[16] Exhausted in their pursuit of extravillage strategies of survival, these migrant hired hands, tenants, and herdsmen were fighting for their right to return to native roots. Not to wage this fight was to allow landlords like Li Baotai to close off the village to anyone they could run out of it. The revolutionary initiatives of the semirooted peasants drew support from the rooted peasant majority because of this frightening realization.

The "contest mentality" of Qilipu's peasant leadership was itself a critical component in the process whereby the CCP and its insurgent army moved toward revolution. It is not enough to look solely at official CCP policy directives on issues like interest reduction. This mode of inquiry, which begins and ends with the CCP as vanguard,[17] draws attention away from the reality being produced through a process influenced by peasant instructions to the party. In recruiting peasants whose protests expressed folk visions of justice and mercy the CCP undoubtedly found itself opening up the possibility for the country people to define their own passage to power. Peter McPhee's great essay makes clear that the folklorization of politics was as important as the politicization of folklore in the development of rural radicalism among the peasants of nineteenth-century Mediterranean France, and that peasant loyalties with the left thereafter "became synonymous with allegiances to their popular culture."[18] Imagine how much greater such a possibility was in the upper zones of China's Taihang Mountains, where peasants did not have to contend with an all-powerful central state and where the CCP itself had not yet become such. Here the CCP was playing to themes in popular culture that reinforced the potency of peasant protest, and peasants were identifying the party's cause with the meaning they gave to their own electrifying actions. Thus, at the level of peasant beliefs, revolutionary legitimacy grew from CCP efforts to help rebels in backhill hamlets like Qilipu create a world in which the values of poor folk would prove decisive in shaping the course of local political struggles.[19]

The conception of justice articulated by the rebellious poor, which comes to us in the wittiest and wildest expressions of folk culture, is in line with the notion that Confucianism was, at bottom, felt to be illegitimate by the country people. Nonetheless, peasant radicalism could never have reached its mercurial breaking point without local power holders having repeatedly violated the socioreligious rights of the rural folk in the decades before the coming of the CCP. The power wielders in Qilipu treated even the modest survival claims in peasant protests as an illegitimate attack on the values of the Great Tradition, and they sought to rationalize their exploitation in an ideology that enabled them to deal with the inconsistency between their beliefs and their immoral actions. Their turn to Confucian morality was of course a natural reaction to a growing peasant challenge to a hegemonic landlord value system. But the tendency of landlords like Li Baotai to rationalize their violations of the popular customs surrounding birth, marriage, and death by flaunting their empty Confucian notions of accountability escalated little squabbles into class collisions. This, plus militarist repression, drove peasants whose remedialist protests started from conservative social concerns toward a radical confrontation with local rulers. The confrontation produced a peasant countersociety capable of developing on its own, in radical opposition to the Confucian model of society and state. The CCP derived its legitimacy in part from supporting the peasants' struggle to replace the Confucian rationalizations of landlord and warlord misrule with their order of folk justice and morality.

What made for a rapid and resilient peasant mobilization here was the undaunted capacity of poor villagers to compete, partly on the basis of local solidarities, with weak outside political forces, particularly Western missionaries and Chinese militarists. Quite apart from anti-Confucian values, the religious beliefs and class experiences of peasants in poor Taihang

Mountain villages coincided to reinforce a shared identity and purpose. Unlike the villages where Roman Catholic priests had attempted to convert Buddhist peasants to a Christianity that lacked a genuine interest in the New Testament's liberating creed that "the last shall be first," Qilipu peasants had not had their folk religious beliefs reworked by the teachings of French, Italian, and Dutch Catholic orders. To be sure, their teachings had engendered peasant resentments that exploded into riots in the day of the Boxers, but the real conversions also had complicated revolutionary mobilization for the CCP during and after the War of Resistance.[20] In this sense, the slowed growth in Catholic missionary work from the outbreak of World War I until the beginning of Guomindang rule was a blessing in disguise.[21] In villages like Qilipu peasants could openly express their folk Buddhist dissent against local power holders without fear of reprimand from foreign priests, and the CCP did not have to contend with splits between Catholic and Buddhist believers. Moreover, in these villages the CCP was able to recruit peasant rebels who themselves could mobilize village-wide followerships on the basis of culturally rooted dissident religious ideas that were still intact and that consequently reinforced the meaning peasants gave to their experienced suffering at the hands of landlords, gentry, and Republican government. Thus, although the Catholic Church equated the CCP with the hammer that struck down peasant religion, many of the vanguard peasant members of the CCP most likely were seen by poor villagers as living Bodhisattvas and the carriers of a prized mother goddess tradition rooted in the soil and soul of peasant China. This tradition, with its apocalyptic possibilities, had outlived the fall of Imperial China, and the CCP was now directing its propensity to collective action against local power holders who seemed determined to destroy its moral defenses. In the Taihang Mountains these peasant mobilizations drew their resiliency not from the CCP transformation of their socioreligious goals, but rather from the fact that the revolutionary army empowered them to remain *free* from the harmful influence of outsiders: bureaucrats, missionaries, and imperialist armies.[22] The Japanese Imperial Army, in particular, did not destroy the ability of these folk mountain villages to compete with its colonial order, for the Japanese were not able to bring the uncharted Taihang hinterland under their control. This fact was as crucial to building national resistance as to sustaining peasant revolution in the border region. It is time, therefore, to turn to the politics of war.

6

Revolutionary Legitimacy,
National Resistance,
and the Tensions of War

The Chinese Communist Party gained legitimacy by enabling peasants to replace the lawless landlords and warlords who had offended their basic sense of justice in the decades leading to the Japanese invasion of China on July 7, 1937. With the backing of the CCP and its armed forces peasants had begun to act out the moral indignation they felt from the failures of local power holders to uphold even a conservative version of *noblesse oblige* and Confucian rights to rule. The revolutionary goals of peasants, in this sense, did not exactly parallel the national resistance objectives of the top and middle-level CCP officials in the Shanxi-Hebei-Shandong-Henan border region government.

The Japanese Invasion and the Development of
Revolutionary Power in the Border Region

The net effect of the Japanese invasion was the weakening of the already weak central government presence, and the perpetuation of the conditions that gave CCP cadres the chance to buttress peasant struggles to take power locally and to involve peasants in building up a more than make-do political economy from the villages, mines, and markets of the border region. Seen in terms of the CCP's prospects for survival and growth, the Japanese invasion proved a plus initially and over the long run. This does not mean, however, that the actual presence of the Japanese army automatically proved a boon to the growth of the peasants' revolutionary power. The Japanese army periodically concentrated its forces to hammer down on the CCP-led peasant movements, shattering the subsistence underpinnings of the revolutionary political economy and swinging the pendulum of power back to the pseudo-Confucian landlords who had ruled the roost before the Liu-Deng army had rushed in. What permitted the CCP to maintain the initiative, and in the process retain legitimacy, was its success in maximizing the gains peasants got from the contradictions in the regional, national, and international politics of our period and minimizing the losses peasants incurred in supporting the Anti-Japanese War of Resistance. Even so, in rising to meet the challenge of war, the CCP was not always able to proceed in perfect congruence with the peasants' goals of survival, roots, and revolutionary anarchism.

According to Chalmers Johnson, the Japanese invasion and the brutality heaped upon peasants by the Japanese army, rather than prewar peasant suffering, created the conditions that prompted the peasants to embrace the Chinese Communists, who "in their post-1937 propaganda . . . concentrated solely on national salvation."[1] Whereas Johnson stresses nationalism without millet, Lucien Bianco later contended that the CCP created the popular basis for its rise to power by supplementing its nationalist appeals with moderate agrarian reforms for the rural people.[2] Still other scholars, such as Mark Selden, emphasize CCP insight in dealing with prewar inequities and CCP initiatives in dismantling illegitimate formations of Republican power as the keys to party-led peasant mobilization for patriotic warfare.[3]

All of these approaches spring from a search for the formula that presumably permitted the CCP to stir up peasant enthusiasm *for resisting the Japanese army*. The problem is, however, that when focused on the emergent CCP-led Shanxi-Hebei-Shandong-Henan Revolutionary Base Area the Japanese invasion did not independently ignite powerful antiforeignism in the peasant masses, and there is little evidence that CCP cadres successfully transformed any real antiforeignism in peasant motivations into forms of revolutionary mobilization that relegated preexisting struggles for survival to a position of secondary importance within the broader political definition of national security posed by the CCP-led border region government.[4]

On the plains, the Japanese presence intensified the ecological disasters and complicated the CCP effort to help peasants recover their means of existence.[5] The Japanese grain requisitions and commodity blockades worsened the effects of the killer droughts stalking tillers in southern Hebei and northern Henan in the first five years of the war. From 1939 until 1942 the Japanese broke open the floodgates on the Fuyang and Dayun rivers, loosing more flood damage in the counties to the south where the CCP was making headway. Meanwhile, in the Japanese-occupied counties along the Beijing-Hankou railway and in the Japanese-Guomindang contested counties (Wuan and Ci *xian*) at the edge of the southern Hebei-northern Henan plain, the swarming locusts continued to spread their devastation.

The harvest crises associated with these disasters neither facilitated social revolution nor favored the growth of national resistance. Local CCP leaders found themselves frantically repairing dikes, distributing seeds for rush makeup planting, and providing relief grain to hungry villagers. In the peak disaster periods, the CCP cadres deemphasized the campaigns to reduce crop rents and recover family lands, which meant they had to surrender local struggles with landlords. If anything, the Japanese-induced devastation further dramatized the survival choices facing the country people, and this greatly increased pressures on the CCP to provide security.

Security, however, was a delusion with the Japanese on the offensive. When the Japanese pushed on across the plains they uprooted hundreds of thousands of peasants, who in turn fled to the Taihang Subregion in the hope of obtaining subsistence and protection there.[6] With this influx of war refugees, the CCP underwent a string of staggering supply crises, and the problems attendant to suddenly arranging food, shelter, and employment for these homeless peasants strained the grain supplies of the Taihang Subregion government right up until the end of the Anti-Japanese War. Worse yet, the Eighth Route Army under Liu Bocheng had to redeploy for river repair work on the open plains some of its detachments involved in producing their own crops on the great Taihang land reclamation project. This not only deprived Liu's subcommanders of the initiative in determining battle position and exposed the troops to intermittent scuffles in which Japanese gunfire reigned supreme; it also made it far less likely that the 129th Division could relieve the villages of the pressure to provide its food grains.

Much of the confusion over the impact of the Japanese invasion stems from the tendency to equate it solely with destruction. To be sure, in mid-1941 the Japanese army unleashed its infamous Three All offensive, a campaign to "kill all, scorch all, and loot all" of the country-dwelling civilians who sided with the CCP-led resistance. But during the early phase of occupation, roughly 1937–40, the Japanese Expeditionary Army and the Japanese Political Council began establishing client governments along the northern rim of the border region. These were designed to neutralize or win over the peasantry in part by replacing the nonreformist Jiang Jieshi officials with Wang Jingwei officials of a more reformist, more Confucian persuasion.[7]

Far more than the CCP's frugal army and financially strained village-base, the Japanese were prepared to offer protection and patronage to the peasantry. Taxed to the bone by wave after wave of Beiyang warlords, bandits, and Guomindang warlords, tillers with a bit of land figured they would retain as much if not more of their produce under the Japanese, and when the Japanese invaded their counties they were neutrals as often as nationalists.[8] In some instances they even seized on the opportunity presented by Japanese penetration to unshackle themselves from Guomindang rule, as when they rebelled against General Dang Enbo in Henan in 1942.[9] Far more than the Guomindang, the Japanese respected land and property rights, handed out seed loans, and offered technical advice on irrigation for the eastern and southern Hebei villages under their occupation.[10] A 1938 report by Liu Shaoqi,[11] head of the CCP North China Bureau, hinted that the party was finding it more difficult to win over the villages receiving foreign protection and patronage for its Anti-Japanese War of Resistance, and by 1941 Liu's concern was shared by some of the border region CCP anti-Japanese war cadres too.

The Japanese thus had every intention of incorporating the border region into their Greater East Asian Coprosperity Sphere, but they certainly did not intend to do this by making the villages more vulnerable to the resource collecting associated with their administration. The Japanese taxed the villages, to be sure, but there is little evidence that *initially* they took so much of the harvest that they stirred rancor and rebellion. Unlike the Central Army they paid—rather than impressed—peasants for road work and war-related porter or scout work, and they evidently attempted to compensate peasants for injuries incurred in performing these tasks.[12]

The direct military presence of the Japanese did not make it any easier for the CCP to continue supporting peasant struggles for survival or cultivating a peasant commitment to its national resistance army. Once the Japanese swept down the Beijing-Hankou rail line in September of 1937 and then concentrated troops and technology in the border region rail towns— Baoding, Shijiazhuang, and Handan in Hebei, Dezhou in Shandong, Yangquan in Shanxi, and Anyang in Henan—they began to impede CCP efforts to liberate the peasantry and build up a national resistance movement with strong intraregional linkages. The CCP received some of its heaviest casualties of the war in the Japanese-garrisoned villages of southern Hebei and northern Henan from 1939 to 1942.[13] In these same years, landlords often led their armed retainers to form the so-called peace preservation committees against the CCP, and they helped the Japanese organize local police forces to keep the "criminals" and "Communists" out of the villages. Moreover, a number of Guomindang commanders, including Sun Dianying and Pang Bingxun, either failed to contest or collaborated with Japanese attempts to garrison the county-level capitals east of the Taihang.[14] General Pang, the Guomindang warlord who had suppressed the Heavenly Gates, fled Lin county in the midst of the CCP fight with the Japanese around 1942, and shortly thereafter showed up at a Beijing conference sponsored by the Japanese general Okamura. By 1943–44 Pang was back in the border region placing his command in the service of a Japanese campaign to crush the Eighth Route Army.[15] In this situation, the CCP armed forces found the going extremely dangerous, and had to engage in holding operations that were of little benefit to the peasants of the occupied markets and towns.

If the odds were so much against the CCP, then what political developments enabled its underdog Eighth Route Army to continue orchestrating peasant movements and organizing national resistance in the border region during the long war years?

To begin with, Mao Zedong and Zhu De persuaded the CCP officers to put aside their competing claims to autonomy of command in order to serve as the armed forces of the party, the peasants, and the whole country. This possibility was in the cards prior to the Japanese invasion, but it was during the War of Resistance that Zhu De recruited a main crack regiment whose role was to assist people's militias against landlords, to help the regular army divisions protect their respective territories in the Taihang, Wutai, and Luliang mountains, and to join with them for strikes against the Japanese. Commander Zhu De's crack regiment, which was stationed in Wuxiang county along the Zhang River in the Taihang area,[16] was able to provide cover for the 129th Division dike workers, and the CCP armed forces thereby restrained the Japanese from wreaking further havoc on the ecology of the border region. Meanwhile, the Liu-Deng 129th Division was able to release some of its units to grow food in the Taihang area throughout the Anti-Japanese War.[17]

Second, the Japanese began alienating the peasantry by substituting terror and outright plunder for protection and patronage. If the Japanese had plans to replace the Guomindang warlord regime with a patron-client Confucian order that would lessen peasant suffering,[18] they undermined these plans by surrendering the villages to the fanatical military police and to extremely cruel landlords.[19] The military police seized peasants suspected of cooperation with the CCP and tortured them mercilessly. Meanwhile, the Japanese officers attempted to rule the villages beyond the fortified towns by relying on the landlords who had refused to heed the peasants' remedialist protests, and who, subsequently, had become the target of the redistributive campaigns being carried out by the peasants under the protection of the Eighth Route Army. It seems these Japanese officers were seduced into becoming the patrons of the local Chinese landlords. Many of them, of course, hailed from feudal landlord families and shared their clients' disdainful and despotic attitudes toward the peasantry. This, plus the existence of interlocking military police and landlord interests in drug-racketeering and rent-racking schemes, explains why peasants eventually came to identify the Japanese with landlord evils and with political order based on yet another harmful vertical division of labor.

In this political context the CCP cadres were able to slip in and out of the semicolonized villages to develop antiforeign resistance by appealing to peasants who equated the Japanese with false cargo prophets and pro-Japanese landlords with false benefactors, both out to fleece poor folk. By the outbreak of the Pacific War in December of 1941 it had become clear that the Japanese army could not sustain its drive in the Shanxi-Hebei-Shandong-Henan border region without resorting to requisition. As in Manchuria and New Guinea during World War II,[20] once the Japanese military position worsened in the border region the peasants were reimbursed less and less for grain, timber, and labor services. By 1942 the Japanese army was engaging in all-out pillage. Consequently, the CCP cadres who were enabling peasants to garner immediate benefits increasingly gained the upper hand in struggles with landlords who were promising peace and patronage with a future Japanese victory.

Finally, revolution and resistance flourished within the border region largely because of the late timing and the political weaknesses of the

Japanese invasion.[21] In the first three years of war the Japanese failed to effectively develop their counterinsurgency operations into the CCP's Taihang Mountain strongholds beyond the Shanxi-Hebei and Shanxi-Henan borders, thereby leaving open the geopolitical gaps in which the oppositionist CCP armed forces could survive, grow, and fight. Hence the commanders of the CCP were able to establish their Anti-Japanese Resistance War bases up in the Taihang and Taiyue mountains beyond the reach of Japanese technology and troop strength.[22] It was not yet the age of counterinsurgency by helicopter and infrared scanning devices. The revolutionary army, therefore, could disperse its troops to assist peasants and concentrate its forces to attack the Japanese—as when the 129th Division teamed up with the 115th to burn twenty-four Japanese airplanes at the Yangmingbao airfield and then wiped out a lone thousand-man Japanese contingent near Mashan village outside the sphere of Japanese military superiority.[23] Just as the initial CCP army victories that established the Taihang base and elevated the confidence of peasants in the army were won in Shanxi at Taigu, Wuxiang, and Licheng in 1938, so the military successes that enabled the CCP to establish its branches in Henan at Lin and Hua county, in southern Hebei at Wei county, and in western Shandong at Linqing and Gaotang all unfolded from the heart of the Taihang Military Subregion from 1937 to 1940. According to Liu Qi, the Shanxi-Chahar-Hebei base area also was founded from the northern Taihang Range through victories scored by the CCP armed forces in the years before 1940, when the Japanese began a drive against the Taihang market towns to the north of Shijiazhuang.[24]

Whether the rise of the CCP was due in part to its Machiavellian maneuverings within the Second United Front remains an important issue. According to both Johnson and Bianco, the Japanese invasion prompted the pro-Guomindang officials to flee their posts, leaving the Chinese Communists to step into the political void.[25] Elaborating on this thesis, Tetsuya Kataoka has asserted that the CCP drew the central government into the War with Japan so that it could build up bases in the counties where the beleaguered Guomindang army was crumbling under Japanese pressure.[26]

In that the Japanese invasion destabilized Guomindang power in the border region, the Johnson-Bianco thesis is close to being correct. The Guomindang officials fled to the cities and the Guomindang troops mutinied and carried out a tumultuous retreat to the countryside in face of the oncoming Japanese army.[27] Whereas the invasion placed a new constraint on the capacity of the Central Army to constrain the CCP guerrilla army in the Taihang Mountains, a number of additional factors seem to have made it possible for the CCP to spread into counties where Guomindang power was on the wane. As we saw in previous chapters, the Chinese Communists—not the Japanese—gave illegitimate pro-Guomindang landlords the boot in the villages of the Taihang area. During the War of Resistance the CCP was able to use land-mine warfare to keep the Japanese out of these villages, and thereby insulate its peasant base from both Guomindang and Japanese interference.[28] Also, the low military priority assigned by the Japanese to the weakly fortified towns of the periphery meant that the Japanese commanders in places like Lin county and Lucheng did not have the strength to do more than occupy the richer market villages linked to the towns by passable dirt roads.[29] This permitted the Liu-Deng 129th Division to send small groups of soldiers down from the high country to build up peasant power, slowly but surely, in the districts beyond the archways of the Japanese-held county-level capitals. Finally, by forging alliances with Guomindang commanders like Fan Zhuxian in northwestern Shandong, General Liu Bocheng was able to keep down the scale of the collaborationist forces employed by the Japanese against the CCP-led border region government in the early phase of the war.[30]

What the political vacuum theory misses, moreover, is that the CCP was expanding outside of the Second United Front in the middle of the Anti-Japanese War. In these years, roughly 1939–42, Jiang Jieshi refused to commit the crack divisions of the Central Army to the defense of the border region; and yet the Guomindang warlord governors in Shanxi and Hebei, Yan Xishan and Lu Zonglin, launched a counterrevolution against the CCP-led peasant movements in the Hebei-Shanxi-Henan triangle. When these second-rate Guomindang units slaughtered two thousand CCP members and captured hundreds of non-Communist patriotic teachers and students from Beijing, Tianjin, and Shijiazhuang in 1939, Liu Bocheng led the 129th Division from the Taihang Mountains to annihilate the Guomindang 41st and 71st armies in Lin county.[31] The Liu-Deng army reportedly had broken all of these Guomindang attacks on the Taihang base by 1942. In this sense, the CCP was expanding its power when the central government's threatened provincial military clients turned the Second United Front into a sham, leaving themselves vulnerable to a Liu-Deng counterattack that had the support of peasants they had pillaged over the preceding decade.[32]

Another explanation for the rise of the Chinese Communists is that of "people's war," the central assumption being that the CCP raised its national resistance army en masse from the peasantry to defeat the Japanese in direct battlefield engagements. The CCP did not recruit its regular army solely or mainly from the rooted peasantry, however. For the most part, the people who joined the Eighth Route Army in the border region were not tillers with ties to the land. They were quasi-peasants, expeasants, and nonpeasants who, like Tito's Partisans in Yugoslavia, had lost their local family roots.[33] By 1944–45 the CCP 129th Division was recruiting in the crowded villages of Wei *xian* and Nangong on the southern Hebei plain, but the vanguard of the main force was drawn initially and largely from the wretched nonpeasants in the Taihang subregion.[34]

Locally, the CCP-led resistance was formed by quasi-peasants who had

Deng Xiaoping and Liu Bocheng, leaders of the 129th
Division of the Eighth Route Army

spearheaded the CCP's village-based revolts—most were marginal and
semi-landless members of the local poor.[35] Along with smallholders who had
made up the backbone of the local Red Spear units, these rural people
formed the village self-defense teams and led the people's militias. En-
grossed in struggles to recapture local roots, they did not join the Liu-Deng
regular army. They often took leave from their self-defense units for family-
related agricultural obligations rather than military reasons, and they invariably returned home to work the land immediately after they had crossed
over county lines to team up with the 129th Division for a military action.

By 1941 the people's militia stood at 350,000, and its membership tripled
over the next four years of the War of Resistance.[36] A 1944 report, *The War
in the Taihang Mountains*, suggests that the militia, or its leadership, was
made up mainly of former migrants, hunters, and bandits.[37] In Lin county
these seminomadic people had migrated to the Taihang, only to return to
their home villages prior to the Japanese invasion, and they were barely
surviving as day laborers when they joined the CCP-led militia from 1938 to
1943. Fu Zhaomu, a homeless migrant, recalls joining the people's militia in
1943:

> When I was three years old my family was poor. This was in 1920. We lived in
> Fengjiakou near the western slope of the Taihang. To escape the drought, we
> went to Shang Huang village in Shanxi's Pingshun county. However, things
> became too difficult for us there. My father died when I was five. Then, in 1922,
> my mother's father, Shu Daoguo, arranged for us to return to Lin county, and
> to live in Yao village. When we came to Yao village we had no house and no

land. We were two families, that of my grandfather and my uncle. Altogether ten of us lived in a run-down temple on the western side of the village.

At first we rented eight *mu* of land from landlord Wei Xiaoguang. We paid fixed rent, at 80 jin per *mu*. But in the very first year there were natural calamities. Drought. Especially locusts. The crops were lost. Even the seeds were lost. All we had was a little property, mainly clothes and jewelry. But Jiang Erxing, the middle man who guaranteed the tenancy for us, took our clothes and jewelry to compensate landlord Wei. Landlord Wei said it wasn't enough. So at the end of the year, even though we had planted the eight *mu* in wheat, he took away the land to rent out to others.

After this our family rented two *mu* from a rich peasant named Shu Fugui. This too was fixed rent. Each year the rent was 150–160 jin per *mu*, or about 300 jin.

We also rented one *mu* of land from the temple association. The fixed rent on this land was 200 jin per *mu* each year. It was some of the richest land in the village. Richer than that of many landlords. This land was near the temple of the Buddhist child-sending goddess.

It was hard to rent the temple land. In the temple association there was one head. He was chosen from the landlords or rich peasants, or the better-off middle peasants. Even the poor peasants sometimes helped the temple head. I remember when landlord Yang Yaorong was the head he employed the middle peasant He Jinji and the poor peasant Xu Laogai to keep order. Xu was really a bad egg. He bullied everyone for the landlords.

With the two *mu* of rich peasant land and the one *mu* of temple land we had three *mu*. But this land could not meet our family needs. So my grandfather and uncle went to work as hired hands in the village and I became a cattle herder of landlord Wei Kailiang. I was about fifteen years old then. The year was 1932, or 1933. I forget. In the first year landlord Wei only gave me food to eat. I also got some worn-out clothes and shoes. In the second year he gave me 60 jin of grain. But then he dismissed me.

Then for three years, from 1934 until 1937, I went to work for landlord Yang Zhenye. He was stingy. I got wages in meals from him. It was hard. So I returned to tilling the temple land. I was a hired hand part of the year, a tenant another part.

Until rent reduction came along we barely survived from one day to the next. Then in 1943 when the peasant association was set up I ran across a member of the Revolutionary Anti-Japanese Government. His name was Li Daoyuan. He came to Lin county from Shihjiazhuang. He had been working in Ren village, just north of Yao village. Li Daoyuan asked me about my family situation. He advised me to join the people's militia. I did this. I received a half-jin of millet per day for militia work and a share of the crops we planted to some cultivable land near here. I still kept my other jobs. For the first time in years my family was earning enough to eat. Thereupon I became the militia instructor as well as a member of the peasant association.[38]

In Qinyuan the militia was made up of former bandits who had fled their villages when the Japanese first threatened the county, and returned several years later upon hearing that the Eighth Route cavalry was establishing people's militias to protect the villages. The militias also involved nonlocals, such as the desperate people who had fled to the Taihang from the Jinan area to hunt and trap their way through preinvasion dearth. With the Japanese getting in the way of their survival these mountaineers took to hunting foreign soldiers as well as wild pigs.

The people's militias were largely county-focused organizations. In the Taihang they helped peasants harvest the grain crops and protect the scarce timberlands to which the Japanese looked for food and firewood. Although devoted primarily to defensive acts, such as laying land mines and evacuating attacked villages, the militias took offensive action too, deposing landlords who were abusing peasants in the presence of the Japanese, intercepting grain coming in on Japanese-held railways, and teaming up with the 129th Division to attack forts and market towns in Japanese hands.[39]

The Qinyuan militia, for example, cut off the water supply and stormed the granary of the Japanese-held market town.[40] Under the leadership of bandits versed in breaking-and-entry, the CCP militia sneaked into the town to fill the wells with donkey dung and dead dogs, so as to contaminate the water and draw the Japanese soldiers to the banks of the Qin River, where they were targets for sniping from the hills. Disguised as peasant women on their way to market, five-man militia squads also entered the town and seized the grain upon which the Japanese depended. Many were killed in Japanese reprisals.

By 1944 there were 90,000 Eighth Route Army troops in the Taihang area. According to Mao Zedong and Zhu De, the vanguard of the regular army was drawn from the *youmin*, or rootless expeasant and nonpeasant riffraff.[41] The CCP, however, was not the only competitor for *youmin* services. When the Japanese occupied Puzhou in 1943, for instance, they reportedly sustained their Three All Campaigns by enlisting hundreds of vagrants and vagabonds from Puzhou and Taiping market towns, and with the aid of these elements they kept the surrounding villages under control until 1944, when the Japanese High Command drastically curtailed its military operations in the Taihang.[42]

Marx had feared the rootless "people without hearth or home" as a dangerous Lumpenproletariat ready to side with a Bonapartist military to bring about a backward-looking restoration with the support of conservative peasants.[43] The Chinese Communist Party was hardly free of this classical Marxist bias. Chen Duxiu, China's Trotsky, had looked on the Lumpenproletariat as an unorganized army of *Ah Qs*—of the dregs, beggars and thieves—who were not capable of the class loyalty and party discipline required of "true revolutionaries." Breaking with the Chen Duxiu line, Mao Zedong envisioned these same wretched human beings as the potential recruits for a vanguard counterforce that could save peasant China from imperialist and militarist domination. To Mao, the CCP turn to the *lumpen* poor was natural and logical. For one thing, CCP leaders like Liu Bocheng,

Peng Dehuai, and He Long had grown up in a world that was teeming with Marx's "rootless proletariat in rags," and they had entered politics by leading armies of *les misérables* to enforce the survival protests of the popular classes during their youth. For another thing, the sheer necessity to survive, militarily, reinforced the compassionate logic of the CCP not turning its back on the poorest rural people. Otherwise, as in Puzhou, the Japanese would turn the *youmin* countryside into a recruiting ground for their plans to put down the peasant movements and smash the CCP-led resistance army.

Among the expeasants who joined the CCP armed forces in the border region were former petty thieves, migrants, and miners.[44] The recruiting grounds for these homeless people were the roadside temples where they congregated to wait for day work or, more usually, to contemplate their next act against lawless Republican officials. Like the intermittently employed people who wandered in and out of the border region coal mines, they joined the 129th Division shortly after Liu Bocheng penetrated the Taihang Range in 1936–37.

The uprooted migrants in the Taihang made up an important pool of revolutionary army recruits. One group was composed of homesteaders from the Henan plain, who hoped to protect their squatter's rights by farming out unmarried sons into the army.[45] Another group was made up of Taihang natives who had gone to Manchuria, only to return home after the Japanese takeover in September of 1931.[46] Over the course of the war these Taihang-based migrants would be joined in the CCP army by former migrants to Manchuria who were fleeing back down to their old home settlements on the plains of Hebei and Shandong. To them, Manchuria had become a second home, and they would fight with the CCP armed forces to reopen the Northeastern frontier where families and friends still lived.[47]

Finally, thousands upon thousands of deserters from defeated Guomindang warlord armies fled into the Taihang-Taiyue area. Contrary to any notion that they were defecting directly into the CCP's popular army, these formerly impressed peasants did not know much about the 129th Division, and those who did come over did not intend to stay on as regulars in 1937–38. They initially welcomed the good will of Commander Liu Bocheng's squad leaders only because they needed help in getting back to home ground.

The CCP armed forces forged alliances with three other groups to wage resistance war in the border region. From 1938 on Ji Degui led units of the 129th Division to link up with the Heavenly Gate members who had been hiding in the Taihang Mountains, and then brought this force down the Zhang River valley to unite with peasants in former Heavenly Gate strongholds like Ren village in Lin county.[48]

In these same years, the CCP army took advantage of the Guomindang failure to accommodate the oppositionist Red Spears. This was not an altogether new alliance. Peng Dehuai, the deputy commander of the Eighth Route Army, had been recruiting the *lumpen* Red Spears from South China hill villages since 1929, and now the Liu-Deng 129th Division was attracting them in border counties like Wei *xian*, Nangong, Hua *xian*, and Neihuang. Official CCP policy was to negotiate with the Red Spear gentry to bring them into the partisan war committees of the Second United Front, but the cadres simultaneously worked alongside the mobilizing Red Spear peasants to overthrow those who actively opposed the redistributive changes and power shifts being engineered locally by the peasant associations.[49]

Lastly, in September of 1936, on the fifth anniversary of the Manchurian incident, Bo Yibo, a member of the CCP North China Bureau, fled Guomindang oppression in Beijing to form a United Front with Yan Xishan and to found the Anti-Japanese Sacrifice League in Shanxi. The young CCP teachers and students in the Sacrifice League worked with peasants to set up provisional county-level administrations and to send Communist party commissars to help reorganize sections of Yan Xishan's National Guard and Shanxi army. Then, on the eve of the fall of Taiyuan, Bo Yibo formed the Dare-to-Die Corps to begin mass work and guerrilla warfare in Xin county in the Taiyue area and in Hong Dong, Zhao Cheng, Xi *xian*, and Xiaoyi in far western Shanxi. Bo subsequently teamed up with the 129th Division and Yang Shoufeng's People's Army to establish the border region government presence in the southern Taihang.[50]

Accompanying the 129th Division in its lowland expeditions from the Taihang were nonpeasant boatmen, porters, and ironsmiths. The ironsmiths of Tiger village along the Jiangjun River apparently had served the Boxers decades before the War of Resistance, and now they were offering their skills to the Taihang Eighth Routers from the war god temples near their villages.[51]

The major mission of the CCP resistance army was to shield the peasants in the liberated counties without relying too heavily on them when the Japanese bore down. We may gain some insight to how this was accomplished by focusing on Wuxiang *xian*, one of the richer grain-producing counties in the Taihang, at the end of the terrible Three All.[52] Before February of 1942 the Japanese had deflated peasant support for the Wuxiang people's militia by killing more than a thousand persons. The peasants were blaming the militia for inviting repression, and the Japanese were enlisting traitors to unearth grain hidden in the hill caves. The Japanese assault was broken only when Zhu De divided his crack regiment into three platoons to carry out the 1942 Autumn Harvest Protection Movement. One platoon continuously tilled its own fields and helped peasants harvest. A second served as a firefighting unit, rescuing villages that were being torched. A third met the Japanese head on. In this way, the *youmin* warriors neither depended on peasants for their survival nor surrendered their resistance war mission to the peasantry's social goals.

The central government claimed that the Liu-Deng army offered the *youmin* the bounty of landlord grain bins and market-town riches. Certainly the *youmin* were attracted to the army by the prospect of sustenance. The 129th Division squad leaders arranged welcome banquets, complete with roast pig, liquor, and tobacco, which the *youmin* received with suspicious gratitude.[53]

The promise of subsistence in and of itself, however, cannot explain why the *youmin* stayed with the Eighth Route Army. For one thing, ex-peasant recruits who deserted the 129th Division were not welcomed back by their home villages.[54] They were refused work and ridiculed for deserting. Many of them, like He Endai from the 5th Company, felt guilty about the market fair reports they received from refugees whose relatives had been killed by the Japanese in areas unprotected by the army. So great were the village pressures for these ex-tillers to return to the 129th Division that the army could afford to be lenient toward deserters. In fact, the CCP county-level governments sent them travel money, and the resistance soldiers praised them for returning to their units.

For another thing, the CCP's internal army campaigns to keep the *youmin* elements in the army were aimed at transforming the quality of their lives. Ma Renyi, a model squad leader in the 129th Division, showed new recruits how to cultivate crops, sent peaches and get-well wishes to wounded soldiers, and taught illiterates how to read, keep personal diaries, and write essays for publication in *The People's Troops*. He also arranged discussion groups in which real and potential deserters could talk openly about their problems. But to change the bandit proclivities and lack of self-respect among these wandering people, the CCP cadres had to stop treating them as less than human. "At first," we are told,

> they were looked down on by others, and they kept to themselves and were apt to desert. We used mockery and punishment, but this created even more suspicion and distrust among them and the other, progressive recruits. So, we changed to praising even their slightest progress, and we adapted Ma Renyi's work style of patience and persuasion.[55]

Participation in the Eighth Route Army offered a form of surrogate kin solidarity for the dispossessed people who had been brutalized by the twin failure of the central government to integrate them into its militarist state-making schemes and of landlord-dominated Republican government to develop employment choices for them in commercially based enterprises. For the rootless *youmin* to join the CCP armed forces was to re-create the strong protective bonds that had been lost when their families and lineages had been pushed off the land. The resistance army was their homecoming and their rerooting, their only hope to re-create a redemptive community in which norms of trust, sharing, and respect might reverse the slide toward hunger, uprooting, and a Hobbesian world. To these people, the Japanese army was but the latest in a long train of predatory armies, and their participation in the resistance army made them aware that the Japanese were a threat to the social bonds that made life possible and worth dying for. In fighting with the 129th Division in the Anti-Japanese War, therefore, they were fighting for the human decencies to be gained through involvement in an emergent revolutionary brotherhood. The willingness of CCP members like Ma Renyi to share the sufferings of war and die alongside them in battle, not CCP appeals to nationalism, cemented their commitment to this fraternity. This willingness removed lingering doubts the *youmin* harbored about being sacrificed to yet another army whose leadership cared more about riding to national power than defending the interest of poor folk.

The democratization of officer-soldier relations signified a final break with Guomindang warlordism and strengthened the *youmin* commitment to the Eighth Route Army. At the company level, the CCP political commissars sanctioned the right of soldiers to hold meetings in order to make decisions on the internal army practices that had dehumanized and destabilized Guomindang commands. The account books of the 129th Division were open to review, and soldiers could challenge officers suspected of embezzling troop pay. In the same years that Jiang Jieshi's officers instituted the death penalty for Guomindang soldiers, Zhu De, Peng Dehuai, and Liu Bocheng were upholding the right of Eighth Route Army soldiers to convene meetings to demand the dismissal of officers who persisted in administering beatings. It was this democratic process, and the security and dignity the soldiers derived from it, not the Japanese threat, that engendered fraternity within the CCP armed forces and produced the solidarity needed for the struggle to drive the Japanese back where they belonged.

Stuart Schram has shown that as early as 1929 Mao Zedong had been recruiting the *youmin* into an oppositionist army in South China.[56] The fundamental question to which the early CCP base area experiments in South China failed to provide a correct political answer, however, was how the *youmin* were to avoid harmful dependency relations with the peasantry. Faced with precarious food and arms-producing resources, the Red Army had fallen short of self-sufficiency in the Jiangxi Soviet. The uprooted soldiers originally had provisioned themselves partly by cultivating mountain land and partly by confiscating the food grains of lowland-dwelling landlords. When the Guomindang warlords reduced the territorial security of the Jinggan Mountain base area, however, a part of Mao's partisan army had fallen back on the rooted peasantry for food, pack animals, and fuel supplies, and the resulting tension doubtless underscored the dangers of overdependency to Zhu De and Liu Bocheng. Consequently, the War of Resistance saw the Liu-Deng army producing its own foodstuffs and even striving for surpluses to be traded in border region markets. By these practices, the 129th Division alleviated much of the tax burden placed on peasants by past armies, though self-sufficiency in grain production was never fully achieved in wartime.[57]

The CCP army eventually extended its nonpredatory practices to its quest for war-related supplies, so that one cannot speak of continuing interdependence between rooted peasants and the uprooted *youmin* army. Instead, the Liu-Deng army ran much of the Resistance War on its own, without making burdensome demands on the peasantry.[58] In the Taihang counties that were free from the direct hammer blows of war, the 129th Division formed a movable storage-supply system.[59] This system faltered from time to time, as when the 1941–42 Japanese Three All and the 1946–47 Guomindang counterrevolution panicked the carriers and carters, but generally it reduced the need to requisition foodstuffs from the villages.

The problem of arms production remained critical throughout the war, but was resolved in part by warlord complicity and Eighth Route Army creativity. Due to the early CCP alliance with Yan Xishan, the Sacrifice League was able to get weapons from the Shanxi arsenal to the Liu-Deng troops in the Taiyue area. In the meantime, the primitive arsenals set up by the 129th Division in Taihang and Wutai Mountain districts beyond the reach of Japanese power began to turn out hand grenades, rifle cartridges, and field artillery shells. By 1940 there were forty-one military-worker factories making arms and equipment for the 129th Division regulars and for the people's militias. In the following year the Liu-Deng army withstood a Japanese assault on the key Liang Guo and Huang Yandong munition plants, which were tucked away under the high cliffs of the Taihang. This success made it possible to move ahead with arms production and supply. By war's end the military-worker factories were employing some twenty thousand persons, who found war plant work highly desirable, especially for the prestige it brought them in their home localities.

Thus, just as the semirooted peasants had saved themselves when the CCP armed forces entered their localities, so now the uprooted regulars saved themselves. The rooted peasants did not depend on the CCP's *youmin* army to carry out the leveling movements inside the villages, and the resistance army did not overly depend on the peasantry to sustain and supply its patriotic guerrilla warfare against the Japanese.

The theory of "people's war" represents a further misconception of how the CCP won the War of Resistance in the border region. The CCP suffered serious military setbacks when its armed forces confronted the Japanese directly in nonguerrilla warfare. The Eighth Route Army was far more successful when it emphasized a "retreat to the hills and blend with the people's militias" strategy of resistance. The Hundred Regiments Offensive, wherein commanders Liu Bocheng and Nie Rongzhen combined one hundred regiments in the summer of 1940 to carry out mobile warfare against the Japanese along the railways crisscrossing southern Hebei, was the exception that proved the logic of this strategy. The CCP armed forces destroyed the Japanese fortifications and disrupted pacification programs, but the Hundred Regiments Offensive depleted the ranks of the regulars and precipitated a Japanese counteroffensive that culminated in the destructive Three All under General Okamura in 1941–42.[60]

These Japanese military campaigns drove the poor Eighth Routers out of the plains back into the Taihang Mountains, where they were able to regroup in poor villages that were not penetrated by the Japanese army. They could regroup in these villages because China's vastness and the start of World War II set limits on Japan's military commitment to North China. That commitment had stabilized at roughly two hundred thousand troops after 1938, and then slipped with the outbreak of the Great Pacific War.[61] Shortly thereafter, from 1942 to 1944 the Japanese commanders in the border region were obliged to transfer better-trained troops to the Pacific theater.[62] The CCP-led anti-Japanese resistance held on in Taihang Mountain villages beyond the reach of an imperialist army that was increasingly turning its attention from the Chinese regions that were to make up its East Asian Coprosperity Sphere toward the theaters of a Pacific war that was threatening its island homeland. Moreover, with the coming of the Pacific War, the Mao Zedong CCP in Yanan and its respective anti-Japanese base area leaderships saw that an informal alliance with Japan's democratic adversaries, the United States and Great Britain, would permit the CCP resistance army to grow as Japan encountered setbacks in what was becoming a war with the great powers over the global economy. Thus, by 1941 officials of the border region government had grown optimistic about Japan's weakened international position. They even began to investigate ways to win over people in the Japanese-occupied areas once the anticipated outbreak of war between Japan and the Soviet Union weakened the value of the pro-Japanese Wang Jingwei currency,[63] though the Japanese-Soviet Neutrality Pact of 1941, which sprang from Stalin's obsession with avoiding a two-front war with Japan and Germany, gave them cause to reconsider Soviet intentions.

The Renewal of Exploitation under the Japanese and the Resiliency of Revolution and Resistance outside of Imperialist Power

With the Japanese occupying the counties along the major railways of the border region peasants once again experienced a setback in their struggles for survival. The Japanese occupation gave landlords a new lease on life. Rather than flee the villages and towns, a large number stayed on to actively welcome the Japanese army in order to reestablish their power locally. These landlords assisted the Japanese in their attempt to smoke out the CCP village branch cadres inside their districts, and they simultaneously began tearing up the subsistence agreements peasants had renegotiated under the shield of the Liu-Deng army. The years 1941–43 saw them turning the tables on tillers in their domains.

To the landless peasants who had to rent land from pro-Japanese land-lords, it suddenly was 1930 all over again. After the landlords of Wuan county linked up with the Japanese army, for example, they shortened the tenure contracts and raised the crop rents of their original tenants in order to withdraw the land and re-rent it to desperate outsiders who would perform labor duties without pay.[64] Just as Japanese investigations of the CCP in Heshun county found that tenants kept more of the harvest in the presence of the 129th Division, so CCP reports lamented the crop rent losses tenants incurred in the districts and counties falling to the Japanese and their landlord collaborators.[65] In Wuan and Pingding, two counties within short reach of the Japanese-held railways, landlords not only took advantage of the political instability brought about by war to collect the rent by force, they also organized district-level police forces to collect "official grain" for the Japanese army from each peasant household.[66] Tenants were required to share the burden of the wheat tax. Those who wanted to retain their insecure leases, and salvage their gleaning rights on the sly, sent food grains to the Japanese tax requisition offices in the name of their landlords right up until 1944–45.

When the Japanese forced the 129th Division to withdraw from its for-merly secure districts, the peasant smallholders who made up the backbone of the Chinese Communist movement in the villages were left at the mercy of landlord usurers. The *Taihang New China Daily News* charged that these landlords subverted interest reduction and land redistribution in several ways during the War of Resistance.[67] They reimposed the same terms of interest that had produced the debilitating indebtedness for peasant land-owners prior to the arrival of the insurgent army, and they seized the peasant smallholders' fertile lands. Just as they transferred their land-tax obligations to tenants, they also attempted to shirk their village tax obligation by insisting that each peasant household pay an equal share of the grain tax to the Japanese occupation governments. Thus they were placing the burden of taxes on the peasant landowners, as they had done under the Guomindang warlords.

But why were the landlords so determined to undercut the survival benefits smallholders had recovered with the coming of the CCP? Initially, the peasant landowners had refused to pay any taxes to any army, and they had badgered the CCP cadres to place the responsibility for troop-support taxes at the gates of landlord households. Peasant anarchism. It had to stop. To landlords, it seemed the smallholders were borrowing to increase their own family incomes, and yet without any sense of gratitude whatsoever these same "little people" were using their mutual-aid groups to reclaim village wastelands, regulate public grain storage, and even collect grain taxes for the border region government. Peasant independence and free-dom. Where would it all lead? To make the smallholders pay taxes through the nose to the Japanese and their puppet administrations, and to refuse them the land and loans they needed for their cooperative production endeavors, would weaken their social capacity to re-create the self-governing free village that had come into being with the Liu-Deng army.

The Japanese occupation also jeopardized the well-being of the rich peasants who had provided gainful employment to landless and jobless tillers and who had paid a portion of their family earnings in taxes to help their home villages. Within the occupied localities the prosperous peasants of the New Democracy lost out to the rich peasants of the prewar Guomindang economy. In both Ten Mile Inn and Long Bow village the few prosperous peasants made their living by renting land and making ruinous loans to marginal villagers during the Anti-Japanese War.[68] By peddling salt for landlords with gabelle interests and selling opium for Japanese officers with a hand in drug traffic, these peasants inadvertently strengthened the leverage of the collaborationist landlords who sought to constrain the peasants' emancipating market initiatives in localities where the CCP armed forces had established firm controls.

Meanwhile, the CCP leadership of the Hebei-Shandong border districts was extremely anxious about wages plummeting with Japanese invasion. The landlords apparently took advantage of the Japanese presence to pare wages. Mediating the sharp disputes over wage cuts between half-starved hired hands and landlords threatened by inflation proved to be one of the biggest headaches of the Resistance War for the CCP's village-level cadres.[69]

Thus, as the Japanese attacked the eastern half of the CCP revolutionary base in 1939−42, the party encountered new hardships, and its attempt to defend its peasant base against the Japanese stumbled into more difficulty.[70] During the 1941−42 Three All along the Hebei-Henan border, for instance, the landlords who had been the target of the peasants' oppositionist revolts in the 1927−32 period came back to organize local vagrants, bandits, and army deserters to forcibly reinstate high rents and usury and to confiscate the crops. In the CCP Sha River district they joined with the Japanese army on April 12−13, 1941, to attack the core villages of the peasant movement. They killed more than a thousand people in Qiankou, Xue, and Yanggu villages, and destroyed a hundred other villages along the Xiao River before Taihang units of the 129th Division drove them back to their fortified positions along the Qingfeng-Puyang highway. In this same fateful spring came the drought that introduced the Henan Famine of 1942, and for the following year the more fortunate peasants survived by eating tree bark and peanut shells. The CCP Taihang Subregion government tried to relieve this suffering by shipping sorghum and beans to the Henan plain, but this precious cargo was subject to Japanese raiding. The cruel truth was that renewed peasant revolutionary survival endured only in villages that did not receive the major thrust of Japanese attacks. In the remote cloud-crowned Taihang area the CCP-led resistance was able to help the village people keep out the Japanese and survive through interrupted redistributive activities such as rent reduction, grain borrowing, and tax relief. But elsewhere, yet another wave of landlord cum militarist "taking" followed the formation of Japanese power until about 1943.

In the Japanese-occupied districts fixed grain taxes were collected by landlords for the Japanese army and the subsistence-first tax-collection practices that had constituted the moral cornerstone of the revolutionary taxation system of the CCP were overturned. If the CCP could move from tax suspension, to "subsistence first," to *heli fudan*, and then to the progressive taxation system in the secure districts of the Taihang Subregion, the party cadres had to discontinue taxes altogether in occupied districts so as to not increase the burden on the peasantry.[71] The CCP cadres in contested districts, where neither the CCP nor the Japanese held sway, still faced landlords who frowned on peasant suggestions that the village grain tax be divided between the protective Liu-Deng army and the predatory Guomindang army.[72] Throughout the war the CCP tried to make up the tax losses in the insecure districts by intensifying production, investigating hidden lands, and increasing taxes in the secure upland basins of the Taihang Range. There were, however, severe limits to this strategy. The CCP armed forces overcame these limits in part by expropriating the grain bins of the landlords who were in collaboration with the Japanese in the lowlands.

Japanese force also followed the CCP development of the free market and popular commerce in the revolutionary base area. After establishing military checkpoints in the market towns along the Beijing-Hankou railway, the Japanese blockaded the products entering the border region from the southern Hebei plain, raided the market villages where peasants and merchants carried on free exchanges, and sent "currency smugglers" and "commodity smugglers" to disrupt the currency system of the border region government. If the Japanese were intending to promote commerce so they could tax it themselves, they did not stop landlords from making a charade of their plans. The landlords deprived peasants of their right to choose between food and money crops, and engaged in speculative grain deals damaging to the price environment that had prevailed in the open peasant markets under the protection of the Liu-Deng army. The changes wrought under the Japanese thus deprived peasants of the benefits of free trade, and undercut the CCP effort to re-create a viable political economy from villages and markets that were short on capital to begin with and that still were served by extremely primitive transport routes.

Many of the skirmishes between the Japanese army and the CCP armed forces sprang from the intensifying struggle for basic commodity markets— especially grain. The Japanese knew that grain was the life-source of the CCP-led peasant movements and the golden bullion that underwrote CCP exports—the border region government exchanged grain to earn the money for purchasing the imports it distributed to develop other primary agricultural products, light industries, and munitions plants inside the revolutionary base area. If the Japanese could get control of the grain by making peasants and merchants exchange their primary goods within the markets of the occupied districts and counties, they could dictate the terms of peasant sustenance and deplete the border region treasury. Throughout the middle phase of the Resistance War the CCP Taihang-South Hebei Bank officials were concerned that Japanese progress in this realm was raising the fear of hunger in the villages and tilting the foreign-exchange rate against the revolutionary order.

With the Japanese troops marching into the base area and leaving the market villages bloody and bare,[73] the CCP called on its Trade Bureau cadres to institute a number of practices to offset the debilitating market consequences of Japanese carnage.[74] To begin with, the peasant associations formed grain accounting committees to adjust the amount of grain leaving the villages for the markets, so that hoarding and speculation by landlords and rich peasants would not leave any peasant family without a subsistence portion of grain. In addition, the villagers formed their own antismuggler teams for arresting and fining merchants who were carrying contraband items from the Japanese-held positions along the railways into the free-trade zones of the base area. Finally, the CCP Trade Bureau cadres had to redouble their efforts to export grain (mainly corn, millet, and sorghum) in exchange for basic commodities produced within the Japanese-ruled counties while they simultaneously placed restrictions on items used by the revolutionary army. Hence we discover a CCP foreign policy that stressed the opening of commodity exchanges in grain and salt, grain and cotton, and grain and lamp oil, while restricting exports such as iron ore, coal, leather, sulphur, saltpeter, nitric acid, and *aqua regia*—the fundamental prerequisites for war. By 1942–43 Luosongjia village in western Hebei and Ren village in northern Henan had become the gateways for exports of the base area, in part because their markets were more advanced. Nevertheless, the CCP continued to suffer in its struggle for the foreign exchange to be earned from exports, and as late as 1944 the South Hebei Bank cadres were reporting that the Japanese were winning the foreign exchange war by a two-to-one margin by virtue of their control of markets along the Beijing-Hankou railway and in the central Hebei plain.

In the final analysis, the CCP was able to firm up the free markets of the border region only by deploying greater concentrations of protective force. Its resistance army was far more successful in preventing the Japanese conquest of peasant markets in the impoverished Shanxi highlands, which held minimal attraction for the Japanese until the massive retaliation of the Three All. All in all sixty-six older marketplaces were re-established by the CCP national-purpose army in the Taihang area during the War of Resistance.[75] The more flourishing markets were in the remote localities of Guaierzhen, Tongyu, Suobao, and Xiying—all sanctuaries to the west of the Taihang escarpment. With few exceptions, the CCP 129th Division was able to prevent the Japanese military from undoing the community-strengthening processes of free trade in these markets and their sister markets in the lowlands to the east—Jencun in Henan, Yangyi, Yuantou, Yecaowan, and eventually Hengshui in Hebei.

The Impact of Japanese Military Presence on Peasant Mobilization and Chinese Communist Party Power

Clearly, the Japanese army was intensifying the war to undercut peasant mobilization and destroy the CCP. Yet the question remains: What, specifically, was the impact of the Japanese military presence on peasant mobilization and CCP legitimacy? To what extent did Japanese muscle prompt peasants to participate in the CCP-led War of Resistance, and thereby facilitate the party's attempt to enable peasants to realize their demands for roots, freedom, and power?

The Japanese army shattered the survival guarantees that were necessary for peasant families to piece their lives back together. The Japanese tore apart the fabric of village society, making it impossible for peasants to reroot in household economies and to generate the income that gave the CCP a productive social base. The warlord armies of Yan Xishan, Wu Peifu, and Pang Bingxun had been violating border region villages for decades, of course, and the Japanese "taking" of 1941–42 was different only because it was conducted by foreigners—the "dwarf devils," as peasants called the small Japanese soldiers. All the peasants could hope for was that the CCP army would make good on its commitment to preserve their chance to reestablish local roots.

With their basic means of existence constantly in peril, most peasants were unable to participate in the Anti-Japanese War. The Japanese presence, with its tolls on labor and its controls on market choices, clearly inhibited peasant involvement in the CCP-led national Resistance War because it intensified starvation and physical weakness.[76] If the border region government wanted assistance from the rural people, its officials first had to find a solution to the problem of livelihood. The peasants equated liberation with relief of family hardships far more than with resistance to physically superior foreign soldiers.

The problem was, however, that the Draconian antiguerrilla tactics of the Japanese shrank the scarce food supplies of the villages, making it more difficult for peasants to work the fields, push the grain mills, and carry the water, and there is no doubt that the spread of war dealt a heavy blow to the already weakened peasant labor force on which the CCP pinned its hopes for economic recovery and rejuvenation.[77] This problem presented itself in 1939–42 when the Japanese went after the guerrilla army in southern Hebei (Daming, Chengan, and Wei *xian*), where death rates reached 15–40 percent and refugee rates climbed to 30–90 percent of the population. It intensified when Guomindang commanders Pang Bingxun and Sun

Dianying implemented unlimited taxation in the Lingchuan war zone, in 1942–43. In Qinyang and Boai every peasant household suffered at least one death. Corpses were piled in mass graves along the major roads, and the bones of the dead were burned and eaten by the living victims of this militarist ravage.

The spread of war, and the internationalization of the preexisting Guomindang pillage, brought an avalanche of new obstacles to the peasant movement, and to the CCP army. The renewed breakup of peasant households was accelerated by a rush of divorce suits brought by women whose frail, wounded, or missing husbands could not support them.[78] The CCP tried to offset further destabilization of the family by organizing village mediation committees, made up of relatives and friends, to persuade women to return to their husbands, then passed an ordinance to prevent other women from ending betrothals to peasant soldiers at war.[79] The situation was so bad that in 1942, at the height of the Three All, Deputy Commander Peng Dehuai visited the Zhang River area in the Taihang to remind CCP officials that the rights of women were to be realized within the reunited peasant family, so that peasant household production for subsistence and national salvation in fact superseded the freedom of women to divorce and marry.[80]

Nor was the CCP able to exploit the crisis wrought by war to further inspire the family mutual-aid-group and village cooperative experiments that were so indispensable to the Great Production Movement. The Japanese were not about to stand by and watch the Chinese Communists extend the mutual-aid exchanges of the settled peasantry into horizontal associations of village solidarity and activism. As with the French in Algeria,[81] the goal of the Japanese was to pulverize the peasants' rediscovered forms of mutual cooperation, leaving the CCP with an insecure, noncohesive peasant base that was less able to collectively pursue its own survival and contribute to the revolutionary army's War of Resistance. In response to Japanese success in this sphere, the CCP cadres often resorted to a mobilization style that created an organizational abscess within the peasant movement. A CCP official put the matter this way:

> In general our party builds on the customary forms of mutual aid and extends these to village-wide arrangements brought together by participation in the peasant associations. In the new districts, however, there often is drought and flooding. The Japanese occupation exacerbates these disasters and adds a pressure of its own. This compels our party to resort to pressures of its own in mutual aid, and this often involves establishing top-down relations with the peasant associations. The peasant forms which can revitalize traditional mutual aid and inspire long run class cooperation were thereby by-passed. This often was done by commandism and a monopolist work style.[82]

When the war turned against the CCP around 1941 the party-induced village cooperatives in southern Hebei collapsed because the peasants were so thoroughly dissatisfied with their performance they withdrew en masse.[83]

The Japanese Three All was based on the logical premise that little families in flight, uprooted from their land, lineages, and livestock, could not find the time or the means to produce enough food crops for sustenance, let alone come together to generate the surpluses the CCP was out to stimulate. So devastated by the Three All were Dazhai village in Xiyang and Yao village in Lin county that peasants had to concern themselves with just staying alive.[84] The peasants who were able to start up continuous family mutual-aid projects in the CCP Great Production Movement lived in villages off the path of the invading Japanese army, and they did not establish the viability of this movement until 1944—the first good harvest year since 1938 and one full year after the Three All had spent its savagery against the Taihang Subregion. In the war-torn localities, the decline of mutual aid correlated with the decline of CCP fortunes, and the peasant movement lost its capacity to elicit collective discipline.

Even in the districts where the CCP was dominant, the mutual-aid groups on which the Great Production Movement was based were stricken with partial paralysis.[85] The basic problem was that when the Japanese scraped a village, stealing oxen or damaging oxcarts and wells, the material blocks on which the profit-share plans inherent in family and lineage cooperation were founded began to crumble. Moreover, peasant families who lost a member of their joint mutual-aid group to sudden Japanese strikes had to scare up the funds for funeral services, and then find ways to compensate for the loss of his labor input. Finally, the peasant mutual-aid-group leaders often had to attend CCP-sponsored war committee meetings to decide how to allocate people and plow animals for war-service work and how to arrange for substitute tilling groups to take care of the fields of members who were performing war-related tasks for the Eighth Route Army's battlefield operations. The loss of plow animals and property, the additional work demands on reduced membership, and the repeated absence of group leaders strained the accepted understandings of mutual exchange, and posed new problems in production.

By 1941−42 the Japanese were making it more difficult for the CCP to inspire the rural people to plan, produce, and save for their own immediate family needs, not to mention the long-run needs of the resistance army.[86] Many peasants were reluctant to renew production as long as the Japanese returned to ruin the dikes and raid the harvest. When the Japanese search-and-destroy operations in southern Hebei deprived the peasants of harvests and left the resistance government with less and less stored grain, the CCP responded by paring its officials by one-half, and by reducing the food provisions of its front-line soldiers to little more than one catty per day. Commanders Peng Dehuai and Liu Bocheng even gave up their regular pay in symbolic support of the urgent need to lighten the burden of government and get production going again.

One should not leap to the conclusion that the Japanese, by their brutal acts, spread the success of the CCP. On the contrary, over the short sweep of the Three All the Japanese occasionally overwhelmed the CCP effort to enable peasants to liberate their villages and markets and the CCP attempt to establish party branches powerful enough to carry on resistance. When the Japanese took over a CCP-held district they recruited the remaining landlord officials and Guomindang police and then proceeded to provide the military wherewithal for wiping out the CCP peasant cadres and war-service workers in the vicinity. The peasants, ill prepared to effectively withstand this repression, did not automatically rise up in solidarity against the Japanese. When the war tilted against the CCP in Wuxiang county during 1941–42 the CCP officials there found themselves having to mediate fights among and within peasant families over the issue of military service.[87] Wives tried to stop husbands from going with the guerrilla army in short-term local actions, parents hid the weapons of sons who declared their intention to fight with the people's militias. Moreover, with the Japanese torching the sorghum fields and gassing the huts and hill caves that gave cover to the CCP, fewer and fewer peasants were willing to risk reprisals by harboring members of the resistance. Repression made peasants fear and hate the Japanese all the more, but it certainly did not create conditions that permitted the CCP to organize the village-based peasant movements for its War of Resistance.

Japanese violence also tried the patience of the peasantry for the CCP attempt to construct a reliable anti-imperialist coalition. Take for example the national salvation elections.[88] In the Taihang area peasants originally participated in these popular electoral contests on platforms that spoke to survival needs, and insisted that landlords abolish rent and absorb the tax levy for troop support so that simple folk could resecure their livelihood. The CCP Taihang district officials arrested and sentenced to "labor-reform" the landlords who took advantage of the Japanese threat to disrupt these elections, but the peasants were upset by the sentences. They feared the landlords would return to the villages to take vengeance. This fear ran so deep that peasants often took the law into their own hands to kill those who violated the popular electoral process. To take another example, when the Japanese stepped up the war in 1941 the peasant guards who manned the CCP detention centers in the Taihang Subregion commenced a reign of terror against former landlords and officials who were apt to escape to the Japanese, and it was not until after the crisis of the Three All that the CCP courts were able to carry out their plan to reform prisoners by letting them retain some of the profits from their own production.[89]

The more serious matter, however, concerned the relationship of the rooted peasantry to the war-related work of the CCP. The CCP originally had won popular acclaim by showing that its revolutionary army did not intend to depend on the villages for survival and its friendship with the peasants was founded on a basic respect for the integrity of their survival routines. With the CCP losing the lifelines of its economy, losing the initiative in trade, and losing the currency wars waged by the Japanese, however, the party cadres had to resort to war-mobilization orders that carried a tremendous social cost for the rooted peasants. The war, with the burden of combat service duties borne by the rural dwellers, threatened to pull the peasants away from their fields and markets, and thereby jeopardize their survival. Unless it somehow eased the burdens of war-service work for the peasantry the CCP clearly ran the risk of imperiling the very basis of its legitimacy with the rural people.

Mobilizing and deploying peasants for war-service work in support of the Eighth Route Army proved one of the CCP's most pressing dilemmas of the War of Resistance. The peasants who had welcomed the 129th Division before the first application of Japanese force did not hesitate to demand a reduction of war-service requests, or even to resist the cadres who treated the villages as war colonies. Two problems would not go away. In the first place, as Ji Dengkui pointed out in reference to Hua county, not all of the peasant activists could separate from their agricultural production routines to support the Anti-Japanese War effort.[90] The mainline CCP cadres were the poorest peasants, and hence all the more preoccupied by problems of land and livelihood. In the second place, the CCP officials in charge of war-service work were obliged to provide assistance and relief to the peasants and miners who were exhausted, sickened, or wounded in the course of their travels to the front lines, and where this help was not instantly forthcoming the resulting popular alienation reduced the prospects for sustaining the Resistance War.[91] The demands of war-service work repeatedly fouled the CCP's relationship with the peasants, and underscored the conditional subsistence basis of peasant participation in the CCP's multiclass nationalist war.

It was in the Taihang Subregion that the CCP first succeeded in adapting the war-service requests of the Eighth Route Army to the subsistence requisites of the peasantry.[92] Here, in the relatively remote counties of Wuxiang, Zuoquan, Pingshun, Licheng, Lin, and Boai, the CCP gained the time and the tactical freedom to experiment with measures to ensure peasants subsistence and security in war-related work. The CCP Rear Service Command (RSC) was formed to ease the burdens of war duties on its peasant base. The practical experiments of the RSC emphasized the minimization of peasant losses in war-service work.

The RSC cadres respected the peasant need to avoid war service tasks that interfered with agricultural production routines. "The most important measure," writes Ding Ling, "was to strictly reduce the war oriented work of the peasants. In general the draft requirement was about three days service per month, and when the peasants were busy during the planting and harvest periods, the party stopped the draft altogether."[93] In addition, the RSC concentrated on recruiting peasants who had both the means and a reason to assist the resistance army. In the Taihang Subregion these peasants often turned out to be the smallholders who owned oxen and carts,[94] and who sent their unemployed sons into the army. When these peasants left their fields for front-line war-service missions, the RSC cadres arranged for others to help cultivate their family lands and allowed their households and mutual-aid groups to reduce grain tax payments.

Another RSC practice involved periodic relief for the peasants going to the battlefields in militia units, stretcher-bearer squads, and transportation teams.[95] The RSC cadres formed auxiliary teams before battles and staggered starts and stops to avoid idle waiting and battlefield exhaustion. They also organized the peasants into carter teams to assist their companions in villages burdened by unusually heavy war-service duties, bringing in the May-June harvest and seeding and fertilizing the fields.

The RSC cadres organized the people's militias under the Liu-Deng army to provide armed escorts for those peasants involved in moving grain, fuel, and ammunition to the battle zones and in evacuating the wounded soldiers from the front lines. And they led the medical teams in providing bandages and blood transfusions for the wounded peasants who were being carried by stretcher bearers to the 129th Division field hospitals. The RSC cadres also handled funeral arrangements, including provisions for a decent burial in the home village. Occasionally, deceased war-service workers received burials in the graveyard for the martyrs that was maintained by the 129th Division.

Still another measure taken by the RSC consisted of outside transactions, such as arranging employment for the peasants who left their home villages to perform tasks for the front-line soldiers, by tilling or harvesting the fields of labor-short peasant families in the localities to which they were assigned. This painstaking task had to be undertaken well in advance of the peasant war service participant departures and confirmed in the course of their travels toward the shifting scenes of battle. At the same time, the RSC cadres arranged for peasants to purchase what the markets at each destination point offered in basic commodities, such as persimmons, coal, and cotton, and to sell these items on the return trip.

Throughout much of the war the RSC was successful in ameliorating the burdens of war-service work and securing a conditional commitment from the peasants of the Taihang to its protracted guerrilla activities on the plains. Yet the pressures of war sometimes engendered production and supply crises that hurt both the war-service workers and the Eighth Route Army. In response to Japanese or combined Japanese-Guomindang warlord strikes, the RSC cadres deployed peasants in war-service tasks during the busy season and doubled the grain taxes in the rear areas to provision the front-line troops, which of course created strain between the rooted peasantry and the RSC cadres who were overdrawing on village resources.[96] The demands on base-area coal miners to participate in war-service work were so great, and the war casualties so high, that by 1945 the CCP-led resistance government faced a crisis in coal production because of the grave shortage of skilled miners.[97]

In the moments of Japanese military ascendancy, when peasants and miners could not count on the CCP and its RSC to alleviate the awful pressures of war, the popular commitment to the party weakened, and the risks rose considerably that national resistance would falter. The commitment of the CCP to improve on the war-service guarantees its RSC cadres had generated against the Japanese in the Taihang, and of the CCP armed forces to send detachments to relieve peasants of the more unbearable assignments, enabled the resistance government to hang on in the highlands and to spread the war down onto the plains in the years 1941 to 1945.

A Hypothesis on Japanese Invasion and the CCP's Resistance War Process—Revolution and Resistance Where the Japanese Were Not

In previous pages we have grasped the geopolitical importance of the Taihang escarpment, and witnessed the CCP raise its banners over the border region by addressing a whole set of social problems in Taihang peasant villages prior to the attempts of the Japanese army to pacify these villages during the Three All phase of its China War. The next question, then, concerns the importance the CCP assigned to these nonpacified mountain villages in the overall development of its Anti-Japanese War of Resistance. If the CCP was able to emerge as the champion of anti-Japanese guerrilla resistance because of the impact of the Japanese army, then we should find a strong positive correlation between the presence of Japanese power and the growth of CCP success in mobilizing peasants for the nationalist cause.[98] The relationship between CCP success and the presence of the Japanese army in the villages of the Taihang, however, was not so simple.

The CCP had to arouse resistance to Japan from occupied, raided, semi-free, and free villages. Semifree and free villages were linked with the rising national resistance fortunes of the CCP, while in occupied villages there was an inverse correlation between established Japanese presence and Chinese Communist power. The raided village was more complex than the others.

Hongshuling, a village on the Qinghua River at the foot of the Taihang in Shanxi's Lucheng county, was occupied by the Japanese from 1942 to 1944, some five years after the Eighth Route Army had entered Lucheng.[99] Here there was fairly firm Japanese control, and the peasants did not follow the CCP. A number of Hongshuling's peasants served as cooks, messengers, and squad leaders in the Japanese army. Moreover, the landlord peace preservation committee managed to requisition grain and repress the CCP women cadres without provoking widespread resistance on the part of the peasantry. In fact, Miao Peishi's report on Hongshuling admitted, once peasants perceived that the Japanese held a strong upper hand the CCP-led resistance could not form a village consensus on how to respond to invasion or rouse the people to resist Japanese demands. Hongshuling was not a solidly "peasant nationalist" village, and even though it had been under the umbrella of the resistance army before the Japanese gobbled it up, the CCP was unable to mobilize it on the basis of nationalist appeals.

Dazhai village in Xiyang county was different.[100] In Dazhai there were no firm Japanese or CCP controls. The CCP's tit-for-tat struggle against the Japanese in this raided (by both sides) village weakened its social fabric. The peasants spent most of their time and labor just trying to recover from the dreadful raids, and were hardly prepared to take the initiative in competing against the Japanese army. Many pro-CCP peasant activists were incarcerated and tortured right up until the liberation of the village on the Festival of the Dead in 1945. Other Japanese-raided villages in Xiyang were completely obliterated, leaving no peasants for the CCP to recruit to its national resistance cause.

In Dazhai the CCP followed the Japanese raids with campaigns to enlist the uprooted peasants in scout, message carrier, and grain porter work for its guerrilla army. Japanese violence created a caste of villageless people who came to equate their survival with service to the CCP armed forces,[101] and in this sense did favor CCP recruiting efforts. But was this *the* key to CCP success? Not really. Sandwiched inside the "free fire zones" that separated the forward flank of the Japanese army from the CCP strongholds deep in the Taihang, Dazhai was somewhat the rarity to begin with. The Japanese were desperate to clear the Chinese Communists out of such villages, and there is little evidence that the CCP gambled away its chances for victory by basing its war-service work or its army recruitment drives in them just when they were being decimated by the Three All.

Caught in the throes of war, Dazhai's peasants wavered until the outcome was no longer in doubt. The Chinese Communists were far more successful in mustering peasant resistance in Donghebao, a village in Pingchuan county.[102] Here the Japanese controls were indirect—they ruled the village through the village chief, landlord Ren Peihou. Located nearly ten *li* from the nearest Japanese outpost, Donghebao remained a low priority to the Japanese throughout the war, and by 1941 it was in the hands of the CCP-led rural revolution. A few hired hands and middle-school youths joined with just one armed CCP cadre, detached from He Long's 120th Division, to win over the village. After deposing the pro-Japanese clique, they compelled Ren Peihou to stop collecting tobacco rents by abnormally big scales and to stop flogging peasants who refused to plant tobacco. The peasants borrowed the name of the CCP cadre's army unit to scribble under the rent-reduction notices they pasted on the walls of surrounding villages, so that their quest for social justice appeared to be the product of the resistance army. Most interestingly, however, the CCP took every precaution against making Donghebao the object of Japanese retaliatory raids. The strategy was not, as the followers of Che Guevara have yet to learn, to turn villages into Dazhai-like death matches, unless the Japanese forced the issue. The strategy was to develop the semifree villages in the interstices of Japan's semicolonial hold on the interior into safe Resistance War strongholds, and to call on the Eighth Route Army to wage guerrilla war to discourage and divert Japanese attention from these seemingly insignificant settlements.

The CCP was betting ultimately on lilliputian homestead villages like Xikou, tucked away on the Taihang skyline of Pingshun county.[103] Here there were firm CCP controls, and the party catered to peasants whose survival concerns were not complicated drastically by invasion and the national emergency. Xikou was on neither central government nor Japanese maps. Its smallholders, tenants, and shepherds were Henan migrants in flight from landlords and Guomindang warlords who had carried out the anti-Communist rioting campaigns in the border region.

Twenty-three-year-old Li Xunda perhaps personified the migrants who shepherded the Chinese Communist movement in villages like Xikou. The son of an itinerant carpenter who had been put to death by militarists, Li had migrated with his mother and brothers to the Taihang during the World Depression in the footsteps of his maternal uncle, who had persuaded a landlord near Xikou to rent one *mu* of hill land to Li. The Li family had settled Xikou as a sanctuary from repression, and they and other Xikou inhabitants were prepared to resist outside authority well before they encountered the CCP. When the 129th Division entered Pingshun in 1938 Li Xunda and the other peasants who joined the CCP concentrated on rousing the hired hands in the employ of Xikou's absentee landlords to help them get back the grain being hoarded in secret bins.

None of Xikou's CCP peasant members followed the regular army to the front lines. They remained in Xikou to fight landlords for the harvest and to form mutual-aid groups for opening up hillslope lands that landlords had captured in the 1920s. They could carry on this fight because Xikou was untouched by the Japanese. It was from unmolested villages like Xikou that the CCP was able to organize the mobilizing peasantry to align with the people's militias for actions against pro-Japanese landlords in the market towns below.

From these indomitable Taihang Mountain hamlets, outside the field of Republican and Japanese force, the CCP resistance was establishing its own protective force around peasants in revolution. If it had not been for these nonpacified highland hideaways, the CCP could not have established the foothold needed in order to build up a strong anti-Japanese base area. Li Yingju's account of the CCP-led resistance in the Lingchuan war zone allows us to link our four-village typology to the process of Resistance War.[104] From the free mountaintop villages of the Pingchuan-Puzhou area the guerrilla army made contact with peasants in the semifree hill villages, then fought for the disputed villages in the upland valleys just beyond the Japanese trench lines, and finally liberated the Japanese-occupied villages,

The terraced hillslopes of untouched Xikou village
in the Taihang high country

which were linked closely with the small market towns on the plain. Thus the process, topography, and controls of Resistance War looked like this to the CCP:

	Japanese	Contested	CCP	CCP
Process	Extremely vulnerable to Japanese invasion	Easily invaded by Japanese	Difficult for Japanese to invade	Impregnable
CCP location and topography	Market-town villages on plains	Ridges, foot-hills, and valleys	Middle hills and wilder-ness	Highlands and moun-taintops
CCP Controls	Occupied—none	Raided—partial and disputed	Semifree—partial and superior	Free—total and uncon-tested

The CCP derived two strategic advantages from supporting the free and semifree villages of the Taihang.[105] First, it based its intelligence system in the natural seminomadic routines of the mountaintop militias. From their mile-high lookouts in the Taihang, for example, shepherd sentries were able to signal hamlets of oncoming Japanese columns, allowing them to prepare for united defensive warfare *(lianfangzhan)*, with its special feature of coordinated multiple-village assistance to any one attacked village. These same unmapped Taihang hamlets were Eighth Route Army telephone station points. In the Taihang part of the Shanxi-Chahar-Hebei base area, for example, the station was in Shahukou one day, Yemapo the next, and Qingshuikou the third, to avoid Japanese reconnaissance. Here the CCP also was able to decentralize its logistic lines, so that the army did not have to develop huge security forces for defending its hundreds of highland outposts.

The CCP, then, was unfurling its Resistance War from highland villages with a long history of hitting back at outsiders, thwarting Japanese plans to fill the political fissure left by the splintered Guomindang military order. The location of these villages outside the field of Republican and Japanese power had a lot to do with the ability of the CCP to align with them successfully. A host of competent scholars have claimed that the CCP based its order in villages where a key institution of state surveillance and control, the *baojia* system,[106] enveloped lineage groupings to create a crosscutting pressure against peasant revolution from below. Yet it seems that the CCP never gained a firm hold on the administrative villages of the border region until the last years of the war, roughly 1943–45. The tiny Taihang Mountain hamlets in which the CCP got going were inhabited by peasants who were free from strong vertical state controls in the market towns below. With the assistance of the Eighth Route Army the popular militias of the upcountry were holding off the landlord peace preservation committees that directed the Japanese patrols from the occupied towns where *baojia* controls prevailed. The pre-1940 gains of the CCP armed forces and Japan's weak and delayed occupation put the uncharted Taihang in the hands of the Chinese Communist movement before the Japanese Three All temporarily challenged this pattern of revolution and resistance.

THE IMPORTANCE OF PEASANT VALUES IN THE CCP-LED PATRIOTIC WAR OF RESISTANCE

A final question. To what extent did the process of peasant mobilization during the Resistance War inspire a peasant identity based on the idea of defending the nation? Wasn't the CCP-led resistance, through supporting the people's militias and leading peasants in war-service work, involving the rural people in an expanding network of contacts that telescoped their political experience and taught them their own interest would be served best by identifying with the national resistance goals of the CCP armed forces?

If the CCP was developing a popular commitment to its national resistance, this was done mainly by involving the semirooted and uprooted peasants in war-related processes that recalled past conceptions of a just society and freedom from illegitimate authority. Otherwise, the nationalist appeals of the CCP did not have legitimacy in the rural world. This is not to deny that the cause of the CCP's resistance army could become acceptable to the peasantry—but acceptable in what sense, and on what specific issues?

The rural Boxer and Red Spear rebels had put forth a slew of antiforeign slogans in their attacks on Qing troops and Western missionaries, but they had not expressed an identity with a nation-state—which imperial China had never been and Republican China had not become. Moreover, the formative encounters of the border region peasantry with nationalism recalled the Guomindang army attempt to establish its own "national interest" by enlisting them in its endless tax drives and its equally burdensome forms of anti-Japanese resistance. These memories were enough to make the rural people extremely suspicious of nationalist-minded outsiders. Even in the Taihang Subregion, where the Chinese Communists in the Sacrifice League were free to demonstrate what Van Slyke rightly calls their "virulent nationalist temper,"[107] the peasants turned deaf ears to the patriotic messages of the Sacrifice League activists who visited the villages, markets, and temples.[108] At first they confused the league with yet another clique of grain tax collectors, and soon began to heed the Japanese propaganda designed to reinforce this confusion.

The national salvation propaganda that did inspire peasants to take up the cause of the CCP often doubled as a pretext for supporting the ongoing subsistence struggles of the country people, and their struggles invariably carried a traditional cultural meaning that was the product of their own perspective.[109] The peasants interpreted the party's national salvation messages in light of their own notions of what had to be done to escape their existential dilemma. Hence, the peasants who did respond to the CCP call to save the homeland were acting to save their families and villages from everything from landlord rent-racking, to Guomindang taxation, to Japanese impressment.[110] The CCP continuously sent its cadres to the villages to persuade peasants to prepare to resist the Japanese, but what CCP headquarters called a peasant-based national resistance war was more akin to a peasant mobilization for survival that posed a direct threat to all outside political authority.

In the hands of heterodox rural rebels the CCP's nationalism took on a distinctively home-grown form. As Liu Shaoqi intimated in 1938, the myth that Commander Zhu De was the lost son of the Ming emperor was taken to heart by members of secret societies who enjoyed a close relationship with the Eighth Route Army.[111] Of course the pro-Ming preferences of the Red Spears and Heavenly Gates had silhouetted the antiwarlord revolts of the late 1920s, and so it was entirely possible for the CCP to enlist those who had participated in this rehearsal for a revolution against hated rulers in its patriotic War of Resistance. The continuity of Han ethnic homogeneity from county to county no doubt simplified the CCP task of convincing

Commander Zhu De addressing his troops and the people, 1942

peasants to bring their coalitions to support the anti-Japanese cause, and counterbalanced the early Japanese effort to enlist peasants in forms of foreign rule that promised a far lighter burden than they had borne under native oppressors.[112] This ethnomythical commitment of the rural people was cemented by the performance of the CCP Eighth Route Army, which invariably stopped the Japanese from sweeping the Taihang villages on the occasion of the old lunar New Year. By 1943, peasants were celebrating this holiday by showering praise on their newfound protector and its liberationist purpose.[113]

Indeed, peasants assigned a bewildering array of folk mythoreligious values to the CCP's rising national fortunes. The peasant outcasts of Dazhai village associated the Eighth Route Army attacks on Japanese-held market villages with the liberation of hungry souls from the yamenlike controls placed on them by the Japanese and their puppet forces.[114] These attacks were staged on the popular Taoist-Buddhist Festival of the Dead, and peasants saw their violence as exemplary behavior within a tradition of aggressive insurgent attacks to free the poor from state-imposed hierarchy and hunger. In Dazhai types of settings, where the social structure had broken up and the Japanese presence made it impossible for the CCP to organize peasants within traditional close-knit familial and village forms, the older festivals provided important cultural events wherein the CCP could form a collective following of rural people—who gave the process their own cultural meaning.

Similarly, the landless peasants of Wangbuchang village in Shanxi's Jincheng county looked upon the Eighth Route Army not merely as a force to relieve immediate hunger or to resolve the impasse of Japanese invasion,[115] but as a savior capable of solving their problems for all time. When the 129th Division troops offered these rural people protection from bandits operating out of Guomindang territory and encouraged them to form village self-defense teams, they said the soldiers were like living Bodhisattvas *(huo pusa)*. To these rural people, the emancipation proclamations of the troops suggested the coming of the kalpa, and they did not relinquish this Buddhist folk belief when CCP cadres stressed national security needs as the main principle of mobilization.

Implicit in the Western image of the CCP success in rousing peasants to participate in the Anti-Japanese War is the assumption that the rural people responded to nationalist appeals by neatly assimilating those appeals into categories that carried the exact meaning of the party's message.[116] But in dealing with peasants who were rising up in revolution to recapture their means of existence, the CCP was dealing with people who had come to define national resistance in terms of a full stomach and liberation from the immoral landlords and lawless militarists who collaborated with the Guomindang and Japanese interventions. What endeared the CCP to the peasantry was the willingness of its resistance army to fight for this Little Tradition version of nationalism. Of course the CCP officials went right on teaching the importance of a broad patriotic United Front of all classes against Japan to the peasant associations, and the resistance army went right on fighting to shift power to anti-Japanese federations in the border region; but the wretched poor continued to experience the national struggle as if it were synonymous with their elemental demands for a tolerable livelihood and an overdue deliverance.

By magnifying the cleavages in the divided Republic of militarists, the Japanese invasion more or less made it possible for the CCP armed forces to continue linking up with the poor and powerless in the preexisting gaps of Guomindang power. With Jiang Jieshi's Central Army giving up on its commitment to a unified defense of the border region, the CCP regular army was able to defeat the second-rate Guomindang warlords during the middle phase of the Anti-Japanese War, roughly 1939 to 1942. From their strongholds in the modern sector of the Hebei-Henan plain the Japanese began to pursue the rise of CCP power, and for the brief duration of the Three All and its afterglow they made some headway in organizing defecting Guomindang officers into their own counterinsurgency operations. But the Japanese presence did not prove a deus ex machina for the Chinese Communist effort to enlist peasants for national resistance. The Eighth Route Army was unleashing the Resistance War from its western mountain sanctuary where peasants who were fighting for their fundamental social rights seldom felt the full weight of Japanese power. Where the CCP was about to be consumed in the inferno of imperialist war its Rear Service cadres resorted to stern measures to make peasants contribute to the resistance. Inasmuch as the Anti-Japanese War was requiring a high level of centralized coordination by the CCP,[117] the tensions of war occasionally edged party cadres to make demands the village dwellers could not tolerate. Without ameliorating the terrible war tolls on its peasant base, as it was able to do in localities where the Japanese presence was either weak or nonexistent, the CCP was unable to involve the rooted peasants in its War of Resistance. Even when peasants supported the CCP-led resistance they clearly were aiming first for what they wanted by way of justice and salvation.

7

Land Revolution and
the War of Liberation

The Anti-Japanese War of Resistance had seen the CCP consecrate its
political order in accordance with the peasants' revolutionary drive to restore subsistence rights. In emphasizing CCP opportunism in the land revolution that followed the War of Resistance Western observers portrayed the
CCP as if it were *initiating* radical land redistribution campaigns in a still
conservative peasant world in order to catapult the villages into a civil war
with the Guomindang. While this interpretation is not totally groundless,
events in the border region in the years 1945 to 1947 do not bear it out. As we
have seen, by 1945 peasants were moving to firm up the rights for which they
had been fighting even before the CCP and its armed forces came to their
assistance during the Resistance War. Emboldened by growing CCP power
vis-à-vis the central government, peasants in the older liberated counties
had begun to extend their struggles for survival and justice to the fundamental question of who would own the land. Their push to take the land was
infused with anti-Confucian folk ideas dating back to Ming times and
beyond, and it was to these ideas that the CCP and its army spoke during the
moment of triumph.

The Origins of Land Revolution and Civil War

Predictably, the Guomindang and the CCP disagreed on the origins of land
revolution and civil war in North China. The central government charged
that the CCP Eighth Route Army, now renamed the People's Liberation
Army (PLA), was expanding eastward into government territory and
imposing land revolution from above to induce passive peasants to attack
their landholding Confucian benefactors. The Chinese Communists responded that Jiang Jieshi and his warlord clients were plotting for civil war
by incorporating Japanese troops into their commands for an assault on the
established CCP base area. Ultimately, the CCP version seems to have been
the valid one, but the geographical manifestations of land redistribution in
the border region demand a qualification of both.

The Guomindang overstated the extent to which the CCP could dictate the course of peasant action in the border region. As we have seen, peasant values infused most of the changes in relations of land and labor in the two decades leading up to the end of the Anti-Japanese War. No one should be surprised, therefore, that the land revolution was triggered in late 1945 and early 1946—in advance of CCP leadership directives—by peasants looking to fulfill their old desires to seize the land.[1] Certainly there were lowland villages where peasants dared not launch into land redistribution without the backing of the PLA, but in the territorially secure Taihang Subregion land revolution was pursued by peasants who had been trying to place this issue at the top of the CCP agenda for nearly ten years. Moreover, from 1945 to 1947 peasants here were left with minimal support in their confrontations with landlords, while the PLA fought a life-or-death war with the Central Army on battlefronts far from its Taihang bastion.

The CCP erred only in overestimating the power of Jiang Jieshi's field forces in 1946–47—as did the Western observers who concluded that the Guomindang could have buried the CCP if only Jiang's men had been more schooled in *Realpolitik* and less prone to military blunder.[2] Indeed, from a purely military standpoint the odds were overwhelmingly in favor of the Soviet-built, American-supplied Guomindang army, which in 1946 outnumbered the PLA four to one, a ratio that reversed completely in the following three years of civil war. It was out of a keen understanding of the desperate position of the Guomindang that Jiang Jieshi launched the counterrevolution against the CCP's Shanxi-Hebei-Shandong-Henan base area on April 12–13, 1947. Even though the United States government was giving the Guomindang massive military aid, and taking every measure short of direct intervention to prevent the regime from collapsing, Jiang attacked the CCP base deliberately in order to elicit an even greater American commitment, for he was desperate to make up for the political base his warlord clients had failed to develop in the countryside. All sides knew that a Central Army rush against the CCP base area would require battles to be fought by battalions and divisions rather than the squads, platoons, and companies of the Anti-Japanese War, and Jiang was gambling that the resulting sudden pressure on the CCP to rally sizable PLA mobilizations would turn the settled peasantry away from the party.

By 1945 the Guomindang was well aware that peasant subsistence and antistate drives had come together with a CCP strategy to decentralize the system of grain production and supply in thousands of peasant villages whose self-defense teams would join in people's militias to protect the decentralized cellular economy of the base area. Moreover, since peasants had thrown landlords out of power and Zhu De and Liu Bocheng had destroyed the spearheads of Guomindang militarism in nearly all of the border region, Jiang Jieshi could not simply mobilize a preexisting power base. Here Jiang would have to fight Liu, who by this time was regarded to be the PLA's Clausewitz, and try to create a brand-new power base in the process of contending with the armed peasant associations. Finally,

Guomindang intelligence understood that increased financial assistance in and of itself was not sufficient to salvage Jiang Jieshi's tenuous position. Peasants joked that with Guomindang soldiers exchanging arms and equipment for food, medicine, and border region government currency Jiang Jieshi was becoming the supply chief of the people's militias.

The Guomindang crack divisions were unleashed against the CCP on April 12–13, 1947. The CCP border region leadership was panicked lest the United States intervene to help Jiang fill the power gaps in which the popular movement had existed since the outset of the Resistance War. This possibility made it even more imperative that the CCP comply with the voiced demands of its peasant base.

Land Revolution Process I:
The CCP Consolidation of Peasant Community

Though the land revolution delivered uneven benefits to different peasant strata, the CCP was fairly successful in cementing the peasantry to a common social purpose in the years 1945–49. The land-to-the-tiller program was to re-create a landowning peasantry with roughly equal shares of land, with the land revolution cadres speaking to the needs of all peasants. The impression given by past scholarship, still widely accepted in Western academic quarters, is that the CCP land revolution processes set peasants against one another and stirred up new insecurities within the villages.[3] This conception was identical to the central government view of land revolution as community disintegration. Doubtless the radical leveling activities of 1945–47 did now and then produce conflict among the peasants. Nevertheless, in both the Taihang area and on the plains of Hebei, Shandong, and Henan the CCP-backed land revolution strengthened the security and solidarity of the village people.

In principle, the CCP was committed to equal redistribution of land, and its cadres were aiming to meet peasant demands for equal ownership of the means of production. The peasants of Wuan county,[4] for instance, took equal redistribution to mean that each person in each household should receive on the average four *mu* of land. By 1947 they had accomplished the following changes:

Table 3.   Effects of Land Redistribution in Wuan County, 1946–47

Social Class Standing	Average Landholding Per Person prior to Liberation in 1945–46	Average Landholding Per Person after Land Redistribution in 1947
Landlord	8 *mu*	4.2 *mu*
Rich Peasant	7.4	5.8
Middle Peasant*	1.5	5.6
Poor Peasant*	1	4–5
Utterly Destitute*	0	4

*90 percent of the population holding only 29 percent of the land in the vicinity of Chengan, Wuan *xian*.

Practically speaking, redistribution neither equalized peasant landholdings nor eliminated the inequities in the property holdings of the emergent middle-peasant community, but it did bring major benefits to the poor peasants by allocating to them the holdings of landlords who had seven to eight times more land and who had used this land to exploit them mercilessly.[5]

These changes in landholdings were being initiated by peasants in their own interest as early as late 1945 and early 1946. Thus, in an important sense, the CCP 1947 Outline Land Law only legitimized the land seizures and redistributions being carried out by demonstrative peasants in the immediate aftermath of the Anti-Japanese War. According to Qi Wu, over three million peasants in the Taihang Mountains had gained land through revolt in 1946–47,[6] and Pepper shows that some ten million peasants in the border region received land through the revolutionary seizures of summer 1946 alone.[7] Clearly, the CCP was only validating a process set in motion by peasants who were taking advantage of the power changes its revolutionary army had carried out during the Anti-Japanese War and the growing struggle for supremacy with the Central Army. CCP officials, foreseeing the collapse (and the crazed reaction) of the Jiang junta, were hastening to generate some political guidelines for this peasant-initiated land revolution.[8]

For much of the peasantry, the basic issue still was survival, and this issue preceded—but did not preclude—the question of peasant community in the land redistribution process. By 1947 peasants along the Shanxi-Hebei border had raised their average holdings to at least three and four *mu*, an important step in a protracted leveling process that enabled them to increase basic food consumption. The harsh fact was, however, that in many villages peasants still could barely produce a year's subsistence yield from these tiny parcels, and had to engage in other endeavors to generate enough income to keep their families at safe levels of protein consumption. The middle peasants who had the better land, plow animals, artisan skills, and market savvy, stood in a superior position in the overall competition with the former landless peasants. Here was a potentially serious problem.

Although land redistribution brought real gains to the poor and utterly destitute peasants, they still envied the middle peasants, and struggled against them in order to compensate for their own limited capacity to produce sufficient crop income.[9] In some instances, the tenants and hired hands who had received land in the first round of land revolution nonetheless seized the land and crops of the middle peasants. In the newly liberated counties on the plains, such acts raised the specter of a middle-peasant retreat from further land revolution and of production cutbacks by peasant-led mutual-aid groups.[10] For the CCP the crucial question in 1947 was how to curtail such attacks while simultaneously meeting poor peasant needs in a way that stimulated peasant community. To understand how this was accomplished, let us look carefully at several dimensions of the so-called middle-peasant problem—land, capital, skills, and property.

As in rural France before the rise of Napoleon, established peasant landowners were in a better position than former landless tillers to purchase land put up for sale on the free market—which every peasant had the right to do.[11] As in the Black Lands Campaign in Ten Mile Inn in Wuan county, the lands of landlords were confiscated for public sale, and for the most part were purchased by the landowning middle peasants.[12] At first the CCP cadres responded by redistributing these lands in order to level the differences between "fat" and "lean" smallholders, but this approach alienated the middle peasants and challenged the cadres to reconsider its divisive effects on the peasantry as a whole. The CCP secretary of the Taihang Subregion attributed this radical leveling to the anarchist tendencies of the poor peasant leagues,[13] and urged CCP officials to come up with less threatening methods.[14] One was the progressive income tax, whereby middle and rich peasants with more productive lands and profitable market relations were to pay a higher income tax. The proceeds were to trickle back to the cash-short peasants for whom landownership was a novel and somewhat feeble experiment. The problem of poor peasant poverty, however, persisted throughout the land revolution, and CCP taxation, however progressive, did not produce significant payoffs for poor peasants. Land reform in fact left this problem unresolved, and all CCP officials could do was strive even harder to convince the cadres that the "hired, poor, and middle peasants are of one family, and the more unified our emancipation the greater our power."[15]

The poor peasants had received land, but their capital was still insufficient and they often lacked the fertile lands, draft animals, and tools and carts for market participation.[16] The harvest failures and flood disasters of the civil war era easily drove them to ruin. During the War of Resistance the CCP had begun creating loan arrangements in the villages, but over time loans had come to serve mainly the middle peasants with cattle and carts, and many poor and landless peasants were left without access to them. In 1947, for example, the poor peasants of Lin county wanted to start up trade, but loans there were still going to owner-cultivators and they could not afford the cost of transportation to the markets in which to buy implements. Because of the higher return they provided for party investment, including the raising of production and paying back of loans, the middle peasants enjoyed priority for loans, and the result of this cruel choice was that poor peasants often remained poor. Moreover, by 1947 rich peasants and landlords had taken over the cooperative loan departments, with the tacit approval of middle peasants, and this tendency was deepening in villages where there had been no post-Resistance War elections. In the Hebei-Shandong-Henan Subregion the CCP responded by organizing poor and hired-hand loan arbitration committees (pingu daiguan pingyi weiyuanhui), so that all loan decisions now passed through the hands of the one-time landless peasants.[17] Here was a check on the discriminating loan processes of the past, and by 1947–48 the poor peasants had begun to gain access to official credit information and loan procedures.

Supplementing the poor peasant loan committees were village skills committees *(cun jishu hui)*,[18] which earlier had excluded poor peasants from their services. The landlord-controlled skills committees of Hojia village in Licheng county, for example, had refused to exchange cultivation techniques with poor tillers, including seed-adjustment procedures for drought. Now, however, the committees were put under the leadership of the poor peasants who made their services available to all tillers, including middle peasants. The poor peasant beneficiaries of hoeing techniques and drought-resistant seeds were far less inclined to encroach upon the crops of middle peasants.

But how and where were former poor peasants to acquire the hoes, oxen, and carts with which to work their newly acquired lands? Were the middle peasants, as previous studies assert, coming away with the lion's share of property, leaving the propertyless peasants with grudges?[19] This was hardly the case. There were two criteria of property redistribution. One was revolutionary performance, applied to peasant actions in uncovering the hidden grain, silver, and livestock of landlords. The formerly landless peasants, not smallholders, led these campaigns to acquire working capital from landlords. When it came to redistributing property *within* the peasantry, however, the peasant associations apparently applied their own internal standards of justice, with emphasis on intraclass mutuality and unity. In the Hebei-Shandong-Henan Subregion the CCP started up wintertime land revolution schools, which encouraged poor peasants who had received land and loans to purchase implements and plow animals together rather than look to solvent landowning peasants for property. This advice was accepted warmly.[20] Yet the livelihood of the poor peasants improved only marginally through education, and they often had to await the expansion of production that came with the solidification of a middle-peasant economy before they could acquire the property needed to improve their lot.

In short, the CCP was behind a land-to-the-tiller movement that was being carried out from below and that had as its immediate goal the reproduction of a peasant society without landlordism and with popular democratic checks on socioeconomic imbalances stemming from competition and hierarchy. The CCP assiduously avoided dividing its peasant base just when its mandate was being tested in civil war. Nor was the CCP-led land-revolution process designed merely to throw the weight of the entire peasant class against all landlords, and ultimately into the imminent war with Jiang's Central Army. The CCP was angling in this direction in theory, but practice informed its cadres that the rooted, villagebound peasants needed help from extravillage fringe groups in consolidating the struggle on the land.

The Land Revolution beyond the Gates of the Gathering Peasant Community: Marginal Militant Groups with Connections to the CCP

When it came to sustaining land revolution in the border region, marginal groups, often made up of women, filled a role the rooted tillers were not capable of assuming. They helped the CCP link up its intervillage revolutionary activities with peasant efforts to consolidate land revolution within the villages.

That peasants were making headway in unifying their communities through land redistribution and forming a united front against landlords within their villages did not necessarily mean that all of the criminal landlords had been dealt with. For one thing, many peasants still thought of their relations with landlords in terms of experiences limited to a single village, and CCP efforts to stabilize peasant society through rent reduction and land redistribution sometimes reinforced this tendency toward localism. Moreover, during the War of Liberation peasants spent most of their spare time in war-service work, and had little time or energy to attend the late evening land revolution meetings of their own villages to investigate landlords who opposed land redistribution and whose holdings were in several villages. For another thing, landlords generally had insulated their household and clan affairs from ordinary peasants, and much of their local leverage owed its origins to economic and political arrangements extending beyond their native villages to other villages, towns, and even counties.

To make up for this limited peasant capacity to uncover the whole range of illegitimate landlord acts, the CCP enlisted several groups of women for whom hatred of landlords and local power holders was tied to a broad and detailed understanding of rural patriarchy. All of these women were wretched, battered, and mobile.

The young women who had turned to laboring in landlord households when their own families had fallen apart in the hungry 1930s made up one such group.[21] By the time of land revolution they had served as housemaids and kitchen hands in as many as a dozen landlord homes, and had some keen insights into the processes of landlord exploitation. They not only knew about the undercover loan and rental arrangements between landlords and peasants in distant villages, they also knew of past landlord connections with Guomindang officers, police, and magistrates. Furthermore, these women were attuned to the ways landlords had cheated their hired hands and beaten the beggars who solicited food at their gates. They sometimes added to and reaffirmed the peasant accusations against landlords by taking secret debt books and blacklists, which landlords had hidden in supposedly safe places, to read aloud before the speak bitterness meetings in the villages.

Small groups of young unmarried women, like the one led by Liu Hulan in Shanxi's Wenshui county, joined the CCP in early 1946 when the party was obliged to realize the peasant demand for land.[22] Born to poor peasant parents who had turned to short-term hired-hand work across several counties in the 1930s, these women had seen many a landlord reduce peasant families and villages to bankruptcy and hunger. They learned about "rolling donkey interest" at an early age, and were quite capable of investigating the intricacies of landlord exploitation for CCP district officials. And since they had lived almost their entire lives inside of CCP-controlled counties where peasant struggles against injustice had taken hold, they did not doubt that the CCP would win. Such women were a force in launching the land revolution among the older hired hands who, though filled with hopes for land, were occasionally prisoners of Confucian hierarchical conceptions about the fate of poor folk. To these women, the lives of hired hands were the lives of their fathers, and they naturally appealed to the women in landless families to urge their menfolk to follow up on their inclinations to take the land.

A third group of female land-revolution activists was composed of professional actresses and opera players. Some of them, such as Zhou Yunfang, barely had survived the abuses suffered under landlords and Guomindang militarists in the border region towns.[23] Zhou had traveled the Henan town opera circuits to Hankou and Su Zhang at the age of fifteen, but as the pay for actors dwindled in the World Depression and the actors' quarters deteriorated she turned back toward the border region in search of work. By 1933, however, opera players there were being dismissed without pay. Zhou Yunfang thereafter joined various vagabond opera troupes, playing in Daokou town in Henan's Hua county one year, Daming in Hebei the next, and Gaotang in Shandong the third. These troupes performed for landlords and Guomindang militarists, who often reneged on promises of pay. During the War of Resistance, therefore, actresses like Zhou joined the Eighth Route Army opera troupes, which provided them with housing and paid them in food-grains and cash. The CCP cadres convinced these women to link their operas to the land revolution in two ways: first, by giving them land in the 1947 land redistributions, and second, by inviting them to speak to peasant audiences about the hardships they had suffered under landlords and the Guomindang. By 1947 actresses like Zhou were traveling with PLA work teams from village to village to perform night dramas for the peasants, commenting on the connections between landlords and militarists who had worsened peasant life, and encouraging tillers to support the PLA war counteroffensive.

Peasants, Party, and the PLA in the Revolutionary Counteroffensive to Liberate the Countryside

From April 1946 to April 1947 the Guomindang army raids against the CCP base areas in North China had intensified. Jiang Jieshi was bent on linking up the Guomindang's planned takeover points in central Shaanxi, Manchuria, and the port cities of Shandong by capturing the North China Plain,[24] and by the autumn of 1946 it was clear to the top-level CCP leadership that the outcome of China's civil war would be determined in the Hebei-Shandong-Henan theater. The growing Guomindang counterrevolutionary offensive had to be turned back. The terrifying paradox, however, was that in drawing peasant support for its counteroffensive the CCP could not always relieve the pressures for war-participation work on the peasantry, so that the tensions that periodically had arisen between peasants and the party during the Anti-Japanese War exploded into real conflicts at the peak of the Guomindang counterrevolution.

In Russia, strains cropped up between the political mission of the Bolshevik army and the social needs of the peasantry after the October Revolution in the problem of provisioning the towns.[25] The stress between the goals of the Chinese Communist PLA and the survival requisites of the peasantry, by comparison, peaked during the revolution at the decisive moment in the civil war, with the dividing lines between peasants and the CCP appearing along the issue of provisioning. The social setbacks resulting from the CCP war-service requirements in many of the clashes with the Guomindang army on the Yellow River Plain proved unbearable for the peasantry.[26] In the Longhai railway counteroffensive, for example, the CCP Rear Service cadres overextended their supply lines in Guomindang territory and led peasants who had committed themselves to a week of war-related tasks into several months of duties. Peasants were delayed from returning to their regular crop routines during the busy season and had to do rush makeup planting right after the exhausting war service tasks. Further, the Rear Service cadres sometimes remained in the villages to carry on land redistribution struggles when they should have been organizing the supply lines and arranging provisions for grain porters and stretcher bearers. In the Hua and Puyang campaigns, where the CCP had been working with the rural people for nearly a decade, there were porter and stretcher-bearer desertions because of inadequate provisions and emotional stress. Finally, where the CCP was unprepared for sudden combat, as was the case in western Shandong's Juancheng *xian*, the CCP Rear Service cadres made arbitrary inductions, prompting peasant draftees to flee, to fight with party induction cadres, and to join in antidraft demonstrations.

One might conclude that the rural people were unwilling to lend their efforts to the whipping of Jiang Jieshi, and that by applying ever larger doses of violence the Guomindang army could have cracked the Chinese Communist movement. The problem, however, was not popular will—there can be no doubt that by 1946–47 the border region peasantry was willing to stand with the CCP against the Central Army. The heart of the matter was that few tillers had the means with which to meet the unpredictable demands of war participation and still survive. In the poor villages on the plains of Hebei, Shandong, and Henan the will was unquestionably there. The peasant capacity to continuously make contributions to the purpose of the PLA, however, was extremely limited. The question, therefore, is how the CCP sustained the contributions the peasants were willing to make to the defeat of the Guomindang without losing the good will built up over the previous decade or begetting a peasant reaction against its mission.

A Hypothesis on Land Revolution and the War of Liberation: The Free Village Revisited

The CCP could count on popular support for the war because of its tenacious commitment to improve peasant livelihood through land revolution. Seen in socioeconomic terms, the CCP was counting on support mainly from a particular type of village. A 1947 report issued by the CCP Hebei-Shandong-Henan Rear Area United Military Headquarters explores this matter in detail. Without a doubt the CCP was drawing its popular support for the War of Liberation from villages in which the overwhelming majority of peasants were smallholders, and in which there were few, if any, landlords.[27] It was running its counteroffensive out of villages where there was a 95 percent middle-peasant dominance and neither the peasant associations nor the Rear Service Command cadres had to contend with landlords who would subvert the land revolution as the war intensified.

Donghuwang village, on the Hebei border, produced the crucial wartime work experience from which the party drew in defeating the 1947 Guomindang. Situated three counties away from the major rail line into southern Hebei, Donghuwang was a village of smallholders whose survival had to be secured, through land revolution and commercial side occupations, if they were to contribute to the War of Liberation. Because the land in Donghuwang was poor a lot of peasants were small merchants, and the CCP district officials could coordinate their war-participation work with their market comings and goings.

What advantages did the CCP derive from running the war out of villages where the land was owned by tillers? First, the Rear Service cadres perceived the peasant contributions to the war to be potentially greater in these smallholder communities. Having recovered their livelihood through interest reduction and market participation during the War of Resistance and through land redistribution in 1946–47, these peasants were capable of contributing grain and carts to front-line troops. Given their past involvement in side occupations and small trade, they also were better prepared than some tenants and poor peasants to perform extravillage war-related transport and repair work, though the latitude they enjoyed in carrying out these tasks still was quite narrow. Moreover, since most of these smallholder communities were on the overcrowded plains, the Rear Service cadres could recruit younger peasants to serve in the PLA against the Central Army, which was sure to turn the clock back to the 1920s if it won. The peasants here would send their sons to fight, and when the CCP did not treat their villages as war colonies they did so.[28]

Second, in relying on the smallholding villages the CCP cadres were temporarily able to skirt the dilemma involved in unifying radical land changes with the War of Liberation processes.[29] The CCP's land-to-the-tiller villages, which were relatively free from peasant-landlord confrontations, were not the ones in which sharp class struggles over the land transpired in this period.[30] If anything, the CCP was linking its Liberation War process to villages where peasants already had resolved livelihood problems associated with usury, land usurpation, and other landlord evils, or where the presence of only a few minor landlords made the need for violent struggle over the land unnecessary. This CCP strategy minimized the chances for landlords to subvert the village leveling process by exploiting war-related issues, and made it rather difficult for the Central Army to sweep the war-supporting revolutionary villages. The Guomindang intelligence officers did not fully comprehend this phenomenon, for they invariably assumed that popular support for the CCP counteroffensive was coming from villages where class conflict was the sharpest, and relied on the bigger landlords to lead their murderous troops to villages where there were ongoing collisions over the land. Of course to many CCP cadres there was no such thing as a village where class tensions were nonexistent and class struggle unnecessary, but they had enough sense not to mobilize villages where landlord−landless-peasant relations erupted into bloody clashes and preoccupied peasants with issues of remorse and retribution as well as the redistribution of land. In short, the CCP was better able to gather support from villages where its cadres were in touch with peasants who had resolved land redistribution matters, and who, in some cases, had already begun to cooperate with a handful of reformist landlords to assist the PLA war effort.

Third, the CCP's national liberation strategy evidently was in part a throwback to the fundamental geopolitical lesson its cadres had learned about revolution and war in the Anti-Japanese War of Resistance. The thousands of smallholder villages from which the PLA drew support for its War of Liberation were in the remote backward counties of the Hebei-Shandong-Henan borderlands. These villages had been free from Japanese rule since the middle phase of the Anti-Japanese War and the Guomindang troops never returned to take them, either in the 1939−42 strikes that shattered the Second United Front or in the 1946−47 counterrevolution, which took as its major targets the main lines of transport and communication on the Yellow River Plain.[31] Just as it had kept the Japanese out of its remote Taihang villages in the Resistance War, so the CCP retained its grip on the dustbowl villages of the plains in face of the Guomindang's heavy attacks in 1947. Here, as ten years before in fortress Taihang, the CCP was able to survive and surge ahead in the gaps of counterrevolutionary power.

Nonetheless, from the standpoint of tillers, the social dilemmas arising from war-service work were just as pressing in 1947 as during the War of Resistance. The CCP encountered endless difficulties in giving sufficient guarantees for war-service workers as the PLA moved into its main counter-offensive in the April–August campaigns of 1947.

Three problems posed a challenge right up until victory. One was how to reestablish the normal agricultural routines of peasants and yet repeatedly send them to the front lines for war-service work.[32] With the Central Army destroying the Yellow River dikes in the 1947 spring season the CCP leadership of the Hebei-Shandong-Henan Subregion suddenly had to find a way to involve peasants in spring cultivation, river repair work, and war duties. The CCP priority was for war-participation work, but peasants wanted to continue spring cultivation and repair the dikes. Thus, when the Guomindang bore down, all sorts of problems arose in the CCP attempt to mobilize villagers within the zones of attack.

The steps taken by the CCP cadres to meet this attack resulted in the depletion of village labor forces and the disruption of production. The diversion of tillers to war-related work left labor forces inadequate to the tasks of May-June harvesting. Storm-troop harvesting was required to gather in the grain crops, but this method failed when the weather was bad.

The demands of war also compelled the CCP to take the mutual-aid group rather than the village as its unit of war-service work, and this weakened the effort to reconstitute the villages whole during the land revolution. Calling middle-peasant mutual-aid leaders away from family fields for war duties, CCP cadres urged women and children to pick up on production within the villages; but they were not able to sustain the output levels they had achieved with their menfolk or substitute themselves in tilling arrangements essential to the survival of the war-service workers from their home villages.

Another problem involved wasting peasant work time and depriving peasants of the income to be earned from side occupations and small businesses.[33] The CCP could not control peasant desertion unless it could assure tillers that their families would not go hungry while they were performing war-service tasks. To resolve this issue, the CCP organized three-way village production committees made up of a chairman from the closest PLA unit, an assistant chairman from the village party branch, and peasant mutual-aid leaders. Still there were problems. For one thing, peasants frequently changed their production plans after these committees had established what seemed necessary for PLA missions, and complained openly about the CCP system of work-point payments for war-related work. Whereas the three-way committees calculated labor power on the basis of labor expenditure and property investment, peasants preferred that points be calculated by the additional variable of time, and that both the time of day (morning, afternoon, and evening) and the season be taken into account. The peasants along the Hebei-Henan border demanded that the CCP cadres abide by what they called their agricultural work-point method and their side-occupation work-point system, so that the three-way committees had to switch from a criterion of labor and time in the main agricultural season to one of goods (oil and cotton) sold in the agricultural off season. Finally, the peasants grumbled when work points were allocated on the basis of privileges derived from political position; they insisted that everyone receive points according to his performance in war-participation work.

Yet a third problem for the CCP was how to carry on land revolution that simultaneously linked into the party's war-participation work plans. A 1947 report by Duan Junyi reveals that land-revolution activities running the gamut from dividing the land to investigating hidden lands preoccupied peasants to the point where they had no time for war-service work.[34] The overwhelming peasant priority was fighting hunger, and war-service plans ran a poor second. Moreover, it was becoming apparent that the peasant reluctance to participate in war-service work could not be chalked up solely to restraints on time or the real dangers of front-line duty. Throughout the border region tillers were more concerned with acquiring land and livestock than with fighting the War of Liberation.[35] The following scheme illuminates the divergence in peasant expectations and the CCP call for civilian sacrifices in intensified warfare at this great turning point in the civil war:

CCP goals
Stage 1: land revolution   Peasants divide the land
Stage 2: civil war   Peasants participate in war-service work

Peasant goals
Stage 1: land revolution   Peasants divide the land; redistribute
                                 property; increase income through trade;
                                 enlarge the family; send children to school
No stage 2—Stage 1 is continuous

To be sure, by this late date significant numbers of peasants saw an important relationship between their own long-term well-being and the success of the CCP armed forces. This made it easier for the cadres to convince them to suspend their land-revolution activities for war-participation work, but the conflict between party-led war and immediate peasant survival remained.

If the aforementioned problems continued to puzzle the CCP in its efforts to inspire rooted peasants to participate on the plane of uninterrupted warfare on which the PLA had to operate regionally and nationally if it were to win, the CCP nonetheless succeeded brilliantly in mediating the ugly disputes growing out of the tensions between peasant survival and party war needs. As Liu Bocheng took the PLA eastward against the Guomindang army in Henan and then southward for the Huai River campaign of 1948, the Rear Service cadres began to surmount the crisis engendered by the incomplete peasant support for the front-line troops.

To begin with, CCP cadres, along with PLA soldiers, assumed an increasing share of the war-participation work that was interfering with peasant

Commanders of the Huai River campaign: *(left to right)*
Ju Yu, Deng Xiaoping, Liu Bocheng, Tan Zhenlin

agriculture. In the Hua county campaign, the CCP officials, their staffs, and the Rear Service cadres rendered assistance for the autumn harvest and seeding, with the impressive result that 70 to 80 percent of the land was seeded during the peak period of civilian war-service work.[36] During the Longhai railway counteroffensive, the CCP magistrate of Qibin took the lead in stretcher-bearer work and long-term-combat service duties. When combined with an equitable work point system, acts like this apparently evoked a decline in desertion rates among war-service workers.

To minimize the problem of peasants losing work time or side-occupation income to production for combat troops, Rear Service cadres redirected small PLA squads away from combat to secret production spots and to war-service work, a practice that was in line with the war-service-work experiences of the CCP in the afterglow of the Three All in the Taihang.[37]

Finally, the Rear Service cadres set up village command posts in conjunction with peasant associations, self-defense teams, and armed work committees, and attempted to honor the peasant demand that they not enlist people in war-related work without giving prior attention to tilling obligations involved with survival. What this meant in practice was that the Rear Service cadres increasingly had to sacrifice their lives in making up for the incomplete peasant war-service contribution, and that their willingness to shoulder the burdens of war endeared them more and more to the peasantry. This CCP initiative, plus the fact that the party was constructing its civilian war-service system from villages that were not beset by all-out class war and in villages not being directly bombarded by the Central Army, permitted the peasants and the CCP to both skirt and smash the counterrevolution on the battlefield.[38]

Land Revolution Process II:
The Merciful, Clever, and Ever-Vigilant Peasantry

In hindsight, it is easy to declare that in the timeless conflict between lord and peasant, landlords were doomed to revolutionary destruction with the help of the CCP. But before the PLA counteroffensives of 1947 the CCP officials were not convinced that victory was just around the corner. Stalin was cautioning that the PLA was not ready, and the United States still was supplying the Central Army. The CCP leadership was certain that the counterrevolution was gaining momentum, and it was worried that popular support was slipping on the lowland plains.[39]

As a party still out of power, in 1946–47, the CCP was making every diplomatic effort to prevent civil war. By the summer of 1947 the first wave of peasant land seizures had provoked a terrible reaction from those landlords who looked to the Central Army to return them to power. The peasant associations, people's militias, and PLA in the old Taihang base were prepared for landlord counterattacks in the event of a sudden Guomindang army rush there, but the swift landlord reaction to the Central Army penetration of the Hebei-Shandong-Henan Subregion caught the CCP county-level officials and peasant cadres off guard, and in village after village landlords took back the grain and mutilated scores of peasant leaders. As a CCP investigation revealed, it was the nonvigilance of the party that enabled landlords to reestablish their power.[40]

One would think that the CCP, with its emphasis on class over patron-client politics, would have been prepared for this development by 1947. And yet landlords frequently succeeded in bringing peasant cadres into their patronage networks, for centuries a key means of diffusing revolts. In many villages the cadres attended private dinner parties sponsored by landlords who toasted the long life of their filial relationships, and in return they protected their hosts from the fury of land revolution. The landlords of Li Ren village, for example, were able to elicit protection even in the wildest moments of struggle on the land:

> In this time of rural panic, when peasants were taking the grain, clothing, and property of landlord exploiters, no one dared restrain them. Nonetheless, the landlords set up tables of liquor and delicacies, invited the peasant cadres to cigarettes and tea, and put on false faces of welcome. They praised the cadres and even volunteered to help peasants transport materials and property. They even offered the cadres their most prized possessions—the young maidens in their households; and they made their daughters-in-law kneel down and weep at the front gates to win the sympathy of the local cadres. This kind of method

proved very successful for the landlords. The peasant activists accepted their smiles and gifts and sympathized with their kneeling and crying, and let them slip from the grip of peasant wrath.[41]

One CCP report lamented that in Ji village, the most progressive land revolution village in a district where the CCP stood superior, 210 out of 420 peasant families still were under the influence of landlords.[42] This included one-third of the middle peasants and one-third of the poor peasants, and the CCP peasant cadres were well within the net too. Clearly, landlords were dampening the spirit of land revolution by cultivating local peasant clienteles, or so it seemed to the CCP officials who penned such reports.

At the same time, the monopolist, undemocratic patron-client work style of the CCP county and district officials was contributing to the demobilization of land revolution activity. Encouraged to look to officials rather than the peasantry for clues to dealing with land revolution and agricultural development, peasant cadres leaned more and more on CCP officials and less and less on their peasant association counterparts, and before long they were attempting to demonstrate their prowess to their superiors by confronting landlords by themselves. By relying on upper-level CCP directives rather than the instructions of supportive peasant groups, they became steadily more vulnerable to landlord patronage and more remote from village grapevines that told of landlord opposition, crippling their ability to instantly mobilize the peasant associations and self-defense teams to respond to landlord counteractions. In this situation many peasant activists temporarily lost the respect of their local followerships, and some lost their lives.

By substituting its patronlike judgments for peasant initiatives, the CCP was drastically undercutting the land revolution. This subjective tendency was particularly strong in production. In Licheng's Songhe village CCP officials blindly "used the methods of the evil gentry" to extend an excellent variety of Golden Queen corn they had developed in other counties, overriding the tillers' right to cultivate their native crops. The cadres "did whatever their superiors told them to do,"[43] but the peasants of Songhe went ahead with their own crop selections, and the benefit they reaped from their decision was more important than internal CCP rectifications in bringing the cadres to their senses.

The tendency of CCP officials to unilaterally pass down directives on the management of peasant production opened up the possibility for landlords to outcompete the party locally. By ordering party cadres to carry out production techniques that had worked well in one village but had little potency in others, the CCP gave landlords the chance to sponsor production approaches that were more respected locally. Such unilateral CCP directives, ignoring peasant opinions freely offered in a spirit of exchange, helped rich peasants and landlords take over the leadership of the village skills committees in Huang Niudi village in Licheng county during the summer of 1947.[44]

The intriguing question is why at this critical juncture the CCP was able to temporarily get away with substituting an emergent patron-client mode of rule for peasant spontaneity and collective action,[45] and correspondingly, how the CCP-led peasant associations were able to survive the reaction and repression brought against them by landlords anticipating yet another Central Army comeback.

As a party without multiple privileges to dispense and with strong bonds to formerly destitute peasant cadres, the CCP was in a good position to deal with the development of despised patronage relations. Not only was there a precedent for this in the 1942–44 Thought Rectifications, the pressures of 1947 prompted the CCP to devote serious attention to a whole set of peasant rules of action that lay beneath the surface of its power and patronage.

The first rule of peasant action was to strike first and be prepared for armed struggle.[46] Many peasant leaders were angry with CCP officials who were unprepared for the landlord violence in the summer of 1947. They often berated the party officials and reminded them that it was only because they had struck first in 1945–46 that landlords had been unable to eliminate the party in 1947. The officials knew better than to question the wisdom of peasant leaders on this matter, particularly those who had lost relatives to the repression that followed the Guomindang coup of April 12–13, 1927.

This is not to say that the CCP was mobilizing peasants to murder landlords willy-nilly.[47] The peasants spared landlords who had demonstrated their good will during the Anti-Japanese War, and even invited them into the community of tillers by offering them land, implements, and livestock. Only landlords who had committed exceedingly evil deeds suffered violent punishment. Even as the central government was describing land revolution as rural mob rage, the CCP generally could not claim a life without first gaining the approval of over 90 percent of the village, and where executions were carried out without this mandate the village people turned their backs to the party.[48] Even in the more destructive moments peasants did not readily yield to CCP directives; the party was obliged to stay within the guidelines of folk justice. Of two thousand landlords arrested in the villages of Hebei's Shouzhang, for example, approximately nineteen hundred were redirected to detention centers or returned to their home villages.[49] These peasants were skeptical of Confucian ideas of humanism, but they were willing to show Buddhist mercy for landlords who refrained from undoing their insurrectionary order.

To be sure, many peasants sought to hedge their bets against the bloodbath that would accompany a Guomindang takeover by accepting patronage from landlords. Some CCP officials took this to mean that peasants still believed that landlords were their benefactors and that landlord rule was reasonable; but the peasants were way ahead of them. Still desperately poor, they accepted patronage from landlords as a means of making up for the local material losses incurred from war participation work. This was their second rule of action, and it was not at all incompatible with immediate survival and futurist liberation. Here were clever peasants with a deep commitment to land revolution, and with a full understanding that landlords were offering patronage only through fear of what promised to be the end of their rule if the PLA should win. Why not accept their patronage and use it to defeat them?

The third rule of peasant action was that absolute democracy—defined as egalitarian, nonhierarchical exchange between CCP officials and ordinary folk—must prevail over cliquish relationships. The Chinese Communists would have us believe they took the lead in rectifying the party work style and the party tendency to tout itself as a new benefactor, and I tend to think there was an understanding within the party that clientele relations weakened individual cadre initiatives to gain collective peasant support of land revolution. The important point, however, is that in 1947 peasant pressure was just as influential on the renewed CCP effort to correct its patron-client approach, and had a lot to do with avoiding yet another counterrevolutionary disaster in the border region. To be sure, local party leaders did not like to hear peasant criticisms of their overdependency on CCP superiors, but, for several reasons, they welcomed the results of the Thought Rectification campaigns. For one thing, by depending less on CCP officials they were in a better position to work with the whole village on issues internal to the peasantry, and to rely on a number of small groups and committees to help them avoid the wrong decisions that divided the village and damaged their reputations. For another, the criticisms and suggestions of their fellow villagers provided the clues that enabled them to stay on top of landlord attempts to subvert the land revolution. Of course this meant that they supported peasant attempts to outproduce landlords and to redistribute land—the one act that seriously weakened the landlord capacity to foster local followerships.

Anti-Confucian Peasant Hegemony in the Land Revolution: Popular Consciousness and Folk Creation Myths at the Moment of Liberation

On the front lines of war the CCP was defeating the counterrevolution by force of arms. Behind the lines its cadres were working side by side with peasants to constrain and defeat the intrigues of landlords. The standard view of this late phase of land revolution is that the CCP inserted itself from outside to politicize the broad mass of peasantry for radical thought reform.[50] As a revolution in popular thinking, however, the land revolution marked yet another stage in the struggle of an anti-Confucian peasantry to re-create society in accordance with its own conception of reality and justice. The involvement of outside CCP officials was limited largely to exchanges with peasants in land revolution committees organized and working on their own.[51] But CCP membership in many villages climbed to 9 percent of the population.[52]

The land revolution committees were competing with landlords who called for a quick demobilization of peasants on the basis of lineage, clan, and local residential ties. To counter their attempts, committee members went from door to door presenting each peasant household with a list of particulars of how landlords had failed to relax the ruthless terms of work life for those who in the past had called them kinsmen.[53] They also prevented landlords from exercising their patriarchal clan standards in judging conflicts with peasants who had been wronged. The revolutionary committees succeeded here partly because clan bonds were not all that strong to begin with and partly because landlords had often proven even more oblivious to the rights of poor peasants who were not from their lineages or clans, which meant the peasants could advance unhesitatingly to class struggle.

The land revolution committees took seven and eight villages, rather than one, as the unit of their attack on landlordism, greatly widening the network of converging peasant identity.[54] A 1947 report on the land-to-the-tiller movement in Wuan county by Wang Tingdong, for example, shows that thousands of peasants were forming their own united struggle meetings, and that their members went from village to village and then into the county town to settle up with landlords there.[55]

The land revolution committees strengthened peasant class allegiances by mediating conflicts over land and harvest rights. When landlords attempted to play middle peasants against poor peasants by encouraging them to join in counterplots against the formerly landless villagers, the committees, on the advice of the CCP, encouraged the rotation and sharing of leadership in the peasant associations, so that the middle peasants did not feel strapped into a "poor peasant dictatorship."[56]

There was relentless pressure for cadres who accepted landlord patronage to denounce themselves publicly. Liu Yongyi, the chairman of Shandong's Fan county peasant association, was one such cadre.[57] In the 1920s Liu's father had lost the family land to a landlord, and then died from overwork during the Depression. Liu and his brother migrated to Manchuria in the 1930s, but his brother starved on the overland trail. Upon returning home around 1938 Liu was banished from his family village for burning the landlord's house, and contemplated joining the Eighth Route Army when it arrived in Fan county. Shortly after Liu joined the peasant association, however, the same landlord offered him one *mu* of land in return for detailed information on the meetings. Liu even rendered protection to this landlord in the opening round of land redistribution. Now, in 1947, Liu Yongyi, like many other formerly destitute peasant activists, was endearing himself to his fellow villagers by public repentance. If the old bonds of reciprocity had been intact, as Tilly has found for peasant-landlord relations in rural Anjou during the French Revolution,[58] the CCP would have found the social climate far less conducive to the cultivation of explicitly peasant allegiances.

One might object that the CCP was transferring peasant allegiances from one-time Confucian landlords to itself, not cultivating the notion that all tillers acting together were to put an end to landlordism and hierarchy. This was a real possibility in villages with a long history of subordination, where there were no preexisting revolutionary arrangements involving peasants, and where the lightning PLA thrusts of the civil war suddenly gave power to the party and poor.[59] But in the early liberated counties of the border region, where peasants had taken power by their own actions with the coming of the Liu-Deng army, the party was working with peasants who believed that they were their own benefactors. And it was this popular conception of revolution that experienced CCP cadres of the older Taihang Subregion promoted in their exchanges with the peasant land-revolution leaders of the lowlands.

In Marxist fashion, many CCP officials still doubted the revolutionary potential of peasants rerooted in family landownership and production, and so they prided themselves in arousing the rural dwellers to trace lines of class association with landlords.[60] These officials discovered, however, that the peasant leaders of the speak bitterness meetings drew their own class lines, and invariably aimed their wrath at landlords who had ruined their families in the recent past. The revolutionary committees often overlapped with temple-based congregations whose members orally reconstructed the process whereby criminal landlords had placed their parents and grandparents in a state of permanent hunger before the coming of the CCP. Thus it was not unusual for one peasant family to inspire another to trace its broken bonds to the wrongdoings of landlords. Little speeches like these sharpened the basis for peasant class anger along lines of shared family experience:

> I am Wang Guo from Wanglou village. My landlord clansman, Wang Guang-san, beat me brutally because I picked two peanut seeds from the field. Landlord Wang not only jailed me for three days and fined me ten packs of cigarettes, he also made me give a dinner and make a public apology before the guests.

> I am Wang Dongyi. I also am from Wanglou village. The same landlord drove my seven member family to bankruptcy and begging during the disaster years, leaving my parents to starve. My sisters then had to flee from Henan to Shanxi where they were kidnapped and sold as slaves.[61]

In a world where landlords had made themselves notorious for replacing patronage with the pistol and the whip whenever the balance of power shifted in their favor, as had happened with the Guomindang volte-face of 1927 and then the Japanese invasion, few peasants were naïve enough to assume that the landlord who suddenly donned the mask of Confucian benefactor would not violently turn on them if the Central Army were to win. The rural people of this border region knew that there was no old regime composed of paternalist landholding patrons to go back to, and they were hardly stricken with guilt or sorrow when they attacked these one-time benefactors.[62] On the contrary, they were out to undo the landlords who had stripped them of livelihood and dignity, and they subjected landlords to popular rituals of shame in which they were expected to show guilt for their sins. The landlords who repented for their sins could save their own lives, but those who were unable to recognize their immorality provoked peasant explosions of rage and physical violence that CCP officials were powerless to control.[63]

In coming together to articulate their bitterness peasants crystallized the class awareness that had been developing before and during the War of Resistance. At the village level this process involved peasant families taking the lead to further expose landlord attempts to subjugate the poor.[64] Landlords were sending fruit and candy before the kitchen god in peasant homes and presenting good-luck charms said to put peasants in touch with the god of wealth and happiness. The peasants rejected these symbolic offerings for vertical community, out of a growing commitment to the collective process whereby they had regained land and reentered commerce. In any given village, however, there were bound to be some peasants who did not recognize the "little favors" done for them by landlords as manipulative behavior. To deal with these peasants, the speak bitterness meetings broke down into small question-and-answer groups run by ten families who had suffered similar injustices at the hands of different landlords. They usually focused on the question, "Is there any such thing as an enlightened landlord?" With the appropriate mixture of pressure and patience, they evidently got the answer they were after:

> After the land revolution committees divided the lands of three landlords who had escaped the dragnet in Ji village, Ma Youtang, a tenant of landlord Ma Youming, said, "I think landlord Ma never refused people when they asked him to loan grain in the past. So isn't he enlightened?"
>
> Another peasant replied, "Oh, you think he is enlightened? Let me ask, then, when you became sick, did you work for him?"
>
> This reminded Ma Youtang of a very bitter experience. "Oh, yes, I remember when I worked with others in the field. In the summer he sent us watermelons to quench our thirst. This made us feel grateful, but it also made us work harder without stopping. Finally, I became exhausted and sick from overwork. When landlord Ma discovered I was sick, however, he fired me." Ma Youtang then broke down and began crying.[65]

Adding to this fermentation of peasant consciousness was a CCP campaign to promote class thinking among its armed forces. In the summer of 1947, the CCP began internal rectifications of its PLA cadres. In Liu Bocheng's division these campaigns were aimed at preventing cadres from landlord families from allowing their parents to subvert land redistribution.

In the course of the land revolution, many landlords had sent their sons into the PLA as a means of obtaining protection, and when land redistribution struck home they often wrote letters pleading for help. The CCP encouraged its cadres to discuss the letters as a test of their own consciousness and feelings toward landlord parents who had lived off the village people without working. After weeks of internal discussion, these cadres wrote letters reprimanding parents for exploiting tillers and recommending the redistribution of their parental lands. These letters were circulated in *The Militia*, and read before the peasant associations as a demonstration of army solidarity with the aims of the land-to-the-tiller movement.[66]

At the same time, demobilized PLA soldiers carried the message of land revolution back to their home villages.[67] These PLA veterans had traveled through hundreds of villages, districts, and counties where land redistribution was in progress, and had a rich experience from which to draw in contributing to the peasants' defeat of counterrevolutionary landlord plots in their native localities. The militancy of these ex-soldiers in keeping the land revolution going was said to match that of the village people, and they generally won acclaim by making speeches and singing songs for the home folk.

With CCP ascendancy, the central government forecast persecution and enslavement for all classes, a topsy-turvy world in which authority relations were improperly ordered—as if the world were turned wrongside up. This viewpoint was not far off the mark, but it was not the mark of the peasantry. Revolution against Republican warlord-landlord government had become the only route to peasant survival, and the process whereby peasants welcomed the CCP armed forces to recapture their means of existence was condemned only by a Guomindang military dictatorship that had drastically redefined the state's relationship to village society. As peasants moved from powerlessness to power and gained confidence that the CCP and its revolutionary army could win, struggles over issues that spelled the difference between life and death increasingly were infused with a seemingly infinite number of folk ideas that called for a radical reordering of the world. These ideas were being expressed with growing frequency and intensity during the land revolution, when it was rumored that a complete reversal of heaven and earth was imminent.[68]

Indeed, the land revolution committees were made up of peasants with goals that transcended the needs of immediate survival. In attacking landlords, the peasants concentrated on delegitimizing the Confucian political values they associated with the hated hierarchy of the past. Much as in Li Zicheng's time, wicked landlords were made to serve meals to peasants and to bow down before them, as they had made peasants do under the Guomindang. The peasants took up residence in the mansions of the landlords whose wealth dated back to the Ming dynasty, and they smeared excrement on those who thought themselves too good to till the land. In the course of the speak bitterness meetings they often went beyond the bitterness felt for the unforgivable landlord injustices of the post-Qing period and called for sweeping away all Confucian authority. The idea of putting an end to elite claims on peasant society and elite negations of the insurrectionary instructions of poor folk caught on throughout the border region.[69]

The ideas peasants expressed for turning the world rightside up were not at odds with CCP-led land revolution and national liberation. E. J. Hobsbawm's classical study on the relationship of peasant rebellion and modern revolution, *Primitive Rebels*, is predicated on the assumption that peasant rebel ontology and the realism of revolutionary leadership seldom converge to lead toward the practical "transfer of power."[70] But peasant millenarian expectations and CCP revolutionary goals to destroy landlordism and to liberate the country were mutually reinforcing in backward China by 1947–48. Within the border region peasants had come to associate land revolution and Liberation War with a return to a world without the state, and the CCP was reaffirming this hoped-for pristine world of the rural folk. Again, the revolution would reconstitute peasant society not in the image of an idealized lost Confucian order, but rather on the basis of a budding folk community stressing ultimately the limitless possibilities for dignity and freedom.

The hope for a world filled with freedom, for an order without imperial hierarchy, was nowhere more jubilantly expressed than in the peasant interpretation of the land revolution as the act of Pan Gu.[71] It was said to be the first time since Pan Gu, the legendary creator of the universe, had swung his axe to open up heaven and break the earth's soil that poor folk had enjoyed the freedom of owning the land and obtaining decent burials— hence the renewed popular expectation for the coming of a heaven on earth in which the rivers, the land, and the streaming skies would become the servant of an all-tillers' world. To this Pan Gu—the Pan Gu of pre-Confucian history—peasants throughout the Taihang sang praise in the land revolution.

Peasants also chose to celebrate PLA victories on July 7 of the lunar calendar,[72] the legendary Lovers' Day—and they associated these victories with a politics that made possible the unfulfilled longings of the Weaver-maiden (Zhi Nu) and the Herdsman (Niu Lang). The Confucian literate classes had relegated the legend of Zhi Nu and Niu Lang to the realm of disorder, unimportance, and impossibility.[73] In popular mythology, however, the story of a celestial wedding of these two lovers had persisted across the centuries. Moreover, implicit in this legend was a rejection of preexisting vertical authority relationships. There was no place in it for active male (Yang) over passive female (Yin), for landlord over peasant, for the sun over the moon, or for the state over the people.

The legend was that Zhi Nu's father, the Sun, had arranged his daughter's marriage to a herdsman, and that this marriage was consummated in the best tradition of heaven and hierarchy. To the dismay of the Sun, however, Zhi Nu and Niu Lang took their marriage as a chance to escape the duties they owed to hierarchy, and with this lovers' pursuit of freedom the stars and galaxies followed disordered courses. Understandably, the Sun was annoyed. He separated the two lovers by placing them on opposite shores of the River of Heaven (the Milky Way), but with the concession, said to stem from his kindness, that Zhi Nu and Niu Lang could meet for one day a year—July 7. On this day, magpies would flock to form a bridge over which Zhi Nu would cross to the Herdsman. To this one meeting the Weaver-maiden and Herdsman looked forward all year, and yet even then they lived in fear that the rains would flood the River of Heaven so that the magpies could not work their unifying miracles.

When peasants celebrated PLA victories on July 7 in the years 1946–47 they were anticipating a permanent uniting of Zhi Nu and Niu Lang, and implicit in these celebrations was a rudimentary folk conception of a reordered universe. Symbolically, the crossing of the River of Heaven was a crossing from a vertical division of society endured in wretchedness under landlords and warlords to a Chinese Communist Party that stressed the reuniting of families no longer haunted by hunger and separation. The coming of the magpies was linked, symbolically, with the coming of the PLA—the people's bridge to freedom. But what if Jiang Jieshi, on whose blue-and-red Guomindang army flag was emblazoned the white sun, were to unleash further flood fury, as was happening in Shandong? The marching song of the PLA reassured peasants that their army was "going forward, going forward, going forward! Marching toward the sun!" Toward power. No need now to fear that the inauspicious political forces were in ascendancy. Revolution personified the myth of the magpies gathering in the myriad. Symbolically, this gathering marked the moment when poor folk enjoyed the right to pass into a world in which they were free at last.

The land revolution was aimed at strengthening village solidarity, though the pressures of both landlord counterplots and the Guomindang counterattack occasionally proved an obstacle to this goal. Because of the thorny matter of matching up the needs of the peasantry with the needs of the PLA counteroffensives, the CCP found it difficult to wage land revolution and liberation war simultaneously. This was especially troublesome on the plains where peasants did not have a long history of combining with the CCP armed forces for mobile warfare. When it came to the War of Liberation, the rural people were most willing to contribute to the PLA defeat of the Central Army. Still, there were continuing tensions between the survival requisites of marginal village dwellers and the combat drives of the PLA. The CCP Rear Service cadres alleviated these tensions partly by drawing from their rich experience with war-service work during the War of Resistance and partly by sacrificing themselves to take up the slack left by the beleaguered peasantry.

Peasants also played a crucial part in defeating the counterrevolution led by landlords. On the plains they came forth to instruct the CCP on its mistaken approach to land revolution, and the CCP heeded their instructions to rectify problems within its own ranks and to prevent landlords from swaying its local cadres away from a class-oriented approach to struggles on the land. Finally, in the Taihang Mountains, where the CCP had rooted itself at the outset of the War of Resistance, peasants were drawing on their own creation myths and popular legends to inform the beginnings of a revolutionary folk order, raised partly in the image of an anti-Confucian yesteryear. For a few long moments, before the rudiments of state-level dictatorship were discovered, the peasants and the CCP turned the world rightside up in this oldest corner of rural China and united with the popular army to extend the revolutionary promise throughout the countryside.

8

Revolutionary Legitimacy in
the Peasant World

However great their stored-up anger, peasants rarely have the power to recapture traditional social rights and rid their villages of tyranny. Usually, they either give up hope or cling to it only to have their heads cut off and sent to the capital to assure some military dictator that his "development program" is proceeding without interruption.

In modern China, a peasantry with its strategies of survival nearly exhausted regained the material basis for its "old designs for living"[1] and realized its own conception of social justice through participation in revolutionary politics. Inasmuch as the Chinese Communist Party derived its mandate to rule China from practices that validated much of what peasants wanted by way of justice and order, it becomes possible to speak of the Chinese Revolution as a folk revolution, that is, as a revolution in the service of the humble folk. In the most fundamental sense, the CCP won by raising a protective shield before the peasant communities whose wretched members championed the social rights and political sovereignty of China's Little Tradition.

Implicit in the theory that peasant revolution was likely to take hold in twentieth-century China because of the weak structural relationship between the imperial state and peasant society[2] is the assumption that the old regime masked a Leviathan with an insatiable appetite for peasant goods. The modern Western scholar, believing with Marx and Lenin that revolution is the negation of tradition, too easily concludes that any change away from yesterday's admittedly imperfect world is automatically better for the peasantry. Of course the demands of the imperial order were real. Of course the imperial polity provided far less in security and services than proclaimed by its paternalist Confucian ideology. Of course it was hierarchical, dictatorial, brutal, and worse. And yet the old regime, for all its liabilities, did attempt to serve agriculture, that is, tillers in their working culture. The physical security it offered from banditry and the food grains it held over for the years of hardship seem far more beneficial when seen against the foreground of pillage and unrelieved hunger in Republican China. At least the intent of the imperial government, however limited, to carry out such promised services was appreciated by tillers anxious to make Confucian government support their quest for survival. The deals that peasants struck with the imperial polity did preserve the autonomy of their villages, incomplete and imperfect as it was. And the peasants preferred it to the political intrusions that intensified with the fiscal crisis of the Republic. The passing of the Qing dynasty thus brought unwanted change, and an unprecedented series of shocks that moved the peasants toward a radical confrontation with the new power holders.

There is appealing logic in the variant of social mobilization theory that argues that the rise of Republican warlord government merely highlighted and intensified a system of illegitimate taking that had been present long before the fall of imperial China.[3] What roused the moral anger of the country people to the point of rebellion, however, was not simply the decay of the old regime, but its supplanting by a militarist order that degenerated into regional and provincial forms of plunderous misrule. If peasants had doubted the value of the paternalistic care they derived from their relationships with the local Confucian spokesmen of the past, what convinced them of government illegitimacy was the new taking process that prevailed after the warlords transformed the Republic of China into their tax gathering machines. The new warlord-gentry plunder was in operation before Jiang Jieshi attempted to incorporate it within his praetorian order and before the Japanese invasion compounded its horrible consequences.

Among the developments that brought on the storm clouds of peasant revolt was the financial crisis of the central government.[4] This crisis, which can be traced ultimately to China's endless debts to the world powers, crippled the Republic. The militarists who marched into the treasuries of the failing Republic did not create the crisis, of course; but the new claims they made on the already bankrupt center did exacerbate it. This, rather than any alleged Chinese Communist Party subversion of the central government, was the tragedy of Republican China.

What moved peasants toward revolution was the process by which Republican militarists shifted the largely foreign-induced fiscal crisis of the post-Qing center onto the villages. Semicolonial China was in debt peonage, a debtor without a creditor in the world political economy. The new Republican military contenders for national power not only raised their armies on the backs of the country people, they also demanded that peasants pay the debts they owed to foreign powers. The new system of rigid taxes which the warlords kept in place during the years of dearth was an important factor in delegitimizing their rule. And when it came to taxation and famine relief the Guomindang warlords gave the country people even more reason to doubt the legitimacy of local Republican power holders.

The new militarist pressure on peasants to plant cash crops to lands customarily reserved for grains evolved from the warlord government attempt to make up for national revenue losses to expansionist foreign powers, such as Japan. The central government under the Jiang junta pursued this practice vigorously, and peasants whose returns from cash crops proved insufficient for simultaneously keeping up with rising taxes and rising food prices quickly learned to equate Guomindang order with hunger, family breakup, and death. When the Guomindang added rampaging inflation to troop support taxes and monetized agriculture, its new, entirely illegitimate national tax put maximum strain on peasant survival. And its attempt to mobilize the peasants for its war with Japan—which in reality amounted to a poorly coordinated internal war against the CCP—exceeded the point of peasant endurance.

Rural class exploitation alone did not trigger widespread peasant revolt, but landlords did anger peasants by violating their elementary understandings of justice and by refusing to heed their protests. Moreover, if Republican warlord government extraction, rather than landlord exploitation, precipitated revolt, the willingness of landlords to collaborate in the tax-collection drives of the Guomindang warlords gave peasants cause to abandon the distinction between vertical and horizontal forms of misrule. The landlord who bore the brunt of peasant wrath during the revolution was usually a man who had replaced the flexible relationships of the past with the fixed rent of his household and fixed taxes of the Guomindang militarist he hosted.

The failure of central government reform, combined with the arbitrary taxation of the Guomindang warlord regime, was an important cause of peasant suffering and indignation. The militarization of the Guomindang led to the development of an antifolk army run by aristocratic officers whose day-to-day performance made clear that the government was not committed to reestablishing a reformist policy incorporating a Confucian mode of rule. Thus the Guomindang attempt to integrate the hungry countryside resulted in peasant alienation from its Confucian hocus-pocus and in peasant protest to avoid its town-based tax machinery: the Chinese Communists entered here.

If Jiang Jieshi was making progress toward building up an army to smash the peasant movements of the Republican era, his emergent warlord center still could not hold. The Guomindang ultimately was a hodge-podge of Chinese-style *caudillos* who fought as Jiang's generals only as long as it suited their individual power goals. Once the Guomindang nationalized their predatory rule, its pacification campaigns were bound to finalize the delegitimization of its purpose. The massive contradiction was that the deep splits between these same Guomindang warlords, along with the continuing fiscal crisis, confounded the central government attempt to directly rule territory, so that the peasants' struggles could make headway in remote noncolonized border areas where delayed modernization slowed the consolidation of militarist power. This phenomenon, combined with the ineptitude of the incumbent's use of force,[5] limited the ability of the Guomindang warlord regime to exercise power and hegemony over the peasants of the periphery in the years before the Japanese invasion: the Chinese Communists survived here.

The interesting question is, what moved peasants from rebellion to revolution, that is, to strike out to overthrow Republican power holders? Was it the diffusion of CCP ideology?[6] Was it the frustrated rising aspirations of the peasantry?[7] Or was it the peculiarities of a particular agrarian ecosystem?[8] None of these factors seems to have been decisive. What moved peasants whose defensive protests started from a nonradical perspective[9] toward a revolutionary mode of politics was the failure of China's suprawarlordism to accommodate them. The Guomindang warlord regime overturned the traditional procedures of conflict resolution, making it impossible for peasants to renegotiate their rights to subsistence via avoidance protest and remedialist rebellion. This new political condition, which crystallized with the Jiang Jieshi coup d'état, created the possibility for peasant involvement in revolution years before Mao Zedong and the CCP began to comprehend and develop it to its logical conclusion.

The more the Guomindang warlords redefined the peasants' protests as "criminal," radicalizing their quest to restabilize their local economies, the more the revolutionary alternative appealed to them. In short, peasants in modern China turned to oppositionist revolutionary politics because a militarist political order defined their defensive response to its new extractive pressure as "illegitimate exit."[10] In this zero-sum situation, they discovered that power relations had to be reordered by revolutionary confrontation if they were to survive. Not to confront the new armed tax Republic was to die. To risk death in revolution was to renew the possibility of life.

The key event that restored life to the village people came with the power shift brought about by the CCP revolutionary army in 1936 37. To be sure, the CCP's organizational strength was important to its political success, but the presence of the Communist party itself hardly explains why peasants found it acceptable and legitimate.[11] The CCP established a foothold in the countryside by reinforcing the renewed initiatives of wretched rural people to regain the rights they had lost in the hungry decades leading up to the Japanese invasion. Clearly, in rooting their party in the survival pursuits of rural people, the Chinese Communists were enabling peasants themselves to exercise maximum influence in reintroducing the most basic of social principles. The CCP was able to achieve an authenticating relationship with them largely by accommodating their determination to reestablish tilling and trading relationships—both among themselves and between themselves and landlords—on their own terms. In this sense, the operational code of the CCP was more in line with the voluntarist practices of anarchist peasants than the authoritarian, manipulative, elite Leninist party depicted in most Western social science research on China. This important practical truth, so easily lost in scholarly understandings of how revolutionaries interact with peasants, is what made the return to traditional morality both revolutionary and legitimate.

Whether the CCP made its greatest strides in the predominantly middle-peasant villages, among the more secure landowning peasants, during the War of Resistance remains an open question.[12] The impetus to revolution seems to have come from semilandless and semirooted sharecroppers, hired hands, migrants, and squatters who had been mistreated by landlords and the lawless Guomindang warlords. Once the CCP anchored its revolution among these semipeasant desperados its officials rediscovered the wisdom of Mao Zedong on the wellsprings of the peasant movement: the poor peasants would make up the vanguard of the revolution in the village world.

Whereas the rebellions of tenants and hired hands were aimed at rectifying the worsening terms of work life under landlords, the goals of landless peasants were not at all incompatible with the mobilizations of the landowning peasants who still made up the rooted village majority.[13] If the CCP thrived in traditionalist owner-cultivator villages, however, it did so in part because many of the less secure peasant smallholders had become the victims of more than just low yields and high taxes. As warlordism and the world market penetrated rural society, these micropeasants were hurt by land usurpation and landlord usury. By the World Depression they were being transformed into part owners and part tenants, and they increasingly shared the same problems facing their landless counterparts, including fixed rents, wild interest rates, and fixed taxes. In this situation, the landless quasi-peasants who carried the banners of the CCP could become intimately involved with the struggles of the poor smallholders. And there is little doubt that in leading the struggles against landlords and local power holders the poorest peasants were acting to reestablish a community of landowning tillers in which they and their smallholding associates would be able to reroot themselves.

The dry zone ecology[14] made these peasant mobilizations all the more volatile and perhaps helped homogenize peasant movements that otherwise were crosscut by different social structural combinations. Unlike their counterparts in the wet rice zones of South China, India, or the Philippines, the peasants of the North China interior could not count on more than one major grain crop from their punished arid plots. Of course it was not the dry crop system per se[15] but rural exploitation *within* the capricious dry zone ecological context that proved conducive to collective-oriented peasant movements. Specifically, the new landlord claims on peasant harvests and peasant income, coupled with the misuse of village water supplies and relief grains, collapsed the dilemmas of different peasants and underscored the logic of attempting collective action to break the chains of injustice. The CCP had only to place its armed forces behind this action and to find the handful of local militants whose lives depended on its success in order to turn a district or county toward an entirely different course of history.

The significant point, however, is that the mobilization potential of the peasantry was determined as much by the geopolitical locations to be taken advantage of by the CCP revolutionary army as by the social structure or ecosystem of rural society.[16] The Taihang Mountains were to North China what the Jinggan Mountains were to South China: a political haven on the periphery of warlord-state and world market development. Here the CCP enjoyed the time and territorial security to link up with peasant movements whose major goal was to destroy the new system of taxation, usury, and tenancy. In this sense, the CCP scored its major successes in peripheral mountainous zones where state development was the weakest and where peasants were the least inclined to accept the centripetal practices of the Guomindang warlord regime.

The other side of the CCP-led peasant struggle was a capitalist revolution.[17] Peasant China was peasant France, 1789–1815, but only in China was there a Communist party to lead a peasant-based bourgeoisie democratic revolution against labor-repressive warlord-landlord rule. Along with peddlers and small merchants, peasants retrieved China's rural markets once the CCP had destroyed the warlord-gentry controls and derailed the market drives of the Japanese. Defining justice in terms of fair prices and market stability, the CCP and its revolutionary army restored markets that sprang from a centuries-old tradition of competitive free trade. Peasant capitalism was thus an integral component of the revolutionary process. Whereas Western scholars have stressed second-order issues such as the CCP accumulation of peasant capital for protostate goals locally or the army's appropriation of surplus for the War of Resistance nationally, the decisive revolutionary practice was the CCP democratization of peasant market participation.

In China this capitalist breakthrough of the common folk was engineered in part by a Communist party that allowed peasants to blend their indigenous subsistence concerns with their natural drive for profit. It is doubtful that peasants distinguish clearly the empirically neat dichotomy drawn by social scientists between subsistence village sector and surplus market sector, where risk taking supposedly reigns supreme. In agrarian China, where peasant perceptions of long-standing social rights comfortably encompassed patterns of interaction that interwove village life with market participation, the revolution had to win by reestablishing the village-serving market.

Revolutionary legitimacy was not established because the CCP merely reinforced a primitive economy à la Marx. The CCP handling of the market was in part a response to a real peasant demand to make capitalism available and beneficial for all. This required, in the first place, that the CCP deny the tendencies within its own emergent political institution to stifle the popular quest for free trade. A genuine Marxist-Leninist party would have fought against the free-trade pursuits of peasant households. Finding itself in a situation in which opposing the peasant desire to accumulate would have been seen as yet another power-hungry act by pseudorevolutionaries, the

CCP did the right thing: it fought against the pressures within its own protostate to hinder popular market participation, and its fight led the village people to further associate the party with their own purpose.

The progressive capitalist potential of the peasantry would not have developed fully in the absence of the revolutionary army's fostering of the free market.[18] It is one thing for peasants to insist on revolutionaries making capitalism democratic. It is quite another for a Communist party to insist that its armed vanguard live and fight by that principle. Without the armed guarantee of grain supply and price fairness, peasants would have become the victims of yet another internal militarist colonization. This enforcement of popular market rights, though taken by peasants as if it were historical inheritance, was a vital contribution to rural revolution by the CCP. Representing a clean break with the parasitic market relations of the recent warlord past, it made the revolution all the more authentic to the rural people.

In sum, China's peasants were not the precapitalist subsistence-level communalists found in Marx's writings.[19] The CCP had to come to terms with individualistic peasant families in search of survival and surplus. No doubt, as Wolf has shown for Latin America and Scott for Southeast Asia, there is a subsistence ethic, and hence a moral basis, to peasant society.[20] This point cannot be overemphasized. But this does not necessarily make peasants any less capitalist. As free-trading familialists in pursuit of the good life, peasants will favor an open competitive market economy over which they have control and through which they can strengthen folk rather than money values. To be sure, traditionalist peasants are a danger to the foreign-influenced capitalist developments in which they become the losers,[21] and our look at China in the World Depression reminds us that peasant resistance to commerce is only rational in such a situation. But, by the same token, the capitalist side of the CCP-led rural revolution illustrates that commercialization need not bring new risks that weaken subsistence guarantees and create preferences for a closed subsistence community.[22] The possibility for "rice-roots capitalism" to develop fully was much greater in pre-1949 China if only because of the weakness of semifeudal and semi-colonial market controls. The CCP decision to re-create an independent home market without subordinating the villages to a new party-imposed division of labor or party-led anti-imperialist war no doubt favored the growth of peasant initiatives in rural marketing, and thereby rooted the revolution even more deeply in the life preferences of the country people.

For those who have no interest in understanding the relationship between the CCP and the peasantry, the integrationist categories implicit in the institutionalized single-party directorship posed by Lenin will provide a reassuring guide to the process whereby peasants moved from powerlessness to power.[23] Of course the CCP originally set out to penetrate, absorb, induce, and indoctrinate the peasants so they would take up its own cause, and its erstwhile cadres still recall that success was dependent on the institutional authority they exercised when it came to peasant revolutionary participation. But this kind of political motivation did not dominate the revolutionary process. The CCP was alive to the demands produced by the peasants' centrifugal struggles, and how easy it is for us to forget that the centralization needed by the party to carry out its anti-imperialist War of Resistance was not needed to realize the revolutionary changes being carried out by the rural folk. The CCP derived its legitimacy by dancing to the demanding tunes of decentralized peasant movements, not by orchestrating its own centrist plan for power. Thus, an alternative theory, one that recognizes the interaction between the CCP and the peasantry while stressing ultimately the popular quest for local sovereignty, is needed if we are to grasp the CCP's authenticating relationship with peasants in the moments when China stood rightside up.

The notion that the CCP penetrated the villages to rouse the peasants for previously unconsidered acts of revolt[24] ignores the now obvious fact that the peasants' revolutionary mobilizations preceded and outpaced the development of party presence. The peasants, moreover, did not hesitate to demand that the CCP accommodate their preexisting mobilizations, so that the outside party member had to accept the countervalues of the humble folk if he was to achieve legitimacy. The truth is that CCP cadres were accepted locally only after being subjected to the disingenuous screenings of the highly suspicious peasantry. Having grown up in a world in which their parents had been persecuted by local power holders, peasants in modern China would retreat from any new outside political redefinition of their family interest. The CCP got its start in the peasant world by sympathetically respecting this popular attitude. At the village level, the CCP was borne along the axis of the peasants' spontaneous protests to escape, and end, Republican rule. Thus, what has been depicted as "institutionalized mass participation" in a revolution to which the CCP gave birth was actually the product of the CCP's relatively limited interaction with a peasantry that was of its own volition turning to revolution.

To speak of peasant mobilization as if the CCP were simply incorporating the villages into its own protostate is to slight the purpose to which the peasants and their party were dedicating themselves.[25] The CCP was rooting its practices in peasant efforts to affirm the autonomy of the village world. Revolutionary legitimacy was attained by strengthening the strategies of survival being pursued by peasants in the fields, temples, and fairs rather than by announcing what some upper level party official thought was the right way to handle things.[26] It was Jiang's Guomindang, not Mao's CCP, that acted autonomously vis-à-vis the village people. The Guomindang's state-making strategy was to incorporate peasants into an extractive political process occurring independent of family or village approval. The CCP, by comparison, was interacting with peasants in ways that obliged its cadres to derive their political regulations in a significant measure from the antistate preferences of the humble folk. The CCP actually sustained peasant interest in its own purpose, and built up its political base, by registering these preferences in its own system of order, including its schools, courts, and militias. The revolution thus grew, and gained ever greater momentum, precisely because the CCP did not impose its own institutionally related demands on the peasants.

There are serious Western scholars, such as Samuel Huntington and Joel Migdal, who cling to the proposition that revolutionaries mount their massive challenges to existing order by inducing formerly inactive peasants to joint Leninist parties capable of providing them with previously unobtainable material benefits.[27] Of course the emergence of the CCP as a politically viable contender was in part dependent on its ability to dispense certain material rewards, but this "party-as-institutional-giver" variable becomes distorted when it is removed from specific regional and national definitions of the revolutionary situation.

In the first place, the CCP was almost as poor as its impoverished peasant base, and the outnumbered, outlawed, and outgunned cadres had little by way of concrete benefits cum patronage to dispense to peasants in exchange for their participation. In the second place, the CCP rose to power without capturing any developed sources of state patronage and without inheriting any existing neocolonial party machine for drawing peasants to its own party organization. The CCP was operating within a bankrupt peasant economy that its army was trying to cut off from the debilitating influences of the global market and the damaging influences of the Guomindang warlords and the Japanese, and this sociopolitical environment set enormous limits on its capacity to generate a "surplus over subsistence" that it could convert into patronage. Furthermore, the CCP's resource base (including depleted land systems, damaged water supply facilities, unavailable investment capital, missing technology, and lack of managerial expertise) made it all the more difficult for the party to generate revenue from the mining and marketing sectors and thereby make the villages dependent on its own extravillage system of patronage. It made little sense for the CCP to create new peasant expectations for party-sponsored patronage when its cadres could not meet the demands fostered by such political dependency—the CCP wisely stressed peasant self-reliance over institutionalized dependency. In the third place, the surpluses taken from the villages went first to food production projects and human relief services for the rural poor—not to any party efforts to reorganize peasant society for its own ends. The war of course intervened to complicate the task of serving the everyday needs of the peasantry,[28] but the surpluses taken for the war were used by and large to sustain the soldiers who tried to keep the Japanese out of the villages and to soften the setbacks peasants suffered when the war spilled over into their lives. In short, the process whereby the CCP saw that a significantly larger share of local produce remained in peasant bellies was far more important in engendering revolutionary legitimacy than was any outside institutional offering.

The notion that the CCP's Marxist-Leninist ideology prepared the peasants to mobilize for revolution underlies most intellectual images of the party's agrarian experience.[29] But as we have seen, the CCP rose to power to a significant extent by developing a political work style in harmony with the peasants' own proposals for self-rule. This work style was partly the child of the CCP's interaction with the popular countryside, but was also a product of political necessity. Alone, half starved, and hunted, the party members could not afford to substitute their own ideology for the values that invested peasant revolt with human purpose and efficacy. Thought Rectification was to prevent the development of party hegemony, not to establish it.

In seeking refuge in the villages, the CCP began to interact with the goals of an infuriated peasantry, and in the process the party had its Marxist-Leninist ideology infused from below by a robust folklore on revolution. I suspect that coming to terms with this folklore was a formidable challenge, and that China's peasants made a compelling case that their seemingly backward ideas ought to prevail in the party's plans for revolutionary order. This conclusion will prove unpleasant only to those who portray the formation of the revolutionary experiment in more familiar ideological categories.[30] For their analyses seldom face up to the fact that the CCP became *the* important friend of the country people. At the village level, the party drew its support from those peasants whose experiences had taken them beyond local roots. Its most audacious supporters hailed from the marginal sharecroppers, hired hands, and herdsmen who made up the revolutionary diaspora. They suffered cruel exploitation in everyday life, and they were prepared by their own experience to carry the revolution to the rooted peasantry. The very fact that they had survived the terrible years of the Republic confirmed them as competent leaders in the minds of their comparatively settled counterparts, who shared their hope for a world in which the peasant was no longer the victim. And they had more than militancy going for them—the uprooting process brought them, dialectically, to new friends who knew about politics and who knew how to place power in the hands of the local poor.

At yet another level, one that spanned village and market town, the carriers of revolution were the professionals who serviced the Little Tradition—the local doctor, the mine clerk, the small merchant, the carpenter or blacksmith, the schoolteacher, the opera singer. Their friendship with peasants grew out of a shared interest in stopping landlords and warlords from manipulating villages, mines, markets, and government to their common disadvantage. Because of their literacy and mobility, they played a crucial part in drafting peasant demands. While they did not share a perfect identity with peasants, they respected the popular values that gave peasant mobilization its liberationist potential—a potential that was shaped by some profoundly religious premises.

This study reconfirms the mutually empowering relationship between religion and revolution in the rural world.[31] In taking up the peasants' revolutionary proposals to eliminate the causes of misery, the CCP drew to its banners the landless desperate peasants who entertained notions of starting history over again outside of the imperial Confucian tradition and without the domination of a state. This desire to get rid of unjust rulers once and for all sprang from the indigenous cultural expressions of the peasants' radically democratic millennialist vision. That they insisted that this vision be realized was for the CCP a reminder of the independent origins of the popular movement, and more. The vision offered a wild card to be played against the aggressively antiheathen forces of militarism and imperialism. In playing it—or in enabling peasants to play it—the CCP embraced the centrifugal Guanyin activities that were at the heart of religious dissent in the Little Tradition. Guanyin, the hope of the poor, remained the cosavior, but the CCP, not the idol behind the mother goddess, took first place as the savior of peasant China.

The anti-imperialist War of Resistance was only one phase of the modern Chinese revolution, and yet any theorist of revolutionary legitimacy must deal with this meeting point between peasant revolution and national liberation. A central question ought to be, as Chalmers Johnson wrote years ago, whether there was an organic interconnection between the origins of the CCP victory and the Japanese invasion.[32] The facts seem to suggest otherwise. Rural revolution and resistance war were largely discrete processes, and the CCP effort to organize the countryside for war did not supersede the survival goals of the peasantry.

The rise of the CCP correlated with the nonpresence of imperialist force. The CCP built its Anti-Japanese base areas in mountainous regions beyond the reach of the Japanese military in the opening moments of invasion. What filled the lives of peasants in these moments was revolution, not Anti-Japanese war. Clearly, then, the capacity of the CCP to successfully carry out its War of Resistance was related to its ability to extend peasant-based revolution in the power gaps of a weakened Republican warlord state and to exploit the inability of Japanese imperialism to integrate the countryside into its order.

For a long time we have been living with the supposition—and that is all it is—that revolutionary success was dependent upon the Japanese invasion and its attendant brutality.[33] The Japanese invasion did increase political instability and did accentuate the social dilemma of the peasantry. It did not, however, ignite *peasant* mobilizations that were in line with the nationalist goals of the CCP. To be sure, Japanese force tracked and challenged the development of revolutionary power, but where the Japanese effectively established their own force around the villages and markets peasants quite often attempted to survive by strategies that did not necessarily benefit the CCP-led partisans.[34] In this sense, the Japanese occupation did not automatically generate the conditions for the growth of "peasant nationalism," and conversely, the CCP-led peasant movements by and large persevered and prospered in villages and districts where the Eighth Route Army did not have to contend with massive Japanese force. These rural localities remained free from imperialist domination, and CCP success in them was not dependent on peasant suffering at the hands of foreign invaders.

Proponents of the theory that the CCP mobilized peasants into a mass citizen army for its anti-imperialist Resistance War[35] would have us think the CCP tore a page from Engels's notion of a militarized revolution of the toiling people, but the party did for peasants only what they could not do for themselves—it formed and led an anti-imperialist army and arranged for peasants to assist the army without radically altering their self-sustaining routines. In the final analysis, the CCP drew its army from the uprooted, rejected noncitizens of the Republic,[36] and then called on its cadres to overcome the limited war contributions of the rooted peasantry. This latter task the CCP accomplished by assuming responsibility for the high-risk assignments of war in place of the peasantry. The great sacrifice entailed allowed the rural people to continuously recapture their means of livelihood through revolutionary mobilization. The willingness of the CCP to undertake this sacrifice established its cadres as morally responsible human beings in the eyes of the peasantry.[37]

To be sure, the CCP spearheaded the movement to resolve the national crisis, and its cadres were the brain trust of a multiclass movement to recapture the motherland. But the movement to involve peasants in saving the nation mostly took shape at local rural levels, and peasants responded to CCP appeals to join in national resistance by words and deeds that brought party intentions in line with their own local self-interest.

The enduring question, therefore, is why CCP appeals to oust the wartime invaders eventually did gain attention within the peasant world. The rather obvious answer is that the Chinese Communists were fortunate enough to be working alongside peasants who took pride in the fact that they had not been assimilated—hence the ease with which they could experience their cooperation with the Communist party's anti-imperialist cause as an extension of antistate resistance that reached back over the centuries.[38] The peasants of the Taihang Mountains carried on their quest for survival from a non-subordinate mentality, and when it came to the politics of liberation, they were determined to place the CCP armed forces in their own Little Tradition category of a messianic deliverer of the poor. The CCP's willingness and ability to fulfill this folk expectation, while actually inspiring the poor to save themselves, fanned the fires of freedom and resistance in the popular countryside.

Given the militarization of modern China, the CCP stress on the strong armed pagan as the necessary source of security, fraternity, and liberty is understandable. Without guns on their side rebellious peasants will be dragged from their hovels, tortured before their loved ones, and dumped in shallow graves. The struggle does not end with death, however, for their tormented souls will demand vengeance, and the local folk will experience revolutionaries as heroic avengers. In explaining revolutionary legitimacy in a country where violence and vengeance became basic it is tempting to portray the CCP rising to power on a wave of raiding and ruin, discovering with destructive peasant rebels that violence and only violence would dignify the struggle for survival.[39]

CCP success in sustaining peasant mobilization cannot be explained solely by reference to the violent application of armed force, however. The revolution was a test of the relative military strengths of the Guomindang and the CCP. But it was also a test of the relative moral strengths of the two contenders. The CCP won by demilitarizing rural authority relations within the territories over which its army and militias exercised control. Within the base areas, flocks of homeless and familyless people took up arms to rectify the suffering and humiliation they knew under the lawless and unrighteous order of militarism and imperialism. But they did not look upon violence as the norm for revolutionary order.

Force, as prescribed by the peasants, was to reestablish the peace of the villages over the war of the towns, cities, and the aborted military state. They, and their party, elected to resurrect the socioreligious codes that traditionally had placed restraints on violence. Like the Anabaptists in the German Peasants' War,[40] China's peasant rebels took up arms to hurry in the millennium, but they built up revolutionary order on the basis of values that symbolized a profound break with militarism and its arrogant mentality.

For Mao Zedong and the CCP, national liberation was to be achieved by force of arms. Unlike Fanon, however, Mao and the CCP came to understand that peasants did not need to confront imperialism head on, or bathe in the blood of the colonial oppressor, in order to attain liberation.[41] And they discovered that there was no need to sacrifice peasant spontaneity to their party's centrally directed anti-imperialist war.

This question—how to break the power of imperialist-backed elite armies that force their way into peasant life through coups at the top—is central to our age. The CCP, in acting as the armed-interest of the popular classes, provided the painfully effective answer to this matter. It is painful to us, not the peasants, for they will die without a counterforce to enforce their interest. Ironically, if the revolution is to win, the popular army must relax the multiple pressures to transform the peasants' world into a colony for national liberation war. The CCP found a way to meet this challenge, that is, to separate the process of warfare from the peasants' struggle for land and livelihood. Rather than thrust peasants into war, the party involved itself in practices to attenuate the peasants' vulnerability to war-related pressures.

Partly the product of a guerrilla tradition of protracted war, these practices worked better where state-military dominance was relatively weak. Just as revolution survived in the power gaps of Guomindang militarism, so the struggle for liberation surged ahead only in the awaited openings of world politics, that is, the moment of faltering outside support for the hated new warlord order. Once the United States defeated the Japanese in the Pacific War, and then declined—rightly—to pay the overhead costs of the Guomindang warlord regime, the CCP armed forces could strike to win the country for ordinary folk. As modern China teaches us, such a decisive moment can hold the promise of something other than the hegemony of a modern nation state.

Notes

ABBREVIATIONS USED IN THE NOTES

CCP   Chinese Communist Party
JPRS   Joint Publications Research Service
PLA   People's Liberation Army
SPRCM   Selections from People's Republic of China Magazines
SPRCP   Survey of People's Republic of China Press

INTRODUCTION

1. Friedrich Engels, *The Peasant War in Germany* (New York: International Publishers, 1966), pp. 35–37, 48–49, 100–101, 122–23, 150. Edward Friedman makes this argument in "The German Peasant War of 1525," in *The Journal of Peasant Studies*, ed. Janos Bak (London: Frank Cass, 1975), pp. 117–23.

2. John King Fairbank, interview with Walter Cronkite, CBS Television (December 1978).

3. James C. Scott has utilized the notion of Little Tradition values to comprehend peasant rebellion in Southeast Asia and Western Europe. His theoretical work deals mainly with subordinated peasants who rebel against firmly established states. My work draws heavily from Scott's framework, but my focus is more on the mentalities of peasants who were revolting to end their subordination to a military order that had not jelled into a strong central state. James C. Scott, "Protest and Profanation: Agrarian Revolt and the Little Tradition," *Theory and Society* 4, no. 1 and no. 2 (1977), pp. 1–38, 211–46.

4. Barrington Moore, Jr., *Social Origins of Dictatorship and Democracy: Lord and Peasant in the Making of the Modern World* (Boston: Beacon Press, 1966), pp. 411, 485, 495.

5. Reinhard Bendix, *Max Weber: An Intellectual Portrait* (New York: Anchor-Doubleday, 1962), p. 92.

6. Christopher Hill, *The World Turned Upside Down: Radical Ideas During the English Revolution* (New York: Viking, 1972).

7. Emmanuel Le Roy Ladurie, *Montaillou: The Promised Land of Error*, trans. Barbara Bray (New York: Vintage Books, 1979).

8. Jack Belden, *China Shakes the World* (New York: Monthly Review Press, 1970), p. 50.

9. "Bo Yibo: New Vice Premier of the State Council," *Issues and Studies* (August 1979): 82–85.

10. Talcott Parsons, ed., *Max Weber: The Theory of Social and Economic Organization* (New York: Free Press, 1964), pp. 155–56.

CHAPTER 1

1. Huang Wei, "The Ancient Yellow River Takes On a New Look," *Lishi yanjiu* [Historical research] no. 6 (20 December 1975), SPRCM (April 1976): 25–28.

2. Sidney L. Greenblatt, ed., *The People of Taihang* (White Plains, N.Y.: International Arts and Sciences Press, 1976), pp. 4–5.

3. The seminal contribution on the Eight Trigrams is Susan Naquin, *Millenarian Rebellion in China: The Eight Trigrams Uprising of 1813* (New Haven: Yale University Press, 1976). Judging from Naquin's study, the mother goddess tradition flourished in some of the same localities where the CCP first gained a foothold—Hua *xian*, Lin Qing, etc. (pts. 1, 3, conclusion).

4. A. E. Glover, *A Thousand Miles of Miracle in China* (London: Pickering and Ingles, 1904), pp. 11–12, 19–20, 34–35, 49–54, 124–30.

5. Institute of Geography, Academia Sinica, *Economic Geography of North China* (Beijing: 1957) (Washington, D.C.: Joint Publications Research, 1958), pp. 102, 170.

6. Cf. Dwight H. Perkins, who writes, "The lower end of the range (400 catties) represents something like a minimum level of subsistence." *Agricultural Development in China 1368–1968* (Chicago: Aldine, 1969), p. 14.

7. Huang Wei, "Ancient Yellow River."

8. Xu Guangdi and Yao Kun, *Hua xian zhi* [Hua county gazetteer] (1867): 1–2; and Wang Puyuan and Wang Weiyuan, *Hua xian zhi* [Hua county gazetteer] (1926–30): 1–2.

9. Huang Wei, "Ancient Yellow River."

10. Frederick Wakeman, Jr., *The Fall of Imperial China* (New York: Free Press, 1975), p. 7.

11. Xu Guangdi and Yao Kun, *Hua xian zhi* (1867): 1–1a.

12. On peasant influences in state migration plans see David N. Keightley, "Peasant Migration, Politics, and Philosophical Response in Zhou and Qin China," University of California–Berkeley Regional Seminar, November 1977, pp. 1–8, 15–23, 32–40.

13. Etienne Balazs, *Chinese Civilization and Bureaucracy*, trans. H. M. Wright (New Haven: Yale University Press, 1964), pp. 6–9.

14. The classic European view of the Chinese empire, reflected in Marx, was one of a despotic center in total control of waterworks and irrigation facilities and hence the sinews of agriculture. Cf. Perry Anderson, *Lineages of the Absolutist State* (London: New Left Books, 1974), pp. 462–83.

15. Cf. John Watt, "Leadership Criteria in Late Imperial China," *Qingshi wenti* 2, no. 3 (July 1970): 31.

16. J. A. Pitt-Rivers, *The People of the Sierra* (Chicago: University of Chicago Press, 1961), pp. 17–19.

17. Jean Chesneaux, *Peasant Revolts in China 1840–1949*, trans. C. A. Curwen (London: Thames and Hudson, 1973), pp. 67–68.

18. Qi Wu, *Yige geming genjudi de chengzhang: Kangri zhanzheng he jiefang zhanzheng shiqi de Jin-Ji-Lu-Yu bianqu gaikuang* [The growth of a revolutionary base: the general conditions of the Shanxi-Hebei-Shandong-Henan border region during the anti-Japanese war of resistance and the war of liberation] (Beijing: Renmin chubanshe [People's press], 1958), pp. 1–7; and Institute of Geography, Academia Sinica, *Economic Geography of North China*, pp. 1–9.

19. This line of argument has been developed for agrarian Asia in James C. Scott, *The Moral Economy of the Peasant: Rebellion and Subsistence in Southeast Asia* (New Haven: Yale University Press, 1976), especially chaps. 1–2.

20. I have developed this point in "The World Turned Downsideup: Three Orders of Meaning in the Peasants' Traditional World," *Modern China* 3, no. 2 (April 1977): 185–215.

21. Joseph Needham long ago pointed out the importance of customary family-centered cooperative relations in Chinese peasant society. "The Past in China's Present," *Pacific Viewpoint* 4, no. 2 (September 1963): 133.

22. Compare with Li Gang, *Qunzhong shenghuo* [Life of the masses], no. 1 (Ji-Lu-Yu kang lian qunzhong shenghuoshe [Life of the masses press of the Hebei-Shandong-Henan district federation of resistance associations], 1944), pp. 24–26.

23. Here I follow the logic of Emmanuel Le Roy Ladurie on *Montaillou: The Promised Land of Error*, trans. Barbara Bray (New York: Vintage Books, 1979), pp. 49–54, 66–67.

24. "Peasant Weather Observer in Central China County," Survey of People's Republic of China Press (SPRCP) (20–24 January 1975), pp. 26–28.

25. Cf. Li Gang, *Qunzhong shenghuo*, pp. 24–26.

26. G. William Skinner, "Marketing and Social Structure in Rural China," pt. I, *Journal of Asian Studies* 24 (November 1964): 3–43; G. William Skinner, "Chinese Peasants and the Closed Community: An Open and Shut Case," *Comparative Studies in Society and History* 13, no. 3 (July 1971): 270–81.

27. Skinner, "Chinese Peasants and the Closed Community," 271–72, 280–82.

28. Ibid., 274.

29. Cf. John R. Watt, "The Yamen and Urban Administration," in *The City in Late Imperial China*, ed. G. William Skinner (Stanford: Stanford University Press, 1977), pp. 369–85.

30. I have developed this point in "Peasants, Capitalism, and Revolution: On Capitalism as a Force for Liberation in Revolutionary China," *Comparative Political Studies* 12, no. 3 (October 1979): 294–98. The point is not inconsistent with Perkins, *Agricultural Development in China*, pp. 169–70, 173–76.

31. Chesneaux, *Peasant Revolts in China*, p. 18.

32. Robert Marks, "Markets and Morals: Peasants and the Question of Food in Eighteenth-Century Guandong," 21st Annual Conference, American Association for Chinese Studies (November 1979), California State University, Long Beach, Cal., pp. 1–18.

33. Glover, *Thousand Miles of Miracle in China*, pp. 6–7.

34. James C. Scott, "Protest and Profanation: Agrarian Revolt and the Little Tradition," *Theory and Society*, vol. 2, 1977, pp. 213–14.

35. Zhao Shuli, "Meng Xiang Stands Up," in *Modern Chinese Short Stories*, ed. W. J. F. Jenner (London: Oxford University Press, 1970), p. 12.

36. Edwin Moise, "Downward Social Mobility in Pre-Revolutionary China," *Modern China* 3, no. 1 (January 1977): 15. Buck's estimate of 17 percent tenancy seems low, but it may not be too far from the mark for the pre-Republican era. J. L. Buck, *Land Utilization in China* (New York: Paragon, 1964), p. 9.

37. Skinner, "Chinese Peasants and the Closed Community," pp. 272–73.

38. On this point, see Wolfram Eberhard, *Chinese Festivals* (New York: Henry Schuman, 1952), pp. 6–9.

39. It is important to distinguish popular temple fair festivities from state festivals. Where the two overlapped the meaning given to these events by peasants was not always the same as that given by officialdom. Cf. Eberhard, *Chinese Festivals*, pp. 8–9.

40. Cf. Wakeman, *Fall of Imperial China*, pp. 29–35.

41. For the concept of instrumental reciprocal relations in peasant societies, see John Duncan Powell, "Peasant Society and Clientelist Politics," *American Political Science Review* 64, no. 2 (1970): 412–18; and James C. Scott, "Patron-Client Politics and Political Change in Southeast Asia," *American Political Science Review* 66, no. 11 (1972): 95–99. Much of the standard literature on peasant society emphasizes peasant dependence on patrons for survival. My assumption is that China's village people tried to maximize their means of survival mainly through family-centered economies. Such an assumption does not, however, rule out the possibility that patron-client relationships were at work traditionally.

42. Barrington Moore, Jr., *Social Origins of Dictatorship and Democracy: Lord and Peasant in the Making of the Modern World* (Boston: Beacon Press, 1966), p. 205.

43. Such doubts were expressed to me by a member of the CCP in a discussion on rural class

relations, Shaoshan, Hunan, July 1979. A discussion with CCP historians in Kaifeng, Henan (April 1980), produced answers far closer to Moore's conception, however.

44. Thus the sociological categories for European feudalism established by Marc Bloch are not so easily transplanted to China. Cf. Bloch, *Feudal Society: The Growth of Ties of Dependence*, trans. L. A. Manyon (Chicago: University of Chicago Press, 1970). For the original version of this point, see Thaxton, "The World Turned Downsideup," 185–225.

45. This is made clear in *Zhongguo nongcun jingji ziliao* [Materials on the Chinese village economy] ed. Feng Hefa (Shanghai: Li Ming Press, 1935), pp. 191–94. See also Kung-chuan Hsiao, *Rural China: Imperial Control in the Nineteenth Century* (Seattle: University of Washington Press, 1960), pp. 384–85. Cf. also R. H. Tawney, *Land and Labor in China* (Boston: Beacon Press, 1966), p. 36. Tawney understood the obligations in tenant-landlord relations, but he sometimes confused what he was witnessing in the 1930s with traditional exchange.

46. For an essay that supports Moore, see Tan Chung, "Nineteenth-Century China Revisited: Chinese Peasant War for Taiping Dreams (1850–1864)," *China Report* (May-June 1978): 20–21.

47. I have dealt with these provisions in landlord-tenant relations in "Tenants in Revolution: The Tenacity of Traditional Morality," *Modern China* 1, no. 3 (July 1975): 323–58. They are detailed in Feng Hefa, ed., *Zhongguo nongcun jingji ziliao*, pp. 191–94. Their previous existence is also confirmed by my "Lin County Village Investigations, Spring, 1980." For a critique of my early elaboration of exchange and dependency in rural China see Ramon H. Myers, "North China Villages during the Republican Period: Socioeconomic Relationships," *Modern China* 6, no. 3 (July 1980): 243–66.

48. This was the practice in North China, but the best source known on it is Morton Fried, *Fabric of Chinese Society: A Study of the Social Life of a County Seat* (London: Atlantic Press, 1956), p. 102.

49. *Gongzuo tongxun* [Work correspondence], no. 11 (Zhonggong zhongyang Ji-Lu-Yu fenqu minyunbu [Civil movement department of the Hebei-Shandong-Henan branch of the Chinese Communist Party], 10 August 1945), pp. 1–17.

50. Cf. J. L. Buck, *Land Utilization in China* (New York: Paragon, 1964), p. 17.

51. In support of this point see Roland Mousnier, *Peasant Uprisings in Seventeenth-Century France, Russia and China*, trans. Brian Pearce (New York: Harper Torchbooks, 1970), p. 271.

52. Ibid., pp. 271–72.

53. Kung-chuan Hsiao, *Rural China*, p. 278; Skinner, "Chinese Peasants and the Closed Community," pp. 272–73.

54. Here I rely on premises borrowed from Eugene D. Genovese's classic *Roll Jordan Roll: The World the Slaves Made* (New York: Pantheon, 1972).

55. But cf. Mark Elvin, *The Pattern of the Chinese Past* (Stanford: Stanford University Press, 1973), p. 244.

56. Ralph Thaxton, "Lin County Village Investigations." See also Zhong Da, "What Is 'Resisted'? What Is Publicized?" *Guangming ribao* (29 November 1974), SPRCP 16–20 (December 16–20, 1974): 1–7.

57. On this point, and on underclass meaning systems in general, see Frank Parkin, *Class Inequality and Political Order* (London: MacGibbon and Key, 1971), pp. 79–102; and Sutti Ortiz, "Reflections on the Concept of 'Peasant Culture' and 'Peasant Cognitive System,'" in *Peasants and Peasant Societies*, ed. Teodor Shanin (Middlesex, Eng.: Penguin, 1973), pp. 322–35. My application of Parkin's elaboration of orders of meaning for European underclasses does not assume that the dominant value system promotes a consistent endorsement of existing inequality by underclasses. Moreover, I assume peasants, rather than mass political parties, to have been the original carriers of countervalues.

58. For the full argument, see Thaxton, "The World Turned Downsideup," 185–215.

59. Huang Xuanwen, *Xiaohe fengyun* [Storm along the Xiao river] *Henan sheng Neihuang*

xian Qiankou cun [The history of Qiankou village in Henan Province's Neihuang county], (Henan renmin chubanshe [Henan people's press], 1976), pp. 1–40.

60. For a suggestive example of this phenomenon, cf. James B. Parsons, *Peasant Rebellions of the Late Ming Dynasty* (Tucson: University of Arizona Press, 1970), pp. 91–92.

61. This view of China is reproduced in many versions. For two examples, see Richard Solomon, *Mao's Revolution and the Chinese Political Culture* (Berkeley: University of California Press, 1971), chaps. 1–2, pp. 515–23, and Leon E. Stover, *The Cultural Ecology of Chinese Civilization: Peasants and Elites in the Last of the Agrarian States* (New York: Mentor, 1974). Perhaps the most complete statement of the major premises of the "integrationist school" is in S. N. Eisenstadt, *Revolution and the Transformation of Societies: A Comparative Study of Civilizations* (New York: Free Press, 1978), pp. 128–34.

62. "Karl Marx: Peasantry as a Class," in *Peasants and Peasant Societies*, ed. Teodor Shanin, pp. 229–37. Gramsci's position is in line with Marx on this issue. Gramsci apparently accepted most of Marx's argument for false consciousness. But he realized the ultimate failure of the "immanentist philosophies" to integrate the "simple people" to their ruling-class ideology. See Antonio Gramsci, *The Modern Prince* (New York: International Publishers, 1975), pp. 42–44, 61–67.

63. For the general argument, see James C. Scott, "Exploitation in Rural Class Relations: A Victim's Perspective," *Comparative Politics* 7, no. 4 (July 1975): 489–532.

64. Wolfram Eberhard, *Lokalkulturen im Alten China*, vol. 1 (Leiden, 1942), vol. 2 (Peking, 1942). For a brilliant affirmation of Eberhard's wisdom see Evelyn S. Rawski, "Popular Religion in East Asia," *Peasant Studies Newsletter* 4, no. 4 (October 1975): 2–6.

65. W. F. Wertheim, *Evolution and Revolution: The Rising Waves of Emancipation* (Middlesex, Eng.: Penguin, 1974), p. 99.

66. Cf. Frederick Wakeman, Jr., "Rebellion and Revolution: The Study of Popular Movements in Chinese History," *Journal of Asian Studies* 36, no. 2 (February 1977): 213. Wakeman's point finds support in the Chinese Communist party documents that, though written in wartime, dealt with ancient Chinese history. The exciting source on this is Shi Liqun, *Zhongguoshi hua* [Talking about Chinese history] (Ji-Lu-Yu Shudian [Hebei-Shandong-Henan bookstore], 1940–41). An article in this work states that "as commercial capitalism developed, the consciousness of the peasantry was raised," p. 20.

67. We lack any serious study of this point. My inference from talks with peasants in Yao village and from Ladurie, *Montaillou*, pp. 44, 70–119.

68. Yang Zhongguo, "Confucius—A Thinker Who Stubbornly Supported the Slave System," and Zhe Zhun, "Confucius' Doctrine of the Mean: A Philosophy of Opposition to Social Change," in *Selected Articles Criticizing Lin Piao and Confucius*, vol. 1 (Beijing: Foreign Languages Press, 1974), pp. 15, 23.

69. Cf. Ortiz, "Reflections on the Concept of 'Peasant Culture,'" 322–35.

70. *Folk Literature*, no. 12 (February 1956): 64. "China: Two Tales about Agricultural Labourers," trans. C. A. Curwen, *Journal of Peasant Studies* 2 (October 1974): 99.

71. Kenneth Evan Sharpe, *Peasant Politics: Struggle in a Dominican Village* (Baltimore: Johns Hopkins University Press, 1977), pp. 141–42.

72. Shu Liqun, *Zhongguoshi hua*, pp. 19–20.

73. This is the thrust of C. K. Yang, *Religion in Chinese Society* (Berkeley: University of California Press, 1961), pp. 214–15, and Daniel Overmyer, *Folk Buddhist Religion* (Cambridge: Harvard University Press, East Asian Series 83, 1976), pp. 1–71. Both Yang and Overmyer recognize the existence of a popular "contest religion" in traditional China, but by and large they treat it as something less than a motive force in the rebellions of the Little Tradition.

74. Cf. Arthur P. Wolf's splendid essay "Gods, Ghosts, and Ancestors," in *Religion and Ritual in Chinese Society*, ed. Wolf (Stanford: Stanford University Press, 1974), pp. 131–40. See also Stover, *Cultural Ecology of Chinese Civilization*, p. 122.

75. My inference from Arthur H. Smith, *Common Proverbs and Common Sayings from the Chinese* (Shanghai: Presbyterian Mission Press, 1914), pp. 202–03; and from Chiang K'uei, *The Whirlwind*, trans. Timothy Ross (San Francisco: Chinese Materials Center, 1977), pp. 150–52. Cf. *Folktales of China*, ed. Wolfram Eberhard (New York: Washington Square Press, 1973), pp. 194–95.

76. This is Overmyer's interpretation, *Folk Buddhist Religion*, pp. 20–30, 42–50.

77. My interpretation of data presented in Wolfram Eberhard, *Guilt and Sin in Traditional China* (Berkeley: University of California Press, 1967), pp. 41–55, 117–18, 121–24. For the theoretical foundations of this interpretation I have relied on Mircea Eliade, *Myths, Dreams, and Mysteries: The Encounter between Contemporary Faiths and Archaic Realities*, trans. Philip Mariet (New York: Harper & Row, 1960), pp. 1–72, esp. 7–10, 42–45, 50–61.

78. On Li Zicheng, the best western historical treatment is Parsons, *Peasant Rebellions of the Late Ming Dynasty*. James P. Harrison best captures the CCP view of this revolt in *The Chinese Communists and Chinese Peasant Rebellions* (New York: Atheneum, 1969), pp. 64, 77–78, and 155–57.

79. From William S. Atwell's splendid paper, "Notes on Silver, Foreign Trade, and the Late Ming Economy," *Qing Shi Wenti* [Problems in Qing history] 3, no. 8 (1977): 1–8, 15–19.

80. Mousnier, *Peasant Uprisings*, pp. 276–77.

81. Zheng Zhou, "A Critique of the Zheng Brothers by the Insurgent Army of Li Zicheng," *Hongqi* [Red flag], no. 9 (1 September 1974). *Li Zicheng fan Ru douzheng xiao gushi* [A little reader on Li Zicheng's anti-Confucian struggle] (Shanghai renmin chubanshe [Shanghai people's press], 1975), pp. 1–12. Cf. Yao Xueyin, *Li Zicheng* (Beijing: Zhongguo qingnian chubanshe [China Youth Press], 1977). Also personal talks with peasant and urban youths in Chengdu and Kaifeng marketplaces, July 1979 and April 1980.

82. Zheng Zhou, "A Critique of the Zheng Brothers."

83. See also Elvin, *The Pattern of the Chinese Past*, pp. 245–46, 254.

84. Mousnier, *Peasant Uprisings*, p. 290.

85. The emphasis on weak traditional political controls and weak center provisioning as facilitators of revolution in the twentieth century is in Moore, *Social Origins*, pp. 162–227; Theda Skocpol, "France, Russia, China: A Structural Analysis of Social Revolutions," *Comparative Studies in Society and History* 18, no. 2 (April 1976): 175–81, 192–95.

86. Compare with how the CCP and the peasants approached the issue during the 1947–48 Land Revolution, as detailed in chap. 7, below.

87. The CCP would show distrust of this type of insurgent in the 1920s and 1930s. On this point see Hong Xuan, "Water Margin and Literature for National Defense," *Xuexi yu pipan* [Study and criticism], no. 12 (14 December 1975); and Hong Cheng, "Ji Jiguang's Thought of Running the Army," *Lishi yanjiu* [Historical research], no. 6 (20 December 1975).

CHAPTER 2

1. R. H. Tawney, *Land and Labor in China* (Boston: Beacon Press, 1966), p. 77. I am indebted to James C. Scott, *The Moral Economy of the Peasant: Rebellion and Subsistence in Southeast Asia* (New Haven: Yale University Press, 1976), chaps. 2–4, for the general theoretical framework of this chapter. China of course was not colonial Southeast Asia. The fiscal crisis of the center and the deep inroads of militarism made peasant hunger much worse in China.

2. *Famine in China's Northwest* (Beijing: China International Famine Relief Commission, 1930), p. 52.

3. The literature of the Western economic school is too voluminous to cite here. The following works, however, stand at its center: John L. Buck, *Land Utilization in China* (New York: Paragon, 1964); Ramon H. Myers, *The Chinese Peasant Economy: Agricultural Development in Hopei and Shantung 1890–1949* (Cambridge, Mass.: Harvard University Press, 1970); Albert Feuerwerker, *Economic Trends in the Republic of China, 1912–1949* (Ann

Arbor: Michigan Papers in Chinese Studies, 1977). The most recent representation, which declares all American-born scholars of modern China to be mistrained dopes, is Ramon H. Myers and Thomas A. Metzger, "Sinological Shadows: The State of Modern China Studies in the U. S.,"*Australian Journal of Chinese Affairs*, no. 4 (1980): 1–29. For a perceptive critique of Myers's *Chinese Peasant Economy*, see Cheryl Payer, "Was the Chinese Peasant Exploited?" *Journal of Peasant Studies* 2, no. 2 (January 1975): 229–36.

4. Myers, *Chinese Peasant Economy*, pp. 13–24, 273–95.

5. Ibid., pp. 290–92.

6. Susan Mann Jones and Philip A. Kuhn, "Dynastic Decline and the Roots of Rebellion," in *The Cambridge History of China*, vol. 10, part I, eds. Denis Twitchett and John K. Fairbank (London: Cambridge University Press, 1979), pp. 111–15, 128–31.

7. Cf. Loh Waifong, "The Board of Revenue and Late Qing Finance," Ph.D. thesis, Harvard University History and East Asian Languages, August 1977, pp. 32–33, 79–80, 133–44.

8. *The Yi Ho Tuan Movement of 1900* (Beijing: Foreign Languages Press, 1976), pp. 114–15. The link between war indemnities and peasant tax burden is well known, but it is seldom explored systematically by the Western economic school. Elizabeth J. Perry, *Rebels and Revolutionaries in North China 1845–1945* (Stanford: Stanford University Press, 1980), p. 153, does a nice job of analyzing it.

9. Ernest Young, *The Presidency of Yuan Shikai* (Ann Arbor: University of Michigan Press, 1977), pp. 44–45.

10. I am indebted to Jerome Ch'en for this insight, in our personal correspondence. Also see Ch'en's *The Military-Gentry Coalition: China Under the Warlords* (Toronto: University of Toronto–York University Joint Center on Modern East Asia, 1979), pp. 134–35.

11. Details on this decline in Qing provisioning are in Paul R. Bohr, *Famine in China and the Missionary* (Cambridge: Harvard East Asia Monographs, 1972), pp. 1–75.

12. See Joseph W. Esherick, *Reform and Revolution in China: The 1911 Revolution in Hunan and Hubei* (Berkeley: University of California Press, 1976), pp. 111–17, showing this change was under way in central China by 1911.

13. Chen Tisi, "Jinan nongcun de xianzhuang" [The present conditions in the villages of Southern Hebei] in *Zhongguo nongcun* [China's peasant villages] 1, no. 11 (Shanghai, 1935): 564.

14. This is the thrust of Hung-Mao Tien's *Government and Politics in Kuomintang China 1927–1937* (Stanford: Stanford University Press, 1972, pp. 2–4, 177, 181.

15. Ibid., pp. 134, 167–68.

16. Ralph Thaxton, "Lin County Village Investigations," 1980. Tien is ambiguous on this point, since he shows that Guomindang and warlord taxes often existed side by side, but then goes on to claim that provincialism undercut the central government's tax base. *Government and Politics of Kuomintang China*, pp. 167–68, 181.

17. Cf. James E. Sheridan, *Chinese Warlord: The Career of Feng Yu-hsiang* (Stanford: Stanford University Press, 1966), p. 24.

18. Here I follow Huntington's logic. No reformist coup d'état followed Jiang Jieshi's intervention, so that from 1927 on the trend was toward reactionary praetorianism. Cf. Samuel P. Huntington, *Political Order in Changing Societies* (New Haven: Yale University Press, 1968), pp. 192–210.

19. My inference from Jui-hua Lo Upshur, "China Under the Kuomintang: The Problem of Unification," Ph.D. thesis, University of Michigan History Department, 1972, pp. 68–73.

20. Theodore H. White, *In Search of History* (New York: Harper & Row, 1978), pp. 150, 162. To White the first cause of inflation was the war, and this was followed by natural disaster and government pillage. *Time* (3 July 1978): 42.

21. Cf. Lloyd Eastman, *The Abortive Revolution: China Under Nationalist Rule, 1927–1937* (Cambridge, Mass.: Harvard University Press, 1974), pp. 187–88, 196, 223–24. Eastman shows that peasants were in trouble and the Guomindang was adding to their woes,

but then he rests his case *for* Nanjing on the assumption that "the rural economy had largely recovered from the depression by 1936–1937." A study that throws light on this issue is Chiang Kia-Ngau, *The Inflationary Spiral: The Experience in China, 1939–1950* (Cambridge, Mass.: MIT Press, 1958), pp. 3–4, 8.

22. The chart has been constructed from Bohr, *Famine in China*, pp. xv, 15–16, 53, 72, 116–31; W. H. Mallory, *China: Land of Famine* (New York: American Geographical Society, 1926), p. 52; *The North China Famine of 1920–21*, pp. 1–13; *Famine Commission Bulletin* 4, no. 4 (Beijing: China Famine Relief Commission, 1922): 22–25; *Famine in China's Northwest*, pp. 1–56; Rewi Alley, *China's Hinterland in the Great Leap Forward* (Beijing: New World Press, 1961), p. 113; Irwin J. Schulmann, "The Origins of the Boxers," ACLS Workshop on "Rebellion and Revolution in North China," Harvard University, 1979, pp. 1–2, and pages to notes. The best study of famine I have run across is François Godement, "Famine in the Warlord Age: The 1928–1930 Crisis in North China," ACLS Workshop on "Food and Famine in Chinese History," Harvard University, 1980, pp. 1–41.

23. Albert Feuerwerker, *Rebellion in Nineteenth-Century China* (Ann Arbor: University of Michigan Center for Chinese Studies, 1975), p. 52, dates the decline in Yellow River administration around 1855 and the time of the terrible Henan floods. Cf. Charles Greer, *Water Management in the Yellow River Basin* (Austin: University of Texas Press, 1979), pp. 41–51.

24. Huang Wei, "The Ancient Yellow River," pp. 27–28. O. J. Todd, *Report on Hydro-Electric Development in Shanxi 1935* (Beijing, 1934), pp. 1–4. Most of the old dikes in Hua *xian* were gone by the 1930s, and the Yellow River was flooding the county every year. Wang Puyuan and Wang Weiyuan, *Hua xian zhi* [Hua county gazetteer] (1926–30): 1–2.

25. Ding Ling, *Yierjiu shi yu Jin-Ji-Lu-Yu bianqu* [The 129th division of the Shanxi-Hebei-Shandong-Henan border region] (Beijing: Xin hua she [New China press], 1950), pp. 41–42.

26. Bohr, *Famine in China*, pp. 42–44, 65–73.

27. Kung-Chuan Hsiao, *Rural China: Imperial Control in the Nineteenth Century* (Seattle: University of Washington Press, 1960), pp. 144–81, especially p. 167.

28. *Famine in China's Northwest*, pp. 4–5. Sheridan, *Chinese Warlord*, p. 26.

29. My inference from White, *In Search of History*, pp. 150–51; and *Seeds for China's Arid Areas* (Beijing: China International Famine Relief Commission, 1930), pp. 1–11. For the general context, see Qi Wu, *Yige geming genjudi de chengzhang*, pp. 155–66.

30. Myers, *Chinese Peasant Economy*, p. 276.

31. Sun Jingxuan, *Huanghe de erzi* [Sons of the Yellow river] (Hubei renmin chubanshe [Hubei people's press], 1978), pp. 3–26, 239–46.

32. Thaxton, "Lin County Village Investigations"; Godement, "Famine in the Warlord Age," 3.

33. Roxanne Prazniak's work on the 1900–10 period anticipates this persistent trend. "Local Uprisings: The Roots of Rebellion and Revolution," ACLS Workshop on "Rebellion and Revolution in North China," Harvard University, 1979. I also have profited from Lucien Bianco, "The Peasant Movement," unpublished draft chapter for *The Cambridge History of China*, vols. 12–13, 1976, pp. 4–11, 16–17.

34. My inference from trips to the border region and from G. William Skinner, "Social Ecology and the Forces of Repression in North China: A Regional-Systems Framework for Analysis," ACLS Workshop on "Rebellion and Revolution in North China," Harvard University, 27 July 1979, pp. 5, 17, 23–24.

35. Thaxton, "Lin County Village Investigations." Cf. Zhuo Ran, "Ji-Lu Huifeizhi" [The record of the criminal societies in Hebei and Henan], in *Zhengfeng* [Rectification] no. 16: 138–39.

36. On this development in general, see Scott, *Moral Economy of the Peasant*, chaps. 3–4; and Samuel P. Huntington and Joan M. Nelson, *No Easy Choice: Political Participation in Developing Countries* (Cambridge, Mass.: Harvard University Press, 1976), pp. 55–57.

37. Thaxton, "Lin County Village Investigations." Perhaps the best source on this is Myers, *Chinese Peasant Economy*, p. 73, in reference to Ssu Pei Ch'ai village: "The absentee

landlord, Lin Feng, undoubtedly spoke for his social class when he said: 'There are no obligations between myself and the villagers of Ch'ai [i.e., Ssu Pei Ch'ai]. I have no obligation to them except to receive my rents in kind or money as determined by our original contract.'"

38. Thaxton, "Lin County Village Investigations." Feng Hefa, ed., *Zhongguo nongcun jingji ziliao* [Materials on the Chinese village economy] (Shanghai: Li Ming Press, 1935), p. 193. Cf. *Luoxiayu de nongcun jingji yu fangzhiye* [The village economy and textile business along the lower stream of the Luo river] (Loyang: Zhongguo gongye Jin-Yu-zhun jingji yanjiushe [Shanxi-Henan China industrial institute]), about 1937 to 1941.

39. Cf. Victor Nee, "Towards a Social Anthropology of the Chinese Revolution," *Bulletin of Concerned Asian Scholars* 2, no. 3 (July–September 1979): 41–42. For a dissenting view see Huang Xuanwen, *Xiaohe fengyun* [Storm along the Xiao river], Henan renmin chubanshe [Henan people's press], pp. 5–6.

40. Huang Wen, "Puyang xian dianhu yundong" [The tenant movement in Puyang county], *Gongzuo tongxun* (work correspondence), 11: 1–4.

41. Thaxton, "Lin County Village Investigations."

42. Cf. Li Xiaoming, *Pingyuan qiangsheng* [The sound of riflefire on the plains] (Beijing: Zuojia chubanshe [Writers' press], 1959). Feng Deying, *Kucai Hua* [The bitter herb] (Beijing: Renmin chubanshe [People's press], 1959), pp. 1–150.

43. Buck, *Land Utilization*, pp. 55–59. Dwight H. Perkins, *Agricultural Development in China 1368–1968* (Chicago: Aldine, 1969), pp. 88–89, and 90–98. Dwight Perkins offers a map that estimates tenancy in the North China region to be in the 0–9 percent range (pp. 88–89). But he at least recognizes widespread variation with the region. Mark Elvin, *The Pattern of the Chinese Past* (Stanford: Stanford University Press, 1973), pp. 254–55.

44. Xue Chao, "Henan zudian zhidu niaokan" [A bird's-eye view of the Henan rental tenant system], *Nongcun bianluan* [Village chaos] (Taipei: Gongfei huoguo shiliao huibian [Materials on the history of the Communist bandit disaster that befell the nation], 1961), pp. 156–57.

45. Compare Xue Chao with Odoric Wou, "The Impact of Differential Economic Change on Society in Henan in the 1920s and 1930s," ACLS Workshop on "Rebellion and Revolution in North China," Harvard University, 27 July 1979, tenancy map.

46. For the point in general, see Qi Wu, *Yige geming genjudi de chengzhang*, pp. 103–4; and Xue Chao, "Henan zudian zhidu niaokan," pp. 156–61. More specifically, see Thaxton, "Lin County Village Investigations"; "Pang cun fadong qunzhong de jiaoxun" [The lesson of mass mobilization in Pang village], Ji-Jin qu dang wei [Hebei-Shanxi district party committee], probably 1944. Among these tenants were former smallholders. Joseph W. Esherick, "Land Distribution in Pre-Revolutionary China," 1979 Association of Asian Studies paper, begins to look at the problem of tenancy in a way that includes former smallholders.

47. J. Lossing Buck, "Land Reform and Economic Development in Asia," in *Land Tenure, Industrialization, and Social Stability: Experience and Prospects in Asia*, ed. Walter Froehlich (Milwaukee: Marquette University Press, 1961), pp. 82–83.

48. I have dealt with this change in "Tenants in Revolution: The Tenacity of Traditional Morality," *Modern China* 1, no. 3 (July 1975): pp. 323–58. Jia Juhou has concluded that 70 percent of the tenants in Republican China were temporary tillers. *The Structure and Determinants of the Tenure System in Modern China 1900–1940* (Taipei: Academia Sinica Institute of Economics, 1977), p. 14. Perkins agrees: see his *Agricultural Development in China*, p. 103.

49. Chen Shouyi and Li Yu, *Jianzu banfa qianjie* [The methods for simple solutions in rent reduction] (Qiqi chubanshe ["July 7" press], August 1944), pp. 21–22.

50. Qi Wu, *Yige geming genjudi de chengzhang*, p. 106.

51. Ibid., p. 22.

52. Ibid., p. 105. Cf. Feuerwerker, *Economic Trends in the Republic of China*, pp. 59 and table 16, part 3. Feuerwerker's data do not show any change but still would suggest that fixed rent was the dominant rental system in North China by Republican times.

53. Xue Chao, "Henan zudian zhidu niaokan," pp. 156–61. Thaxton, "Lin County Village Investigations."

54. Huang Xuanwen, *Xiaohe fengyun*, pp. 7–8.

55. Feng Hefa, ed., *Zhongguo nongcun jingji ziliao*, p. 193. Also see Huang Xuanwen, *Xiaohe fengyun*, pp. 7–8.

56. Xue Chao, "Henan zudian zhidu niaokan," pp. 156–61. Thaxton, "Lin County Village Investigations." Compare Myers, *Chinese Peasant Economy*, p. 108. Myers found it difficult to conclude that changes in *fenzu* or sharecropping reflected recent developments, but the evidence on Henan suggests otherwise.

57. Xue Chao, "Henan zudian zhidu niaokan," pp. 156–61.

58. Ibid., pp. 159–61. Li Gang, *Qunzhong Shenghuo* [Life of the masses], no. 1 (Ji-Lu-Yu kang lian qunzhong shenghuoshe [Life of the masses press of the Hebei-Shandong-Henan district federation of resistance associations], 1944), pp. 12–14.

59. Ji Dengkui, "Hua xian chajian yundong jianbao" [A report on the investigation of the rent reduction movement in Hua county], *Qunzhong yundong cailiao* [Materials for the mass movement] (Ji-Lu-Yu qu dangwei minyunbu [Civil movement department of the Hebei-Shandong-Henan district party committee], probably 1945), pp. 33–34, 36–37.

60. Qi Wu, *Yige geming genjudi de chengzhang*, pp. 105–6. Thaxton, "Lin County Village Investigations."

61. Qi Wu, *Yige geming genjudi de chengzhang*, pp. 106–7.

62. Buck, *Land Utilization*, p. 14.

63. Ji Dengkui, "Hua xian chajian yundong jianbao," pp. 26–27, 34. Cf. Isabel and David Crook, *Revolution in a Chinese Village: Ten Mile Inn* (London: Routledge & Kegan Paul, 1959), pp. 28–29.

64. Ji Dengkui, "Hua xian chajian yundong jianbao," p. 35.

65. Qi Wu, *Yige geming genjudi de chengzhang*, pp. 106–7.

66. Xue Chao, "Henan zudian zhidu niaokan," pp. 159–61.

67. Ibid.

68. Li Gang, *Qunzhong shenghuo*, p. 12.

69. Thaxton, "Lin County Village Investigations."

70. Ibid.

71. Qi Wu, *Yige geming genjudi de chengzhang*, pp. 106–12.

72. Thaxton, "Lin County Village Investigations."

73. *Henan nongcun diaocha* [Henan village investigations], Xingzhengyuan nongcun fuxing weiyuanhui bian [edited by the Administrative Research Staff of the Committee on Village Rejuvenation] (Shanghai: Shang Wu Bookstore, 1934), pp. 8–19, 30–35, 42–52. For supportive evidence see Crook and Crook, *Revolution in a Chinese Village*, pp. 20–25. Qi Wu, *Yige geming genjudi de chengzhang*, p. 101; and Joseph W. Esherick, "Rural Social Economic Change in North China," ACLS Workshop on "Chinese Communist Base Areas," Harvard University, 1978, pp. 7–8, 19–20. Esherick has documented the failure of a rich peasant economy to develop in Shandong. He does not, however, explore the decline which I believe took place in the rich peasant economy of Republican China.

74. Thaxton, "Lin County Village Investigations."

75. William Hinton, *Fanshen: A Documentary of Revolution in a Chinese Village* (New York: Random House, 1966), pp. 28–31.

76. Thaxton, "Lin County Village Investigations," *Pang cun fadong qunzhong de jiaoxun*. The novels on this period also testify to this change. See, for example, Mu Xiang, *Jinyang Qui* [Taiyuan autumn] (Beijing: Jiefang jun wenyi chubanshe [Liberation Army literature and arts press], 1962), pp. 1–50. Ma Feng, *Luliang Shan yingxiong zhuan* [The heroes of the Luliang mountains] (Beijing: Renmin chubanshe [People's press], 1977), pp. 1–111.

77. A superb study on the tendency of newly developing governments to transform the nature of patron-client relationships and to ignore older reciprocal obligations to the villages is Robert E. Gamer, *The Developing Nations: A Comparative Perspective* (Boston: Allyn and

Bacon, 1976), chap. 4. Gamer's work has helped me clarify many of the thorny conceptual issues raised in this chapter.

78. Sidney L. Greenblatt, ed., *The People of Taihang* (White Plains, N.Y.: International Arts and Sciences Press, 1976), pp. 75-76.

79. Qi Wu, *Yige geming genjudi de chengzhang*, p. 106.

80. Huang Xuanwen, *Xiaohe fengyun*, pp. 56-57. Cf. "Rentlessly Create a New Land," *Chinese Sociology and Anthropology* 10, no. 1 (Fall 1977), p. 12.

81. Qi Wu, *Yige geming genjudi de chengzhang*, pp. 106-12; Li Gang, *Qunzhong shenghuo*, pp. 12-14.

82. Qi Wu, *Yige geming genjudi de chengzhang*, pp. 109-10. According to Qi Wu this interest rate was taken every half-year. I have used the lower figure of 60 percent per year.

83. Ibid., p. 109.

84. Ibid., p. 110.

85. *Nu Yingxiong Liu Hulan* [The heroine Liu Hulan] Renmin chubanshe [People's press], 1975, pp. 10-11. Liu Qi, *Zhanzheng jiguan* [Impressions of war] (Beijing: Jiefang wenyishe chuban [Liberation Army literature and arts press], 1978), p. 18.

86. Qi Wu, *Yige geming genjudi de chengzhang*, p. 11.

87. Cf. Crook and Crook, *Revolution in a Chinese Village*, pp. 24-35. *Jikucun enchou ji* [The kindness and hatred of Jiku village] (Beijing: Zhongguo qingnian chubanshe [China youth press], 1964), pp. 1-75.

88. Huang Wen, "Puyang xian dianhu yundong," 1-15.

89. Jack Chen, *A Year in Upper Felicity: Life in a Chinese Village During the Cultural Revolution* (New York: Macmillan, 1973), p. 131.

90. Charles Tilly, "Routine Conflicts and Peasant Rebellion in Seventeenth-Century France," in *Power and Protest in the Countryside: Studies of Rural Unrest in Asia, Europe, and America*, ed. Robert Weller and Scott Guggenheim (Durham: Duke University Press, 1982).

91. Cf. Scott, *Moral Economy of the Peasant*, chap. 4, for the analytical thrust here.

92. White, *In Search of History*, p. 151.

93. Qi Wu, *Yige geming genjudi de chengzhang*, pp. 108-9. Compare Sidney D. Gamble, *North China Villages: Social, Political and Economic Activities Before 1933* (Berkeley: University of California Press, 1963), pp 31, 209.

94. Qi Wu, *Yige geming genjudi de chengzhang*, p. 106.

95. For late Qing I have drawn from *Xinhai Gemingshi* [History of the 1911 revolution], ed. Zhang Kaiyuan and Lin Zengping (Beijing: Renmin chubanshe [People's press], 1980), p. 275. For the Republican period, see Belden, *China Shakes the World*, pp. 98-99.

96. Huang Xuanwen, *Xiaohe Fengyun*, pp. 26-29.

97. Thaxton, "Lin County Village Investigations." General Pang Bingxun occupied the village in which I interviewed (Yaocun) and the older peasants remember him to this day. According to Odoric Y. K. Wou, Pang Bingxun was the commander of the Jili 3rd Reserve Brigade in 1919-1920 and a client of Wu Peifu, *Militarism in Modern China: The Career of Wu Peifu, 1916-39* (Canberra: Australian National University Press, 1978), pp. 63-65. The Guomindang historians Lung-hsuen and Chang Ming-kai list Pang as the commander of the 40th Corps in the First War Zone which encompassed the Zhang River-Lingchuan area. *History of the Sino-Japanese War 1937-45*, trans. by Wen Ha-hsiung (Taipei: Chung Wu Publishing Co., 1971), pp. 190, 289.

98. Thaxton, "Lin County Village Investigations." Cf. Zhuo Ran, "Ji-Lu Huifeizhi," 138-39.

99. See *Jiang Jieshi tongzhi qu de zhengqing shilu* [On the record of human kindness in the districts under the control of Jiang Jieshi] (no publisher, no date), pp. 2-3, 11-12, 19-20. Cf. *Lost Chance in China: The World War II Dispatches of John S. Service*, ed. Joseph W. Esherick (New York: Vintage, 1975), pp. 12-13.

100. *Henan nongcun diaocha*, pp. 79-80.

101. White, *In Search of History*, p. 151.

102. Thaxton, "Lin County Village Investigations." Young has shown the gentry to have been imposing higher taxes on peasants in Henan with the aid of the New Army. *Presidency of Yuan Shikai*, p. 18. This phenomenon no doubt continued into the 1920s and 1930s.

103. Thaxton, "Lin County Village Investigations."

104. Eastman, *Abortive Revolution*, pp. 201–2.

105. *Shandong sheng zhangonghui zhaokai diyici quansheng zai zhengfu daibiao huiyi* [A report to the first provincial financial and economic delegation conference sponsored by the Shandong wartime works committee] (May 1940), pp. 9–10.

106. Feng Hefa, ed., *Zhongguo nongcun jingi ziliao*, pp. 194–95. On the question of increasing force in order to increase taxes see Myers, *Chinese Peasant Economy*, pp. 85–88.

107. For this view, see Ramon Myers, "The Commercialization of Agriculture in Modern China," in *Economic Organization in Chinese Society*, ed. W. E. Willmont (Stanford: Stanford University Press, 1972), pp. 179, 183, 187.

108. Leonard M. Outerbridge, "Grains for China's Arid Areas," *China International Famine Relief Report* (1931): 20–21.

109. *Luoxiayu de nongcun jingji*, pp. 51–52.

110. Compare with Myers, who makes the point but does not give it proper emphasis. *Chinese Peasant Economy*, pp. 42–43.

111. Chen Tisi, "Jinan nongcun de xianzhuang," p. 564. Cf. Esherick, ed., *Lost Chance in China*, p. 13.

112. Compare with Arthur N. Young, *China's Nation Building Effort, 1927–1937* (Stanford: Hoover Institution Press, 1971), pp. 20–22, 54–59. Young's preoccupation with increased government extraction of revenue being the key measure of effective political development makes him oblivious to this point. Feuerwerker also shows that the central government increased salt revenues after 1928, but he does not explore the social consequences for the peasantry. *Economic Trends*, pp. 77–79.

113. Huang Xuanwen, *Xiaohe fengyun*, pp. 4–5, 55–58.

114. Cf. Greenblatt, ed., *People of the Taihang*, pp. 268–69. A superb study of this phenomenon, which was developing everywhere, is Linda Grove's "Creating a Northern Soviet," *Modern China* 1, no. 3 (July 1975), pp. 254–57.

115. S. A. M. Adshead, *The Modernization of the Chinese Salt Administration 1900–1920* (Cambridge, Mass.: Harvard University Press, 1970), pp. 138–41.

116. Ibid., pp. 45–47, 50, 140–41.

117. Wou, "Impact of Differential Economic Change," pp. 2–3.

118. Huang Xuanwen, *Xiaohe fengyun*, pp. 47–48.

119. Chen Tisi, "Jinan nongcun de xianzhuang," pp. 563–65.

120. Adshead, *Modernization of the Chinese Salt Administration*, pp. 45–50, 140–41.

121. *Yan* [Salt] (Hong Kong: Qi shi nian dai zazhi she [Decade of the seventies press], 1976), pp. 26–30.

122. From a China trip report by Boston epidemiologist Elaine Shiang, Fall 1979, p. 4.

123. Crook and Crook, *Revolution in a Chinese Village*, pp. 32–33.

124. *United States Department of Agricultural Statistics*, 1941, pp. 9–10, 48–50, 101–2, 116–17, 320–22. The world market price of peanuts stood at 9 cents a pound in 1919 and 4 to 5 cents per pound for most of the 1920s, then fell to 1 to 2 cents. The price in China, however, probably was less than the world market price because of monopoly international power in output markets and Nationalist government taxes. I am indebted to agricultural economist William Grisely for conversations on this topic.

125. "Ji-nan pochan de nongcun" [The bankrupt villages of southern Hebei] (Henan province history research institute library, about 1935). This source details the rise and collapse of peanut prices in Qiankou village, Neihuang *xian*, on the Hebei-Henan border from 1921 to 1935.

126. See Yeh-Chien Wang, "Economic Depression and China's Monetary Reform in 1935," 1–2. Peng Kuanghsi, *Why China Has No Inflation* (Beijing: Foreign Languages Press, 1976), pp. 26–27. John King Fairbank, *The United States and China* (Cambridge, Mass.: Harvard University Press, 1979), pp. 265, 326. On the internationalization of banking and currency "reform" in China also see Ann Trotter's fine study, *Britain and East Asia, 1933–1937* (Cambridge: Cambridge University Press, 1975), pp. 148–67.

127. My inference from Marvin D. Bernstein, *The Mexican Mining Industry 1890–1950: A Study in the Interaction of Politics, Economics, and Technology* (Albany: State University of New York, 1964), pp. 95–99, 102–4, 112–14, 130–31, and 281–82.

128. This is the position of Arthur N. Young, a leading spokesman of the Western economic school, in *China's Wartime Finance and Inflation, 1937–1945* (Cambridge, Mass.: Harvard University Press, 1965), pp. 2–8, 131–37, and throughout. But Young offers little convincing evidence that the central government had balanced its budget and brought inflation down to a tolerable level by the Japanese invasion of 1937. Though Young points to the Japanese invasion as the trigger to rampant inflation, in another work he expresses concern that the central government would "overstrain the currency and economy and take the easy but dangerous path of inflationary financing of development." *China and the Helping Hand, 1937–1945* (Cambridge, Mass.: Harvard University Press, 1963), p. 10.

129. Yeh-Chien Wang, "Economic Depression," 1–2; and Peng Kuanghsi, *Why China Has No Inflation*, pp. 26–27.

130. Qi Wu, *Yige geming genjudi de chengzhang*, p. 113. Also see Cheryl Payer, "Western Economic Assistance to Nationalist China, 1927–1937," Ph.D. thesis, Harvard University Department of Government, 1971, pp. 120–25.

131. Ma Feng, *Liu Hulan zhuan* [On Liu Hulan] (Beijing: Zhongguo qingnian chubanshe [New China youth], 1978), pp. 296–97.

132. Shanxi banks had been in trouble since 1917–18, but it was during the early 1930s that the collapse took place. Cf. Yeh-Chien Wang, "Economic Depression," 7–8, 10–15, 17–18. Payer, "Western Economic Assistance to Nationalist China," pp. 169–70.

133. On this point, Eastman's work comes close to the bull's-eye. *Abortive Revolution*, chap. 5.

134. Wou has shown that several border region towns at important railway junctures did spawn some light industry in the 1900–30 period. "Impact of Differential Economic Change," 10–14. Nevertheless, this town-based industry did not integrate the massive numbers of unemployed peasants.

135. My inference from Theodore W. White and Annalee Jacoby, *Thunder out of China* (New York: William Sloane, 1961), p. 173. Sheridan, *Chinese Warlord*, pp. 248–49. Godement, "Famine in the Warlord Age," 16–20.

136. Institute of Geography, Academia Sinica, *Economic Geography of North China*, pp. 126, 166. Owen Lattimore, *Inner Asian Frontiers of China* (New York: American Geographical Society, 1951), pp. 12–13. Owen Lattimore, *Manchuria: Cradle of Conflict* (New York: Macmillan, 1932), pp. 178–94.

137. The best source on Nanjing's appeasement is Eastman, *Abortive Revolution*, pp. 245–47, 263.

138. From Yi Shou Wang's insightful "Chinese Migration and Population Change," Ph.D. thesis, University of Minnesota Geography Department, 1972, 72–74, 95–96, 132–33.

139. Wang shows overland migration off from one million per year in the late 1920s to 200,000–800,000 in the 1930–37 period. Wang's estimates are not exactly in line with Tawney's, but his interpretation fits nicely with the thesis advanced in the coming chapter (which uses Tawney's data). *Chinese Migration*, pp. 59–61, 64–69.

140. Donald G. Gillin, *Warlord Yen Hsi-shan in Shansi Province, 1911–1949* (Princeton: Princeton University Press, 1967), pp. 31–33, 49, 127.

141. Eric A. Nordlinger, *Soldiers in Politics: Military Coups and Governments* (Englewood Cliffs, N. J.: Prentice-Hall, 1977), pp. 2–21, 141–78, 207.

142. My inference from Edmund S. K. Fung's superb study of *The Military Dimensions of the Chinese Revolution* (Vancouver and London: University of British Columbia, 1980), pp. 142–44, 257–58.

143. Here I rely on several sources: Thaxton, "Lin County Village Investigations." F. F. Liu, *A Military History of Modern China* (Princeton: Princeton University Press, 1956), pp. 13, 40, 108, 112–24, 136–37, 150–51. Sheridan, *Chinese Warlord*, pp. 15, 26–27.

144. The term is a more active version of "alternative symbolic universe" as developed in Scott, *Moral Economy of the Peasant*, pp. 237–40; and Peter L. Berger and Thomas Luckmann, *The Social Construction of Reality* (New York: Anchor-Doubleday, 1967), pp. 106–12.

145. Hinton, *Fanshen*, p. 40.

146. Tenant activists in Qingshui and Liulin villages, for example, say they first met in the jails of Baihe town in northern Shanxi. Ma Feng, *Wo de diyige shangji* [My first superior] (Beijing: Renmin chubanshe [People's press], 1977), pp. 46–47.

147. On the process whereby this symbolic defiance embedded itself in the culture of powerless peasants elsewhere see Scott, *Moral Economy of the Peasant*, pp. 231–34.

148. Huang Xuanwen, *Xiaohe fengyun*, pp. 7–8.

149. Wang Li, *Mingtian* [Tomorrow] (Beijing: Zuojia chubanshe [Writers' press], 1955), pp. 1–4.

150. Peter A. Lupsha, "Explanation of Political Violence: Some Psychological Theories Versus Indignation," *Politics and Society* 2, no. 1 (Fall 1971): 96–101.

151. Qi Wu, *Yige geming genjudi de chengzhang*, p. 108.

152. Zhao Shuli, *Changes in Li Village* (Beijing: Foreign Languages Press, 1953), pp. 32–86.

153. Qi Wu, *Yige geming genjudi de chengzhang*, p. 111.

154. Ibid., pp. 111–12.

155. Ma Feng, "Cun chou" [Village hatred], *Wo de diyige shangji*, pp. 1–27.

156. Cf. Kenneth Olenik, "Teng Yen-ta and the Theory of Mass Revolution in Kuomintang Ideology," *Asian Thought and Society* (September 1978): 178–92. Cf. Upshur, *China Under the Kuomintang*, pp. 55–56.

157. Compare with A. J. Cherepanov, *The Northern Expedition of the National Revolutionary Army of China*, trans. Martin Wilbur (New York: Columbia University Press, 1970), pp. 15, 71, 212–23.

CHAPTER 3

1. For the starting points for this chapter I am indebted to James C. Scott, *The Moral Economy of the Peasant: Rebellion and Subsistence in Southeast Asia* (New Haven: Yale University Press, 1976), pp. 205–25. The emphasis here is more on self-help and oppositionist revolt than remedialist protest. Perhaps the political context in China was less conducive to restoration and bargaining.

2. Samuel L. Popkin, *The Rational Peasant: The Political Economy of Rural Society in Vietnam* (Berkeley: University of California Press, 1979), pp. 33–35.

3. *Zhongguo jindai nongye shi ziliao* [Source materials on China's modern agricultural history], ed. Zhang You-yi, in *Sanlian Shudian* (Beijing: Sanlian Bookstore, 1957), pp. 206–14, 217. Compare with Ramon Myers, "The Commercialization of Agriculture in Modern China," in *Economic Organization in Chinese Society*, ed. W. F. Willmott (Stanford: Stanford University Press, 1972), pp. 179, 183, 187; and Dwight H. Perkins, *Agricultural Development in China, 1368–1968* (Chicago: Aldine, 1969), p. 31.

4. Myers suggests, correctly, that this was the case for small producers in both North China and Taiwan in the early twentieth century. "Commercialization of Agriculture," 179–87.

5. Cf. Richard A. Kraus, "Cotton and Cotton Goods in China 1918–1936: The Impact on the Traditional Sector," Ph.D. thesis, Harvard University Department of Economics, 1968, pp. 1–160, esp. 115–45.

6. Kraus's rigorous quantitative study of peasant responses to changes in production levels detects this pullback among peasants who were tilling cash cotton on land customarily reserved for cereals in the early years of the Great Depression. "Cotton and Cotton Goods in China," 45–46, 49, 73, 160.

7. J. L. Buck, *Chinese Farm Economy: A Study of 2,866 Farms in Seventeen Localities and Seven Provinces in China* (Chicago: University of Chicago Press, 1930), p. 95.

8. Donald G. Gillin, *Warlord Yen Hsi-shan in Shansi Province, 1911–1949* (Princeton: Princeton University Press, 1967), pp. 98–99.

9. Ramon H. Myers, *The Chinese Peasant Economy: Agricultural Development in Hopei and Shantung 1890–1949* (Cambridge, Mass.: Harvard University Press, 1970), p. 67.

10. Cf. Phil Billingsley, "The Rise of Banditry in Republican China," unpublished manuscript, 1982, pp. 87–92.

11. This involutionist approach to survival refers to peasant attempts to develop social arrangements to cope with low levels of per capita production stemming from insufficient technological advances and tremendous population pressures. It was first noted by Clifford Geertz, *Agricultural Involution: The Process of Ecological Change in Indonesia* (Berkeley: University of California Press, 1963).

12. Cf. Xiu Rong, "Bursting Out of a Sea of Suffering," *Chinese Sociology and Anthropology* 10, no. 3 (Spring 1978): 27–39, esp. 31.

13. *The North China Famine of 1920–21* (Beijing: Report of the Beijing United International Famine Relief Committee, 1922), pp. 1–15.

14. Qi Wu, *Yige geming genjudi de chengzhang*, pp. 155–77. Cf. Zhao Yukuan, "A Tattered Quilt Coat," in *Rentlessly Create a New Land*, part 2, pp. 19–26.

15. Qi Wu, *Yige geming genjudi de chengzhang*, pp. 155–77.

16. Thaxton, "Lin County Village Investigations." Cf. Les Ross, "The Legacy of the Pre-Liberation Period," unpublished manuscript, pp. 3, 9, fn. 20; *The North China Famine of 1920–21*, pp. 12–13, 15, 19.

17. Thaxton, "Lin County Village Investigations." Two examples of this process are Zhang Ruyun, Guo Shigang, and Li Jiaming, "The Tragedy of the People of 'Lucky Star Locust,' " in Sidney L. Greenblatt, ed., *The People of Taihang* (White Plains, N.Y.: International Arts and Sciences Press, 1976), pp. 35–37; and Xiu Rong, "Bursting Out of a Sea of Suffering," pp. 28–29.

18. Thaxton, "Lin County Village Investigations."

19. From trips to the border region, and from Jean Chesneaux, *The Chinese Labor Movement 1919–1927*, trans. H. M. Wright (Stanford University Press, 1968), pp. 12–35.

20. Chesneaux, *Chinese Labor Movement*, pp. 89–94; David D. Buck, *Urban Change in China: Politics and Development in Tsinan* (Madison: University of Wisconsin Press, 1978), pp. 141, 148, 155.

21. Chesneaux, *Chinese Labor Movement*, pp. 10–11, chap. 4; and Liu Baoshan, "A Blood Debt Law Suit," in *Rentlessly Create a New Land*, part 1, p. 72.

22. Chesneaux, *Chinese Labor Movement*, pp. 89, 94.

23. Myers, *Chinese Peasant Economy*, pp. 50–51, 75–76, 90–91, 110–11.

24. Thaxton, "Lin County Village Investigations"; Zhao Shuli, *Xiaxiang ji* [A collection on the countryside] (Beijing: Zuojia chubanshe [Writers' press], 1953), pp. 103–12.

25. I am indebted to G. William Skinner for this point. Made in a talk before the ACLS Workshop on "Rebellion and Revolution in North China," Harvard University, 1979.

26. From trips to the region, and from Li Yingju, *Nu youji dui zhang* [A woman guerrilla commander] (Beijing: Jiefangjun wenyishe [Liberation Army literature and arts press], 1979), pp. 225–29.

27. From Shih-ta Chen's fine study of "Enclave Growth in an Open Agrarian Economy: Manchuria Under Japanese Colonialism," Ph.D. thesis, Cornell University, 1973, pp. 33–34, 45.

28. Thaxton, "Lin County Village Investigations"; Myers, "Commercialization of Agriculture," p. 188; Shih-ta Chen, "Enclave Growth in an Open Agrarian Economy," pp. 32, 44–45, 139–42.

29. Thaxton, "Lin County Village Investigations."

30. In developing this point, I have benefited from correspondence with Jerome Ch'en, including his report on the visit of the North American Delegation on Socialism and Revolution, *Ideology and History* (June–July 1980): 162.

31. Cf. Ramon H. Myers, "North China Villages during the Republican Period: Socioeconomic Relationships," *Modern China* 6, no. 3 (July 1980): 243–66.

32. We must not confuse the plight of villages like Ten Mile Inn and Long Bow with that of villages in the upper reaches of the Taihang. The former were satellites of landlord-dominated market towns. Cf. Isabel and David Crook, *Revolution in a Chinese Village: Ten Mile Inn* (London: Routledge & Kegan Paul, 1959), chaps. 1–2, and William Hinton, *Fanshen: A Documentary of Revolution in a Chinese Village* (New York: Random House, 1966), pp. 1–17, 29–34.

33. Liu Qi, *Zhanzheng jiguan* [Impressions of war] (Beijing: Jiefangjun wenyi chubanshe [Liberation Army literature and arts press], 1978), pp. 1–50.

34. Thaxton, "Lin County Village Investigations."

35. A scholar who understands that the Manchurian migrations grew out of peasant work-life difficulties in North China and that the peasant migrants often resisted the permanent resettlement schemes of warlord governors in the Northeast is Ronald Suleski, "Regional Development in Manchuria," *Modern China* 4, no. 4 (October 1978): 419–34.

36. Cf. Vera Vladimirovna-Vishnyakova, *Two Years in Revolutionary China*, Steven I. Levine, trans. (Cambridge, Mass.: Harvard University Press, 1971), pp. 7–8.

37. Yue Feng and Wang Tian, "Land," and Pei Feng, Li Zhikuan, Zhang Fengru, and Liu Zhong, "A Poor Blacksmith Becomes a Master of the Country," in Greenblatt, ed., *People of Taihang*, pp. 64–80, 267–84; cf. *Jikucun enchou ji* [The kindness and hatred of Jiku village] (Beijing: Zhongguo qingnian chubanshe [China youth press], 1964), pp. 1–100.

38. Yue Feng and Wang Tian, "Land," in Greenblatt, ed., *People of Taihang*, pp. 64–71; Thaxton, "Lin County Village Investigations."

39. Cf. Yang Hsiao, *The Making of a Peasant Doctor* (Beijing: Foreign Languages Press, 1976), pp. 44–47.

40. Cf. Sidney D. Gamble, *North China Villages: Social, Political and Economic Activities before 1933* (Berkeley: University of California Press, 1963), pp. 83–95, 203–5, 300–301.

41. The pilfering of crops in the Taihang area would prove to be a problem even for the CCP during the War of Resistance.

42. *Gongzuo tongxun* [Work correspondence] no. 35, Sixiang zijue zhibao ligong tuanjie kongsu zhuanhao [A special issue on achieving self-confidence and self-assessment in rendering service to the solidification of the accusation movement] Dang nei kanwu [Internal party publication] Ji-Lu-Yu dangwei chuban [Published by the Hebei-Shandong-Henan party committee] (10 July 1947), pp. 1–52.

43. According to Phil Billingsley, Henan was on its way to becoming a bandit world in the early 1920s. "Banditry in China, 1911–1928," Ph.D. thesis, University of Leeds, 1974, chap. 6.

44. Thaxton, "Lin County Village Investigations," and Guo Youfan, "Oral History Raw Notes on the Tianmen hui."

45. Guo Youfan, "Oral History Raw Notes on the Tianmen hui." Compare with Mark Mancall and Georges Jidkoff, "The Hung Hu-tzu of Northeast China," in ed. Jean Chesneaux, *Popular Movements and Secret Societies in China, 1840–1950* (Stanford: Stanford University Press, 1972), pp. 125–31.

46. Sun Tan Wei, *A Village Moves to Socialism* (Shanghai: China Reconstructs, Supplement, 10 November 1956), p. 15.

47. Odoric Wou, "The Impact of Differential Economic Change on Society in Henan in the

1920s and 1930s." ACLS Workshop in "Rebellion and Revolution in North China." Harvard University, 27 July 1979, p. 19. Cf. *Lo xia yu de nongcun jingji*, pp. 31–32.

48. On sharing cave housing, see Wang Xitang, Lian Buwang, and Yao Yixin, "The Poor People's Cave," in *People of Taihang*, p. 199. On relatives lending land, see "A Shepherd Becomes a College Professor," in *People of Taihang*, pp. 247–48. On money loans, see Feng Tianrong, "Happily Turn Over, Never Forget Our Roots," in *Chinese Sociology and Anthropology* 10, no. 3 (Spring 1978): 57.

49. Thaxton, "Lin County Village Investigations."

50. Mutual crop-watching most likely correlated more with the lineage-based middle-peasant village. The decline of protection is strikingly evident in Hinton, *Fanshen*, chaps. 3 and 4.

51. For an example of this, see Zhao Shuli, *Changes in Li Village* (Beijing: Foreign Languages Press, 1953), pp. 15–27.

52. Sun Tan Wei, *A Village Moves to Socialism*, p. 7; Zhao Shuli, *Xiaxiang ji*, pp. 103–12; Thaxton, "Lin County Village Investigations."

53. Liu Guangpu and Chen Futong, "A Woman Farmhand," in *People of Taihang*, p. 188.

54. Thaxton, "Lin County Village Investigations." Compare with chap. 5.

55. Ibid. Cf. Pei Feng et al., "A Poor Blacksmith," p. 272.

56. Ji Dengkui, "Hua xian chajian yundong jianbao" [A report on the investigation of the rent reduction movement in Hua county], Qunzhong yundong cailiao [Materials for the mass movement] (Ji-Lu-Yu qu dangwei minyunbu [Civil movement department of the Hebei-Shandong-Henan district party committee], probably 1945), pp. 21–45.

57. Li Gang, *Qunzhong shenghuo* [Life of the masses], no. 1. (Ji-Lu-Yu kang lian qunzhong shenghuoshe [Life of the masses press of the Hebei-Shandong-Henan district federation of resistance associations], 1944), pp. 12–17.

58. Thaxton, "Lin County Village Investigations."

59. Yue Feng, "Land," pp. 73–75.

60. Thaxton, "Lin County Village Investigations."

61. This strategy also had its limits. Cf. Liu Baoshan, "A Blood Debt Law Suit," pp. 76–84.

62. Zhao Shuli, *Changes in Li Village*, pp. 17, 113. Liu Baoshan, "A Blood Debt Law Suit," pp. 69–74.

63. Cf. chap. 5. Also see "Suffering 'Divine Colt' Changes to a New Day," *Chinese Sociology and Anthropology* 10, no. 1 (Fall 1977): 54–55.

64. Liu Baoshan, "A Blood Debt Law Suit," pp. 55–56.

65. Cf. Mu Xiang, *Jinyang chou* [Taiyuan Autumn] (Beijing; Jiefangjun wenyi chubanshe [Liberation Army literature and arts press], 1962), pp. 19–22.

66. Lu Yingju, *Nu you jidui zhang*, pp. 151–52.

67. See chap. 5. Cf. Zhuo Ran, "Ji-Lu Huifeizhi," *Zhengfeng* [Rectification] no. 15 (1935): 139–40.

68. On the litigations, see Zhao Shuli, *Changes in Li Village*, p. 20; and Liu Baoshan, "A Blood Debt Law Suit," pp. 72–81. On salt price protests, compare with chap. 5 and Linda Grove, "Creating a Northern Soviet," *Modern China* 1, no. 3 (July 1975): 257. These "petitionist" or *qingyuan* protests sprang up throughout North and South China in the 1920s. In general, see *Diyici guonei geming zhanzheng shiqi de nongmin yundong* [The peasant movement in the period of the first internal revolutionary war] (Beijing: Renmin chubanshe [People's press], 1958), pp. 146–47.

69. Tai Hsuan-chih, *Hong qiang hui* [The Red Spear society 1916–1949] (Taipei: Shihuo chubanshe [Shihuo press], 1973), pp. 1–84, especially pp. 83–84.

70. Cf. R. Slawinski, "The Red Spears in the Late 1920s," in Chesneaux, ed., *Popular Movements*, pp. 202–7.

71. Jean Chesneaux, *Secret Societies in China in the Nineteenth and Twentieth Centuries*, trans. Gillian Nettle (Hong Kong: Heinemann Books, 1971), p. 190.

72. Ibid., pp. 189–91; Chesneaux, *Peasant Revolts*, p. 85.

73. Tai Hsuan-chin, *Hongqiang hui*, p. 84.

74. Elizabeth J. Perry, *Rebels and Revolutionaries in North China 1845–1945* (Stanford: Stanford University Press, 1980), pp. 152, 177–80, 205–7.

75. Slawinski, "The Red Spears," 202–7.

76. Lucien Bianco, "Secret Societies and Peasant Self-Defense, 1921–1933," in Chesneaux, ed., *Popular Movements*, pp. 221, 275.

77. Baba Takeshi, "The Red Spear Society: Its Ideology and Organization," *Studies in Society and Economy* 41 (1975): 72–75.

78. Ibid.

79. This interpretation has benefited significantly from my reading of Marvin Harris, *Cannibals and Kings: The Origins of Cultures* (New York: Vintage Books, 1977), pp. 110–17.

80. Tai Hsuan-chih, *Hongqiang hui*, pp. 83–90.

81. Ibid., pp. 85–86.

82. Ibid., pp. 91–96.

83. For the conception underlying this point I am indebted to Jean A. Meyer, *The Cristero Rebellion: The Mexican People Between Church and State, 1926–1929* trans. Richard Southern (Cambridge: Cambridge University Press, 1976), pp. 102–3; and Emmanuel LeRoy Ladurie, *Montaillou: The Promised Land of Error*, trans. Barbara Bray (New York: Vintage Books, 1979), pp. 62–63.

84. The standard version, offered by Perry, is that the Red Spears and other secret societies lacked the religious zeal that characterized the popular millennial movements of the past. *Rebels and Revolutionaries in North China*, pp. 176–77. The documentation on the Red Spears and Heavenly Gates, however, indicates they flew the flag of Little Tradition millennialism. Moreover, all but the Heavenly Gates were said to have come from the Eight Trigrams religion. Cf. "Ji-Lu Huifeizhi," *Zhengfeng*, no. 15: 140–41.

85. Tai Hsuan-chih, *Hongqiang hui*, pp. 197–202.

86. Ibid., pp. 190–91.

87. Xiang Yonlong, "Hongqiang hui de qiyuan ji qi shanhuo" [The origins and prospects of the Red Spear society] in *Dongfang zazhi* [Far Eastern miscellany] 24, no. 21 (1927): 35–36.

88. Tai Hsuan-chih, *Hongqiang hui*, pp. 190–92.

89. I am indebted to Richard Bernstein for this information. Bernstein's portrayal of the Red Spears, is, however, in line with Chesneaux-Perry. Cf. "The Red Spear Society," unpublished ms., 1974, pp. 51–57.

90. Huang Xuanwen, *Xiaohe fengyun* [Storm along the Xiao river] (Henan renmin chubanshe [Henan people's press], 1976), pp. 1–2, 16–17, 27–38, 47–51.

91. Guo Youfan, "Oral History Raw Notes on the Tianmen hui; Baba Takeshi, "Red Spear Society," pp. 63–65, 71–80.

92. Zhuo Ran, "Ji-Lu huifeizhi," *Zhengfeng*, no. 14: 118–20.

93. Guo Youfan, "Oral History Raw Notes on the Tianmen hui."

94. Zhuo Ran, "Ji-Lu huifeizhi," *Zhengfeng*, no. 16: 138–40.

95. Guo Youfan, "Oral History Raw Notes on the Tianmen hui."

96. Cf. Zhuo Ran, "Ji-Lu huifeizhi," *Zhengfeng*, no. 15: 139–40.

97. Guo Youfan, "Oral History Raw Notes on the Tianmen hui."

98. Ibid.; Zhuo Ran, "Ji-Lu huifeizhi," *Zhengfeng*, no. 14: 118–20.

99. Baba Takeshi, "Red Spear Society," pp. 79–80; Zhuo Ran, "Ji-Lu huifeizhi," *Zhengfeng* no. 14: 119–20.

100. Charles Tilly, *From Mobilization to Revolution* (Reading, Mass.: Addison-Wesley, 1978), pp. 73–75.

101. Jerome Ch'en, *The Military-Gentry Coalition: China Under the Warlords* (Toronto: University of Toronto—York University Joint Center on Modern East Asia, 1979), pp. 177–85.

102. From Bi-Monthly Famine Commission Bulletin 5, no. 4 (April 1928): 23–24.

103. Cf. Gillin, *Warlord Yen Hsi-shan*, pp. 98–99, 194; "Report on the Peasant Movement in Henan," *Documents of the Chinese Communist Party 1927–1930*, trans. and ed. Hyobom Pak (Hong Kong: Union Research Institute, 1971), pp. 238–52; "Foreign Capital and Peasantry in Henan," *Agrarian China*, Institute of Pacific Relations (Chicago: University of Chicago Press, 1938), pp. 176–79.

104. Tilly's summary of Gabriel Ardant's work on France has been most useful in the formulation of this issue—which was far more serious in China given the pressures of imperialism. *From Mobilization to Revolution*, pp. 205–6.

105. Zhuo Ran, "Ji-Lu huifeizhi," *Zhengfeng* no. 14: 19.

106. William Hinton, "Two Ways to Read the 'Red Book,'" *New China* (Summer 1977): 22.

107. Qi Wu, *Yige geming genjudi de chengzhang*, p. 145. Thaxton, "Lin County Village Investigations."

108. Qi Wu, *Yige geming genjudi de chengzhang*, pp. 100–104.

109. Ibid., p. 115.

110. Compare with Carl E. Dorris, "People's War in North China," Ph.D. thesis, Kansas University History Department, 1975, pp. 134–35.

111. William H. McNeill, *Plagues and Peoples* (New York: Anchor Books, 1976), pp. 137–38.

112. We still lack a study that places these microlevel influences in migration in the context of the larger systemic changes at work in the North China region.

113. Thaxton, "Lin County Village Investigations"; Pei Feng, "A Poor Blacksmith," 267–78.

114. Shih-ta Chen, *Enclave Growth in an Open Agrarian Economy*, pp. 167–69.

115. R. H. Tawney, *Land and Labor in China* (Boston: Beacon Press, 1966), pp. 105–6.

116. Li Yingju, *Nu youji duizhang* [A woman guerrilla commander] (Beijing: Jiefangjun wenyishe [Liberation Army literature and arts press], 1979), pp. 225–29.

117. Pei Feng, "A Poor Blacksmith," 267–68.

118. *Gongzuo tongxun* no. 35: 42–44.

119. Li Yingju, *Nu youji duizhang*, pp. 225–29.

120. Thaxton, "Lin County Village Investigations." The warlords attempted to reinstitute the *baojia* throughout China. I suspect this system was not firmly in place in the nonmarket and nonadministrative villages. On this point, compare Zhao Shuli, *Changes in Li Village*, pp. 1–3, and chap. 5. A study that shows *baojia* strengths in one border region administrative village is Crook and Crook, *Revolution in a Chinese Village*, pp. 1, 6, 15, 27. Cf. Victor Nee, "Towards a Social Anthropology of the Chinese Revolution," *Bulletin of Concerned Asian Scholars* 2, no. 3 (July–September 1979): 40–50.

121. Guo Youfan, "Oral History Raw Notes on the Tianmen hui."

122. G. Rolf Tiedemann, "Rural Conflict in North China, 1868–1935," paper presented to ACLS Workshop on "The Chinese Communist Base Areas," Harvard University, 1978, pp. 14–16.

123. Guo Youfan, "Oral History Raw Notes on the Tianmen hui." Feng Deying, *Kucai hua*, suggests a similar development in eastern Shandong.

124. Compare Sun Tan Wei, *Village Moves to Socialism*, p. 5, and chap. 5.

125. Sun Tan Wei, *Village Moves to Socialism*, p. 9.

126. Qi Wu, *Yige geming genjudi de chengzhang*, p. 113.

127. Cf. Ji Dengkui, *Huaxian chajian yundong jianbao*, pp. 21–45; *Gongzuo tongxun* no. 11, pp. 1–20.

128. Wang Tingdong, "Wuan xin qu chubu shixian" [The initial accomplishments in the new districts of Wuan county], in *Bianqu zhengbao* [Border region government news] (1946–47): 1–4.

129. See chap. 5; Zhuo Ran, "Ji-Lu huifeizhi," *Zhengfeng* no. 14: 119–20. Cf. Mu Xiang,

Jinyang Qiu [Taiyuan autumn] (Beijing: Jiefanjun wenyi chubanshe [Liberation Army literature and arts press], 1962), pp. 1–400.

130. *Jikucun enchou ji*, pp. 1–35.

131. Within the border region peasants were extremely skeptical about approaching the courts. They did, however, undertake litigations in Henan, Shanxi, and Shaanxi. For a couple of suggestive accounts of law suits over land and water rights see Mu Xiang, *Jinyang Qiu*, and *Jikucun enchou ji*, pp. 1–20.

132. "Gaozhuang Hen" [A law suit of hatred] (Zhengzhou: Henan renmin chubanshe [Henan people's press], 1965), pp. 37–51. Cf. Zhao Shuli, *Changes in Li Village*, pp. 3, 10–11, 29; Liu Baoshan, "A Blood Debt Law Suit," 76–81.

133. Thaxton, "Lin County Village Investigations."

134. Guo Youfan, "Oral History Raw Notes." Cf. Zhuo Ran, "Ji-Lu huifeizhi," *Zhengfeng* no. 14: 118–20. Esherick, *Lost Chance in China*, pp. 12–15.

135. Theodore H. White and Annalee Jacoby, *Thunder out of China* (New York: William Sloane, 1961), pp. 175–76.

136. Discussions with historian Pang Shouxin, Henan Province History Research Institute, 1980; Zhuo Ran, "Ji-Lu huifeizhi," *Zhengfeng*, no. 16: 138–39.

137. Discussions with Pang Shouxin.

138. Guo Youfan, "Oral History Raw Notes."

139. Ibid.; Zhuo Ran, "Ji-Lu huifeizhi," *Zhengfeng*, no. 16: 139–40. Bernstein, "Red Spear Society," 51–57.

140. Guo Youfan, "Oral History Raw Notes"; Zhuo Ran, "Ji-Lu huifeizhi," *Zhengfeng* nos. 13–16.

141. My inference from Liu Danian, *Meiguo Qinhua Jianshi* [A brief history of American aggression in China] (Beijing: China Bookstore, 1950), pp. 55–56.

142. Liu Guangpu, "A Woman Farmhand," in *People in Taihang*, pp. 180–88.

143. Cf. *Jikucun enchou ji*, pp. 1–60.

144. This argument, and the supporting evidence, was presented in Ralph Thaxton, "When Peasants Took Power," Ph.D. thesis, University of Wisconsin Department of Political Science, 1975. Much of it reappears with different emphasis in Perry, *Rebels and Revolutionaries in North China*, pp. 190–94.

145. Thaxton, "Lin County Village Investigations." Zhuo Ran, "Ji-Lu huifeizhi," *Zhengfeng* nos. 15, 16. A good source on Guomindang iconoclastic attacks on peasant religion is C. B. Day, *Chinese Peasant Cults* (Taipei: Cheng Wen, 1969), chap. 13. Cf. Tai Hsuan-chih, *Hongqiang hui*, pp. 203–5. Perry also begins to comprehend this point, *Rebels and Revolutionaries in North China*, pp. 177, 180–81, 205.

146. "Henan nongmin baodong" [The peasant explosions in Henan], reprinted in *Nongcun bianlun*, pp. 822–23. The Guomindang was unable to lead the Henan Red Spears because its cadres were insufficient, unwilling to combat gentry exploitation, and arrogant to "backward" peasants. Similarly, Vishnyakova-Akimova reports that the CCP cadres were violently attacked when they went among the Red Spears of Loyang. *Two Years in Revolutionary China*, pp. 118–20.

147. Han Wenzhou and Yao Longchang, "A Home Given by Chairman Mao," in *People of Taihang*, pp. 14–25. Cf. Liu Guangpu, "A Woman Farmhand," pp. 180–88. *Jikucun enchou ji*, pp. 1–20.

148. This is implicit in James M. Polachek, "Mao's 'Moral Economy' and the Kiangsi Soviet," *Journal of Asian Studies*, in press, pp. 17–19, 20–28, 36, and 41 in the original unpublished Davis Center manuscript, 16 October 1981.

149. Baba Takeshi, "Red Spear Society," 63–67. Tai Hsuan-chih, *Hongqiang hui*, pp. 190–205.

150. Huang Xuanwen, *Xiaohe fengyun*, p. 27.

151. The seminal contribution on this topic for South China is Angus W. MacDonald, *The Urban Origins of Rural Revolution* (Berkeley: University of California Press, 1978), pp.

142–44, 221–23, 281–85, 316–17. For an interpretation that places emphasis on the irresponsibility of the CCP, see Roy Hofheinz, Jr., *The Broken Wave: The Chinese Communist Peasant Movement, 1922–1928* (Cambridge, Mass.: Harvard University Press, 1977), pp. 263–305.

152. This army henceforth will be referred to as the Mao-Zhu army or the Liu-Deng army, in either case the "army of the people." The term is Edward Friedman's, among others. See *Backward Toward Revolution: The Chinese Revolutionary Party* (Berkeley: University of California Press, 1974), pp. 128, 219.

CHAPTER 4

1. On the timing of the Red Army arrival in the Taihang-Taiyue area see Hu Ch'iao-mu, *Thirty Years of the Communist Party of China* (London: Lawrence and Wishart, 1951), p. 43; Miao Ch'u-huang, *A Short History of the Chinese Communist Party* (Beijing: Hsueh Hsi Magazine Press, 1956), p. 62, "Bo Yibo," *Issues and Studies*, p. 85; Mu Xin, "Tongyi Zhanxian shenglide yiqukaige" [A victorious episode of the United Front], in *Shehui kexue zhanxian* [The battlefront of social science], no. 4 (1979): 1–5.

2. Ralph Thaxton, "Lin County Village Investigations." Compare with chap. 5.

3. Zhao Shuli, *Xiaxiang ji* [A collection on the countryside] (Beijing: Zuojia chubanshe [Writers' press], 1953), p. 103.

4. Mu Xiang, *Jinyang Qiu* [Taiyuan autumn] (Beijing: Jiefangjun wenyi chubanshe [Liberation Army literature and arts press], 1962), pp. 1–40.

5. Ralph Thaxton, "Lin County Village Investigations." Cf. Agnes Smedley, *The Great Road: The Life and Times of Chu Teh* (New York: Monthly Review Press, 1956), pp. 215, 219; Jan Myrdal, *Report From a Chinese Village* (New York: William Heinemann, Ltd., 1965), pp. 78–79.

6. For the initial argument see Hamza Alvai, "Peasants and Revolution," *Socialist Register Reprint* (1965): 19–20.

7. Thaxton, "Lin County Village Investigations." *Qunzhong shenghuo* [The life of the masses] no. 3, Ji-Lu-Yu bianqu kang lian zhonghui qunzhong shenghuoshe [Life of the masses press of the federation of resistance associations in the Hebei-Shandong-Henan border district], 1944, pp. 1–31.

8. Ji Dengkui, "Hua xian chajian yundong jianbao" [A report on the investigation of the rent reduction movement in Hua county], Qunzhong yundong cailiao [Materials for the mass movement], Ji-Lu-Yu qu dangwei minyunbu [Civil movement department of the Hebei-Shandong-Henan district party committee], probably 1945, p. 53.

9. Huang Xuanwen, *Xiaohe fengyun* [Storm along the Xiao river] (Henan: Henan renmin chubanshe [Henan people's press], 1976), pp. 9–10.

10. Cf. Li Xiaoming, *Pingyuan qiangsheng* [The sound of rifle fire on the plains] (Beijing: Zuojia chubanshe [Writers' press], 1965), pp. 1–150.

11. Qi Wu, *Yige geming genjudi de chengzhang: Kangri zhanzheng he jiefang zhanzheng shiqi de Jin-Ji-Lu-Yu bianqu gaikuang* [The growth of a revolutionary base: The general conditions of the Shanxi-Hebei-Shandong-Henan border region during the anti-Japanese war of resistance and the war of liberation] (Beijing: Renmin chubanshe [People's press], 1958), pp. 155–67.

12. Ibid., pp. 167–68.

13. Ibid., pp. 168–70.

14. *Gongzuo tongxun* [Work correspondence] no. 8, Ji-Lu-Yu bianqu zhengfu Taihang xing shu ban gong dai bian chuban [Published by the Taihang district editorial office of the Hebei-Shandong-Henan district government], 22 December 1947: pp. 19–20.

15. Qi Wu, *Yige geming genjudi de chengzhang*, p. 171; Ding Ling, *Yierjiu shiyu Jin-Ji-Lu-Yu bianqu* [The 129th division of the Shanxi-Hebei-Shandong-Henan border region] (Beijing: Xin Hua she [New China press], 1950), p. 44.

16. *In Guerrilla China* (New York: China Aid Council, 1943), pp. 36–37.

17. Ding Ling, *Yierjiu shiyu Jin-Ji-Lu-Yu bianqu*, pp. 39–45.

18. For example, see Philip Selznick, *The Organizational Weapon: A Study of Bolshevik Strategy and Tactics* (New York: McGraw-Hill, 1952).

19. Cf. Liu Bocheng, "Women zai Taihang Shan shang" [When we were in the Taihang mountains], in *Renmin Ribao* [People's daily], 21 June 1962. Reproduced in *Xinghuo liaoyuan* [A single spark can ignite a prairie fire] (Beijing: Xin Hua shudian [New China bookstore], 1977), pp. 128–29. Mu Xin, "Tongyi zhanxian shenglide," 6. On CCP membership in Shijiazhuang see Jerome Ch'en, report on the visit of the North American Delegation on Socialism and Revolution, *Ideology and History* (June–July 1980), p. 86.

20. "Pingshun diaocha yundong" [The Pingshun investigation movement], no date, pp. 55–58.

21. Zhao Ziyang, *Hua xian qunzhong shi ruhe fadong qilaide* [How the masses of Hua county rose up] (Zhonggong zhongyang Ji-Lu-Yu fenjuyin [Printed by the Hebei-Shandong-Henan subbureau of the central committee of the Chinese Communist Party], 26 May 1946). Written and finished October 1944, pp. 33–65. The quote is from pp. 64–65.

22. See Miao Peishi, *Hong Shu Ling* [Red Tree Hill village] (Beijing: Gongren chubanshe [Workers' press], 1950), p. 21; *Qunzhong shenghuo* no. 3, pp. 9–18. Thaxton, "Lin County Village Investigations."

23. *Qunzhong shenghuo* no. 3, pp. 5–7.

24. Huang Wen, "Puyang xian dianhu yundong" [The tenant movement in Puyang county], in *Gongzuo tongxun* [Work correspondence], no. 11: 5.

25. For a sophisticated version of this theory in reference to China see Joel Migdal, *Peasants, Politics and Revolution* (Princeton: Princeton University Press, 1974), pp. 226–52, especially p. 247. Cf. Samuel L. Popkin, *The Rational Peasant: The Political Economy of Rural Society in Vietnam* (Berkeley: University of California Press, 1979), pp. 243–55, 259–65.

26. For the general picture, see Qi Wu, *Yige geming genjudi de chengzhang*, pp. 99–131.

27. Liu Bocheng, "Lun youji zhanzheng" [On guerrilla warfare], in *Balujun junzheng zazhi* [The military and political affairs magazine of the Eighth Route army] no. 4 (15 April 1939): 8.

28. There are several rich CCP publications on the tenant movements in the border region. For the Taihang see Lai Ruoyu, *Sisi nian dongji yilai jianzu yundong zongjie* [A summary of the 1944 winter season rent reduction movement] (1945). On northern Henan see Ji Dengkui, *Hua xian chajian yundong jianbao* (1945 [?]), pp. 21–45. For the Hebei-Shandong-Henan border see *Gongzuo tongxun* no. 11 (1945); and *Jianzu jianxi zengzi qunzhong yundong kaizhan* [The mass movement for the reduction of rent and interest and the unfolding of wage increases] (Ji-Lu bianqu dangwei [The Communist party Hebei-Shandong border district committee] 1 January 1943). On the Shandong Bohai base area see *Guanyu pubian jiancha jianzu jianxi gaishan gongren daiyu zhengce zhichi guangda gongnong jiben qunzhong de zhishi* [Concerning the ordinary investigation of rent and interest reduction, the policy of improving workers' treatment and wages, and the instructions for organizing the broad masses of workers and peasants] Bohai qu dangwei [Bohai district party committee], June 1944).

29. *Falinghui bian Jin-Ji-Lu-Yu bianqu zhengfu bian* [A complication of laws and directives edited by the Shanxi-Hebei-Shandong-Henan border region government] (Tao Fen shudian [Tao Fen bookstore], July 1945), pp. 1–39, condition no. 19.

30. Ibid., condition no. 22. Cf. Qi Wu, *Yige geming genjudi de chengzhang*, pp. 99–131.

31. Ji Dengkui, *Hua xian chajian yundong jianbao*, pp. 21–45; *Jianzu jianxi zengzi qunzhong yundong kaizhan*, pp. 1–24.

32. Ji Dengkui, *Hua xian chajian yundong jianbao*, pp. 27–34; *Qunzhong shenghuo* no. 3, pp. 1–113.

33. Qunzhong shenghuo no. 3, p. 15.

34. Xiao Chun, "Qinlaozhuang chajian yundong jingyan" [Experiences of the movement to investigate rent reduction in Qin Laozhuang], in *Gongzuo tongxun* no. 11, pp. 65–80.

35. *Jianzu jianxi zengzi qunzhong yundong kaizhan*, pp. 5–8.

36. Thaxton, "Lin County Village Investigations."

37. Xiao Chun, "Qinlaozhuang chajian yundong jingyan," 65–80. Compare with Qi Wu, *Yige geming genjudi de chengzhang*, pp. 116–17; Mark Selden, *The Yenan Way in Revolutionary China* (Cambridge, Mass.: Harvard University Press, 1971), p. 234; and Tetsuya Kataoka, *Resistance and Revolution in China: The Communists and the Second United Front* (Berkeley: University of California Center for Chinese Studies, 1974), p. 249.
38. Ji Dengkui, *Hua xian chajian yundong jianbao*, pp. 21–45.
39. Qi Wu, *Yige geming genjudi de chengzhang*, pp. 116–17; *Jianzu jianxi zengzi qunzhong yundong kaizhan*, p. 3; and Chen Shouyi and Li Yu, *Jianzu banfa qian jie* [The methods for simple solutions in rent reduction] (Qiqi chubanshe yin xing [The "July 7" press], August 1944), pp. 3–6.
40. Qi Wu, *Yige geming genjudi de chengzhang*, pp. 99–116.
41. *Gongzuo tongxun* no. 11, pp. 1–20.
42. Ji Dengkui, *Hua xian chajian yundong jianbao*, pp. 24–35; cf. Zudian guanxi diaocha cankao cailiao [Reference materials on the investigation of rental tenant relations] (November 1945–January 1946), pp. 1–14.
43. Ji Dengkui, *Hua xian chajian yundong jianbao*, pp. 33–35.
44. Thaxton, "Lin County Village Investigations."
45. Li Gang, *Qunzhong shenghuo* [Life of the masses], no. 1, Ji-Lu-Yu kang lian qunzhong shenghoushe [Life of the masses press of the Hebei-Shandong-Henan district federation of resistance associations], 1944, pp. 12–14.
46. Ji Dengkui, *Hua xian chajian yundong jianbao*, pp. 33–36; *Jianzu jianxi zengzi qunzhong yundong kaizhan*, pp. 38–42; *Guanyu pubian jiancha jianzu jianxi gaishan gongren diayu zhengce*, pp. 75–84.
47. Ji Dengkui, *Hua xian chajian yundong jianbao*, pp. 33–36; *Guanyu pubian jiancha jianzu jianxi gaishan gongren diayu zhengce*, pp. 42–44.
48. Ji Dengkui, *Hua xian chajian yundong jianbao*, pp. 46–53.
49. Thaxton, "Lin County Village Investigations."
50. Qi Wu, *Yige geming genjudi de chengzhang*, p. 116; *Jianzu jianxi zengzi qunzhong yundong kaizhan*, pp. 8–9; *Guanyu pubian jiancha jianzu jianxi gaishan gongren daiyu zhengce*, p. 24.
51. *Jianzu jianxi zengzi qunzhong yundong kaizhan*, pp. 8–9; cf. Kataoka, *Resistance and Revolution in China*, pp. 124–25.
52. Qi Wu, *Yige geming genjudi de chengzhang*, p. 127.
53. Kataoka, *Resistance and Revolution in China*, pp. 253, 255–56.
54. Qi Wu, *Yige geming genjudi de chengzhang*, p. 128.
55. Thaxton, "Lin County Village Investigations."
56. "Pangcun fadong qunzhong de jiaoxun" [The lesson of mass mobilization in Pang village] Ji-Jin qu dangwei [Hebei-Shanxi district party committee], probably 1944, pp. 15–19.
57. *Gongzuo tongxun* no. 8, pp. 1–17.
58. Ibid., pp. 1–3.
59. *Mofan shiji: ganbu xuexi cailiao zhiyi* [Model achievers: study guide materials for cadres] Jinan yinhang gongshang guanli [The South Hebei Bank industrial and commercial management] (Jinan yinhang bafenhang ganbu kebian [Edited by the cadre section in the eighth branch of the South Hebei bank], 1946), pp. 1–14.
60. Mao Zedong, *Selected Works* (Beijing: Foreign Languages Press, 1967), vol. 3, p. 114; cf. Kataoka, *Resistance and Revolution in China*, pp. 129, 253. Kataoka does not specify which peasants were included among the two-thirds of the rural people who were largely exempt from taxes during the early war years. But poor smallholders and landless peasants paid few if any taxes. The Crooks tend to confirm this was the case (Isabel and David Crook, *Revolution in a Chinese Village: Ten Mile Inn* [London: Routledge and Kegan Paul, 1959], pp. 46–47).
61. The best source on middle-peasant involvement in mutual aid and production is Li Chunlan, *Shengchan yundong xiaozongshu zhi yi* [A book in the little reader on the production movement] *Hezuo huzhu shengchan de huo yangzi* [A living model in cooperative mutual aid]

(Qian Rugui he Houshangu cun [Qian Rugui and Houshangu village], Ji-Lu-Yu shudian [Hebei-Shandong-Henan bookstore], May 1946), pp. 1–46. Cf. Li Gang, *Qunzhong shenghuo*, pp. 19–26.

62. *Gaishan dui de jingji douzheng jiaqiang genjudi jingji jianshe wenti tigang* [Outlines for problems in unfolding the struggle against the enemy and strengthening the economic reconstruction of the base areas] (Zhanxianshe [Frontline press], 1943).

63. Qi Wu, *Yige geming genjudi de chengzhang*, pp. 127–28.

64. On the harmful effects of this line see Trygve Lotviet, *Chinese Communism 1931–1934: Experience in Civil Government* (Sweden: Scandinavian Institute of Asian Studies Monograph Series no. 16, 1973), pp. 151–54.

65. "Jian You baodong xiangqing ji qi jyauxun" [Information on the lessons of rebellion in Jian You] *Bianqu zhengbao* [Border region government news] (1945–46): 20–22.

66. Huang Wen, "Puyang xian dianhu yundong," 5–27.

67. Thaxton, "Lin County Village Investigations."

68. Liu Moyuan, "Wen miao de jinxi" [Present and past of the literary temple], in *Peifang zazhi* [Magazine of the north] no. 3, Jin-Ji-Lu-Yu bianqu wenlian bian [Shanxi-Hebei-Shandong-Henan literary federation] (1946).

69. Compare with Edward Friedman, who makes the point in reference to social bandits for early Republican China, *Backward Toward Revolution: The Chinese Revolutionary Party* (Berkeley: University of California Press, 1974), pp. 130, 160.

70. Thaxton, "Lin County Village Investigations."

71. "Jieshao Pingshun xian tonglei shui pingyi gongzuo" [Introducing our integrated tax appraisal work in Pingshun county], in *Bianqu zhengbao* [Border region government news] (1945–46): 20–21.

72. *Shandong sheng zhangong hui minggai diyici quansheng caizhengfu daibiao huiyi* [A report to the first provincial financial and economic delegation conference sponsored by the Shandong province wartime works committee] (May 1940), pp. 11–14.

73. "Jieshao Pingshun xian tonglei shui pingyi gungzuo," pp. 20–21; *Shandong sheng zhangong hui*, pp. 11–14.

74. "Jieshao Pingshun xian tonglei shui pingyi gungzuo," pp. 20–21.

75. *Zhongguo nongcun jingji fazhan de daolu* [The course of the Chinese peasant economy], no date, p. 6.

76. Cf. Belden, *China Shakes the World*, pp. 97–104, 131–32.

77. Li Chunlan, *Shengchan yundong xiaozongshu zhi yi*, pp. 1–46.

78. Thaxton, "Lin County Village Investigations."

79. On Shanxi, compare with chap. 5; on Hebei see Crook and Crook, *Revolution in a Chinese Village*, pp. 46–47; on Shandong see *Shandong sheng zhangong hui*, pp. 13–14.

80. "Shouzhang qin zidong shougao qi nongye shengchan" [The leader lifts his own hands to boost agricultural production], in *Renmin de jundui* [The people's troops] (9 June 1946).

81. Ding Ling, *Yierjiu shi yu Jin-Ji-Lu-Yu bianqu*, pp. 39–45.

82. "Jiulingwu budui shengchang fenhong jihua" [The profit share production plan of the 905th troop unit], in *Renmin de jundui* [The people's troops] (18 April 1946).

83. *Tongyilei jin shui banfa* [The method of unified progressive income tax], Taihang di qi xingzheng ducha zhuanyuan gongshu [Special inspector's office of the Taihang seventh administrative unit] (Jin-Ji-Lu-Yu bianqu tongyilei jin shui zhanxing shuizi caoan [A draft of the temporary tax principles for the unified progressive tax of the Shanxi-Hebei-Shandong-Henan border region], 1 April 1945), pp. 1–10.

84. Qi Wu, *Yige geming genjudi de chengzhang*, pp. 99–131.

85. Li Chunlan, *Shengchan yundong xiaozongshu zhi yi*, pp. 1–46.

86. See John L. H. Keep, *The Russian Revolution: A Study in Mass Mobilization* (New York: Norton, 1976), chap. 31.

87. Liu Bocheng, for example, had studied military history and strategy in the Soviet Union, and he apparently had a good understanding of problems in the Russian Revolution.

88. From *Taihang qu maoyi gongzuo li nian lai zhongyao jueding zhi shi mingling bi mi wenjian yi jiaopin* [The secretly filed materials on the past years' important decisions, directives, and orders on Taihang district trade work], *Cankao ziliao de san bian shangye maoyi lei di yi ji* [The first book on categories of business and trade in the third edition of reference materials] (Taihang qu Jinan yinhang zonghang gong shang guanliji chuban [Taihang district South Hebei bank headquarters, bureau of industry and commerce], December 1945), pp. 1–100; and *Taihang qu yinhang gongshang gongzuo cankao ziliao bianji weiyuanhui* [Editorial committee for work reference materials for the Taihang district bank industry and commerce work] (2 September 1945), pp. 1–15.

89. Jeffery Paige, *Agrarian Revolution: Social Movements and Export Agriculture in the Underdeveloped World* (New York: Free Press, 1975), p. 17.

90. *Zhongguo nongcun jingji fazhan de daolu*, pp. 9–10.

91. Liu Bocheng, "Women zai Taihang Shan shang," 126–44.

92. Belden, *China Shakes the World*, pp. 100–101, 106–7.

93. *Taihang qu yinhang gongshang gongzuo*, p. 24.

94. Gongzuo cankao: Jin-Ji-Lu-Yu bianqu maoyi zongqu [Work references: Shanxi-Hebei-Shandong-Henan border region trade bureau headquarters] no. 2 (20 October 1947), pp. 14–18.

95. *Taihang qu maoyi gongzuo*, pp. 1–5.

96. Ibid., pp. 1–56.

97. Ibid., pp. 1–4.

98. Robert Marks, "Markets and Morals: Peasants and the Question of Food in Eighteenth-Century Guandong," 21st Annual Conference, American Association for Chinese Studies (November 1979), California State University, Long Beach, Cal., pp. 1–18.

99. Cf. Belden, *China Shakes the World*, pp. 105–6.

100. *Taihang qu maoyi gungzuo*, pp. 1–100; *Taihang qu yinhang gongshang gongzuo cankao ziliao*, pp. 2–11.

101. *Shandong sheng zhangong hui*, p. 7; *Gongzuo cankao: Jin-Ji-Lu-Yu bianqu maoyi zong qu*, pp. 1–20.

102. *Taihang qu maoyi gongzuo*, pp. 1–73; and *Taihang qu yinhang gongshang gongzuo*, pp. 1–20.

103. "Ning Jiannian shi aimin hao banyang" [Nian Jiannian is a beloved model of the people], in *Renmin de jundui* [The people's troops] (24 February 1946).

104. Mao Zedong, "Instructions on the Army's Participation in Production and Construction Work," *Miscellany of Mao Zedong Thought* (I) (Springfield, Va.: JPRS, 1974): 3. Yanjin siren zuo maimai" [Prohibit private business operations], in *Renmin de jundui* [The people's troops] (9 June 1946).

105. *Taihang qu maoyi gongzuo*, pp. 1–73.

106. Thaxton, "Lin County Village Investigations." *Pingyuan zazhi* [The magazine of the plains] no. 1, *Xiangcun yishu* [Village art], *Zenyang gaizao miaohui* [How to transform the temple fairs], *Ji Zong Luoyou xiangyan dahui de gaizao* [Notes on the transformation of Zong Luoyou's big incense meeting], pp. 1–10.

107. In developing this point I have benefited from Cyril S. Belshaw, *Traditional Exchange and Modern Markets* (Englewood Cliffs, N. J.: Prentice-Hall, 1965), pp. 53–83.

108. Li Chunlan, *Shengchan yundong xiaozongshu zhi yi*, pp. 19–20.

109. *Gongzuo cankao: Jin-Ji-Lu-Yu bianqu maoyi zongqu*, pp. 16–18.

110. *Pingyuan zazhi*, pp. 1–10.

111. Karl Polanyi, *The Great Transformation* (Boston: Beacon Press, 1957), pp. 1–75; Christopher Hill, *The World Turned Upside Down: Radical Ideas During the English Revolution* (New York: Viking, 1972), pp. 1–45, 274–91.

112. Barrington Moore, Jr., *Social Origins of Dictatorship and Democracy: Lord and Peasant in the Making of the Modern World* (Boston: Beacon Press, 1966) chap. on England. Cf. Hill, *The World Turned Upside Down*, pp. 16, 289.

113. Here I respect the foundations of Eric R. Wolf, *Peasant Wars of the Twentieth Century* (New York: Harper & Row, 1969), pp. 276–82; and James C. Scott, *The Moral Economy of the Peasant: Rebellion and Subsistence in Southeast Asia* (New Haven: Yale University Press, 1976), chaps. 1–2. Cf. Marvin Harris, *Cultural Materialism: The Struggle for a Science of Culture* (New York: Random House, 1979), pp. 297–304.

114. Ma Feng, *Wo de diyige shangji*, pp. 37–38.

115. For this interpretation see Moore, *Social Origins*, pp. 226–27. Moore's point is better taken in reference to the post-1956 PRC state.

116. Cf. Qi Wu, *Yige geming genjudi de chengzhang*, pp. 171–76.

117. Edward Banfield, *The Moral Basis of a Backward Society* (New York: Free Press, 1958), pp. 139–52. Banfield also stressed the importance of childhood socialization in fostering images of immoral society.

118. Cf. Crook and Crook, *Revolution in a Chinese Village*, pp. 161–65; and Li Chunlan, *Shengchan yundong xiaozongshu zhi yi*, pp. 19–46.

119. *Guanchéng shengchan yundong zhong de jige wenti* [Several problems in the mutual aid movements around Guancheng], Gongzuo tongxun [Work correspondence] no. 17 (Zhonggong Ji-Lu-Yu qu dang wei minyunbu bian [Civil movement department of the Hebei-Shandong-Henan district bureau of the CCP], probably 1945), pp. 1–4, 34–35.

120. Qi Wu, *Yige geming genjudi de chengzhang*, pp. 175–76.

121. Ibid., pp. 172–73.

122. *Zhongyuan ernu* [Sons and daughters of the central plains], in *Henan minbing geming douzheng gushi ji* [A collection of stories on the revolutionary struggles of the Henan people's militia] (Henan renmin chubanshe [Henan people's press], 1975), pp. 138–60.

123. I am indebted to Popkin for this point. *Rational Peasant*, p. 267, and personal correspondence.

124. Polanyi, *The Great Transformation*, p. 75.

125. *Taihang qu sifa gongzuo gaikuang Xu quzhang zai Taihang qu sifa huiyi shang zhi zongjie baogao* [The general conditions of judicial work in the Taihang district—department director Xu's summary report to the judicial conference of the Taihang district] (Taihang xin shu [Taihang Administrative Office], 1946). Trans. by Wallace Douglass in *Chinese Law and Government* 6, no. 3 (Fall 1973): 14–25.

126. Li Chunlan, *Shengchan yundong xiaozongshu zhi yi*, pp. 1–46.

127. *Taihang qu yinhang gongshang gongzuo cankao ziliao*, pp. 1–70.

128. Qi Wu, *Yige geming genjudi de chengzhang*, p. 95.

129. Ibid., p. 100.

130. Lai Ruoyu, *Sisi nian dongji yilai jianzu yundong zongjie* [A summary of the 1944 winter rent reduction movement], 1945, pp. 3–6.

131. See *Liandui gongzuo* [Company work] (Jin-Ji-Lu-Yu qu zhengzhibu [Shanxi-Hebei-Shandong-Henan political department], 1946), pp. 1–20.

132. Joseph W. Esherick, ed., *Lost Chance in China: The World War II Dispatches of John S. Service* (New York: Vintage, 1974), p. 218.

133. Franz Schurmann, *Ideology and Organization in Communist China* (Berkeley: University of California Press, 1966), p. 24.

134. See, for example, Amos Perlmutter, *The Military and Politics in Modern Times* (New Haven: Yale University Press, 1977), p. 229.

135. See Belden, *China Shakes the World*, pp. 89–96; Zhao Shuli, *The Tale of Li Youcai's Rhymes*. Notes by Susan S. H. MacDonald (London: Cambridge University Press, 1970).

136. Qi Wu, *Yige geming genjudi de chengzhang*, pp. 99–131 for the context.

137. "Liang Liangui," in *Qunzhong shenghuo*, no. 3: 83–90.

138. Cf. Mao Zedong, *The New Stage* (Chungking: New China Information Committee, 1938). Cf. Mao Zedong, "The Identity Between the National and the Class Struggle," *Selected Works*, vol. 2 (Beijing: Foreign Languages Press, 1965), p. 215.

139. Shi Liqun, *Zhongguo shi hua*, pp. 19–22.

140. "Liu Bocheng jiangjun songhui da xigua" [Commander Liu Bocheng sends back a big watermelon], in *Min Bing* [The militia] (22 August 1947).

141. The premises in this line of analysis are to be found in Marvin Harris, *Cannibals and Kings*, and "Cannibals and Kings: An Exchange," *The New York Review of Books* (28 June 1979): 51−53.

CHAPTER 5

1. Liu Jiang, *Taihang fengyun* [The Taihang storm] (Beijing: Zuojia chubanshe [Writers' press], 1962), pp. 1−532.

2. It is possible to test this particular novel, and others like it, by oral history work undertaken at the village level, by establishing connections between the writers and places and events in these works through interviews. The interviews can be checked against the novel itself and the memories of peasants in the locality about which it was written. I began work in this direction in the spring of 1980, but I have relied entirely on other, written sources to check and supplement *The Taihang Storm*. These include Bai Ping, "Fenghuang shan jiande hongqi" [The red flag on Phoenix mountain] in *Hongqi piaopiao* [The red flag flutters], vol. 8, pp. 122−40; *Zuo Zhuan jiangjun zai Taihang shan shang* [Commander Zuo Zhuan in the Taihang mountains] in *Hongqi piaopiao* [The red flag flutters], vol. 5, pp. 138−48; and *Renmin de jundui* [The people's troops], which provide running accounts of Liu Bocheng's activities in the Taihang. For a relevant personal memoir see Jiang Xianshan, *Zhandou zhe de ri zi* [Days of fighting] (Shanghai: Xin Wenyi chubanshe [New literary press], 1953), pp. 1−82. For a critical review of *The Taihang Storm* see Li Xifan, *Cun xin ji* [A collection from the heart], *Geming nongcun de bianqian shi* [The changing history of a revolutionary peasant village] (Beijing: Zuojia chubanshe [Writers' press], 1962), pp. 21−23.

3. Compare with chaps. 2, 3, and 4.

4. Bai Ping, "Fenghuang shan," pp. 122−40.

5. Benjamin I. Schwartz, *Chinese Communism and the Rise of Mao* (New York: Harper Torchbooks, 1967), pp. 198−200.

6. Ramon de Jaegher, *The Enemy Within* (New York: Doubleday, 1952), pp. 45−47.

7. Compare this position with the writings of Mao Zedong and Lu Dingyi on religion in Donald E. MacInnis, *Religious Policy and Practice in Communist China* (New York: Macmillan, 1972), pp. 11, 30−31. Whether religion reinforced class in China's peasant wars is by no means settled, even within the high circles of official CCP history.

8. The Red Spears, in this case, refers to the marginal oppositionist members of the secret society discussed in chap. 3.

9. The term "long-haired bandit rebels" refers to the Taipings. Landlords also used this term to refer to the Boxer and Red Spear rebels.

10. Compare Daniel Overmyer's position in *Folk Buddhist Religion* (Cambridge: Harvard University Press, East Asian Series 83, 1976), pp. 18, 26, 42−44, with my review of his work in *The Journal of Asian Studies* 37, no. 1 (November 1977): 105−7. In developing this point, I have benefited from Kitsiri Malalgoda, "Millennialism in Relation to Buddhism," in *Comparative Studies in Society and History* 12, no. 4 (October 1970): 424−41.

11. Cf. Liu Bocheng, "Women zai Taihang shan sheng," [When we were in the Taihang Mountains], in *Renmin Ribao* [People's daily], 21 June 1962. Reproduced in *Xinghuo liaoyuan* [A single spark can ignite a prairie fire] (Beijing: Xin Hua shudian [New China bookstore], 1977), pp. 128−31. According to Liu Jiang and Liu Bocheng, the CCP armed forces were entering southeast Shanxi through Hongtong, Zhaocheng, Wenshui, Taigu, and Zuoquan along the Zhang river.

12. Compare with Frantz Fanon, *The Wretched of the Earth* (New York: Grove Press, 1963), pp. 126−27.

13. De Jaegher, *Enemy Within*, pp. 38−39, 73−84, 155−56.

14. The CCP members in the Sacrifice League were working mostly in the temples around

the county seats and market towns. Cf. *Cong Ximenghui kan Shanxi minzhong yundong* [The Shanxi civil movement from the viewpoint of the sacrifice league] (Huang He chubanshe [Yellow River press], July 1939), pp. 1–80.

15. Barrington Moore, Jr., *Social Origins of Dictatorship and Democracy: Lord and Peasant in the Making of the Modern World* (Boston: Beacon Press, 1966), pp. 201–13.

16. In developing this interpretation and the link between microlevel (village) and macro-level (region) revolutionary developments implicit in it, I have profited from exchanges with G. William Skinner in the ACLS workshop on "Rebellion and Revolution in North China," Harvard University, Summer 1979.

17. For a good critical analysis of this mode, see Michael Walzer, "A Theory of Revolution," *Marxist Perspectives* 2, no. 1 (Spring 1979), p. 24.

18. Peter McPhee, "Popular Culture, Symbolism and Rural Radicalism in Nineteenth-Century France," *The Journal of Peasant Studies* 5, no. 2 (January 1978): 238–53, especially 243–44, 250.

19. For several works that understand the promise of peasants in rebellion to substitute their own countervalues for the ideas of the dominant political groups, see Mao Zedong, "Report on an Investigation of the Peasant Movement in Hunan," *Selected Works of Mao Zedong*, vol. 1 (Beijing: Foreign Languages Press, 1965); Fanon, *Wretched of the Earth;* and Christopher Hill, *The World Turned Upside Down: Radical Ideas During the English Revolution* (New York: Viking, 1972).

20. William Hinton, *Fanshen: A Documentary of Revolution in a Chinese Village* (New York: Random House, 1966), pp. 58–68, 143–46.

21. According to K. S. Latourette, Roman Catholic missions received financial setbacks from World War I. *A History of Christian Missions in China* (New York: Macmillan, 1929), chaps. 28–29. On the general point, compare Ian Liden's study of the relationship of Catholic presence to peasant religion and rebellion in Africa, *Catholics, Peasants, and Chewa Resistance in Nyasaland, 1889–1939* (London: Heinemann, 1974).

22. For a similar argument on Cuba, see Bert Ussem, "Peasant Involvement in the Cuban Revolution," *Journal of Peasant Studies* 5, no. 1 (October 1977): 106–7.

CHAPTER 6

1. Chalmers A. Johnson, *Peasant Nationalism and Communist Power: The Emergence of Revolutionary China 1937–1945* (Stanford: Stanford University Press, 1962), p. 4; and see especially chaps. 1–2, pp. 2–14.

2. Lucien Bianco, *Origins of the Chinese Revolution, 1915–1949* (Stanford: Stanford University Press, 1971), pp. 151–55, 166.

3. Mark Selden, *The Yenan Way in Revolutionary China* (Cambridge, Mass: Harvard University Press, 1971), pp. 77, 115, 231, 277–78.

4. For my preliminary essay on the priority of peasant subsistence over CCP national resistance goals, see Ralph Thaxton, "On Peasant Revolution and National Resistance: Toward a Theory of Peasant Mobilization and Revolutionary War with Special Reference to Modern China," *World Politics* 30, no. 1 (October 1977): 24–57.

5. See Qi Wu, *Yige geming genjudi de chengzhang: Kangri zhanzheng he jiefang zhanzheng shiqi de Jin-Ji-Lu-Yu bianqu gaikuang* [The growth of a revolutionary base: the general conditions of the Shanxi-Hebei-Shandong-Henan border region during the anti-Japanese war of resistance and the war of liberation] (Beijing: Renmin chubanshe [People's press], 1958), pp. 156–61, 167–77.

6. Ibid., pp. 156–57, 162–64. As of 1939 there were at least three million refugees in the border region. From 1939 to 1942 CCP agrarian development programs reduced this number significantly, but the Japanese Three All had added yet another million refugees by 1942–43.

7. There are two excellent studies of this: John Hunter Boyle, *China and Japan at War 1937–1945: The Politics of Collaboration* (Stanford: Stanford University Press, 1972); and

Gerald E. Bunker, *The Peace Conspiracy: Wang Ching-wei and the China War, 1937–1941* (Cambridge, Mass.: Harvard University Press, 1972). Boyle's study more than Bunker's suggests that Wang Jingwei's Guomindang was anti-Confucian. But surely the Japanese saw something of traditional Confucian paternalist rule in the old-style officials surrounding Wang. Cf. Boyle, *China and Japan at War*, chap. 5.

8. Referring to the initial Eighth Route operation in Wuan *xian* in 1937–39, Crook and Crook point out, "The greatest obstacle which the Communists encountered in organizing resistance was that the peasants' spirit had been almost completely shattered by the abuses and ruinous exactions of the Guomindang troops. The latter's extortions had in the end become so great that peasants thought bitterly that the Japanese could hardly be worse; and that perhaps they might even be better." Isabel and David Crook, *Revolution in a Chinese Village: Ten Mile Inn* (London: Routledge & Kegan Paul, 1959), p. 34. The proclivity of peasants to assume a neutralist position in war is dealt with by Geoffrey Blainey, *The Causes of War* (New York: Free Press, 1973), pp. 186–205.

9. Jack Belden, *China Shakes the World* (New York: Monthly Review Press, 1970), pp. 50, 98; cf. Joseph W. Esherick, ed., *Lost Chance in China: The World War II Dispatches of John S. Service* (New York: Vintage, 1974), p. 19.

10. For a Guomindang report on these Japanese provisions see *Lun xianqu zhi de weihulu zhengce* [The enemy and puppet road protection policy in the occupied counties and districts] (Chongqing: The Special Economic Investigation Office of the Guomindang Central Bureau of Investigation and Statistics, 1943), pp. 1–15.

11. Henry G. Schwartz, *Liu Shao-ch'i and "People's War": A Report on the Creation of Base Areas in 1938* (Lawrence: Kansas University East Asian Research Publications, 1969), pp. 45–47, 49–50.

12. *Lun xianqu zhi de weihulu zhengce*, pp. 6–12.

13. Liu Bocheng, "Women zai Taihang Shan shang" [When we were in the Taihang Mountains], *Renmin ribao* [People's daily] (23 June 1962), reproduced in *Xinghuo liaoyuan* [A single spark can ignite a prairie fire] (Beijing: Xin Hua shudian [New China Bookstore], 1977), pp. 127–38. Cf. Sun Yuanfa, "Banian chenggang de Jin-Cha-Ji bianqu" [The steeling of the Shanxi-Chahar-Hebei border region], *Jeifang ribao* [Liberation daily] 10 July 1944.

14. Compare with John S. Service, "Willingness of Chinese Military Leaders to Become 'Puppets,'" in Esherick, *Lost Chance in China*, p. 49.

15. Israel Epstein, *The Unfinished Revolution in China* (Boston: Little, Brown, 1947), pp. 316–17. Ralph Thaxton, "Lin County Village Investigations."

16. The Japanese came after Zhu De's crack regiment in 1938. Zhu held them off until the height of the Three All in southeast Shanxi. Cf. Liu Baiyu, *Hongyan de shiyue* [A time of redness] (Shanghai: Wenxue chubanshe [Literary press], 1978), pp. 42–49.

17. On Liu Bocheng's 129th Division land-reclamation projects see Ding Ling, *Yierjiu shiyu Jin-Ji-Lu-Yu bianqu* [The 129th division of the Shanxi-Hebei-Shandong-Henan border region] (Beijing: Xin hua she [New China press], 1950), pp. 39–45. On He Long's 120th Division efforts see Wang Cheng, "In Memory of He Long," *Renmin ribao* [People's daily] (28 July 1977).

18. According to Boyle, General Kita had concluded, "It was necessary to go back to Confucian times to find a really satisfactory system for the rule of the Chinese people." *China and Japan at War*, p. 6.

19. See Michael Lindsay, *The Unknown War: North China 1937–1945* (London: Bergstrom and Boyle, 1975), pp. 5–7. This section also has benefited from Saburō Ienaga, *The Pacific War: World War II and the Japanese, 1931–1945* (New York: Pantheon, 1978), pp. 47, 51–52, 160–71.

20. Writing of how the local people of Madang greeted the Japanese as cargo prophets in the early phase of occupation, Harris points out that as the Japanese military situation in Madang deteriorated and as the Japanese began impressing and pillaging, the natives were less inclined to expect patronage from any foreign occupying forces, including those of the

Australians and Americans. Marvin Harris, *Cows, Pigs, Wars and Witches* (New York: Vintage, 1974), pp. 141–43.

21. Lindsay, *Unknown War*, pp. 5–7.

22. Liu Bocheng, "Women zai Taihang Shan shang," 126–29. Liu Bocheng, "Lun youji zhanzheng" [On guerrilla warfare], in *Balujun junzheng zazhi* [The military and political affairs magazine of the Eighth Route army] no. 4, (15 April 1939): 1–8. Huang Xuanwen, *Xiao he fengyun* [Storm along the Xiao river] (Henan renmin chubanshe [Henan people's press], 1976), pp. 62–63.

23. Liu Bocheng, "Women zai Taihang Shan shang," p. 127.

24. Liu Qi, *Zhanzheng jiguan* [Impressions of war] (Beijing: Jiefangjun wenyi chubanshe [Liberation Army literature and arts press], 1978), pp. 1–25.

25. Bianco, *Origins of the Chinese Revolution*, pp. 151–52. Like Johnson, Bianco's premises are that "with social concerns relegated to the background, the accent was on national resistance"; and that "the CCP's greatest ally was the Japanese Army, whose atrocities left the peasantry in such desperate straits that it had no recourse but to seek the Red Army's protection."

26. Tetsuya Kataoka, *Resistance and Revolution in China: The Communists and the Second United Front* (Berkeley: University of California Center for Chinese Studies, 1974), chap. 5, especially pp. 143, 161–65, 178–80.

27. Liu Bocheng, "Women zai Taihang Shan shang," 126–30.

28. "Pingding duidi douzheng yu qunyun qingkuang de jieshao" [An introduction to the conditions of the struggle with the enemy and the mass movement in Pingding], in *Bianqu zhengbao* [Border region government news] (1946): 41–45.

29. Thaxton, "Lin County Village Investigations." William Hinton, *Fanshen: A Documentary of Revolution in a Chinese Village* (New York: Random House, 1966), p. 72.

30. Liu Bocheng, "Women zai Taihang Shan shang," 131.

31. Ibid., 134–36.

32. I am indebted to Johnson for the leads to this point. *Peasant Nationalism and Communist Power*, pp. 13–14.

33. See Bogdan Denitch, "Violence and Social Change in the Yugoslav Revolution: Lessons for the Third World?" *Comparative Politics* 8, no. 3 (April 1976): 469–70. Denitch shows this was the case for Yugoslavia, but he assumes, as does Johnson for China, that war proved to *the* precipitant of peasant uprooting and social mobilization.

34. Cf. "Gonggu heping tuijin bianqu minju jianshe" [Consolidate the peaceful advancement of the border region democratic construction], in *Bianqu zhengbao* [Border region government news] (1946): 4–5.

35. See Zhu De, *On the Battlefronts of the Liberated Areas* (Beijing: Foreign Languages Press, 1952), pp. 73–75, and (1962), p. 65; Ji Dengkui, "Hua xian chajian yundong jianbao" [A report on the investigation of the rent reduction movement in Hua county], *Qunzhong yundong cailiao* [Materials for the mass movement], (Ji-Lu-Yu qu dangwei minyunbu [Civil movement department of the Hebei-Shandong-Henan district party committee], probably 1945, pp. 21–45; Hua Shan, *The Shepherd Boy Hai Wa* (Beijing: Foreign Languages Press, 1974), pp. 1–3, 11; Hinton, *Fanshen*, pp. 89–91, 115, 182; Thaxton, "Lin County Village Investigations."

36. *Canzhan gongzuo* [War participation work] no. 13, Ji-Lu-Yu qu houfang zongjie zhanbu [Hebei-Shandong-Henan district rear area military headquarters department] (1947), p. 32.

37. *Zhandou zai Taihang Shan shang* [The war in the Taihang mountains], Lianfang jun zhengzhibu xuanchuanbu [Propaganda department of the joint military-political department] (August 1944), pp. 40–60, especially 56–60. For a supporting personal account, see Ge Lan, *Yang tietong de gushi* [The story of Yang Tietong] (Beijing: Zuojia chubanshe [Writers' Press], 1955), pp. 1–2.

38. Thaxton, "Lin County Village Investigations."

39. Belden, *China Shakes the World*, pp. 55–58, 229–37; Sun Tan Wei, *A Village Moves to Socialism* (Shanghai: China Reconstructs, supplement 10, November 1956), pp. 3–36; Liu Qi, *Zhanzheng jiguan*, pp. 12–13; Li Yingju, *Nu youji dui zhang* [A woman guerrilla commander] (Beijing: Jiefangjun wenyishe [Liberation Army literature and arts press], 1979), pp. 738–822, 872–958.

40. Ge Lan, *Yang Tietong de gushi*, pp. 1–115.

41. This argument owes its origins in part to Edward Friedman, "Mao Zedong Backward Toward Revolution," unpublished manuscript, University of Wisconsin, 1975, pp. 8–15. Typical of Mao's watered-down references to the *youmin* is his statement that "of course it is inadvisable to have too many of them." *Selected Works of Mao Zedong*, vol. 1 (Beijing: Foreign Languages Press, 1951), p. 81. But Mao made clear that the *youmin* were the army fighters who did not fear death and hence were pivotal in the formation of the armed forces. Mao Zedong, *Miscellany of Mao Zedong Thought*, vol. 2 (Springfield, Va.: JPRS, 1974), pp. 421, 425. For Zhu De's reference to these rootless elements see Agnes Smedley, *The Great Road: The Life and Times of Chu Teh* (New York: Monthly Review Press, 1956), p. 301.

42. Li Yingyu, *Nu youjidui zhang*, pp. 232–70.

43. See Karl Marx, *Class Struggles in France 1848–50* (New York: International Publishers, 1964), pp 50–51; Karl Marx, "The Eighteenth Brumaire of Louis Bonaparte," in *The Marx-Engels Reader*, ed. Robert C. Tucker (New York: Norton, 1972), pp. 522–23. There is no one systematic comparative treatment of the role of *lumpen* elements in revolution or counterrevolution. For an interesting start on France, which attempts to show the irrelevance of Marx's *lumpenproletariat* as a sociological category, see Mark Traugott, "The Mobile Guard in the French Revolution of 1848," *Theory and Society* 9, no. 5 (September 1980): 683–720.

44. Liu Bocheng, "Women zai Taihang Shan shang," 126–32; Gongzuo tongxun [Work correspondence] no. 35, Sixiang zijue zhibao ligong tuanjie kongsu zhuanhao [A special issue on achieving self-confidence and self-assessment in rendering service to the solidification of the accusation movement], Dang nei kanwu [Internal party publication], Ji-Lu-Yu dangwei chuban [Published by the Hebei-Shandong-Henan party committee] 10 July 1947, pp. 1–121, especially 40–45; Zhanyoubao [Comrades-in-arms newspaper] supplement no. 3, Ji-Lu-Yu jun qu zhengzhibu zhanyoubaoshe bianyin [Published by the Comrades-in-arms press of the political department of the Hebei-Shandong-Henan military district] 15 July 1945, 1–20. Cf. Zhi Xia, *The Railway Guerrillas* (Beijing: Foreign Languages Press, 1966), pp. 1–12.

45. Sun Tan Wei, *Village Moves to Socialism*, pp. 3–36.

46. Li Yingyu, *Nu youji duizhang*, pp. 225–29.

47. Cf. Ma Feng and Ke Ming, *Chunyingde gushi* [The story of spring heroes] (Beijing: Huabei renmin chubanshe [North China people's press], 1953), pp. 22–42.

48. Thaxton, "Lin County Village Investigations."

49. For a pro-Guomindang source that understood this possibility and warned the Guomindang commanders of the consequences of using forceful methods to deal with the Red Spears, see Gao Yiqing, "Jin-nan de Hongqiang Hui" [The Red Spears of southern Shanxi] in *Xibei Lunheng* [Northwest forum]: 19–21. On the Peng Dehuai-Red Spear connection see Polachek, "Mao's 'Moral Economy' and the Kiangsi Soviet," *Journal of Asian Studies*, forthcoming, pp. 27–28 in the original unpublished Davis Center manuscript, 16 October 1981. For the Liu-Deng-Red Spear praxis see Li Xiaoming's popular novel [The sound of rifle fire on the plains] (Beijing: Zuojia chubanshe [Writers' press], 1965, pp. 1–150.

50. Belden, *China Shakes the World*, pp. 43–53, 71–78; "Bo Yibo: New Vice Premier of the State Council," *Issues and Studies* (August 1979): 84–85; Guo Youfan, "Oral History Raw Notes"; Mu Xin, "Tongyi Zhanxian Shenglide yiqukaige" [A victorious episode of the United Front], in *Shehui kexue zhanxian* [The battlefront of the social science], no. 4 (1979), pp. 4–7.

51. Guan Hua, *Jiangjun He* [Along the Jiangjun river] (Beijing: Zhongguo qingnian chubanshe [China youth press], 1977), pp. 1–5, chaps. 12–20.

52. Hua Shan, *Yingxiong de shiyue* [Ten months with the heroes] (Tianjin: Renmin wenxue chubanshe [People's literary press], 1949), pp. 1–19; and Su Di, "Zhu De's Model Guard Movement," in *Zhandou zai Taihang Shan shang*, pp. 61–62.

53. *Zhanyoubao* no. 3, pp. 1–10, 16–20.

54. Ibid., pp. 17–19.

55. Ibid., pp. 15–16.

56. Stuart R. Schram, "On the Nature of Mao Zedong's 'Deviation' in 1927," *The China Quarterly*, no. 18 (April–June 1964): 65–66.

57. I am indebted to Gregor Benton for keeping me honest on this point. The truth is that no ordinary army could live off its own agriculture *in wartime*. However, the CCP army was no ordinary army, and its soldiers produced more than just grain on lands that were free from war.

58. The sources on this point are *Renmin de jundui* [The people's troops], 1946; Qi Wu, *Yige geming genjudi de chengzhang*, pp. 99–131; *Zhanqin gongzuo aiguo siwei zhancheng jingyan* [On war-service work experiences in the war of self-defense for the beloved ancestral land] (Bianqu zhengtongbao zhu yishang zaizheng ganbu zhanqin ganbu [Border region government publication no. 7, issued by the government finance and war service cadres], Jin-Ji-Lu-Yu bianqu zhengfu mishu bianji [Compiled by the secretarial office of the Shanxi-Hebei-Shandong-Henan border region government], 10 July 1947), pp. 1–20.

59. Compare with Polanyi's description of a similar mobile grain provisioning system conceived by Xenon's Asian army. Karl Polanyi, *The Livelihood of Man*, ed. Harry W. Pearson (New York: Academic Press, 1977), pp. 131–32.

60. *Taihang qu maoyi gongzuo li nian lai zhongyao jueding zhi shi mingling bi mi wenjian yi jiaopin* [The secretly filed materials on the past years' important decisions, directives, and orders on Taihang district trade work], Cankao ziliao de san bian shangye maoyi lei di yi ji [The first book on categories of business and trade in the third edition of reference materials] (Taihang qu Jinan yinhang zonghang gong shang guanliji chuban [Taihang district South Hebei Bank Headquarters, Bureau of Industry and Commerce], December 1945), pp. 8–17.

61. Lincoln Li, *The Japanese Army in North China 1937–1941* (Tokyo: Oxford University Press, 1975), pp. 6, 13–14, 219–23, 225–28.

62. Ibid., p. 223.

63. Taihang qu yinhang gongshan maoyi gongzuo cankao ziliao bianji weiyuanhui [Editorial committee for work reference materials for the Taihang district bank, industry, and commerce work], 2 September 1945, pp. 6–7.

64. Wang Tingdong, "Wuan xin qu chubu shixian" [The initial accomplishments in the new districts of Wuan county] in *Bianqu zhengbao* [Border region government news], 1946–47: 1–3.

65. Cf. Tanaka Kyoko, "Mass Mobilization: The Chinese Communist Party and the Peasants," Ph.D. thesis, Australian National University History Department, July 1972, p. 93.

66. Wang Tingdong, "Wuan xin qu chubu shixian," 1–3; "Pingding duidi douzheng yu qunyun qingkuang de jieshao," p. 41; see also *Zudian guanxi diaocha cankao cailiao* [Reference materials on an investigation of rental tenant relations] (November 1945–January 1946), pp. 1–14.

67. "Jiaqiang xin jiefang qu gongzuo" [Strengthen the work in the newly liberated areas], in *Taihang xin hua ribao* [Taihang New China daily news], 1946.

68. Crook and Crook, *Revolution in a Chinese Village*, pp. 65–66, 122–23; Hinton, *Fanshen*, pp. 34–35, 132–36.

69. *Jianzu jianxi zengzi qunzhong yundong kaishan* [The mass movement for the reduction of rent and interest and the unfolding of wage increases] (Ji-Lu bianqu dangwei [The Communist Party Hebei-Shandong border district committee] 1 January 1943), pp. 25–34.

70. Huang Xuanwen, *Xiao he fengyun*, pp. 82–103. Cf. Sun Tan Wei, *Village Moves to Socialism*, pp. 3–33; and Rewi Alley, *Travels in China 1966–1971* (Beijing: New World Press, 1973), p. 115.

71. *Lun Shui Gongzuo* [Directives on tax work] (Jin-Ji-Lu-Yu bianqu shi dangwei chuban [CCP tenth district of the Shanxi-Hebei-Shandong-Henan border region government], March–June 1945), pp. 1–10.

72. Thaxton, "Lin County Village Investigations."

73. Ibid. The Japanese generally went after the market villages. Their targets were merchants involved in the border region economy, not peasants.

74. *Taihang qu maoyi gongzuo*, pp. 56–100.

75. Ibid.

76. A revealing source on this is Zheng Weisan, *Kangri zhanzheng yu nongmin yundong: Zai ershi diyi ci minyun gongzuo huiyi shangde baogao* [The war of resistance and the peasant movement: A report given at the First Civil Movement work conference of the Second Division], 14 April 1941, pp. 2–3. *Xinsijun ershi zhengzhibu chuban* [New Fourth army, second division, Political Department], 14 April 1941, pp. 2–3.

77. Qi Wu, *Yige geming genjudi de chengzhang*, pp. 143–77, especially 164–65.

78. *Taihang qu sifa gongzuo kaikuang* [The general conditions of judicial work in the Taihang] (Taihang xinshu [Taihang administrative office], 1946), trans. by Wallace Douglass, *Chinese Law and Government* vol. 6, no. 3 (Fall 1973), pp. 9–10.

79. Ibid., pp. 10, 13, 21. I have drawn this information from Kay Ann Johnson's brilliant *Women, the Family, and Peasant Revolution in China: The Political Limits of Change in the Countryside* (Chicago: University of Chicago Press, 1982), chap. 6.

80. Peng Dehuai, "Guanyu Huabei genjudi de gongzuo baogao" [Report concerning work in the North China base areas], in *Gongfei* [The Communist bandits] 3: 346–406. Cited in Johnson, *Women, the Family, and Peasant Revolution in China*, chap. 6.

81. Eric R. Wolf, *Peasant Wars of the Twentieth Century* (New York: Harper & Row, 1969), pp. 215–16, 240–41; Qi Wu, *Yige geming genjudi de chengzhang*, pp. 99–131.

82. *Jizhong fazhi yi jiusiwu nian yi hou jiefang de xin zhu jingyan* [A collection of the experiences of the newly liberated areas of 1945 and after], Jin-Ji-Lu-Yu bianqu zhengfu mishu chu bianji [Edited by the Shanxi-Hebei-Shandong-Henan border region government secretariat] no. 12 (July 1947), pp. 12–13.

83. Ibid., pp. 7–14; Qi Wu, *Yige geming genjudi de chengzhang*, p. 173.

84. "Dazhai Matures in Struggle," *Lishi Yanjiu* [Historical Research] no. 1, 20 February 1976); Sun Tan Wei, *Village Moves to Socialism*, pp. 15–22.

85. *Jizhong fazhi yijiusiwu nian yi he jiefang de xin zhu jingyan*, pp. 1–28.

86. For the general context, see Qi Wu, *Yige geming genjudi de chengzheng*, pp. 99–196; and Ding Ling, *Yierjiu shiyu Jin-Ji-Lu-Yu bianqu*, pp. 35–45.

87. Hua Shan, *Yingxiong de shiyue*, pp. 1–4, 10–20; cf. Yuan Jing, *Xin Ernu yingxiong zhuan* [The new heroic sons and daughters] (Beijing: Renmin wenxue chubanshe [People's press], 1977), pp. 1–43.

88. *Taihang qu sifa gongzuo*, pp. 39–45, 52–65; Zhao Shuli, *Changes in Li Village* (Beijing: Foreign Languages Press, 1953), pp. 207–12.

89. *Taihang qu sifa gongzuo*, pp. 66–78.

90. Ji Dengkui, *Hua xian chajian yundong jianbao*, pp. 42–43.

91. Li Yiqing, *Dongyun minli yu zuzhi minli* [The mobilization and deployment of civilian power] (Taihang xingshu yin [Taihang administrative office] 1 May 1947), pp. 1–40. Cf. *Zhanqin gongzuo ai guo siwei zhanzheng jingyan*, pp. 1–2.

92. Li Yiqing, *Dongyun minli yu zuzhi minli*, pp. 1–20.

93. Ding Ling, *Yierjiu shiyu Jin-Ji-Lu-Yu bianqu*, pp. 39–45.

94. *Zhanqin gongzuo ai guo siwei zhangzheng jingyan*, pp. 23–24.

95. Li Yiqing, *Dongyun minli yu zuzhi minli*, pp. 1–20.

96. *Ji-Lu-Yu qu shige yue zhanqin gongzuo jingkuang* [The conditions of ten months of combat service duties in the Hebei-Shandong-Henan district], *Canzhan gongzuo* [War participation work] no. 13, Ji-Lu-Yu qu houfang zongzhi huibu bian [Command Headquarters of the

Hebei-Shandong-Henan rear area] (10 June 1947), pp. 1–22. Cf. Li Yiqing, *Dongyun minli yu zuzhi minli*, pp. 1–40. Cf. Liu Zhong, "Recalling the Great Victory of Shandang," in *The Great Turning Point* (Beijing: Foreign Languages Press, 1962), pp. 40–41; Belden, *China Shakes the World*, pp. 319–20, 350.

97. "Rong fuzhuxi wuyuejiuri zai bianqu meiye huiyi shang dui jiqi yao taolun de zongjie" [A summary of Vice-chairman Rong's May ninth border region coal business meeting discussion about the feasibility of using machinery in the coal pits], in *Bianqu zhengbao* [Border region government news] (15 June 1945): 12–15.

98. This is the logic of Johnson, *Peasant Nationalism and Communist Power*, chaps. 1–2.

99. Miao Peishi, *Hongshuling* [Red Tree Hill village] (Beijing: Gongren chubanshe [Worker's press], 1950), pp. 1–5, 12–13, 40–42, 45–47, 90–92, 98–110.

100. See "Dazhai Matures in Struggle"; and William Hinton, "Two Ways to Read the 'Red Book,'" *New China* (Summer 1977): 22–27. I owe much of this Dazhai interpretation to personal exchanges with Edward Friedman.

101. For this conception of the war-related mobilization process in Dazhai I have relied in part on Denitch, "Violence and Social Change in the Yugoslav Revolution," pp. 469–72.

102. Ma Feng, *Chunying de gushi*, pp. 1–121.

103. I have gleaned this account from Sun Tan Wei, *Village Moves to Socialism*, pp. 3–36, esp. 8–18; Li Xunda, "Lin Biao's Reactionary Program for Restoring Capitalism," in *Workers, Peasants, and Soldiers Criticize Lin Biao and Confucius* (Beijing: Foreign Languages Press, 1976), pp. 24–27; and Rewi Alley, *Travels in China*, p. 115. Also see Hua Shan, *The Shepherd Boy Hai Wa*, pp. 54–59.

104. Li Yingju, *Nu youji duizhang*, pp. 1–955; Thaxton, "Lin County Village Investigations."

105. *Renmin zhanzheng weili wuqiong* [The infinite power of the people's war] (Beijing: Renmin chubanshe [People's press], 1973), pp. 62–65; Liu Qi, *Zhanzheng jiguan*, p. 4. In developing this conception I have benefited from Jeffrey Race, *War Comes to Long An: Revolutionary Conflict in a Vietnamese Province* (Berkeley: University of California Press, 1972), pp. 178–79.

106. Victor Nee, "Towards a Social Anthropology of the Chinese Revolution," *Bulletin of Concerned Asian Scholars* 2, no. 3 (July–September, 1979), pp. 41–47. The insightful source on *lijia* as a system designed to diminish the power of state over society is John R. Watt, *The District Magistrate in Late Imperial China* (New York: Columbia University Press, 1972), pp. 111–15. Also see Franz Shurmann, *Ideology and Organization in Communist China* (Berkeley: University of California Press, 1966), pp. 409–10, 423.

107. Lyman P. Van Slyke, *Enemies and Friends: The United Front in Chinese Communist History* (Stanford: Stanford University Press, 1967), p. 133.

108. *Cong ximenghui kan Shanxi minzhong yundong*, p. 57.

109. Cf. James C. Scott, "Protest and Profanation: Agrarian Revolt and the Little Tradition," *Theory and Society* 4, no. 2 (1977), pp. 216, 222–28, 240–41.

110. Thaxton, "Lin County Village Investigations." My Yao village interviews suggest that the peasants who answered the CCP's patriotic call to arms did so in the name of their urgent social needs, and that they seldom knew about the *specific* political conditions in the CCP's United Front agrarian program for reducing rent and interest.

111. Liu Shao-ch'i, *Collected Works* (Hong Kong: Union Research Institute, 1969), vol. 1, p. 74. I am indebted to Lowell Dittmer for calling this to attention. *Liu Shao-ch'i and the Chinese Cultural Revolution: The Politics of Mass Criticism* (Berkeley: University of California Press, 1974), p. 188.

112. For a more optimistic estimate of colonialism's death knell in Asia see Epstein, *Unfinished Revolution in China*, chap. 1.

113. *Zhandou zai Taihang Shan shang*, pp. 19–20.

114. Hinton, "Two Ways to Read the 'Red Book,'" 22–27.

115. "Zhangzhi sizhongdui jiji canjia qunyun" [The Zhang river branch of the fourth middle

troop enthusiastically participates in the mass movement], in *Renmin de jundui* [The people's troops] (11 April 1946).

116. Cf. Scott, "Protest and Profanation," 216–41.

117. Barrington Moore, Jr. has pointed out that war is a phenomenon with built-in pressures for centralization. I take him seriously. See *Political Power and Social Theory* (New York: Harper & Row, 1965), pp. 1–4.

CHAPTER 7

1. See Mark Selden, *The People's Republic of China* (New York: Monthly Review Press, 1979), pp. 29–30. Cf. Ma Feng, *Liu Hulan zhuan* [On Liu Hulan] (Beijing: Zhongguo Qingnian chubanshe [China Youth Press], 1978), pp. 273–74.

2. Compare with Lucien Bianco, *Origins of the Chinese Revolution, 1915–1949* (Stanford: Stanford University Press, 1962), pp. 179–85.

3. On South China see C. K. Yang, *Chinese Communist Society: The Family and the Village* (Cambridge, Mass.: MIT Press, 1959), pp. 144–45; on North China see Tanaka Kyoko, "Mao and Liu in the 1947 Land Reform: Allies or Disputants?" *The China Quarterly*, no. 75 (September 1978): 574, 593.

4. Wang Tingdong, "Wuan xin qu chubu shixian" [The initial accomplishments in the new districts of Wuan county], in *Bianqu zhengbao* [Border region government news] (1946) 47: 1–3.

5. Compare with Edwin Moise, "Land Reform in China and North Vietnam: Revolution at the Village Level," Ph.D. thesis, University of Michigan, 1977, pp. 41–42.

6. Qi Wu, *Yige geming genjudi de chengzhang: Kangri zhanzheng he jeifang zhanzheng shiqi de Jin-Ji-Lu-Yu bianqu gaikuang* [The growth of a revolutionary base: the general conditions of the Shanxi-Hebei-Shandong-Henan border region during the anti-Japanese war of resistance and the war of liberation] (Beijing: Renmin chubanshe [People's press], 1958), p. 278.

7. Suzanne Pepper, *Civil War in China* (Berkeley: University of California Press, 1978), p. 290.

8. Cf. Selden, *People's Republic of China*, pp. 29–30.

9. Tanaka implies that middle peasants were resented by poor peasants because the former's gains were poor peasant losses. Surely this was not the case. The middle peasants only recovered and retained what was theirs in the land revolution, while the poor peasants actually gained *more* than they previously had possessed. "Mao and Liu in the 1947 Land Reform," 591.

10. *Gongzuo tongxun* [Work correspondence] no. 31, Tudi gaige huiyi zhuanhao [Special issue on the land revolution conference], Dang nei kanwu [Internal party publication], Zhonggong Ji-Lu-Yu qu dangwei minyun bu [Published by the Chinese Communist Party Hebei-Shandong-Henan district committee of the civil movement department] (1 June 1947), pp. 33–35.

11. See Albert Soboul, *The French Revolution 1787–1799* (New York: Vintage, 1975), pp. 558–59.

12. Isabel and David Crook, *Revolution in a Chinese Village: Ten Mile Inn* (London: Routledge & Kegan Paul, 1959), pp. 120–21.

13. Ibid., p. 135.

14. Compare with William Hinton on the tendency of cadres to carry out land revolution from an "absolute equalitarian" viewpoint. William Hinton, *Fanshen: A Documentary of Revolution in a Chinese Village* (New York: Random House, 1966), pp. 489–92.

15. Wang Tingdong, "Wuan xin qu chubu shixian," p. 19.

16. *Gongzuo tongxun* no. 8, p. 103.

17. Ibid., pp. 1–5.

18. Ibid., pp. 15–22.

19. Crook and Crook provide a splendid analysis of this issue and the mistaken ways the

CCP at first attempted to handle it. *Revolution in a Chinese Village*, chaps. 8–9.

20. *Gongzuo tongxun* [Work correspondence] no. 35, Sixiang zijue zhibao ligong tuanjie kongsu zhuanhao [A special issue on achieving self-confidence and self-assessment in rendering service to the solidification of the accusation movement], Dangnei Kanwu [Internal party publication] Ji-Lu-Yu dangwei chuban [published by the Hebei-Shandong-Henan party committee], 10 July 1947, pp. 37–38.

21. *Gongzuo tongxun* no. 31, pp. 28–31.

22. *Nu Yingxiong Liu Hulan* [The woman hero Liu Hulan] (Beijing: Renmin chubanshe [People's press], 1975), pp. 1–20. Cf. Ma Feng, *Liu Hulan zhuan*, pp. 283–305.

23. Zuo Xian, *Jiuyiren fanshen ji* [Remembrances of the transformation of the old artists and actors] Xin Hua shudian Huadong zong fen dian faxing [Published by a branch of the East China bookstore], 1951, pp. 1–16, 21–27, 30–40, 45–59. The relatively conservative outlook of these opera performers contrasts sharply with the cosmopolitan leftism of Jiang Qing, whose early career was launched from the small cities skirting the border region. Cf. Roxane Witke's fascinating portrayal, *Comrade Chiang Ch'ing* (Boston: Little, Brown, 1977), pp. 63–88.

24. For a study that understands this possibility, see C. P. Fitzgerald, *Mao Zedong and China* (New York; Penguin, 1976), pp. 78–81. For one that doesn't, see Jacques Guillermaz, *A History of the Chinese Communist Party 1921–1949*, trans. Anne Destenay (London: Methuen, 1972), pp. 375–401.

25. For an interesting anarchist polemic on the way the Bolsheviks bore down on the popular countryside to provision their town-based army, see Peter Arshinov, *History of the Makhnovist Movement 1918–1921*, trans. Lorraine Perlman and Fredy Perlman (Detroit: Black and Red, 1974).

26. *Ji-Lu-Yu qu shige yue zhanqin gongzuo jingkuang* [The conditions of ten months of combat service duties in the Hebei-Shandong-Henan district], *Canzhan gongzuo* [War participation work] no. 13, Ji-Lu-Yu qu huofang zongzhihuibu bian [Command headquarters of the Hebei-Shandong-Henan rear area], 10 June 1947, pp. 1–22, especially 3–7 and maps.

27. *Canzhan gongzuo* [War participation work] no. 13, Ji-Lu-Yu qu huofang zongzhihuibu bian [Command headquarters of the Hebei-Shandong-Henan rear area], 10 June 1947, pp. 5–10, especially 7. This report was widely circulated in the border region, and it became a guide to war-service work there during the War of Liberation.

28. Ralph Thaxton, "On Peasant Revolution and National Resistance: Toward a Theory of Peasant Mobilization and Revolutionary War with Special Reference to Modern China," *World Politics* 9, no. 1 (October 1977): 46–49. The best source on this, however, is Pepper, *Civil War in China*, pp. 290–91.

29. For this view, see Pepper, *Civil War in China*, pp. 289–92, 305, 311. The thrust of Pepper's argument on the Jiang Jieshi clique as a desperate takeover regime is well taken, though her concern is more with the cities. Moreover, I share her assumption that the CCP won the civil war in North China, rather than Manchuria, largely on the basis of a legitimizing pre-1946 performance. Where I disagree is on how the land revolution fits into the events that came before it and whether the CCP abandoned its rationale for modifying class conflict in militarily insecure areas in favor of carrying on land redistribution and civil war. I do not believe victory in the civil war was dependent on "initiating class struggle." That had been going on for a long time, and the CCP was trying not to mix the two in the more insecure military areas.

30. *Canzhan gongzuo* no. 13, pp. 1–10.

31. Ibid. Thaxton, "Lin County Village Investigations." Donghuwang and Yao village were similar in that after 1943 the Guomindang never returned to take them.

32. Cf. Jack Belden, *China Shakes the World* (New York: Monthly Review Press, 1970), pp. 319–20, 350; *Canzhan gongzuo* no. 13, p. 1.

33. *Canzhan gongzuo* no. 13, pp. 1–10.

34. Duan Junyi, "Guanyu jinhou zhanqin gongzuo de zhiling xin" [Concerning the current and past instructions on war service work], in *Canzhan gongzuo* no 13: 1–4. According to Klein

and Clark, Duan's whereabouts during the War of Resistance were unknown. Documents like this one, however, support their guess that he was active in war-related work in the Henan-Hubei area. Duan was working with the Liu-Deng army in the Ji-Lu-Yu area. Donald W. Klein and Anne B. Clark, *Biographic Dictionary of Chinese Communism, 1921–1965*, vol. 2 (Cambridge, Mass.: Harvard University Press, 1971), pp. 873–74.

35. *Canzhan gongzuo* no. 13, pp. 1–10.

36. *Ji-Lu-Yu shige yue zhanqin gongzuo jingkuang*, pp. 1–22, especially pp. 2–7.

37. Ibid.

38. Cf. Thaxton, "On Peasant Revolution and National Resistance," pp. 47–50. The important point here is that the CCP arrangements involving peasants in war-related work often collapsed in the event of crisis, and the CCP immediately had to step in and take up the slack left by the peasantry.

39. Hinton's *Fanshen*, pp. 482–83, leaves the impression that the CCP was fairly confident of victory in this period. My sources suggest that CCP confidence had been shaken by landlord successes in demobilizing CCP branches and by CCP difficulties in mobilizing the villages for war-participation work.

40. *Gongzuo tongxun* no. 35, pp. 43–44.

41. *Gongzuo tongxun* no. 31, pp. 27–28.

42. *Gongzuo tongxun* no. 35, pp. 2–4, 39–47, 61–65.

43. *Gongzuo tongxun* no. 8, pp. 17–18.

44. Ibid., pp. 15–17.

45. Compare this interpretation of the CCP relationship to peasant mobilization with Jacques Elliul's analysis of Communist political institutions and revolutionary mass mobilization in general. *Autopsy of Revolution*, trans. Patricia Wolf (New York: Knopf, 1971), pp. 122–42. Selden is superb on this point. *People's Republic of China*, p. 29.

46. Thaxton, "Lin County Village Investigations." Cf. Feng Deying, *Ying chun hua* [The promise of spring] (Beijing: Jiefangjun wenyishe [Liberation army literature and arts press], 1961), pp. 1–41.

47. *Gongzuo tongxun* no. 31, pp. 32–33; Feng Deying, *Ying chun hua*, pp. 1–22, 27–35.

48. Any decision to kill people was to have the support of over 90 percent of the peasantry, and this was to include the middle peasants. *Gongzuo tongxun* no. 35, pp. 26–27, 66–67.

49. Ibid., pp. 49–50.

50. Cf. Yang, *Chinese Communist Society*, p. 136; Hinton, *Fanshen*, throughout; and Ben Stavis, "China and the Comparative Analysis of Land Reform," *Modern China* 4 (January 1978): 70.

51. The interpretation here is similar to Pepper's. Her emphasis, however, is on the CCP as an outside catalyst for land revolution among a not fully committed peasantry. *Civil War in China*, pp. 246, 297–98.

52. *Gongzuo tongxun* no. 35, p. 17. In some parts of the region landless-peasant membership in the CCP was four times greater than middle-peasant membership during the land revolution.

53. "Dazhai Matures in Struggle," *Lishi Yanjiu* [Historical research] no. 1 (20 February 1976): 20. Nonetheless, the documentation sometimes mentions clan participation in the War of Liberation. Cf. *Ji-Lu-Yu shige yue zhanqin gongzuo jingkuang*, pp. 1–22.

54. *Gongzuo tongxun* no. 35, pp. 40–41, 51–52, 61–62, 75–76.

55. Wang Tingdong, "Wuan xin qu chubu shixian," pp. 5–7.

56. *Gongzuo tongxun* no. 35, pp. 23–25; no. 31, pp. 47–48.

57. Ibid., no. 31, pp. 42–44.

58. See Charles Tilly, *The Vendee* (Cambridge, Mass.: Harvard University Press, 1964).

59. For an example of this see *Jikucun en chou ji*, pp. 79–94.

60. "Jaiqiang xin jiefang qu gongzuo" [Strengthen the work in the heavily liberated areas], in *Taihang xinhua ribao* [Taihang New China daily news], 1946, pp. 49–50. Cf. Karl Marx, "The Eighteenth Brumaire of Louis Bonaparte," in Tucker, pp. 515–16. Frederick C. Gamst

makes a similar assumption about peasant China. *Peasants in a Complex Society* (New York: Holt, Rinehart and Winston, 1974), p. 50. Otherwise, Gamst provides an excellent introduction to peasantry.

61. *Gongzuo tongxun* no. 35, pp. 50–55.

62. Ibid., pp. 1–52; Thaxton, "Lin County Village Investigations."

63. My inference from *Gongzuo tongxun* no. 35, pp. 1–121.

64. Ibid., pp. 1–52.

65. Ibid., p. 61.

66. *Minbing* [The militia], "Chedi suqing dizhu yishi" [Uproot and eliminate landlord ideology] (22 August 1947).

67. Cf. Feng Deying, *Ying chun hua*, pp. 35–39.

68. Ibid., p. 6.

69. This same vision is alive and well in the border region today. Thaxton, "Lin County Village Investigations."

70. E. J. Hobsbawm, *Primitive Rebels* (New York: Norton, 1959), pp. 58–59, 62.

71. Crook and Crook, *Revolution in a Chinese Village*, p. 134; Liu Jiang, *Taihang fengyun* [The Taihang Storm] (Beijing: Zuojia chubanshe [Writers' press], 1962), pp. 429–54.

72. Cf. Ma Feng, *Luliang Shan yingxiong zhuan*, pp. 420–23.

73. Padraic Colum, *Myths of the World* (New York: Grosset and Dunlap, 1977), pp. xii, 237–41.

CHAPTER 8

1. The term is Richard Critchfield's, and is drawn from his brilliantly done "Critchfield's Villages," *The Humanities* (1979): p. 16.

2. Barrington Moore, Jr., *Social Origins of Dictatorship and Democracy: Lord and Peasant in the Making of the Modern World* (Boston: Beacon Press, 1966), chap. 4; Theda Skocpol, "France, Russia, and China: A Structural Analysis of Social Revolutions," *Comparative Studies in Society and History* 18, no. 2 (April 1976): 175–81, 192–95.

3. Moore, *Social Origins*, chap. 4.

4. For a nice treatment of this causal factor in modern revolutions see Crane Brinton, *The Anatomy of Revolution* (New York: Vintage Books, 1965), p. 252. The internationally linked fiscal crisis of the state is also dealt with in splendid fashion by Theda Skocpol, *States and Social Revolutions: A Comparative Analysis of France, Russia, and China* (London: Cambridge University Press, 1979), pp. 60–64, 73–74.

5. Brinton, *Anatomy of Revolution*, pp. 252–53.

6. The best accounts in this tradition are Maurice Meisner, "The Chinese Communist Revolution," in *Revolutions: A Comparative Study*, ed. Lawrence Kaplan (New York: Vintage, 1973), pp. 315–54; and Jerome Ch'en, "The Development of Mao Tse-tung's Thought, 1928–49," in *Ideology and Politics in Contemporary China*, ed. Chalmers Johnson (Seattle: University of Washington Press, 1973), pp. 78–114, especially 90–95, 111–12.

7. For this theory see Ted Robert Gurr, *Why Men Rebel* (Princeton: Princeton University Press, 1970), pp. 47–55. Gurr also has conceived of a type of relative deprivation in which popular expectations remain unchanged while the means to fulfill those expectations are undermined. This is very close to Scott's notion of why peasants rebel, but Gurr's assumption is that values lose their potency under pressure. My position is that values may be reinforced by exploitation and deprivation.

8. This is the qualified position of Elizabeth J. Perry, *Rebels and Revolutionaries in North China 1845–1945* (Stanford: Stanford University Press, 1980), conclusion.

9. For two studies that deal with the nonrevolutionary intent of rebelling peasants see Henry A. Landsberger, "The Role of Peasant Movements and Revolts in Development: An Analytical Framework," *International Institute for Labor Studies Bulletin* (February 1968):

8–33; and Edward Friedman, *Backward Toward Revolution: The Chinese Revolutionary Party* (Berkeley: University of California Press, 1974), p. 222.

10. Compare with Albert O. Hirshman, *Exit, Voice, and Loyalty: Responses to Decline in Firms, Organizations, and States* (Cambridge: Harvard University Press, 1970). Hirshman reminds us that "exit" from institutions of declining performance is not simply a "freely allowed" response. There is no exit without penalty of some kind. Although Hirshman does not explore the issue in depth, penalties tend to grow ever more severe for people who decide to exit by putting an end to governments whose performance is basically parasitic. The clear summary of Hirshman is in Charles Tilly, *From Mobilization to Revolution* (Reading, Mass.: Addison-Wesley, 1978), pp. 27, 71–72.

11. For this argument, see Roy Hofheinz, Jr., "The Ecology of Chinese Communist Success," *Chinese Communist Politics in Action*, ed. A. Doak Barnett (Seattle: University of Washington Press, 1969), pp. 3–77. The broader, generalized, and more sophisticated application is Samuel P. Huntington, *Political Order in Changing Societies* (New Haven: Yale University Press, 1968), pp. 264–343.

12. Compare my position with that of Carl E. Dorris, a proponent of the middle-peasant thesis for China who nonetheless cites tenancy rates of 50 percent in the Shanxi mountain districts where the CCP thrived. "Peasant Mobilization in North China and the Origins of Yenan Communism," *The China Quarterly* 68 (December 1976): 706. The general theory is developed in, again, Eric R. Wolf, *Peasant Wars of the Twentieth Century* (New York: Harper & Row, 1969), pp. 291–92. Wolf's argument, with which I tend to agree, is that peasant landholdings plus tenuous control from outside power holders gave the middle peasants leverage, and this, combined with day labor, clandestine trade, and migration carried on in the shadows of local power, added mobility and hence the opportunity to link up to peasant protests. All of these ingredients were present in the case at hand. The leaders of the revolts, however, were not the more secure landowning "middle peasants." We have seen they were landless peasants and poor smallholders who had lost the land and business income necessary for family security. Also see Hamza Alavi, "Peasants and Revolution," *Socialist Register Reprint* (1965).

13. To the political scientist looking for the process whereby the CCP rose to power, this issue might seem irrelevant, but it becomes important when we discover that a contingent of the China field has concluded from the middle-peasant thesis that rent and interest reduction did not play a significant part in the process whereby the CCP formed its popular base and fostered the conditions for peasant contributions to the Anti-Japanese War of Resistance. This is the view of Suzanne Pepper, *Civil War in China* (Berkeley: University of California Press, 1978), pp. 233–37, 274–76, 327. A more plausible argument is that the CCP officials were developing their power base in accordance with the tremendous social structural variations within the peasant movements they encountered from locality to locality.

14. The importance of the dry-zone factor was first stressed in Ralph Thaxton, "The World Regained: The Rise of Peasant Revolution and Responsible Party Government in Hebei-Shandong-Henan Border Districts, 1915–45," ACLS Workshop on "Rebellion and Revolution in North China," Harvard University (July–August 1979). Compare Donald S. Zagoria, "Asian Tenancy Systems and Communist Mobilization of the Peasantry," in *Peasant Rebellion and Communist Revolution in Asia*, ed. John Wilson Lewis (Stanford: Stanford University Press,1974), pp. 29–49. Zagoria deals mainly with monsoon wet-rice Asia.

15. Compare with Perry, who does not look closely enough at localized forms of horizontal exploitation within Huaibei's allegedly dry-cropping environment. *Rebels and Revolutionaries*, pp. 260–61.

16. Wolf's *Peasant Wars*, pp. 292–93, is most helpful on this point.

17. Ralph Thaxton, "Peasants, Capitalism, and Revolution: On Capitalism as a Force for Liberation in Revolutionary China," *Comparative Political Studies* 12, no. 3 (October 1979): 294–98. This message, though lost in the political climate fostered by McCarthyism, stands out

in Jack Belden, *China Shakes the World* (New York: Monthly Review Press, 1970), pp. 463–70, 490–96; Friedman, *Backward Toward Revolution*, pp. 222–23; and Peter Schran, *Guerrilla Economy: The Development of the Shensi-Kansu-Ninghsia Border Region, 1937–45* (Albany: State University of New York Press, 1976), pp. 127–252.

18. The Bolsheviks evidently did not care to apply this wisdom to the Ukraine. See Peter Arshinov, *History of the Makhnovist Movement, 1918–1921*, trans. Lorraine Perlman and Fredy Perlman (Detroit: Black and Red, 1974), pp. 69–71, 174–76.

19. Karl Marx, *Pre-Capitalist Economic Formations* (New York: International Publishers, 1964), pp. 38, 79–81.

20. Wolf, *Peasant Wars*, conclusion; and James C. Scott, *The Moral Economy of the Peasant: Rebellion and Subsistence in Southeast Asia* (New Haven: Yale University Press, 1976), chaps. 1–2, conclusion.

21. E. J. Hobsbawm, *The Age of Capital* (New York: Scribner, 1975), pp. 108–21.

22. The arguments and counterarguments on this issue are to be found in Wolf, *Peasant Wars*; G. William Skinner, "Chinese Peasants and the Closed Community: An Open and Shut Case," *Comparative Studies in Society and History* 13, no. 3 (July 1971): 270–81, and Terry A. Rambo, "Closed Corporate and Open Peasant Communities: Reopening a Hastily Shut Case," *Comparative Studies in Society and History* 19, no. 2 (April 1977): 179–87.

23. For this view, see Roy Hofheinz, Jr., *The Broken Wave: The Chinese Communist Peasant Movement, 1922–1928* (Cambridge, Mass.: Harvard University Press, 1977), chap. 12; Joel Migdal, *Peasants, Politics, and Revolution* (Princeton: Princeton University Press, 1974), pp. 237–56; and Skocpol, *States and Social Revolutions*, p. 193. Nonetheless, the strength of Skocpol is to doubt the CCP capacity to engineer rural revolution from below by virtue of its organizational presence alone, pp. 257–61.

24. This notion is advanced in Migdal's *Peasants, Politics, and Revolution*, pp. 232, 248–49; and Skocpol's "France, Russia, and China," pp. 193–94, 200–201.

25. Migdal, *Peasants, Politics, and Revolution*, pp. 226, 235; Hofheinz, *Broken Wave*, pp. 302–3.

26. For the point in reference to peasant demands in the Mexican revolution, see John Womack, Jr., *Zapata and the Mexican Revolution* (New York: Knopf, 1969), p. 129.

27. Huntington, *Political Order in Changing Societies*, pp. 275–77; Migdal, *Peasants, Politics, and Revolution*, pp. 240–42; cf. Samuel L. Popkin, *The Rational Peasant: The Political Economy of Rural Society in Vietnam* (Berkeley: University of California Press, 1979), pp. 263–64. Popkin's conception of "revolutionary surplus" is in reference to the Vietnamese case, but his thesis on peasant mobilization as party-building is in line with Huntington and Migdal.

28. No doubt the CCP was compelled by politics to spend for war over revolution. Dorris is the most convincing proponent of this genre of "people's war" thinking. "Peasant Mobilization in North China," pp. 697–703, 711–12.

29. Meisner, "Chinese Communist Revolution," p. 348.

30. In just about every Western intellectual account of the modern Chinese revolution. Nor are revolutionaries above this presumptuous assumption. On Cuba compare Che Guevara, *Episodes of the Revolutionary War* (New York: International Publishers, 1968), p. 157.

31. Friedman, *Backward Toward Revolution*, pp. 156–58, 219–23. In developing this point I also have profited from Jean A. Meyer, *The Cristero Rebellion: The Mexican People between Church and State 1926–1929*, trans. Richard Southern (Cambridge: Cambridge University Press, 1976), pp. 193–98, especially 197.

32. Chalmers A. Johnson, *Peasant Nationalism and Communist Power: The Emergence of Revolutionary China* (Stanford: Stanford University Press, 1962), chaps. 1–5.

33. Ibid., chaps. 1–2, especially pp. 2–5, 7, 11.

34. Implicit in Wolf's judgment that peasants remain powerless without outside force is the assumption that they are sensitive to political change, and furthermore that they will adjust their strategies of survival to such change. I have relied on this assumption throughout. Wolf, *Peasant Wars*, p. 290.

35. The best-developed version is Mark Selden, "Revolution and Third World Development: People's War and the Transformation of Peasant Society," in *National Liberation: Revolution in the Third World*, ed. Norman Miller and Roderick Aya (New York: Free Press, 1971), pp. 214–48, especially 226–27. In developing the alternative presented here I have benefited from W. B. Gallie, *Philosophers of Peace and War: Kant, Clausewitz, Marx, Engels and Tolstoy* (Cambridge: Cambridge University Press, 1978), chap. 4.

36. This is in line with Friedman, *Backward Toward Revolution*, pp. 218–19.

37. Compare Mao Zedong, "Problems of Strategy in China's Revolutionary War," in *Selected Military Writings of Mao Zedong* (Beijing: Foreign Languages Press, 1963), pp. 75–95.

38. This interpretation derives in part from my reading of Nathan Wachtel, *The Vision of the Vanquished*, trans. Ben and Sian Reynolds (New York: Barnes and Noble, 1977), pp. 5, 9–10, 26–30.

39. Cf. Frantz Fanon, *The Wretched of the Earth* (New York: Grove Press, 1963), pp. 131–35. The social science variant of this view for China is Skocpol, "France, Russia, and China," p. 200. The argument is made with due caution and clarity by Perry, *Rebels and Revolutionaries*, pp. 246–47. Her strength is to show that the CCP did not merely incorporate the predatory raiding style in order to reflect it. Her weakness is to leave us without any understanding of what the CCP did in fact *do* in order to gain legitimacy.

40. Norman Cohn, *The Pursuit of the Millennium: Revolutionary Millenarians and Mystical Anarchists of the Middle Ages* (New York: Oxford University Press, 1970), pp. 252–70.

41. This, I believe, is the grave error in Fanon, *The Wretched of the Earth*, pp. 136–44.

Index

Temple-based activities. *See* Religion
Tenants and tenants' rights. *See* Landlords
Theater and opera, 15, 16, 20, 90, 202. *See also* Folk culture
Thought Rectification *(1942–44)*, 130, 210, 211, 212, 215, 229
Three All offensive. *See* War of Resistance
Tilly, Charles, 45, 78, 213
Tito, Josip Broz, 166
Trade: CCP Bureau of, 117–21, 179; and competition, 9–10, 50, 64, 116–21 passim, 125–26, 200, 226; free, CCP emphasis on, 116–28, 134, 136, 178–80, 184, 225–26; with Japan, 50, 119; local, 8–10, 52, 100, 178, (revival of) 119–21, 123–29, 199; middleman *(yahang)* in, 118; village-serving market, 225. *See also* Economic conditions; Transportation
Tradition. *See* Great Tradition; Little Tradition
Transportation, 102, 205; central government and, 36, 49, 52, 100; uncertainty/risks of, 8, 117, 119–20, 178. *See also* Railways; Trade; Water

United Front *(1936)*, 171, 193. *See also* Second United Front
United States, xiii, 30, 50, 175; and Jiang Jieshi, 32, 87, 196, 197, 209, 233
Usury. *See* Economic conditions

Van Slyke, Lyman P., 191
Village(s): "allied village meetings," 131–32; central government and, 58; cooperatives of, *see* Collectivization; drought and, 3; extravillage networks and labor forces, 19, 62; family/intravillage networks, 8, 10, 13, 37; free, 186, 189–90, 204–09; freeholding, 10, 69 (*see also* Land ownership); fringe elements in, 200–02; government of, 112; Japanese impact on, 162–65, 180–90, 194; and local authority, 3; Qilipu, 138–59; raided/occupied, 186–90; self-defense systems of, 71, 155, 193; skills committees of, 200; and temple-based activities, *see* Religion; and trade (village-serving market), 9, 225 (*see also* Trade); and village autonomy, 10–11, 70, 100, 111, 132, 221, 227; and village welfare, 42. *See also* Peasant(s)

Wages. *See* Economic conditions
Wang Hongyin, 56

Wang Jingwei, 31, 91, 162, 175, 263n7
Wang Manxi, 153, 156
Wang Tingdong, 213
War in the Taihang Mountains, The (*1944* report), 167
Warlords, 31, 48, 49, 51, 52, 76, 80, 87, 91, 221; Beiyang (Northern), 30, 35, 45, 46, 73, 85, 162; Fengtien, 46, 77, 78, 85; revolts against, 2, 60, 68, 70–71, 77–78, 129, 134, 191; secret society alignment with, 72, 74; taxation by, 35, 45–46, 68, 73, 74, 77, 84, 114. *See also* Guomindang warlord regime
War of Liberation (civil war), xvii, xix, xx, 16, 195–219
War of Resistance, xvii, xix, xx, 32, 46, 54, 85, 91–103 passim, 107–22 passim, 125, 128, 132, 139, 152–59 passim, 160–94, 195–205 passim, 211, 215, 218–19, 224–31 passim, 250n41, 263n8; Hundred Regiments Offensive, 174–75; Three All Campaigns, 162, 169, 171–77 passim, 182–93 passim, 208, 263n16. *See also* Japan
Warring States period, 54
Water: irrigation, 3, 15, 41, 57, 69, 96, 162; rights to, 12, 42, 58, 69–70, 84, 109, 122, 224; transport by, 29, 53, 81, 99, 102. *See also* Droughts; Floods; Transportation
Weber, Max, xvi, xviii
Wertheim, W. F., 18
Western missionaries. *See* Religion
Western views, xiii, 18, 25, 220, 228, 236n14; of CCP, xiv–xvi, xx, 30–31, 98, 112, 135, 138, 195–97, 223, 225; of economic history, 28–29, 30, 35, 37, 40, 45, 51, 55, 59, 80, 94, 197
Wolf, Eric R., 226
Women, 62, 67, 80, 110, 140, 181; in CCP cadres, 186, 201–02, 206; and prostitution, 81, 125
World War II, 164, 175, 233
Wuan county: Black Lands Campaign in, 199; Japanese Army in, 161, 176; land redistribution in, 197, 213
Wu Guang, 1
Wu Peifu, 45, 54, 70, 72, 85, 180, 245n97

Yang Dayong, 94
Yang Shoufeng, 171
Yan Xishan, 31, 97, 147, 153, 166, 171, 174; and landlords, 43, 47–48; Opium Bureau of, 116; peasant opposition to, 122, 141; and salt traffic, 49, 143; vs. secret societies,